WILLIAM SHAKESPEARE

Coriolanus

Edited by John Ingledew M.A., Ph. D.

Longman

Longman Group Limited
Longman House
Burnt Mill, Harlow, Essex.

This edition © Longman Group Ltd 1975

First published 1975
Third impression 1981

ISBN 0 582 52747 3

Filmset by Keyspools Ltd, Golborne, Lancs.
Printed in Hong Kong by
Commonwealth Printing Press Ltd

Contents

Acknowledgements

WE ARE grateful to the following for permission to reproduce copyright material:

Associated Book Publishers Ltd. for an extract from *The Imperial Theme* (1931) by G. Wilson Knight, published by Methuen & Co. Ltd; Longman Group Limited for extracts from *Angel With Horns*, 1961 by A. P. Rossiter; Macmillan Ltd. for extracts from *A Miscellany* by A. C. Bradley, reprinted by permission of Macmillan London and Basingstoke and The University of California Press for extracts from *Shakespeare's Tragic Frontier* by Willard Farnham, 'originally published by the University of California Press; reprinted by permission of The Regents of the University of California.'

WE ARE also grateful to the following for permission to reproduce copyright photographs:

British Museum, page xxiv; Courtauld Institute of Art and The Marquess of Bath (Longleat), page lxvii; Douglas H. Jeffery, pages xc, xci, 50, 51, 92, 93, 134, 135, 176 & 177; Mander and Mitchenson Theatre Collection, page xii; State University of Utrecht, page lxi; The Mansell Collection, page lvii. The illustrations which run through the text are taken from the 1973/74 production of the Royal Shakespeare Company at the Aldwych Theatre, London; with Nicol Williamson as Coriolanus, Margaret Tyzack as Volumnia, Christopher Howard-Lee as Martius, Wendy Allnutt as Virgilia, Edwina Ford as Valeria, Mark Dignam as Menenius, Walter Brown as Lartius, Nicholas Selby as Cominius, Philip Locke as Brutus, John Nettleton as Sicinius and Oscar James as Aufidius.

THE AIM of the edition of *Coriolanus* in the *New Swan Shakespeare Advanced Series* is to ensure that the reader fully understands and appreciates the play itself. To this end it pays unusual attention to explanation of the text. A large number of points that other editions take for granted or touch upon inconclusively are now treated at length, and besides dealing with such matters as archaic language and allusions to customs no longer current, the notes explain briefly certain rare words still alive in modern English which happen to occur in the play (e.g. *viand, muniments*). Help is also given with complicated syntactical constructions and with patterns of imagery which may not be obvious at first sight. The content of the play, its historical, social and philosophical bases, and the conventions implied in the way characters react to one another may be strange to many readers; these matters too are treated in detail. Nevertheless the total extent of the notes on the left-hand pages is not very great. There are two reasons why the notes can be comparatively short and yet comprehensive. First, the language of the explanations is simple and direct. Second, in other editions much space has frequently been given to alternative readings of the text of the play, and to various conjectures about what difficult passages really mean. The present edition omits nearly all speculation of this kind. Where the meaning is doubtful, numerous alternative explanations are not given; instead, the editor has chosen the one which seems to him to fit the context most satisfactorily; if *one* possible alternative definitely serves to give a clearer meaning, this is added.

Some background knowledge is essential to a full understanding of the play. Certain passages can be explained only in the light of some aspect or other of the 'world view' of Shakespeare's day, or by some piece of information about the ancient world in which the action supposedly takes place, or about Shakespeare's view of this ancient world. Some of these things will be unknown to many readers, especially those who are not very familiar with the English background to Shakespeare's plays. Such information is given briefly so as to clarify the meaning of the passage in question, but no attempt has been made to provide a far-reaching account of the whole subject. Readers who are completely familiar with the English background will occasionally be able to ignore notes of this type, but others may find them useful, since they will remove difficulties rooted not in the use of the language but in the Shakespearian ethos.

At the back of the book there is an index which glosses and gives the location of all the difficult or unusual words in the text. By reference to the location in the text the student will find a note which will in most instances expand the brief equivalent in the glossary. The index will also help him to trace passages in the play: if he remembers a key word likely to be included in the index, he can look it up and find there a line reference in the text. In this way the glossarial index is also an index to the notes.

Elaborate criticism of the play is not given, although some passages of literary criticism relating to it are reproduced, and further sources are indicated in the bibliography. A study of these sources can however wait until the play is thoroughly known and appreciated for its own sake.

All the help offered, in the form of notes, glosses and introduction, has only this end in view, that the student should understand the play, since the way to enjoy it fully is to understand fully what it means.

Introduction

Meaning and method in *Coriolanus*

The events of *Coriolanus* take place in the early years of Rome's history, shortly after the defeat of Tarquinius Superbus, the last king of Rome, around 496 B.C., and the subsequent establishment of the Roman Republic. The play tells the story, regarded by most historians as largely mythical, of the great warrior–hero Coriolanus who is given the opportunity to become consul and political leader of the state, but throws it away through pride and inability to compromise his patrician dignity and conceal his contempt for the plebeians. Accused of treason and expelled from the city, he offers his services to Rome's enemy, the Volscians, and leads their armies against his native city. The intercession of his family saves Rome from destruction but ensures the death of Coriolanus at the hands of the enraged Volscians.

Whether or not the story is historical is unimportant for us, since through it Shakespeare explores issues which have a profound bearing on the lives of men in any age, whatever their political institutions might be. His subject is power – how it is won, held, and lost – and its effect both on those who wield it and those who have to live under it. He had earlier investigated the nature of power in such plays as *Richard II* and *Henry IV, parts 1 and 2*, but without the same close scrutiny found in *Coriolanus*. The word 'power' occurs 38 times, more than any other noun in the play, and is on everyone's lips. Indeed the whole action of the play could be said to be the dramatic manifestation of the power struggle.

We learn that the 1933 production of *Coriolanus* at the Comédie Française in Paris resulted in rioting at each performance between, on the one hand, those of right-wing sympathies who saw Coriolanus as martyr–hero defending civilized values against an anarchical mob and their power-hungry leaders, and on the other, those of left-wing persuasion who saw him as a would-be fascist dictator. This confrontation testifies that the play has an immediacy of appeal and application for twentieth century audiences. At the same time it illustrates a danger which we must avoid in our approach to the play, namely, the distortion of its meaning through the tendency to squeeze it into the mould of our own political beliefs or situation.

ix

Coriolanus, written in 1608–9, was a late play, Shakespeare's last extant tragedy, displaying all the complexity, ambiguity, paradox and irony that distinguish his mature work. It is the product of a lifetime of thought about politics and observation of its effect on men. It is not a manifesto for any particular political party or programme, nor does it offer easy solutions to the multiplicity of problems which have beset men through the ages in their attempts to forge political institutions which will ensure law and order without endangering social justice and human liberties.

In order to be receptive to what the play is saying we must first shed our political prejudices and preconceptions. Secondly, we must learn what we can of the current thought and outlook of Shakespeare's age, since these are inevitably mirrored in the play, and differ in many ways from present-day attitudes and ideas. Thirdly, we must remember that we are dealing with a play, and not treat it as if it were life, a novel, or a doctor's casebook. Our critical approach must be to take events in the order in which the dramatist unfolds them to us, relating each event in the sequence to what has gone before. If the dramatist is doing his job well, character and action will be so interwoven that what happens will influence and change his characters and thus shape succeeding events. In *Coriolanus* this organic relationship of character and event, of cause and effect, is extremely tight and coherent. Our final appreciation will be determined by the whole action, though of course the dramatist relies heavily on the ending – the catastrophe or dénouement – to convey the ultimate impression and meaning he intends. Our response to people and events in drama, while related to our response to life, is different in all kinds of subtle ways. We are more indulgent in literature than in real life to vicious but attractive characters, like Falstaff in *Henry IV* for example. We are more moved by tragic events. This is because dramatic art is not life, but a simplification and selection from it, so that paradoxically, while we may remain detached spectators, we are more simply and directly involved in the drama without all the distractions, complications and qualifications of real life. We have to accept that plays create their own world, and it is within the limits of the play's world that we have to judge its people and events. Most play-goers make these adjustments instinctively, accepting for the duration of the play the existence, for example, of magic and monster in *The Tempest*, fairies in *A Midsummer Night's Dream* or the Ghost in *Hamlet*. The meaning of a Shakespearian play is the impression that the playgoer carries away with him from the theatre, and this is an amalgam made up of the intellectual significance of the words spoken, the acting performance – which is largely dictated by the words of the text – and the tone or atmosphere generated by the imagery and the rhythmic and melodic effects of the poetry.

A useful starting point is the indication provided by the title of the First Folio of 1623, *The Tragedy of Coriolanus*, which suggests that Shakespeare's age saw it as a tragedy rather than a 'History' or 'Life'. And it is not, as some would have it, the tragedy of Rome, but that of a man, Coriolanus. The play supports this: a quarter of the lines of this long play are spoken by the hero, who appears in eighteen of its twenty-nine scenes, and even when he is not present he dominates the action, since the other characters spend their time discussing him. He is the centre of attraction in the play, and it is his story. As even his enemy Brutus concedes, 'All tongues speak of him.'

The renaissance conception of tragedy, we need to remind ourselves, was the rise (sometimes) and the fall (always) of a great man (or sometimes couple, as in *Antony and Cleopatra*) through a blend of causes which must include some serious moral flaw in his character. Fate, fortune and chance might help to shape the tragic fall, but the Shakespearian protagonist always has free will, and somewhere makes a wrong moral choice which inevitably brings suffering, punishment and death. Thus far, Coriolanus conforms to the pattern. He rises to the position of Rome's supreme magistrate, and falls through pride and anger, which lead to his treachery and death. Reduced to the simplest terms, his career exemplifies the dictum that pride must have a fall, but there is much more to it than that.

Coriolanus's tragedy is that of the outsider, the self-alienated man, whose idealism destroys his humanity and wrecks his life. He is led, by a combination of nature and upbringing, to dedicate himself to an unattainable form of human conduct, and this dedication gradually but inevitably separates him from his fellow-men and finally brings about the disintegration of his own personality. He struggles to accommodate reality to his obsessive vision, and his failure leads to the breakdown of this ideal and the collapse of his moral nature. His story is tragic – and the process of this tragedy is analysed on pp. xxvi–xxxv – because he is a great man, of enormous force and vitality, of undoubted ability and intelligence, a patriot possessed of many fine human qualities, whose destruction was neither necessary nor inevitable, and whose passing leaves his world that much poorer.

For renaissance Europeans the Romans were the greatest nation that had ever lived, and their history was better known, largely because it was more fully and skilfully written about, than any other. Renaissance man studied history, not from an academic desire to reconstruct accurately the events of the past, but rather with the moral purpose of deriving lessons from it for application in the present and future. Coriolanus was one of Rome's great men, and Shakespeare was drawn to his story not because of an intellectual interest in the evolution of the Roman republic in the fifth century B.C., but because it reached out across the twenty centuries between them with something to say to him and his contemporaries.

The ideal of the epic hero as it had come down from the Greeks, and pre-eminently from Homer, through the Romans, was that of a man of almost

Coriolanus as portrayed in the theatre:

John Vandenhoff mid-1830's

Mr Phelps 1860

Henry Irving 1901

Laurence Olivier 1938

godlike proportions, great in deeds and fame, a man abundantly endowed with *virtus*, that is, male force and energy, the classical ideal of masculinity. Military prowess, courage, anger, magnanimity and a single-minded pursuit of honour were the essential qualities of the 'virtuous' man. In trying to push beyond merely human limitations he was frequently aggressive, boastful, cruel, irate, and thus at odds with the conception of the Christian hero, whose perfection demanded contrary qualities like love, patience, humility and prudence. Many of Shakespeare's contemporaries, men like Sir Philip Sidney, Sir Walter Raleigh, the Earls of Essex and Oxford, nourished on the classics, attempted to put this ideal into practice, often with disastrous results. It was given dramatic expression in such plays as Marlowe's *Tamburlaine*, Chapman's *Bussy D'Ambois*, and several plays on Julius Caesar.

Shakespeare, however, was critical of it. In *Troilus and Cressida*, some years earlier, he had taken the hallowed Homeric story of the Trojan War with its great heroes, Achilles, Hector, Ajax and the rest, and turned it on its head, saying, in effect, 'Let us look at these great heroes as they really were', and exposing them as self-centred bullies, cowards and lechers, a compendium of the Seven Deadly Sins. The play is Shakespeare's mock-epic. In *Julius Caesar* and *Antony and Cleopatra* he has humanized these great Romans, showing their defects as well as their virtues, so that by the time we come to *Coriolanus* we are conditioned not to expect a simple glorification of the warrior-hero.

In Plutarch's *Life of Marcus Coriolanus*, his source-book, Shakespeare read:

> Now in those days valiantness was honoured in Rome above all other virtues; which they call *virtus*, by the name of virtue itself, as including in that general name all other special virtues besides.

He used this passage, but with a significant twist. Cominius, praising Coriolanus, says

> It is held
> That valour is the chiefest virtue, and
> Most dignifies the haver. If it be,
> The man I speak of cannot in the world
> Be singly counterpoised.
>
> (II.ii.80)

The phrases 'it is held' and 'if it be' concede that other views are possible, and invite us to question this conception of 'virtue'.

Cominius's eulogy points up one essential quality of the epic hero – his uniqueness. He stands monolithically, 'like a great sea-mark', above the rest of humanity. Even in his chosen element of war Coriolanus is something of a solitary, as we see in his single-handed capture of Corioli. He also stands apart in many ways from his fellow-patricians and their order, as for example in his hostility to some of their customs (on which their prerogatives depend), in his rejection of praise, for which he is several times rebuked, and his opposition to their doctrine of political expediency. His pride, too, another heroic quality, cuts him off from fellowship with the citizens. As Shakespeare's contemporary, the Frenchman Pierre de la Primaudaye, put it

> And indeed God hath made man of a mild and communicable nature, apt to society, and to live with company, not solitarily, as savage beasts do. Therefore there is nothing more contrary to his nature, and to that end for which he was created, than this vicious pride, whereby he is so puffed up and swelleth in such sort, as if he were some other nature and condition than human, and as though he meant to live in some other estate and degree than of man.

(*The Second Part of the French Academy*, translated by T.B. (1594) p. 330.)

This viewpoint is expressed in the criticism of Brutus, his enemy,

> You speak o' the people
> As if you were a god to punish, not
> A man of their infirmity

(III.i.80)

and of Menenius, his friend:

> He wants nothing of a god but eternity and a heaven to throne in.

(v.iv.21)

The play has several major themes which are explored through the story of Coriolanus. Firstly, it demonstrates the impossibility and irrelevance of a pursuit of the heroic ideal, whether in Shakespeare's world or our own, and the likelihood that it will lead to tragic disaster. Secondly, it asserts the necessity of human interdependence; and thirdly, the need for integrity and wholeness in the individual and in society at large.

It is no accident that the central and unifying image of the play is that of the body and its functioning. The Fable of the Belly (i.i.82; see also p. liii), found in Plutarch, the classical argument for the interdependence of the members of the body politic and the harmonious integration of society which is the true end of all political endeavour, accorded perfectly with Shakespeare's intentions, and he extends the metaphor throughout the play. It was reinforced by the theological analogy of the Church as the Mystical Body, whose head is Christ and whose limbs are the members of the Church, developed in St. Paul's First Letter to the Corinthians:

> For Christ is like a single body with its many limbs and organs, which, many as they are, together make up one body. . . . The eye cannot say to the hand, 'I do not need you'; nor the head to the feet, 'I do not need you.' Quite the contrary: those organs of the body which seem to be

more frail than others are indispensable, and those parts of the body which we regard as less honourable are treated with special honour. . . . God has combined the various parts of the body, giving special honour to the humbler parts, so that there might be no sense of division in the body, but that all its organs might feel the same concern for one another. If one organ suffers, they all suffer together.

1 *Corinthians* 12 – New English Bible.

This passage with all it implied, so intimately known to the Elizabethans,* would inevitably be evoked by Menenius's Fable of the Belly. The transference of the metaphor from the church to the state gave an almost sacramental standing to the idea of the body politic as a divinely-appointed institution which it was blasphemous to attack or undermine in any way.

Coriolanus, we see, has a conception of the integrity of the body politic, revealed as he recommends to the Senate the dissolution of the tribunate,

> Your dishonour
> Mangles true judgement, and bereaves the state
> Of that integrity which should become't,
> Not having the power to do the good it would,
> For th'ill which doth control't

(III.i.157)

but this turns out to be simply the unrestricted power of the Senate, which he sees as dishonoured by any limitation of that power. The plebeians are no part of this integrity. They are not even complete beings, but 'fragments' (I.i.208), 'not Romans' although 'calved i' th' porch o' th' Capitol', but 'barbarians' (III.i.238), and he attempts to rob them of their humanity by the string of animal epithets he hurls at them. Ironically he cannot do without this very humanity he is denying; however despicable they may be, he cannot fight his wars without them. His fame and honour, which rest on deeds and are the centre of his life, depend upon these 'shreds'. His attempt to exclude them is thus impotent from the start. Part of his tragic dilemma is that to the degree that he fulfils his ideal of the supreme and solitary epic hero, to the same degree he unfits himself for political office, and for life generally.

But Coriolanus's heroic aspiration is not the only obstruction to the unity of the Roman polity. Apart from the national opposition between Roman and Volscian which is only broken down, and that temporarily, by Coriolanus and Aufidius, and for selfish reasons by the spies Adrian and Nicanor, there are also class barriers within Rome between patricians and plebeians, functional barriers between senators and tribunes, as well as divisions within these

---

* Although Elizabeth died in 1603, the adjective and noun *Elizabethan* is used in this edition, as normally, to refer also to that part of Shakespeare's life and work which fell within the reign of her successor, James I.

groups, and contention and misunderstanding within the family. All these are caused by tension resulting from the pull of the personal and individual against the demands of the public or collective. Selfishness and egotism blind everyone to the need for integration and also to his own disintegrative influence. Rome is a fatally divided city.

Shakespeare had portrayed the mob in *Henry VI, Part 2* (1590/1) and in *Julius Caesar* (1599) with a good deal of hostility. Although their irrationality, mutability and violence reappear in *Coriolanus* there are significant differences in his treatment of them which support the idea that he was consciously reflecting the English social scene in 1607, which witnessed a rising of the peasants in the midland counties, centred in Shakespeare's native county of Warwickshire. The gentry had been enclosing arable land, turning it into pasturage for sheep as the wool trade flourished. These lands had been held in common for centuries and tilled by the peasants, who now found themselves deprived of their land and livelihood. About a thousand of them (known as 'Levellers' or 'Diggers' from their practice of knocking down the enclosing walls and hedges and digging up the pastures) assembled, as a contemporary witness put it, 'furnished with many half-pikes, piked staves, long bills and bows and arrows and stones' to try to rectify the failure of government proclamations intended to deal with the shortage of grain and other foodstuffs – a situation having affinities with the play's opening scene. They were bloodily suppressed, mainly by the local gentry, some forty or fifty killed and many injured.

The First Citizen's rallying cry, 'You are all resolved rather to die than to famish?' (I.i.3) echoes the assertions of the leaders of the 1607 insurrection. In the Oxfordshire rising of 1597, the leader Bartholomew Stere argued that rather than starve 'it is better to die manfully than to be pined to death'; his aim was 'to help the poor commonalty [common people] that were ready to famish for want of corn', and this same situation prevailed ten years later and must have been familiar to Shakespeare, himself a countryman. He hardly mentions the complaints about usury which figure largely in Plutarch's account, and makes much more of the corn shortage, and in general presents the citizens with a good deal of sympathy. Shakespeare owned land in Warwickshire and there is evidence that he was opposed to the enclosure of land. He gives the citizens a strong case which the patricians ignore to their cost.

The manifesto of the Diggers of 1607 shows how widespread the concept of the body politic was:

> We as members of the whole do feel the smart of these encroaching Tyrants who would grind our flesh upon the whetstone of poverty so that they may dwell by themselves in the midst of their herds of fat wethers.

We notice the pathetic plea of these men to be treated as integral to the body politic, their sense of the tyranny of their exclusion which has resulted in their degradation, and the isolation of the gentry who 'dwell by themselves'. The play reflects this aspect of the Jacobean social scene from the start. The people, starving and mutinous, speak of their rake-like thinness, while the patricians surfeit, 'their storehouses crammed with grain' (I.i.68), and 'our misery is as an inventory to particularize their abundance' (I.i.17) – or as the Diggers had put it, 'There is none of them but do taste the sweetness of our wants.' The First Citizen's cry, 'The gods know, I speak this in hunger for bread, not in thirst for revenge' (I.i.20), has the ring of truth about it. Despite their suffering they show signs of fair-mindedness, as in the Second Citizen's defence of Coriolanus, and their goodwill towards Menenius and willingness to listen to him; and later their readiness to reward Coriolanus for his services to Rome with their votes predisposes us in their favour. They have a dim apprehension of their rightful place in the commonwealth:

> Ingratitude is monstrous, and for the multitude to be ingrateful were to make a monster of the multitude; of the which we, being members, should bring ourselves to be monstrous members.
>
> (II.iii.9)

While Coriolanus sees them as fragments – voices, teeth, faces that need washing and stinking breaths – and Menenius describes them as 'multiplying spawn', Shakespeare does not let us forget that they are people:

> Not that our heads are some brown, some black, some abram, some bald, but that our wits are so diversely coloured.
>
> (II.iii.16)

They are aware of their individuality, the patricians blind to it. We are given a strong sense of their essential good nature which only requires a moderate dose of humanity to respond warmly. That the price of the consulship is 'to ask it kindly' as one of them says, is totally reasonable, but a lesson that Coriolanus is too proud to accept. On the battlefield, sharing a common purpose, and excited by action, he can at times treat them as human beings and find them responding, but here in the market-place he cannot, and reverting to mockery and sarcasm, brings about his own downfall.

Menenius at first appears to be capable of overcoming the class barriers and of communicating with the people, but serious doubts are soon raised in our minds. His Fable is clever rhetoric, but highly inapt. His argument that the Belly/Senate supplies the members/citizens with food, and that they

> do back receive the flour of all,
> And leave me but the bran
>
> (I.i.131)

is a travesty of the truth – a fact visually impressed upon us by the sight of the sleek and well-fed Menenius telling the ragged starvelings in front of him that they have been getting all the food and he the husks. It is one of the dramatist's shrewdest ironies that the speaker is a well-known gourmet and epicurean. His phrases, 'my countrymen', 'masters', 'my good friends, mine honest neighbours', which suggest his belief in their unity as Romans, are seen a few seconds later to be a deception. As soon as the crisis is over he is telling them what he really thinks of them:

> Rome and her rats are at the point of battle;
> The one side must have bale.
>
> (I.i.148)

For him Rome is the patrician order; the people are Rome's enemies, the 'beastly plebeians', not humans even, but vermin, a view echoed soon after by Coriolanus:

> The Volsces have much corn; take these rats thither
> To gnaw their garners.
>
> (I.i.235)

Menenius also has a concept of the state, which he sees as a vast impersonal force, following its course uncontrolled by human influence:

> the Roman state, whose course will on
> The way it takes, cracking ten thousand curbs
> Of more strong link asunder than can ever
> Appear in your impediment.
>
> (I.i.57)

Events prove him woefully wrong. The course of the Roman state, like a human body, is very much at the mercy of human agents, as he later discovers.

When Cominius reports the failure of his peace mission in v.i, Menenius ludicrously, but consistently with his character, attributes it to the fact that Coriolanus had not had his breakfast:

> he had not dined.
> The veins unfilled, our blood is cold, and then
> We pout upon the morning, are unapt
> To give or to forgive.
>
> (v.i.50)

Ironically, he does not perceive the application of this to the citizens, whose coldness for war springs largely from those unfilled veins which it is the Belly/Senate's function to see replenished. It is their hunger which causes their insurrection, which in turn leads to the appointment of the tribunes who are the agents of Coriolanus's disgrace. Cause and effect can be seen too in the looting of the soldiers in I.v. For Coriolanus, war means the chance of fame; for them, the opportunity of booty. Cominius understands this and uses it as an incentive to make them fight:

> Make good this ostentation, and you shall
> Divide in all with us.
>
> (I.vi.86)

Coriolanus, blind to their condition and needs, merely curses them. Cominius, despite his stronger sense of the realities and his unquestionable patriotism, shares the patrician exclusion of the plebeians from organic membership of the state. They are 'goodly things', to be used cynically when needed, ignored when not.

Volumnia is even more strongly separatist. Behind her curses

> Now the red pestilence strike all trades in Rome,
> And occupations perish
>
> (IV.i.13)

there is no awareness that her position and that of her class depends on these same workmen, and Sicinius's complaint that Coriolanus's friends

> rather had,
> Though they themselves did suffer by't, behold
> Dissentious numbers pest'ring streets, than see
> Our tradesmen singing in their shops and going
> About their functions friendly
>
> (IV.vi.5)

has some justification. The plebeians, we should notice, are not social parasites, the idle and unemployed, but everywhere represented as men who work and have to go off to fight for Rome. Volumnia has imbued Coriolanus with her own dismissive contempt for them, as creatures whose function is to shut up and do what they are told:

> woollen vassals, things created
> To buy and sell with groats, to show bare heads
> In congregations, to yawn, be still and wonder,
> When one but of my ordinance stood up
> To speak of peace or war.
>
> (III.ii.9)

But if the patricians are blind to their responsibilities and to any conception of a homogeneous social entity of which the citizens are an essential part, the tribunes and their followers are equally exclusive. The First Senator's warning that civil dissension is the way 'To unbuild the city and to lay all flat' provokes the myopic response:

> SICINIUS What is the city but the people?
> CITIZENS   ` True,
>   The people are the city.

(III.i.198)

This definition of the commonwealth which excludes the patricians is fatally incomplete, as they are soon to discover. When Coriolanus threatens the city which is 'but the people', tribunes and plebeians turn in total helplessness to the patricians to get them out of trouble. That the tribunes in their pride have exalted their own small part of the political function into the whole, so that they cannot see beyond their noses, is illustrated with neat irony in their complacent conviction that they have established peace at the very moment when Coriolanus is poised to burn Rome to the ground (IV.vi). Their blindness has been pointed out by Menenius:

> You know neither me, yourselves, nor anything.

(II.i.62)

> O that you could turn your eyes toward the napes of your necks, and make but an interior survey of your good selves! O that you could!

(II.i.34)

They can't, but ironically again, neither Menenius nor anyone else makes this 'interior survey' of which he speaks.

Shakespeare, it must be stressed, is not taking political sides. There is no doubt that he shared the current political belief in the hierarchy of the three estates, king, nobles and commons, and would have supported Aristotle's assertion, so widely echoed by renaissance political theorists, that of the three forms of government, dictatorship, oligarchy and democracy, the last was the lowest and least desirable. His political and social philosophy is given full expression in the Archbishop of Canterbury's metaphor of the commonwealth of the bees in *Henry V* (I.ii), and by Ulysses on order and degree in *Troilus and Cressida* (I.iii). In *Coriolanus* the integrity of the state is destroyed by the egotism of individuals and the selfishness of groups which blind them to the nature and needs of the body politic and the mutual interdependence of its members. Nobody escapes censure.

Wishing to explore the themes outlined above, Shakespeare's problem was how best to give them dramatic embodiment. The first requirement was balance, and he achieves this in various ways. The first is to place the audience in the favoured position of knowing more about people and events than any single character in the play. Every character's views are partial and limited by prejudice or ignorance, and we see where their judgement of each other goes wrong and why. This creates an ironic distance between us and the characters, preventing total identification of ourselves with any of them. All sides are given a measure of truth and powerful motives for action, and this creates dramatic tension. There are no exemplary characters whom we can fully trust or follow. Shakespeare constantly employs the technique of attracting us towards an individual or group one moment and repelling us the next, so that we are precluded from making snap judgements about them, and forced into a detached and questioning attitude about them and their motives and behaviour. For example, the play begins by presenting multiple viewpoints about Coriolanus's nature. His military exploits are variously interpreted:

> FIRST CITIZEN   Though soft-conscienced men can be content to say it
> was for his country, he did it to please his mother, and
> to be partly proud, which he is, even to the altitude of
> his virtue.
> SECOND CITIZEN   What he cannot help in his nature, you account a vice
> in him.
>
> (I.i.29)

The debate continues in II.iii where the citizens are puzzled by his manner, one holding that 'He flouted us downright' (148), another defending this as just 'his kind of speech', while Brutus plans what to do 'If, as his nature is, he fall in rage' (247). The question of just what Coriolanus's nature is, and how far it is responsible for his tragedy, is, like so many other questions in this play, left unanswered. Later Aufidius proffers three possible reasons for Coriolanus's fall from power – pride, defective judgement or inherent nature – again without coming to any conclusion, thus guiding our response into a balanced inconclusiveness. As in life, some questions have no answers.

Menenius on his first appearance is hailed by the plebeians as an honest man who has always loved them. We soon see that neither statement is true, thus forcing us to be sceptical about the reliability of what Menenius says, and about their judgement. When the tribunes wind up the scene with their comments we perceive that these are twisted by envy of Coriolanus and so not wholly dependable. Shakespeare brings them in with these comments repeatedly – at the end of II.i, II.ii, at II.iii. 140, the end of II.iii and the beginning and end of IV.vi – and always the same reservations have to be made.

The play follows a dialectical mode, running to extremes, from thesis to antithesis, from which we endeavour to form a synthesis; it is a play of 'violentest contrarieties' among which we seek a middle way. The First Citizen's words to Coriolanus,

> You have deserved nobly of your country, and you have not deserved
> nobly
>
> (II.iii.80)

which Coriolanus calls an 'enigma', might well serve as a motto for the method of the play. G. Wilson Knight has usefully drawn attention to the use of pairs of contrasting images which run through it: lions and hares, foxes and geese, oaks and rushes, a bear scattering children, a boy and a butterfly, men and geese, the cat and the mouse, eagles and crows, and many more, all pointing to the extremes of Roman society. We see it too in reactions to simple events. When Coriolanus, 'a bear who lives like a lamb', returns from war, Volumnia knows 'not where to turn', Virgilia weeps to see him triumph, and Menenius exclaims, 'I could weep/And I could laugh, I am light and heavy', and promises to 'make my very house reel tonight'. Hate turns to love and back again with lightning rapidity: 'Friends now fast sworn . . . shall within this hour . . . break out/To bitterest enmity' (IV.iv.12) – as we see exemplified by Coriolanus and Aufidius.

If it is a world of extremes, it is also a world of uncertainties. Here Shakespeare's major technical weapon is irony. There is a thick web of situational ironies in which events turn out in ways which, though fully and logically motivated, are altogether unexpected. All the triumphs of the play turn immediately to disaster: Coriolanus's triumphal entry into Rome is swiftly followed by his ignominious banishment; the resulting triumph of the tribunes is equally short-lived, cut off at the very moment of self-congratulation; Volumnia's triumphal return to Rome is paid for at once by the death of her son; Aufidius's revenge turns sour on him the moment he gets it, and so on.

Things and people are not what they seem. Spying and treachery are rife, people assume roles and set out to deceive – Coriolanus, Menenius, Volumnia, Aufidius and the tribunes all 'act', and the citizens are notoriously inconstant. Coriolanus who boasts of his constancy and is described as 'the rock, the oak not to be wind-shaken' by the Volscian guards (v.ii.104) is twice a traitor. Nothing is sure in the quicksands of Roman politics.

In this grim world comedy is necessarily muted. What there is is found in Menenius, arising out of his deception of the people with his clever tongue; in the mindless unreliability of the plebeians; in the muddle-headed hypocrisy of the servants of Aufidius, and in Menenius's exchange with the Volscian guards, who out-talk this accomplished rhetorician and expose his high-sounding words as 'lies'. Comedy thus serves a serious and chastening purpose in the play.

Shakespeare took pains to render the Roman world faithfully. He achieves this partly by a brilliantly imaginative assimilation of the Roman scene and outlook, and partly by his use of detail. His references to the Tiber, the Capitol, the market-place, gates, walls and buildings of the city, give us the solid feel of Rome, and this is enhanced by the wealth of classical allusions – to Jupiter, Juno, Mars, Hercules, Pluto, Neptune, Deucalion, Phoebus, Triton, the Hydra, Hector, Hecuba, Ulysses, Cato, the Tarquins. At the same time, in his usual fashion, he ties this ancient world indissolubly to his own by numerous contemporary details: the orange-wife and faucet-seller, mummers, balladmakers, mountebanks, tailors, harvest men tasked to mow, ladies sewing spots, the kitchen malkin in her richest lockram, Hob and Dick; stalls, bulks and windows, roof-ridges, pictures hanging on the wall, graves i' th' holy churchyard, the tide rushing under London Bridge, bowls, stocks, coxcombs, spectacles, the plague, grace before meat, the lottery, fawning greyhounds on the leash, crab-trees and nettles, and scores more. The Shakespearian magic effects this with no sense of incongruousness, and brings the ancient world and his own age into close relationship. It is the real world that he presents, hard, stony, metallic and brittle, in which each event has a natural and logical cause.

Shakespeare did not sentimentalize the story or soften its harshness. The play is a tragedy and the Roman world is not finally regenerated, yet paradoxically the play leaves us with an impression of final optimism, in that we perceive that events do not have to be like this. No supernatural agency such as Fate or Destiny propels Shakespeare's characters into action; their tragedy springs from corrigible human weaknesses, and at numerous points in the action they are given warnings and offered opportunities to make the right choice. There is a strong sense of a residual human goodness, obscured and frustrated by man's attempt to be an island, to cut himself off and erect barriers against his fellow-men, springing from egotism and selfishness. The diagnosis is explicit, the cure implicit, and the situation perennial.

The text of *Coriolanus*

Reference is made in the *Introduction* and Notes to the First Folio. A folio is simply a book made up of sheets which have been folded once before printing, giving two leaves or four pages of print. The First Folio, published in 1623, seven years after Shakespeare's death, was the first collected edition of his plays, printing thirty-six of them, eighteen for the first time, including *Coriolanus*. The First Folio is thus our sole authority for the text of the play, and bibliographical scholars are generally agreed that the manuscript, or copy, given to the printers was Shakespeare's original autograph manuscript, often known as 'foul papers', or else a reliable transcript of it. The play is rich in stage directions which were certainly provided by the author, since many of them, such as 'Holds her by the hand, silent' are derived from Plutarch, Shakespeare's source for the play. There are many others which, like this one, reflect Shakespeare's concern with the stage production of his play, with details of position, movement and gesture, which are frequently important in

30

The Tragedy of Coriolanus:

Actus Primus. Scæna Prima.

*Enter a Company of Mutinous Citizens, with Staves,
Clubs, and other weapons.*

1. *Citizen.*

Efore we proceed any further, heare me speake.

All. Speake, speake.

1. Cit. You are all resolv'd rather to dy then
to famish?

All. resolv'd, resolv'd.

1. Cit. First you know, *Caius Martius* is chiefe enemy
to the people.

All. We know't.

1. Cit. Let us kill him, and wee'l have Corne at our
owne price. Is't a Verdict?

All. No more talking on't, Let it be done, away, away

2. Cit. One word, good Citizens

1. Cit. We are accounted poore Citizens, the Patricians good: what Authority surfets one, would releeve us,
If they would yeelde us but the superfluity while it were
wholsome, we might guesse they releeved us humanely:
But they thinke we are too deere, the leannes that afflicts
us, the object of our misery, is as an inventory to particularize their abundance, our sufferance is a gaine to them.
Let us revenge this with our Pikes, ere we become Rakes.
For the Gods know, I speake this in hunger for Bread,
not in thirst for Revenge.

2. Cit. Would you proceede especially against *Caius
Martius.*

All. Against him first: He's a very dog to the Commonalty.

2. Cit. Consider you what Services he ha's done for his
Country?

1. Cit. Very well, and could be content to give him
good report for't, but that hee payes himselfe with bee-
ing proud.

All. Nay, but speake not maliciously.

1. Cit. I say unto you, what he hath done Famously,
he did it to that end: though soft conscienc'd men can be
content to say it was for his Countrey, he did it to please
his Mother, and to be partly proud, which he is, even to
the altitude of his vertue.

2. Cit. What he cannot helpe in his Nature, you account a Vice in him: You must in no way say he is coue-
tous.

1. Cit. If I must not, I neede not be barren of Accusations he hath faults (with surplus) to tyre in repitition.
                                Showts within.
What showts are those? The other side a'th City is risen:
why stay we prating heere? To th'Capitoll.

All. Come, come.

1. Cit. Soft, who comes heere?
                    Enter Menenius Agrippa.

2. Cit. Worthy *Menenius Agrippa*, one that hath al-
wayes lov'd the people.

1. Cit. He's one honest enough, would al the rest were so.

Men. What workes my Countrimen in hand?
Where go you with your Bats and Clubs? The matter
Speake I pray you.

2. Cit. Our busines is not unknowne to th'Senat, they
have had inkling this fortnight what we intend to do, w^{ch}
now wee'l shew em in deeds: they say poore Suiters have
strong breaths, they shal know we have strong armes too.

Men. Why Maisters, my good Friends, mine honest
Neigbours, will you undo your selves?

2. Cit. We cannot Sir, we are undone already.

Men. I tell you Friends, most charitable care
Have the Patricians of you for your wants.
Your suffering in this dearth, you may as well
Strike at the Heaven with your staves, as lift them
Against the Roman State, whose course will on
The way it takes: cracking ten thousand Curbes
Of more strong linkd asunder, then can ever
Appeare in your impediment. For the Dearth,
The Gods, not the Patricians make it, and
Your knees to them (not armes) must helpe. Alacke,
You are transported by Calamity
Thether, where more attends you, and you slander
The Helmes o'th State; who care for you like Fathers,
When you curse them, as Enemies.

2 Cit. Care for us? True indeed, they nere car'd for us
yet. Suffer us to famish, and their Store-houses cramm'd
with Graine: Make Edicts for Usury, to support Usurers; repeale daily any wholsome Act estableshed against
the rich, and provide more piercing Statutes daily, to
chaine up and restraine the poore. If the Warres eate us
not uppe, they will, and ther's all the love they beare
us.

Men. Either you must
Confesse your selves wondrous Malicious,
Or be accus'd of Folly. I shall tell you
A pretty Tale, it may be you have heard it,
But since it serves my purpose, I will venture
To scale't a little more.

2 Cit. Well, Ile heare it Sir: yet you must not thinke
To fobbe off our disgrace with a tale:
But and't please you deliver.

Men. There was a time, when all the bodies members
Rebell'd against the Belly; thus accus'd it:
That onely like a Gulfe it did remaine

                                            I'th

The first page of Coriolanus *from the First Folio (1623), which has been reduced from the original
size of 34 cms × 22 cms.*

creating exactly the atmosphere he wanted. One obvious example of this is I.iii, in which we are told that Volumnia and Virgilia 'set them down and sew', a scene of quiet domesticity which contrasts effectively with the bustling scenes of public disorder and clamour of war which precede and follow it.

The compositors in the printing house of Isaac Jaggard, in converting their handwritten copy into type did an average job of work by the standards of the time. There were two of them: the first, identified as Compositor A, was the more accurate workman, while the second, Compositor B, tended to take more liberties with the text, so that modern editors have to make more emendations to the pages he set up than to those composed by his companion. Both, however, were experienced compositors and produced together not more than about thirty errors of substance in the text. Many of these are obvious typographical errors, easily corrected; others can be righted by reference to Plutarch. For example, the First Folio at I.i.57 has the nonsense reading, 'Thou wast a soldier/Even to Calues wish', which derives from Plutarch's statement, 'For he was even such another, as Cato would have a soldier and a captain to be', and so is easily amended. Elsewhere an editor can only make an intelligent guess at what the author intended.

The present edition modernizes spelling and punctuation and regularizes the lineation which is very wayward in some 300 lines, with the compositors printing lines that have either more or fewer than the ten syllables of the blank verse line. Sometimes they seem to have been trying to save space, sometimes they could not get the whole line into the narrow column of the Folio and so carried the extra material over into the next line, capitalizing the first letter as if beginning a new line. In this way subsequent lines of a speech would often be thrown out of correct lineation. A number of errors of speech-attribution in the Folio are also corrected here, and variation in the spelling of people and places is replaced by a single spelling in each case. Caius Martius is called Coriolanus in speech headings and stage directions after I.ix.65, and throughout the Notes and *Introduction*. The Folio has division into five acts, but no scene divisions. The former have been retained, although they have no structural significance and were probably not Shakespeare's; the latter have been provided for the convenience of the reader.

The principal characters in *Coriolanus*

Coriolanus, with 3410 lines, is one of Shakespeare's longest plays. Of this total Coriolanus has 24%, Menenius 14% and the five figures of Volumnia, Aufidius, Cominius, Brutus and Sicinius some 8% each. The remaining 20% is divided between 31 small parts – those of Virgilia, Valeria, Titus Lartius, Adrian and Nicanor and the usual auxiliaries such as citizens, soldiers, senators, officials, attendants and messengers whose large numbers convey the desired atmosphere of the bustle and activity of the Roman political world.

CORIOLANUS as Shakespeare presents him is a hero in the renaissance tradition, one who impresses his powerful personality on all around him, whether favourably or not. In order to sustain his conception of a hero tragically dedicated to an impossible epic idealism, Shakespeare had to transform Plutarch's portrait, of an anti-social boor whom nobody could talk to, in many ways. Firstly he makes him more independent of his mother, by omitting Plutarch's detail that 'at her desire [he] took a wife also, by whom he had two children' and that he did not leave his mother's house after his marriage. He carefully makes Coriolanus bid farewell to his wife before his mother on his banishment (IV.i) and greet her first in the pleading scene (V.iii), and generally accents his love for her, all contrary to Plutarch's narrative.

Secondly, he increases his heroic stature. He adds the detail that in the fight against the tyrant Tarquin, Coriolanus 'slew three opposers' and invents his personal slaying of Tarquin. Plutarch's phrase that he made 'the enemy afeared with the sound of his voice and grimness of his countenance' is transmuted in Titus Lartius's words to

> but with thy grim looks and
> The thunder-like percussion of thy sounds
> Thou mad'st thine enemies shake, as if the world
> Were feverous and did tremble.
>
> (I.iv.58)

The attribution of the Jove-like power of thunder to Coriolanus, later seconded by Cominius's assertion that his voice compared with those of other men was like thunder beside a drum (I.vi.25), and the image of the trembling world, give him a cosmic force which is reinforced elsewhere as we are told that 'he waxed like a sea' (II.ii.96) and 'struck/Corioli like a planet' (II.ii.110). This aura of the elemental and godlike is carefully built up through the play. Even the inimical tribune Brutus reports on his divine bearing,

> As if that whatsoever god who leads him
> Were slyly crept into his human powers,
> And gave him graceful posture.
>
> (II.i.208)

The Messenger adds that

> The nobles bended
> As to Jove's statue.
>
> (II.i.254)

He is 'godded' by Menenius (v.iii.11) who compares him to Hercules (IV.vi.100) and comments that 'He wants nothing of a god but eternity and a heaven to throne in' (v.iv.22); Aufidius addresses him as 'Mars', would as soon believe him as believe Jupiter (IV.v.100), and 'sanctifies himself with's hand' (IV.v.188); the Volscian lords greet him 'as if he were the son and heir to Mars' (IV.v.184) and Cominius remarks that for them

> He is their god. He leads them like a thing
> Made by some other deity than Nature.
>
> (IV.vi.91)

The Volscian soldiers 'use him as the grace 'fore meat' (IV.vii.3), and Volumnia affirms that he has always striven

> To imitate the graces of the gods.
>
> (v.iii.150)

He is free from covetousness and ambition for power, chaste, honest, not given to flattery. Coriolanus is widely loved and admired; not just by his wife and mother as we might expect, but also by Valeria, Menenius, Titus Lartius, Cominius and even his enemy Aufidius who reports that 'The senators and patricians love him too' (IV.vii.30) whereas in Plutarch many of them are hostile to him. He is the eagle, the osprey 'who takes it/By sovereignty of nature' (IV.vii.34), 'the rarest man i' the world' (IV.v.155), 'best man i' th' field' (II.ii.94), 'Beyond the mark of others' (II.ii.86), 'too noble for the world' (III.i.254). The two neutral Senate officials pronounce him brave and worthy, the citizens agree that 'if he would incline to the people, there was never a worthier man' (II.iii.34), and even the Tribunes grudgingly concede some of his virtues. The praise comes from all sides. Shakespeare makes him more sagacious in predicting the Volscian war in I.i and more noble in that he does not intrigue to propel the Volscians into war after his exile or spare the patrician lands with the politic purpose of driving a wedge between the patricians and plebeians in Rome, as in Plutarch. His anger in the play is directed against the whole city, which makes him a much more terrifying figure, approximating the hero Achilles in his remorseless anger.

Coriolanus, then, is unquestionably the hero. His faults, like his virtues, are on a grand scale, particularly the pride and anger which lead to his treason. Many, while conceding this, would deny that he is a *tragic* hero, chiefly on the grounds that he is inhuman, machine-like, cold, a man who knows nothing of himself and learns nothing, one in whom there is no inward struggle. There is a degree of truth in some of these charges, but they are usually accompanied by discussions of his character which distort by simplifying the complexity of Shakespeare's characterization. The sharp differences of opinion about him among the other characters of the play draw attention to the many paradoxes of his nature. For example, it is running counter to the text to assert, as many do, that his modesty is an inverted pride, an unwillingness to accept praise from people he regards as inferior, and hence a false modesty. He declares his distaste for flattery on numerous occasions: alone with Lartius (I.v.16), with the army (I.ix.13,28,41), and on his return to Rome (II.i.157). His mother grieves him when she praises him, he tells us (I.ix.15). While he generously gives a full account of Lartius's part in the battle, he avoids talking about himself (I.vi.46), and during the electioneering it is clearly agony for him to boast of his exploits and show his wounds. Several reliable characters comment on his modesty and there is nowhere the slightest suggestion that it is hypocritical or an unconscious form of pride. To fight bravely is as natural to Coriolanus as breathing, and he who hates to flatter others understandably hates to hear his 'nothings monstered'. It is perfectly possible, of course, for modesty to co-exist with a pride in one's social rank. The point is worth labouring because his modesty is just one quality which sets up a tension between his nature and his idealism, since boasting is one of the accepted characteristics of the epic warrior.

We go wrong, then, in seeking to argue away the paradoxes that Shakespeare carefully built into his hero. In similar fashion he is both constant, as he claims, and inconstant, arrogant and humble, patriotic and treacherous, conservative and revolutionary, uncompromising and yet willing to sacrifice principle, manly and immature, warmly human and coldly unfeeling. All this is in keeping with the antithetical mode of the whole play, earlier discussed. The tension between his nature and his upbringing makes him a divided man, and this is the essence of his tragedy. It is one of the play's deeper subtleties and a source of pathos, that his mother, to whom no man is more closely bound, who has helped to 'frame' him both in body and spirit, and who thinks she knows him through and through, should understand so little of his real nature. He is not nearly so 'absolute' as she imagines.

We see the cracks in Coriolanus's psychological armour if we consider him in his chosen element of war. The epic warrior is basically a solitary figure, an individual seeker after personal honour and fame whose appropriate form of action is the single combat. In this role Coriolanus is pre-eminent, and Shakespeare stresses his isolation and 'singularity'. As Plutarch tells it, he enters Corioli with other Roman soldiers; in the play 'He is himself alone/To answer all the city' (I.iv.51); he is acclaimed by the Roman troops and asks, 'O, me alone? Make you a sword of me?' (I.vi.76); he boasts in epic style to Aufidius, 'Alone I fought in your Corioli walls' (I.viii.9), an action praised by the Herald, 'Know, Rome, that all alone Martius did fight/Within Corioli gates' (II.i.151), and later by Cominius, 'Alone he entered/The mortal gate of th' city' (II.ii.107) and 'cannot in the world/Be singly counterpoised' (II.ii.83). It is, too, the subject of his final, fatal boast, 'Alone I did it' (v.vi.116).

This isolation, however, severely limits his worth as a commander. Our first glimpse of him at war, invented by the dramatist, is disconcerting. He is making a bet with Titus Lartius, which ominously he loses, and this suggests that like Troilus and Hector in *Troilus and Cressida* and Hotspur in *Henry IV, part 1*, all would-be epic honour-seekers, he regards war as a sport (later confirmed by Cominius's account of how he turned 'terror into sport' (II.II.102); it also points to a certain recklessness of nature. Before battle he threatens to kill his men if they run away. As a method of leadership it fails signally and they are soon in full flight, evoking his curses; it is in marked contrast with the leadership of Cominius who, forced to retreat, praises his men, and keeps them together as a fighting unit which forms the nucleus of the force which finally defeats the Volsces. The result of Coriolanus's vilification of his troops is that they refuse to follow him – which he later refers to as 'their mutinies and revolts' (III.i.126) – despite the unheroic incentive he holds out to them:

> If you'll stand fast, we'll beat them to their wives.
>
> (I.iv.41)

His stirring battle-cry, 'Mark me, and do the like', is ignored, as he needlessly endangers his life by dashing alone into the city, 'to the pot' as his mutinous men laconically put it. In the eyes of Titus Lartius it is a 'noble' action; to an ordinary soldier 'foolhardiness'. We notice once again the dramatist's method of presenting conflicting viewpoints for our consideration. It is the steady old soldier, Titus Lartius, who leads these same men to the rescue of Coriolanus who is seen within 'bleeding, assaulted by the enemy'. Elizabethan soldiers of this swashbuckling kind, despite their personal courage, men like the Earl of Essex, Sir Richard Grenville and Sir Edward Stanley, who needlessly risked their own lives, were censured as poor leaders by the military theorists of the time. Emerging from the city, Coriolanus hurries off to confront Aufidius in single combat, a detail invented by Shakespeare, and overcomes him in epic fashion. With skilful ambiguity Shakespeare both establishes Coriolanus's heroism on the battlefield and also questions its value.

The tensions between his nature and his military ideal cause him to shut off his humanity. They reach into the heart of his family life. His mother has inculcated in him a love of war and rejoices at the thought of his 'bloody brow', which provokes from Virgilia the prayer, 'O Jupiter, no blood!' (I.iii.36), an exchange which neatly sums up their opposed attitudes. Coriolanus, although he loves his wife, follows his mother, and it is clear that Young Martius, who mercilessly tears the butterfly to pieces, is being brought up to be another Coriolanus. The latter loves 'this painting', blood (I.vi.68); he is 'a thing of blood' who runs 'reeking o'er the lives of men' (II.ii.116), 'death's stamp' (II.ii.104). Yet humanity keeps breaking through. He tells how he saw his

Coriolan host taken prisoner,

> But then Aufidius was within my view,
> And wrath o'erwhelmed my pity.

(I.ix.84)

The epic challenge of Aufidius's presence submerges Coriolanus's humanity, but it surfaces again after the battle as he pleads for the man's release. He is aware that humanity and war are at odds. We see the disruption of his values in the way he transfers to the battlefield the terms of romantic love as he greets Cominius:

> in heart
> As merry as when our nuptial day was done,
> And tapers burned to bedward!

(I.vi.30)

It is clearly an attitude derived from his mother,

> If my son were my husband, I should freelier rejoice in that absence wherein he won honour than in the embracements of his bed where he would show most love

(I.iii.2)

and is echoed, significantly, by that other aspiring hero, Aufidius, as he greets Coriolanus at IV.v.111. Coriolanus's two references to those he has widowed and deprived of sons (II.i.167, IV.iv.2) show a consciousness of the human effects of his warring. Too often he is viewed as a machine rather than a person. Menenius, it is true, tells Sicinius that 'he moves like an engine, and the ground shrinks before his treading' (v.iv.17), but this reflects his chagrin at the failure of his peace mission, and is said in ironic ignorance of the powerful feelings we have just witnessed in Coriolanus in the previous pleading scene (v.iii).

Coriolanus's first moral crisis occurs in III.ii when his mother and friends are urging him to seek pardon from the plebeians in order to secure the consulship. He is bewildered by his mother's disapproval of his behaviour; her advice that he should dissemble contradicts all she has taught him and demands that he should be false to his nature. It is not that he is afraid of her; it is love and respect he exhibits, not fear. Even Sicinius says 'he loved his mother dearly' (v.iv.14). Coriolanus gives way because he is persuaded that this will save Rome from civil war. As the Senator puts it:

> There's no remedy,
> Unless, by not so doing, our good city
> Cleave in the midst and perish.

(III.ii.26)

Menenius adds that the crisis requires it as 'physic/For the whole state' (33).
The shrewdest point in Volumnia's argument is her exposure of a fundamental weakness in her son's epic posture:

> I have heard you say,
> Honour and policy, like unsevered friends,
> I' th' war do grow together.
>
> (41)

Coriolanus will use 'policy', that is, deception, to gain his ends in war; for
example, he will 'take in a town with gentle words'.

> If it be honour in your wars to seem
> The same you are not, which for the best ends
> You adopt your policy
>
> (46)

why not, she asks, in peace-time. It is, as Menenius remarks, 'a good demand'
and Coriolanus has no answer. Clearly he has conceded that the practical
exigencies of war sometimes demand a sacrifice of principles to expediency.
His willingness 'to seem the same he is not' in war undermines his insistence
that it is dishonourable to dissemble in peace-time. His agony of spirit is no
less real because of his inconsistency, however:

> Must I
> With my base tongue give to my noble heart
> A lie that it must bear? Well, I will do't.
> Yet were there but this single plot to lose,
> This mould of Martius, they to dust should grind it.
>
> (99)

He accepts the humiliation for the sake of Rome; what is often taken as weak
selfishness or fear of his mother is for him an act of considerable self-sacrifice.
As he thinks of what is demanded of him he veers again – 'I will not do't' (120)
– but at his mother's warning, 'Come all to ruin' (125) he finally acquiesces.
Ultimately Coriolanus's tragedy is that his idealism prevents him from living in
the real world. He is constantly forced to deny human relationships. As
Sicinius observes, his nature 'easily endures not article/Tying him to aught'
(II.iii.185). His words as he is exiled – 'I banish you' (III.iii.121) – are magnilo-
quent, but a characteristic blinking of the facts. His career is one of progres-
sive isolation. When he leaves Rome he is on good terms with his family and
friends, but once alone his outraged pride and anger consume him and he
casts them all off. In 'mere spite' he will fight 'with the spleen/Of all the under
fiends' (IV.v.88), the expression suggesting the element of diabolical possession in his switch from love to hate, a 'slippery turn' for which he attempts to
blame the 'world'. He tries to evade responsibility for the ruin of his family

which his revenge involves by the simple process of denying his relationship with them:

> Wife, mother, child, I know not.
>
> (v.ii.78)

Although he breathes fire on Rome, he is no 'lonely dragon' as he claims. He needs the Volscians now as much as he needed the Roman troops he cursed in Act I. He acts as if he were a god to punish the Romans, and 'not/A man of their infirmity' (III.i.81). It is an arrogant pride, which has to be punished.

His second and final crisis, and one foreshadowed by and intimately tied to the first, is the arrival of his family seeking mercy for Rome. The reality of their physical presence dispels his fantasies and breaks his resolution:

> Shall I be tempted to infringe my vow
> In the same time 'tis made?
>
> (v.iii.20)

He tries now to deny natural feelings:

> But out, affection!
> All bond and privilege of nature, break!
> Let it be virtuous to be obstinate.
>
> (24)

It is a straight fight between his concept of *virtus* and nature, which nature wins as he looks at Virgilia:

> What is that curtsy worth? Or those dove's eyes,
> Which can make gods forsworn? I melt, and am not
> Of stronger earth than others.
>
> (27)

This realization of his common humanity is a new insight. One of the major ironies of the scene is that his mother's plea, so clever and eloquent, is not really needed; he is won over before she speaks. The sight of Volumnia bowing is

> As if Olympus to a molehill should
> In supplication nod, and my young boy
> Hath an aspéct of intercession which
> Great Nature cries 'Deny not'.
>
> (30)

He struggles blasphemously to assert his individualism against great Nature, vowing

> I'll never
> Be such a gosling to obey instínct, but stand

> As if a man were author of himself
> And knew no other kin.

(34)

Talking to his wife he seeks to deny reality:

> These eyes are not the same I wore in Rome.

(38)

Although he concedes that 'like a dull actor' he has forgotten his part, an explicit self-admission that he has been dissembling, he still tries to have it both ways, to enjoy the extremes of love and revenge:

> Best of my flesh,
> Forgive my tyranny, but do not say,
> For that, 'Forgive our Romans.' O, a kiss
> Long as my exile, sweet as my revenge!

(42)

The phrase 'Long as my exile' speaks eloquently of the agony of his separation from love, the price he has paid for living a lie. His prayer, too, that his son should 'prove/To shame unvulnerable . . . standing every flaw,/And saving those that eye thee' (72), shows a consciousness of his own failure to be proof against shame, withstand adversity and save those dependent on him. Rather, as his mother says, he will 'bear the palm for having bravely shed/Thy wife and children's blood' (117). When he exhorts his mother

> Tell me not
> Wherein I seem unnatural

(83)

he is still trying to make the 'seeming' into a 'being', appearance into reality, but he cannot sustain it:

> Not of a woman's tenderness to be,
> Requires nor child nor woman's face to see.
> I have sat too long.

(129)

Even here he tries to cling to his concept of masculine *virtus* by dismissing a man's natural feelings as 'a woman's tenderness', and tries physically to break away, but is restrained by his mother's command 'Nay, go not from us thus' (131). Her final appeal is too much for him and as Shakespeare's stage direction puts it, he 'holds her by the hand, silent', an eloquent sign both of his inner turmoil and of his reconciliation with nature and love. That his eyes 'sweat compassion' (196) is a further sign of this. Part of the reality he now accepts is the imminence of his own death, of which, pathetically, his family seem to be unaware. Aufidius interprets the action correctly:

> I am glad thou hast set thy mercy and thy honour
> At difference in thee.
>
> (200)

The 'honour' he speaks of is, of course, treachery. Mercy, we learn, is the one thing, apart from 'eternity and a heaven to throne in' which he has lacked (v.iv.23). Paradoxically, he is most godlike now that he has accepted his humanity. His end follows swiftly and inevitably. This great and moving climactic scene establishes Coriolanus beyond doubt as tragic hero.

A heavy use of soliloquy would be out of place in this man of action so un-accustomed to reflection. The three soliloquies he is given – his self-disgust at vote-begging (II.iii.101), his reflections on the world's slippery turns (IV.iv.12), and his thoughts as his family approaches (V.iii), present us not with his thought-processes, but with his present suffering, a reality denied or ignored by many who do not accept him as tragic hero. Apart from the evidence of suffering contained in these soliloquies we have public situations where he is on the rack, as in his submission to the tribunes and people in III.iii:

> SICINIUS   I do demand
> If you submit you to the people's voices,
> Allow their officers, and are content
> To suffer lawful censure for such faults
> As shall be proved upon you.
> CORIOLANUS   I am content.
>
> (43)

> SICINIUS   Answer to us.
> CORIOLANUS Say, then. 'Tis true I ought so.
>
> (61)

This requires greater heroism from this proud man than anything he has met on the battlefield. Things, says Menenius, 'might have been much better, if/ He could have temporized' (IV.vi.16). Part of Coriolanus's tragedy is that, trapped in the mould which his nature and upbringing have cast him in, he cannot change, temporize or find a mean between extremes.

It is mistaken zeal, because destructive of the tragedy Shakespeare has care-fully created, to invent a non-existent regeneration for Coriolanus. He dis-covers, it is true, the power of nature and human affection, but this is limited we notice to his family. His boast on returning to the Volscians that he is

> No more infected with my country's love
> Than when I parted hence
>
> (v.vi.71)

accentuates his continued blindness and avoidance of reality. He learns almost nothing, and falls as easily to Aufidius's cry of 'traitor' as he had into the traps of the tribunes; the vulnerability of his consistency and simplicity has a quality of greatness in it and is a moving incident on the stage. It is also sad that having shed his identity while seeking revenge on Rome – 'He was a kind of nothing, titleless', as Cominius reports (v.i.13) – he should, in regaining selfhood, be simply the same aspiring epic hero as before, 'Coriolanus':

> like an eagle in a dovecote, I
Fluttered your Volscians in Corioli.
Alone I did it.
>
> (v.vi.114)

It is tragic, but profoundly true.

MENENIUS is mentioned briefly in Plutarch as 'one of the pleasantest old men and the most acceptable to the people', sent by the Senate to pacify them, which by the use of 'good persuasions and gentle requests', including the Fable of the Belly, he succeeds in doing. Shakespeare enlarges these meagre details into the second largest part in the play, and one much prized by actors for its rich scope.

Menenius is a patriot, a shrewd, affable, worldly-wise man able to understand and talk to the common people, who loves Coriolanus as a father and is loved by him. As a figure in the drama, he has several important functions to perform. Primarily, he exists to interpret Coriolanus to us, which he does through straightforward description, through reminiscence, praise, and his bustling efforts to secure the consulship for him. He exposes, through his closeness to him, the hero's strengths and weaknesses: 'As I do know the consul's worthiness/So can I name his faults' (III.i.276). Menenius's practical common sense and moderation enable him to comment authoritatively on the absence of these qualities in Coriolanus. His constant pleas for calm, peace, temperate behaviour, and his warnings to Coriolanus that he will 'mar all', stress the important point that the hero does not act in ignorance, but has a choice open to him at all stages of the action.

Just as Menenius's virtues illuminate Coriolanus's failings, so his faults show up the hero's virtues. Having created this sensible, efficient, and in many ways attractive man, Shakespeare had to be careful to prevent him from becoming a rival or a superior to his protagonist in our minds. Hence he is given serious flaws. With characteristic paradox Shakespeare shows that his flaws spring from these same virtues. In constantly having to pour oil, keep the peace and restore the order which Coriolanus's rash impetuosity has disturbed he is forced into flattery and hypocrisy. His pacific and compromising nature leads him to approve and embody Volumnia's doctrine of 'policy'.

He tells his fable 'since it serves my purpose', and this we discover is to 'fob off' the complaints of the citizens. Once he has disarmed in debate the First Citizen his 'good friend' becomes a 'rascal' and the 'great toe', and the people, his 'neighbours' and 'masters' become 'rats', 'garlic-eaters', the 'beastly plebeians' whose 'stinking greasy caps' 'make the air unwholesome'. The tribunes, at a dangerous moment are 'worthy', but when no longer in a position of power are 'musty chaff . . . smelt above the moon'. We can believe them in their moment of triumph when they report that Menenius 'is grown most kind of late' (IV.vi.11). Even this 'kindness' is a pose which he drops at the first hint of trouble, as he echoes the anger and scorn of them voiced by Cominius. Menenius tends to go with any wind that is blowing.

Menenius's self-portrait in II.i usefully points out the lack of self-awareness in the tribunes, but ironically demonstrates that the criticism applies to himself too, when he claims 'What I think I utter' (II.i.47). In a few moments he is telling the tribunes, 'He (i.e. Coriolanus) loves your people' (II.ii.61). What he calls 'speaking fair' and 'haply amplifying', the Volscian guards more bluntly call 'lies', and we are reminded forcibly that Coriolanus is not like this, and we prefer his honesty to Menenius's diplomacy and dishonesty. When he says of Coriolanus, 'His heart's his mouth' (III.i.256), it is at once both criticism and praise of Coriolanus and of himself. Similarly, Menenius's self-confessed epicureanism points up Coriolanus's freedom from materialism. Although he does not lack courage, there is nothing heroic about the aged senator; he accuses himself and the other patricians of cowardice in allowing the expulsion of Coriolanus, and his consciousness of the difference between himself and the hero whom he 'gods' and feels is 'too noble for this world' makes his worship of him totally convincing, and plays no small part in building him up as tragic hero.

Shakespeare also prevents us from feeling close sympathy with Menenius by making him a 'humorous' man, both in the Elizabethan sense of an eccentric or oddity – what we would call 'a character' – and in the modern sense of 'amusing'. His conviction that he can persuade Coriolanus to spare Rome, especially if he is asked after a good meal, is both absurd and vain, and he is punished by being made the comic butt of the guards who characterize him as a 'decayed dotant' with his 'half-pint of blood'. His pride is punctured and his judgement falters: he is wrong in thinking he is painting Coriolanus 'in the character' when he describes him as a merciless tiger, a dragon and a machine, and wrong in forecasting the failure of Volumnia's peace mission. It is paradoxically at this moment of his humiliation that we feel most sympathy for him. Critics who argue that his heart is not broken and that this is comedy are going against the text. Coriolanus himself sees that he has 'a cracked heart' and Menenius testifies to it as he stumbles off with the mockery of the guards in his ears:

> I neither care for the world, nor your general . . . He that hath a will to
> die by himself fears it not from another.
>
> (v.ii.97)

Though conditioned by the prejudices of the patrician group to which he
belongs, Menenius is a good man who works for Rome's good as he sees it and
whose world falls to bits when his 'son' who has called him 'Thou old and
true' now rejects him. The destruction of his morale is part of the play's
tragedy.

VOLUMNIA is greatly altered and enlarged by Shakespeare. He powerfully
intensifies the relationship between mother and son, making Volumnia a
type of matron revered by the Romans, austere and imperious, and accenting
her formative influence over her son. In the opening scene the First Citizen
tells us that his exploits were performed 'to please his mother' (I.i.30).
On her first appearance she remarks with evident satisfaction that Coriolanus's son would 'rather see the swords and hear a drum than look upon
his schoolmaster' (I.iii.53), to which Valeria replies, 'O' my word, the father's
son', and when she describes how he tore the butterfly to pieces, Volumnia
complacently comments 'One on's father's moods' and later describes the boy
as her son's 'epitome' (v.iii.68). From all this, and from Coriolanus's phrases in
IV.i, 'You used to say' and 'When you were wont to say', we get a strong sense
of her guiding hand throughout his life, as we do from her claim 'Thou art my
warrior;/I holp to frame thee' (v.iii.62). She boasts that she sent him as a
young boy to 'a cruel war' 'where he was like to find fame'.

Of her love for Coriolanus there is no question, but it takes strange forms.
She urges Virgilia, with seeming lack of feeling, to rejoice more at her husband's absence than his loving embraces, derives comfort from his danger,
talks with equanimity about his 'bloody brow', and would rather have eleven
sons 'die nobly for their country, than one voluptuously surfeit out of action'
(I.iii.22). She must be the only mother in literature or life to thank the gods
that her son is wounded (II.i.112).

Yet it is mistaken to see her simply as masculine and unfeeling, or some kind
of human monster. Coriolanus's love for her, Valeria's preference for her as
against Virgilia, and the admiration of Menenius and the other patricians
establish her humanity. She is clearly maternal and fiercely possessive as
phrases like 'my boy Martius' (II.i.93), 'my warrior' (v.iii.62), 'my good
soldier' (II.i.160), 'my gentle Martius' (II.i.161) and 'my first son' (IV.i.32)
indicate, and she is agonized at his banishment. She realizes what she is
sacrificing when she sends him off to war

> when yet he was but tender-bodied, and the only son of my womb;
> when youth with comeliness plucked all gaze his way; when, for a day

of kings' entreaties, a mother should not sell him an hour from her beholding.

(I.iii.5)

Yet she subordinates her maternal feelings to her passionate patriotism. For her, Rome is paramount, and she is, in the patrician view, 'Our patroness, the life of Rome' (v.v.1). Her assertion

> The breasts of Hecuba
> When she did suckle Hector, looked not lovelier
> Than Hector's forehead when it spit forth blood
> At Grecian sword, contemning.

(I.iii.38)

concedes the beauty of motherhood but grotesquely equates it with spurting blood, since wounds 'become a man' in her view, an attitude she inculcates in her son who loves 'this painting', blood. The unnatural distortion of her values is brought out by the normal femininity of Virgilia.

Shakespeare is careful not to attempt to define the precise degree of her responsibility for making Coriolanus what he is. Clearly a good deal of culpability is removed from his shortcomings when we consider her influence over him, but Shakespeare has to be careful to retain freedom of will for his protagonist. We cannot blame everything on Volumnia. He fosters this ambiguity carefully by making it apparent that Coriolanus is both like and unlike his mother.

He is like her in his courage – and she herself claims 'Thy valiantness was mine' (III.ii.129) – his dedication to heroic service, his disdain for the plebeians whom he calls 'dogs' and she 'cats', and his exaltation of the patrician order. Like her he is choleric, and clearly inherits it from her. She exults at being 'in anger, Juno-like':

> Anger's my meat. I sup upon myself,
> And so shall starve with feeding.

(IV.ii.50)

This same self-consuming rage is found in her son:

> I tell you, he does sit in gold, his eye
> Red as 'twould burn Rome, and his injury
> The gaoler to his pity.

(V.i.63)

They have numerous expressions and tricks of speech in common; for example, a habit of sarcastically echoing the words of their adversaries, as in Coriolanus's contemptuous 'They say' (I.i.176) and 'Shall remain' (III.i.88) and

Volumnia's 'I would he had' (IV.ii.33). Her imagined picture of him cursing his troops

> 'Come on, you cowards! You were got in fear,
> Though you were born in Rome.'
>
> (I.iii.31)

is her son to the life, as we see in the next scene.

Yet there are important differences. In the first place she is consumed by a political ambition which he feels nothing of. She has dreamed of and planned for his consulship, while he appears to have given it no more than a passing thought. When it is offered he is ready to assume it as a duty and as what he has deserved, but he would take no initiative to secure it for himself. She sees even his wounds as stepping stones to the consulship and assumes without question that he will show them to the people, unaware of the torture to him of such an action. He senses the difference between them over this issue:

> Know, good mother,
> I had rather be their servant in my way
> Than sway with them in theirs.
>
> (II.i.191)

Her habit of praising him is offensive to him. While they are both choleric by nature, as we have seen, she has sufficient self-control to use her anger prudently:

> a brain that leads my use of anger
> To better vantage.
>
> (III.ii.30)

His anger is more truly Achillean, spontaneous and unpolitic, and his inability to control it makes him a puppet in the hands of his opponents, the tribunes and later Aufidius.

A further rift appears when she disapproves of his handling of the crowd and consequent loss of their supporting vote, a fact which deeply disturbs him:

> I muse my mother
> Does not approve me further.
>
> (III.ii.7)

He is simply expressing the attitudes she has taught him in a way she has hitherto approved and shared. Her advice now that he should dissemble until he has power in his hands horrifies him. 'Would you have me/False to my nature?' he asks. Her reply

> You might have been enough the man you are,
> With striving less to be so

(19)

suggests that she does not understand what he is. At the same time we see when she points out his inconsistency in using policy on the battlefield but refusing to do so in the city, that he has been blind to this aspect of himself. She tells him,

> I would dissemble with my nature, where
> My fortunes and my friends at stake required
> I should do so in honour.

> (62)

While we are intended to weigh her notion of honour in which the end justifies the means, we are also meant to see that this is an honest statement of her standpoint, while Coriolanus with characteristic flinching from unpleasant realities finds it impossible to accept that his concept of honour is basically the same as hers. Volumnia raises the incredibly difficult political problem of how a private code of honour is to be reconciled with public needs. If he is prepared to use policy to 'take in a town' and so save bloodshed, is she altogether wrong in doing the same to save Rome?

The deep shock of discovering an unpleasant truth about himself, and of finding that his mother is not the paragon he has always imagined she was, may well help to explain his moral disintegration after his banishment. As he leaves Rome he rebukes her (a reversal of their usual relationship), although gently, for not practising the precepts she has taught him. There is surely ironic bitterness in his observation

> You were used to load me
> With precepts that would make invincible
> The heart that conned them

> (IV.i.9)

and as we have seen, he attempts to deny her existence. Yet his natural human feelings and his training prove too strong for him. She is still for him 'Olympus' and he a 'molehill'. Her great appeal in v.iii, in which this clever and formidable woman uses every possible trick and argument, overwhelms him. Ironically, although all her efforts have been to make a man of him, she keeps him in many ways a boy – a fact which the watchful Aufidius observes and finally exploits to destroy him.

AUFIDIUS is another character virtually created by Shakespeare, who gives him an integral part in the action.

He has two main functions. The first is to act as a contrast to Coriolanus, whose role as epic hero is enhanced by his defeat of this great warrior. For this purpose Aufidius has to be given a sufficient degree of nobility and courage to make him a worthy opponent, but not so much that he diminishes Coriolanus.

Since the latter has serious faults, so too must Aufidius, but they have to be of a meaner nature. He has to be introduced early into the action, and before the two meet there are a dozen references to Aufidius who is quickly built up as 'noble', 'great', 'fell' and 'the very heart of hope' of the Volscians by various characters – Coriolanus, Cominius, a Senator, Volumnia and Virgilia – while he is shown in the second scene of the play displaying his powers of leadership among the Volscians at Corioli.

From Coleridge onwards there has been a strain of criticism insisting that Shakespeare was careless in making Aufidius an incredibly inconsistent figure. It is a charge which needs rebuttal, since Shakespeare foresaw it and successfully provided against it. We are all familiar today with what psychology calls the love-hate relationship, which has always been a feature of the battlefield, and is found no less today in the boxing ring and athletics arena. It is a feeling which may be shared by both victor and vanquished, though more commonly by the latter for the former. We recognize, in the hatred which these two heroic aspirants express for each other, the stock boasts, defiance and attitudinizing demanded by the conventions governing the literary creation of epic figures, which stem from ancient times. Coriolanus, for example, tells us that he sins in envying Aufidius's nobility

> And were I anything but what I am,
> I would wish me only he
>
> (I.i.217)

and

> Were half to half the world by th' ears, and he
> Upon my party, I'd revolt, to make
> Only my wars with him. He is a lion
> That I am proud to hunt.
>
> (219)

It is a statement that causes us to question the nature of his patriotism, and proves deeply ironic, since Coriolanus 'revolts' for just the opposite reason; when his patriotism is in conflict with his egotism it goes under, as we see. The 'lion' epithet, however, suggests an admiration for Aufidius at odds with his subsequent statement, 'I do hate thee/Worse than a promise-breaker' (I.viii.2) which provokes Aufidius to similar defiance:

> We hate alike.
> Not Afric owns a serpent I abhor
> More than thy fame and envy.
>
> (3)

Later Aufidius embraces this noble Mars. The 'hatred' is a pose, cloaking an admiring envy which seeks to increase personal honour by vanquishing the opponent. They are both making the expected gestures. Their attraction towards each other is evident in the fact that Coriolanus seeks asylum with Aufidius; he is right in assuming that if any man will understand his predicament it is Aufidius, who most resembles him. It is seen reciprocally in Aufidius's response, which is generous, however romantic and emotional. He knows that Coriolanus like the osprey 'takes it/By sovereignty of nature' (IV.vii.34), that he has always beaten him and always will, and that he more nearly approaches the heroic ideal after which he himself is striving.

Aufidius's long emotional speech of welcome to Coriolanus reveals the loving admiration that underlies his rivalry:

> I loved the maid I married: never man
> Sighed truer breath. But that I see thee here,
> Thou noble thing, more dances my rapt heart
> Than when I first my wedded mistress saw
> Bestride my threshold.
>
> (IV.v.110)

This transference of the language of love to the epic warrior and the things of war, paralleled in Coriolanus's greeting of Cominius as we have seen (I.vi.29), manifests the emotional distortion and inversion of normal values which lies at the heart of the tragedy of both men. Aufidius's murder of Coriolanus, which has caused so much critical disapproval, exemplifies this same tendency to take the lower for the higher; it is both psychologically convincing and consistent with his character as Shakespeare has developed it. He plants the motivation early, in Act I, where Aufidius, having been humiliated in front of his men in the single combat with Coriolanus which Shakespeare invents for him, determines to 'potch at him some way,/Or wrath or craft may get him' (I.x.15). He is aware of the deterioration in himself caused by the frustration of his heroic aspirations:

> My valour's poisoned
> With only suffering stain by him; for him
> Shall fly out of itself.
>
> (I.x.17)

As in plays like *Henry IV* and *Troilus and Cressida*, Shakespeare intends us to question the value of a concept of honour which is destroyed by defeat.

There is nothing gloating or mean in Aufidius's welcome to Coriolanus in Antium. He offers him half his command, unaware in his romantic enthusiasm that to share his powers equally with one who is his superior is an impossibility. We see this simple truth at once as his servants transfer their allegiance to Coriolanus who has always 'thwacked' their general and 'scotched him and notched him like a carbonado' (IV.v.179). We are not surprised to learn from

Aufidius's lieutenant that his troops 'still fly to the Roman' (IV.vii.1) and 'use him as the grace 'fore meat'. Aufidius is placed in what for him is the intolerable position of having either to relinquish his epic ambitions or to reassert them by destroying Coriolanus. He decides, as his nature demands, and as we might have known he would, to 'renew me in his fall' (v.vi.48). Since this cannot be achieved by fair means he turns, through the pressures of rage, shame and frustration, to foul, as he had resolved he would in I.x. With effective irony Volumnia's vision of her son standing on Aufidius's neck (I.iii.44) is reversed finally with Aufidius standing on the slain Coriolanus; what she had envisaged as a moment of triumph for Coriolanus is an occasion of degradation for Aufidius, one in which he quickly and consistently switches from anger to self-disgust. His baseness at this point underlines Coriolanus's moral superiority.

Aufidius's second function is to interpret Coriolanus to us, which, as one who shares a similar philosophy and who is aware to some extent of his own inner processes, he can credibly do. No character is better placed to conjecture upon the reasons for Coriolanus's fall in Rome. In his proffering of three tentative explanatory causes, Shakespeare keeps him true to his vacillating and uncertain nature, and at the same time guides our response to the hero, which as we have said earlier, prohibits facile conclusions and forces us to suspend judgement.

In short, Shakespeare gives Aufidius just as much attention as the plot demands, and just the kind of character that his role necessitates. Like Coriolanus, Aufidius is trapped, divided, and morally corrupted by his dedication to an unworkable code of conduct. Something of the ridiculousness of this code is conveyed by the debunking comments of Aufidius's servants:

> Our general himself makes a mistress of him, sanctifies himself with's hand, and turns up the white o' the eye to his discourse
>
> (IV.v.187)

We are forced to evaluate the conception of honour which underlies this behaviour towards a man who is betraying his country.

The tribunes SICINIUS and BRUTUS have come in for a great deal of harsh criticism. Plutarch, who disliked them, calls them 'seditious' and 'flattering' and insists that they 'had only been the causers and procurers of this sedition' in Rome. In several respects, however, in filling out Plutarch's bones, Shakespeare gives them a stronger case. To begin with, as he presents it, the civil insurrection springs not from their initiative, but from famine and oppression, and it is the people who are after Coriolanus's blood. The appointment of five tribunes, among them Brutus and Sicinius, takes place as a result of this unrest and is an attempt by the Senate to appease it.

On their entry in I.i the tribunes make no attempt to inflame the situation, but remain silent until everyone leaves, and then comment on events. At once we are aware that they are unreliable commentators, since their remarks about Coriolanus are slanted by their envy of his greatness and their annoyance at his contempt for them. He is certainly proud, as they say, but not impious as they claim. Sicinius's conjecture

> But I do wonder
> His insolence can brook to be commanded
> Under Cominius

(I.i.247)

tells us more about Sicinius himself than about Coriolanus, who shows no reluctance to serve under Cominius. His pride does not take the form of jealousy or power-seeking as they suggest. Their twisted comments, a blend of truth and untruth, cause us to weigh carefully all they say in the situations in which Shakespeare frequently places them, alone on the stage like the chorus in an ancient Greek tragedy which interprets and comments upon the action. The first scene thus ends in a balanced but explosive state, with each faction seeming to have some truth and justification but misunderstanding the other to some extent through prejudice or ignorance.

An interesting feature of their characterization is that Shakespeare makes no attempt to distinguish one from the other; they are as alike as two pins and each echoes the other to such an extent that it is difficult at the end of a scene to remember who said what. Possibly this was a deliberate device to suggest the ubiquity and colourlessness of this political type, the power-seeking demagogue. The other characters often lump them together as a unit:

> MENENIUS Do you two know how you are censured here in the city . . . ?
> BOTH Why, how are we censured?

(II.i.19)

They frequently speak together like a chorus in this way. Menenius insists that they 'can do very little alone' (31), and he applies his strictures to them both simultaneously. They are 'a brace of unmeriting, proud, violent, testy magistrates' (38), 'two such wealsmen as you are' (49), 'a pair of strange ones' (73), 'a pair of tribunes that have wracked for Rome' (v.i.16). They are physically undifferentiated also: both are old, bald, bearded and lacking 'good faces'.

They are hypocrites, liars and schemers, mean-spirited and petty, and their behaviour frequently repels us. Nevertheless, when all that is unpleasant about them has been said, it remains true that our sympathies are sometimes with them. They are patient and even polite in the face of Menenius's insults in II.i, and we concede that they are right in their view that if Coriolanus becomes consul, 'Then our office may/During his power go sleep' (II.i.211) since he is an enemy to the people's 'liberties and charters' (II.iii.169), although they go too far in accusing him of being 'ambitious past all thinking' (IV.vi.31). Coriolanus is not interested in power for its own sake, as they appear to be, but he would certainly curtail their power if he were consul.

Brutus's reaction to the news of Coriolanus's threat to Rome, 'Would half my wealth/Would buy this for a lie' (IV.vi.159), with its apparent suggestion that he has made a fortune out of his tribuneship, and that he would sacrifice only half of it for Rome's sake, tells badly against him. On the other hand the tribunes work assiduously at their appointed task of protecting the interests of the people. From their point of view they are correct in seeing Coriolanus as their enemy and opposing his election. They take pride in Rome's new-found peace, illusory though it proves to be:

> This is a happier and more comely time
> Than when these fellows ran about the streets
> Crying confusion.
>
> (IV.vi.27)

Shakespeare also gives them an incisive gift of speaking home truths and of putting their finger on Coriolanus's weaknesses that no one else displays.

> You speak o' the people
> As if you were a god to punish, not
> A man of their infirmity.
>
> (III.i.80)

Brutus's words here and Sicinius's question

> Where is this viper
> That would depopulate the city and
> Be every man himself?
>
> (III.i.262)

show a shrewd understanding of Coriolanus's presumptuous pride. This understanding is seen also in Sicinius's perceptive comment that mercy is the godlike attribute which Coriolanus lacks (V.iv.23).

Brutus's professed willingness to support Coriolanus's candidature

> If he remember
> A kinder value of the people than
> He hath hereto prized them at
>
> (II.ii.55)

may not be whole-hearted, but the condition is reasonable, and one which would have secured the office for Coriolanus had he heeded it. Similarly,

Sicinius's sound advice

> If you will pass
> To where you are bound, you must inquire your way,
> Which you are out of, with a gentler spirit,
> Or never be so noble as a consul

(III.i.54)

is ignored. In fact it is not so much the malignancy of the tribunes, as Coriolanus's persistent refusal to listen to their warnings that brings about his expulsion. Despite the 'lessoning' from the tribunes (which closely parallels Volumnia's rehearsal of *her* actor, Coriolanus) the people are anxious to give him their votes; it is his mockery which makes them wish to withdraw their support, and leaves them ripe for the manipulations of the tribunes. Brutus's question

> Why shall the people give
> One that speaks thus their voice?

(III.i.118)

is a fair one that goes to the heart of the problem. Despite all that may be said in their favour, however, we deplore the trickery they employ against Coriolanus in planning to 'put him to choler straight' (III.iii.25) by calling him traitor, a device which works all too easily. They make no pretence of giving him a fair trial and despicably prod the citizens into whooping him out of the gates. After this we applaud the scourging Volumnia gives them in the next scene.

   Their political error is, ironically, very much the same as Coriolanus's: that of exalting their own part of the body politic to the exclusion of the rest. They have no understanding of the wider political perspective and are soon in trouble. Like Coriolanus they are unwilling to accept a reality that endangers their illusions. Their response to the report of the Volscian invasion is not to investigate the truth of the report, but to deny its possibility and order the messenger to be whipped, an act of tyrannical injustice whose irony is not lost on us. When it proves true they are silent, frightened and helpless.

   It is impossible to like the tribunes, those perennial political types, and we feel a poetic justice in the manhandling which the plebeians give to Brutus and threaten to give Sicinius. But though their ends are selfish and their methods unscrupulous, to a degree which swings us over to Coriolanus's side, we have to ask ourselves whether their political ethics are so very different from those of Volumnia and her son. They all dissemble for their own chosen and limited ends.

VIRGILIA is virtually Shakespeare's own creation. His problem was to create a character at once subordinate to Volumnia's dominance, yet independent, and a worthy wife for Coriolanus – one whom he loves and who loves him.

Virgilia's most remarkable characteristic is her silence, very much 'a speaking silence'. We may be surprised to discover that though she appears in six scenes, she speaks only 34 lines. Her presence, however, is very much felt.

Virgilia has three main functions. The first is to serve as a foil to Volumnia, her feminine tenderness and hatred of bloodshed in strong contrast to the opposite qualities in Volumnia. The second is to tell us something about Coriolanus. The fact that these two very different women love Coriolanus so deeply is an indication of a lovableness and humanity in him too often over-looked, but certainly demonstrated, however briefly, in his regard for Virgilia. The third is to stand as a representative and reminder of a different way of life and set of values from that which dominates Rome. She refers to her womb 'That brought you forth this boy, to keep your name/Living to time' (v.iii.125), impressing on us her creative love and life-giving quality, which we feel Coriolanus would have done better to heed than the death-dealing role his mother trained him for.

Virgilia's polite submissiveness to Volumnia – notice her deference in that fascinating scene, i.iii – and to her husband ('My lord and master'), and her piety (five of her lines are prayers to the gods for help, which succinctly convey her anguish at the thought of her husband's wounds, or his departure) are not to be construed as weakness of character. On the contrary they were qualities highly prized as becoming a Roman matron and appreciated in an Elizabethan one. Her general decorousness makes all the more admirable her refusal to be browbeaten by Volumnia or wheedled by Valeria into breaking her vow not to leave her house until Coriolanus returns. Indeed, we feel that her 'solemness' is a more fitting attitude than the 'mirth' of the other two while the outcome of the war is uncertain.

Virgilia shows her spirit also when she joins Volumnia in her attack on the tribunes in iv.ii. Her outburst to Sicinius, 'He'd make an end of thy posterity', provoked by her love for Coriolanus and frustration at her loss of him, is so uncharacteristic of her that it impresses on us the stress she is under, and how hard it is in this harsh and violent Roman world to preserve her more civilized values. Finally, her fibre is seen in her resolution to commit suicide rather than watch her husband ravage Rome.

Coriolanus aptly calls her his 'gracious silence'. Her restraint and quiet weeping when all the others are acclaiming her husband's triumph, are a visual image of her love, more impressive and eloquent than all their clamour. In numerous ways the dramatist gives her prominence and accentuates Coriolanus's love for her, omitting Plutarch's statement that Coriolanus married at Volumnia's desire and never left her house. He inverts Plutarch's order, 'When he had taken leave of his mother and wife' to 'Farewell, my wife, my mother' (iv.i.20) and 'Come, my sweet wife, my dearest mother' (iv.i.48).

In the great pleading scene, Plutarch tells us 'first he kissed his mother and embraced her a pretty while, then his wife and little children'. In the play he first addresses Virgilia, and in the most loving terms:

> O, a kiss
> Long as my exile, sweet as my revenge!
> Now, by the jealous queen of heaven, that kiss
> I carried from thee, dear, and my true lip
> Hath virgined it e'er since.

(v.iii.44)

Disturbingly, apart from the love expressed here, we see his obsession with his exile and consequent revenge, the passion which has swamped love. Before these words he has revealed to us in soliloquy the power which only the sight of her has over him:

> What is that curtsy worth? Or those dove's eyes,
> Which can make gods forsworn? I melt, and am not
> Of stronger earth than others.

(27–9)

We should be chary of accepting the common view that it is simply Volumnia's power over him that makes him relent. The play says something different. Virgilia is a sad and isolated figure, helpless in the face of the violence, both moral and physical, which surrounds her and even invades her home in the shape of Volumnia and Valeria.

The characterization of Virgilia is a masterpiece of dramatic economy.

Shakespeare's use of his source-material

Shakespeare's main source for *Coriolanus* was Plutarch's *Life of Martius Coriolanus*, one of his *Parallel Lives of the Greeks and Romans*, in which he narrated the life of a great Greek, then of a Roman counterpart, concluding with a 'Comparison' between them. In this case the parallel life was that of Alcibiades, and the *Comparison of Alcibiades with Martius Coriolanus* also furnished some ideas and details for the play. Plutarch, a Greek writing in the first century A.D. when Greece was under Roman domination, was an immensely popular and influential writer with readers in the sixteenth century, when his original Greek was translated into Latin and thence into the vernacular languages. It was the French translation in 1559 by Jacques Amyot, Bishop of Auxerre, which Sir Thomas North translated into English in 1579, and this was the version Shakespeare used in writing *Julius Caesar, Antony and Cleopatra, Coriolanus* and *Timon of Athens*.

Plutarch explains that his intention was

> not to write histories but only lives. For the noblest deeds do not always show men's virtues and vices; but oftentimes a light occasion, a word or some sport makes men's natural disposition and manners appear more plain than the famous battles won.

His primary interest, then, is not history but biography, and his probing into human behaviour and its motives, and into the minutiae of personality was the secret of his fascination for renaissance readers. His analytic approach to character and his attempt to get behind human action to its causes – which is always one of the chief concerns of any dramatist – were unusual among ancient classical writers. As Amyot, discussing the difference between history and biography, explains to his readers,

> One [history] is more interested in things, the other [biography] in persons; the one is more general, the other more private; the one has to do more with the things that are outside the man, the other with things that come from within him; the one with events, the other with consultations.

With his accent on the personal and private, the individual differences of disposition and manners, on the 'consultations', that is, the thought and underlying motives, we need not be surprised that Plutarch was one of Shakespeare's favourite authors.

Most Roman historians are overtly propagandist: they see with Roman eyes, and are influenced by their political ideology, republican or imperialist, so that their work suffers a consequent simplification or distortion, and their presentation of character a loss of roundness and inwardness. As a Greek, Plutarch is free from the political bias; his interest in great men is much more judicial and impartial. His approach is summed up in his quotation from Euripides:

> The good and bad cannot be kept apart
> But there is some commingling.

This attitude is reflected in his statement that Coriolanus's upbringing shows that

> a rare and excellent wit, untaught, doth bring forth many good and evil things together, like a fat soil bringeth forth herbs and weeds that lie unmanured [i.e. untilled].

Any dramatist using Plutarch as a source-book finds a balance of good and bad qualities built into his characters. In place of the immaculate hero and the deep-dyed villain of myth or melodrama, Plutarch gives us fallible human beings, and this feature of his biographies is mirrored in Shakespeare's play, adding in large measure to its strength and interest, and also to its complexity.

Plutarch's balanced impartiality is reflected not only in his general attitude, but also in his style. He is fond of an antithetical sentence structure, in which one point of view is balanced against another, with Plutarch declining to take sides. His work is full of phrases like 'on the one hand . . . on the other' and 'although . . . yet', and in this poised detachment Shakespeare is a kindred spirit with him.

Surprise has been expressed that Shakespeare should have found in the *Life of Martius Coriolanus* a suitable subject for drama, though in more recent years the personal and political dilemmas which it explores have been seen to be highly pertinent to our own lives and times. Shakespeare's own age certainly saw its relevance. Alexandre Hardy, the French dramatist, whose *Coriolan* was written probably before the end of the sixteenth century though not published until 1625, remarked

> few subjects are to be found in Roman history which are worthier of the stage

and many French dramatists after Hardy wrote plays about Coriolanus. There is no evidence that Shakespeare knew Hardy's *Coriolan* (or that Hardy knew Shakespeare's play), which makes it all the more interesting that two dramatists should independently perceive the dramatic possibilities of Plutarch's biography.

Elizabethan dramatists felt free to take certain liberties with the facts of history. Modern historians tell us that the historicity of Coriolanus is doubtful, and that even if he did exist, at the beginning of the fifth century B.C., a good deal of Plutarch's life of him must be conjectural or legendary. Neither Plutarch nor the sixteenth century, however, questioned his existence, and Shakespeare's attitude to and use of the *Life* of him is identical in all important respects with his approach to the lives of Julius Caesar, Brutus and Mark Antony, all undoubtedly historical figures, although, since Coriolanus was a much less well-known figure than they, he was freer to invent. In all three Roman plays we find the same basic fidelity to the narrative, character-drawing and general spirit of Plutarch's account, and the same kind of retention, alteration and omission of details, determined by Shakespeare's dramatic needs.

To begin with the omissions, Shakespeare cuts out anything irrelevant. Plutarch is given to digression, particularly on Roman custom or manners, a habit of comparing one event or personality with another, often with a moralistic aim, none of which was to Shakespeare's purpose. He therefore omits Plutarch's conjectures about the origin of the award of the oak garland, his digression about the use of first, second and third names among the

Romans, their custom of making their wills verbally immediately before battle, the gradual corruption of public officials in Rome, his discussion of the nature and operation of sorrow, and whether it is possible for statues to speak, his comparison of Coriolanus with Epaminondas and his frequent quotations from Homer.

Of the events described by Plutarch he excises the dispatch by the Senate of many of the dissident plebeians from Rome to the city of Velitres which had been depopulated by the plague, and the war between Rome and the Antiates which occurred between the original death sentence on Coriolanus and the later hearing of his appeal against it. The inclusion of these events would have dissipated the speed and tension that Shakespeare had carefully built up at these points. He omits also the minute account of Coriolanus's subjugation of the various cities of the Latins on his way to attack Rome, preferring the increased effect of terror which the unbelievably swift appearance of Coriolanus at the gates of Rome produces among the Romans, and the powerful impression of the burning and single-minded intensity of Coriolanus's anger and desire for revenge on Rome, which is much less forcefully suggested in Plutarch.

Interestingly, too, Shakespeare excludes all reference to the supernatural. North's Plutarch describes the reported appearance of the gods Castor and Pollux at the Battle of Lake Regillus in which Coriolanus distinguished himself, cites portents and omens, 'sights and wonders in the air' attributable to the banishment of Coriolanus, and mentions the report that the statue of the goddess Fortuna had spoken. It would seem that the dramatist was concerned to make his ancient story credible and immediate to his contemporaries, what Samuel Johnson praises as his power of 'approximating the remote', and to stress the free will of his characters, unconstrained in any way by the intervention of the gods.

The omission of all this material gave a tightness and coherence to what remained. Shakespeare's next task was to create that linking of events in which one thing is seen to lead necessarily or credibly to the next, and this necessitated certain alterations of the source-material. While Plutarch gives a chronological account of Coriolanus's life, the dramatist begins near his final crisis and fills in, with considerable skill, such earlier events as we need to know. This is done in a convincingly natural manner, for example, in I.iii when his womenfolk reminisce about him at home while he is away at the war, and in II.ii when Cominius delivers his formal eulogy of Coriolanus before the Senate, rehearsing all his former exploits.

Other major structural changes concern his compression of time, juxtaposing events which occupied some four years of Rome's history, so that they appear to follow continuously without intermission through a short period. Plutarch describes two disturbances of the people: the first before the

Volscian war, in which the people, justifiably angered by the broken promises
of the Senate and oppressed by usurers, withdrew to the Mons Sacer to stage
a passive demonstration, and the second after the war, caused by famine.
Shakespeare collapses the two into one, starting the play with it and making it
the mainspring of the whole action. He also runs together Coriolanus's
triumphal return from the wars and his candidature for consulship, making
the latter the reward for his services, though in Plutarch they are unconnected
and separated in time. Whereas Shakespeare makes his arrest follow immediately and spring out of his anger at the malevolent intriguing of the
tribunes and his denunciation of them, in Plutarch there is no connection, and
the arrest follows a Senate speech about the free distribution of corn. Shakespeare also simplifies a complicated political situation by omitting Plutarch's
narration of a divided Senate, some favouring the plebeians and later opposing
the repeal of Coriolanus's banishment when he threatens the city, and a
divided people, some opposing his arrest, so that even with a rigged vote he is
banished by a majority of only three plebeian votes. These changes result in a
condensed, smooth-flowing action which heightens the political conflict by
making the two factions, patrician and plebeian, internally united and
mutually antagonistic.

Shakespeare made changes to Plutarch's narrative with the general aim of
illuminating his protagonist by developing other characters as foils and contrasts to him. Menenius and Aufidius, who are practically independent crea-
tions, and Volumnia, who is greatly expanded, are in this group. Many others,
little more than names in Plutarch, like Cominius, Titus Lartius, Virgilia and
the Tribunes, are given flesh and blood in the play. The 'little children' of
Coriolanus mentioned by Plutarch are effectively reduced to Young Martius
in the play (although Shakespeare once alludes to his 'children'). The discussion of him by Volumnia, Virgilia and Valeria in I.iii is a subtle method of
characterizing Coriolanus, since his likeness to his father as a boy is stressed.
What they say about the boy tells us something about them. The fact that
Young Martius is an only child is exploited by Shakespeare to achieve powerful pathos in v.iii. The emotional intensity of this scene would have been more
difficult to create with two or more children. A number of characters are invented, like the two Senate Officials who act like the chorus of the ancient
Greek tragedy, giving us information and reflecting various opinions of
characters and events, like Adrian and Nicanor, and the Lieutenant of Aufidius, part of whose purpose is to convey some of the narrative details reported
in Plutarch.

This leads to a consideration of Shakespeare's main technical problem —
that of converting narrative prose, largely of reported action, into poetic
drama. He certainly made the most of one feature of Plutarch's style, namely
his fondness for inventing direct speech for his characters. There are fifteen

examples in the *Life* varying in length from one line (on three occasions) to two pages, though the average is about fifteen lines. Many of them are remarkably vivid, well-constructed, and moving, and these Shakespeare incorporated into the play where he could do so consistently with his purposes, with the minimum alteration necessary to turn them from prose to effective blank verse. To give just one example, the beginning of Coriolanus's speech to Aufidius at Antium

> If thou knowest me not yet Tullus, and, seeing me, dost not perhaps believe me to be the man I am indeed, I must of necessity bewray myself to be that I am

becomes in the play

> If, Tullus,
> Not yet thou know'st me, and seeing me dost not
> Think me for the man I am, necessity
> Commands me name myself.

(IV.v.50)

A similarly close dependence on sentence structure, phraseology, vocabulary and the order of the words is found commonly in the play. We have it in Menenius's Fable of the Belly, often cited as an example of Shakespeare's close dependence on his sources. However, when we examine this closely we find that Menenius's speech of 14 lines in Plutarch is expanded to 45 lines in the play, and the whole is made *dramatic* by the interpolation of remarks by the First Citizen and the injection of a humorous dialogue between the two.

Volumnia's great plea in v.iii follows the order and often the phrasing of Plutarch very closely (Plutarch's 64 lines becoming 73 in Shakespeare) but largely because it is a brilliant piece of writing, instinct with drama and emotional force, and coincided perfectly with Shakespeare's intentions at that point. Similarly, Coriolanus's speech to Aufidius in Antium in IV.v (29 lines in Plutarch and 40 lines in the play) is closely followed but broken up with interjections by Aufidius to create dramatic dialogue. Interestingly, however, Aufidius's terse reply (3 lines in Plutarch), simply thanking Coriolanus, which did not give the dramatist what he wanted, is ignored and replaced by a long metaphorical speech of 34 lines, revealing Aufidius as a highly emotional man, torn between envy and admiration, establishing further Coriolanus's superiority to him, and by the introduction of a psychological instability preparing us for his later treachery.

Of the remaining speeches of Plutarch, three – Valeria's to Volumnia and Virgilia suggesting they all go to plead for mercy from Coriolanus, Volumnia's reply to this, and the words attributed to the statue of Fortuna – are omitted entirely from the play, and on the rest there is very little verbal dependence, though the ideas they contain are sometimes worked into the play. A typical example of this group is Coriolanus's plea for his friend in Corioli. Plutarch reports:

> 'Only this grace,' said he, 'I crave and beseech you to grant me. Among the Volsces there is an old friend and host of mine, an honest wealthy man, and now a prisoner, who, living before in great wealth in his own country, liveth now a poor prisoner in the hands of his enemies; and yet, notwithstanding all this his misery and misfortune, it would do me great pleasure if I could save him from this one danger, to keep him from being sold as a slave.'

In the play this becomes

CORIOLANUS I sometime lay here in Corioli
      At a poor man's house; he used me kindly.
      He cried to me; I saw him prisoner,
      But then Aufidius was within my view,
      And wrath o'erwhelmed my pity. I request you
      To give my poor host freedom . . .
  LARTIUS Martius, his name?
CORIOLANUS   By Jupiter, forgot!

(I.ix.81)

There is almost total independence in language. Shakespeare invents the detail of the friend begging for mercy, and Coriolanus's preoccupation with Aufidius (a recurring note). He turns this wealthy man into a poor one thus extending the range of Coriolanus's human sympathy, so that we conclude that it is not the poverty of the Roman plebeians that angers him but their cowardice. We also get a degree of self-awareness in Coriolanus, often overlooked, in his consciousness of the effect which his anger has on his pity, and finally Shakespeare adds the enormously effective stroke of making Coriolanus forget the man's name. Here then Shakespeare uses Plutarchan material as a starting point for developments of his own, enriching and complicating Coriolanus's character.

It is sometimes asserted that the poetic quality of Plutarch's prose made the task of converting it into dramatic blank verse an easy one. But apart from an occasional simile and metaphor, which the dramatist took over if it suited him, Plutarch's narrative is remarkably plain and unadorned. As rendered by North it is often racy and vigorous, but just as often tortuous and wordy, with long meandering sentences, heavy antithetical clauses and piled-up nouns and adjectives. Amyot, apologizing for his own jerky style, blames it on 'Plutarch's peculiar manner of inditing, which is rather sharp, learned and short, than plain, polished and easy'. Montaigne congratulates Amyot on having

> so successfully-happy been able to explain an author so close and thorny and unfold a writer so mysterious and entangled.

It is not, then, *how* Plutarch wrote, so much as *what* he wrote that captivated the sixteenth century.

The metaphor of the play, Shakespeare's chief stylistic distinction, is all his own. Even where he is closest to Plutarch we suddenly come across an image which makes the passage leap into life, as in Coriolanus's speech attacking the free grant of corn we find

> Even when the navel of the state was touched,
> They would not thread the gates. . . .
>
> (III.i.123)

>   which will in time
> Break ope the locks o' th' Senate and bring in
> The crows to peck the eagles.
>
> (137)

The 'navel' metaphor cleverly suggest a combination of ideas: sensitivity, life-line, the vital centre of things, and connects up with the 'body' image which pervades the play and is discussed fully on p. lxxiii of this *Introduction*. The 'threading-of-the-gates' image is vivid and compressed, with a powerful visual suggestion. The 'broken locks' conveys succinctly Coriolanus's conviction of the criminality of their policy of appeasement which will render even the most sacred things vulnerable, while the crows pecking at the eagles suggests an inversion of the natural order as well as conveying his contempt for the plebeians and his conviction of the superiority of the patrician order to which he belongs, the eagle being the supreme or royal bird, the crow a scavenger.

Whereas Plutarch's description is frequently generalized, Shakespeare's is always moving in the direction of the concrete and the particular, rooted firmly in sensory experience, often developed from the most homely subjects, but tellingly impressing a picture on the mind. Plutarch, for example, describes the youthful warrior Coriolanus as 'a stripling', while Shakespeare makes him 'sixteen'; Plutarch says he fought 'many battles', Shakespeare specifies seventeen; Plutarch tells us he bestrode a fallen Roman soldier and 'slew the enemy with his own hands', Shakespeare adds to this a graphic picture of the action:

> When with his Amazonian chin he drove
> The bristled lips before him
>
> (II.ii.88)

and also subtly suggests his link with his mother through that word 'Amazonian'.

Sometimes a chance word in Plutarch will start the image-making process. Plutarch described the Romans who would not fight the Volscians as 'house-doves' which doubtless was the spark for Coriolanus's spirited defiance of Aufidius in the last scene 'like an eagle in a dovecote, I/Fluttered your Volscians in Corioli', and quite possibly accounts for Virgilia's 'dove's eyes' which proved so devastating in v.iii.

We can thus see Shakespeare constantly at work, shaping and enriching his source material to fit dramatic situation and character. Plutarch offers a frame-work of events, guiding-lines in character relationships, illustrative anecdote and dialogue snatches, detachment, integrity, commonsense. Yet it must be stressed that four-fifths of the play's lines owe nothing to him. Of the twenty-nine scenes no fewer than sixteen are Shakespeare's invention, and these include some of the best: the domestic scene in Coriolanus's home (I.iii), all the Aufidius scenes except IV.v and the last (I.ii, I.viii, I.x, IV.vii), the exchanges between Menenius and the Tribunes and Brutus's description of the crowd thronging to see Coriolanus's triumphant return to Rome (II.i), the crucial scene in which Volumnia persuades her son to dissemble to the people (III.ii), her attack on the Tribunes after Coriolanus's departure (IV.ii), the Adrian–Nicanor scene (IV.iii), the humbling of the Tribunes (IV.vi), the scene in which Menenius is persuaded to seek Coriolanus's mercy (V.i) and Volumnia's triumphal entry (V.v). Apart from Volumnia's great appeal, the play's most powerful emotional effects are achieved where Shakespeare is relying most heavily on his own imaginative powers. The comic or humorous element is entirely his. All the changes he makes are those of an experienced dramatic craftsman, directed towards shaping Plutarch's amorphous material into a closely-integrated and fluent dramatic unity.

Apart from the major debt to Plutarch, Shakespeare almost certainly made minor use of *The Roman History of T.Livy*, translated by Philemon Holland in 1600, for a few details in Menenius's Fable of the Belly, for which he certainly used also William Camden's *Remains of a Greater Work Concerning Britain* and William Averell's *A Marvellous Combat of Contrarieties*.

The theatre of Shakespeare's day

To know something of the theatre for which Shakespeare wrote, of its conventions, possibilities and limitations, so different from the modern theatre, is to have a deeper understanding of the nature and meaning of the plays themselves.

The earliest permanent theatres in Elizabethan times reflected many of the

A view of London in the early 17th century showing St. Paul's Cathedral and the Globe theatre on the South Bank (from an engraving by Visscher 1616).

structural features of the inn-yards and the bull-baiting and bear-baiting arenas of the time. Like many of them, they were two- or three-storeyed and round, octagonal or square, the buildings surrounding an open-air auditorium on all sides. An 'apron' stage, or 'platform', projected forward from one wall with the audience sitting or standing around three sides of it. The first to be built was The Theatre, and between its erection in 1576 and the closing of the theatres by the Puritans in 1642 we learn of the existence of nine public theatres in London. Their life span was short, usually a few years, and only three or four were in operation at any one time during this period. In the latter part of his career, Shakespeare was writing plays for performance in the private theatres, which were smaller, roofed-in, rectangular structures catering to more sophisticated audiences of about 700 people. If we accept 1608 as the date of composition of *Coriolanus* then it was written for production at The Globe, the public theatre owned by the acting company to which Shakespeare belonged, the King's Men, built in 1599 (see Visscher's view of London, p. lvii). From 1609 the King's Men also used the Blackfriars, a private theatre, and it is possible that *Coriolanus* or a simplified adaptation of it may have been acted there. However, the play as we have it is on the same large scale as *Antony and Cleopatra* written a few years before for the public theatre and demanding the same theatrical resources, space being not least among them.

The extant building contract for the erection of the Fortune Theatre in 1600 provides much useful detail about Elizabethan theatres. The Fortune was a square theatre, measuring 80 feet on the outside, with an auditorium 55 feet square on the inside. The stage jutted forward halfway, 27 feet 6 inches, and was 43 feet wide, thus leaving a narrow gap of 6 feet on either side where the audience could stand. A significant feature of these theatres was their smallness. Although they could hold some 2500 people, no member of the audience could be more than 25 yards from the furthest player, while the great majority were very much nearer. This created an intimacy between player and spectator which had a powerful influence on the construction of the plays. The soliloquy and the aside, two common conventions in Elizabethan drama, were credibly employed with a stage on which the actor could go right forward with the audience on three sides of him and confide or whisper his thoughts to them. This is difficult on the average stage in use today, in which the audience, sitting in darkness, look from a distance into a kind of lighted room, cut off from them often by the proscenium arch or frame around the stage.

We should notice, too, the largeness of the stage itself, occupying almost half the area of the theatre. It made possible scenes in which groups or individuals could be so far apart that they could realistically be represented as not seeing, hearing or recognizing each other. We have an example of this where

Coriolanus, entering at one side of the stage, is not recognized in the distance by his close friend Cominius:

> Who's yonder
> That does appear as he were flayed? O gods!
> He has the stamp of Martius, and I have
> Before-time seen him thus.
>
> (I.vi.21)

Similarly a good deal of space is needed for v.iii where Coriolanus catches sight of his family and describes their approach for 17 lines before they reach him, and of course for the battle scenes and crowd scenes which figure so prominently in the play.

The stage was raised some four feet above ground level, so that both the groundlings or 'penny stinkards' standing on the flat auditorium and those paying more and sitting in the surrounding galleries could see and hear more easily. Wooden panelling stretching around the front and sides of the stage prevented the audience from seeing beneath the stage and created an enclosed 'underground' area successfully exploited by many dramatists. Since the main stage was uncurtained it was important for the dramatist to ensure that it was cleared naturally, within the action of the play, of bodies or stage properties. The stage direction at the end of the play 'Exeunt bearing the body of Martius' illustrates this and the text tells us explicitly how it was done, as Aufidius instructs his men:

> Take him up.
> Help, three o' th' chiefest soldiers; I'll be one.
> Beat thou the drum, that it speak mournfully,
> Trail your steel pikes.
>
> (v.vi.148)

Aufidius, that is, with three of his men, bears Coriolanus off the stage. The hero is given a military funeral, with pikes at the trail and the slow drum beat contributing to the sombre finality of the play, while in practical terms it avoids the clumsiness of having the dead body getting up and walking off the stage, which would destroy the required effect. The ladders which Lartius calls for in the assault of Corioli in I.iv, and the cushions provided by the Senate officials in II.ii would be brought in and removed as a natural part of the action of the scene.

Most Shakespearian scholars have conjectured the existence of an inner stage (known variously as the 'study', 'discovery-space' or 'enclosure'), a recessed alcove or room in the centre of the wall at the back of the stage, between the two side doors, curtained off and thus presenting the dramatist with a valuable opportunity to extend the dimensions of his play by varying the setting, presenting scenes in small enclosed spaces, like a bedroom, cave, tent, study or cell, and making possible effective contrasts with the major, public or large-scale scenes on the main stage. None of the few surviving drawings of the interior of the Elizabethan theatre shows an inner stage, nor is it mentioned in any of the literature of the time, but so many of the stage directions of the Elizabethan plays demand some such acting area for their performance that its existence is a reasonable hypothesis. In the drawing of the Swan Theatre (see p. lxi) the large double doors at each side of the back wall, when opened back, with a curtain drawn across, some feet behind the doors, would make such an acting area. One obvious use for an inner stage in *Coriolanus* is in I.iv where it would represent the gates of Corioli, flung open when the Volsces rush out to the attack and later closing in Coriolanus. Another is in I.ix where the inner stage curtain would represent the entrance to Cominius's tent.

Above the main stage was the upper stage, with a light railing or balustrade along the front of it. This too had a curtain a few feet back from the railing, so that when closed it created a narrow passage or terrace, and when opened provided another room for indoor scenes. The upper stage was clearly used for I.iv where we have the stage direction, 'Enter two Senators with others, on the walls', that is, of Corioli. Doubtless for such a scene the railing would be replaced by a piece of representational battlement or wall which we know to have been a stage property of Philip Henslowe's company. The upper stage was built at a height of about seven feet and thus made possible scenes which enabled actors (who in Elizabethan times were much shorter than modern man – about 5 feet 2 inches on the average) to jump safely to the main stage below, as they have to in several plays. Many domestic scenes were performed on the upper stage, and it is probable that I.iii would be acted here or on the inner stage below. In either case the stools on which Volumnia and Virgilia sit could be on stage before their entry, revealed as the curtains opened, then concealed at the end of the scene by the closing of the curtains, and so removed unseen to make ready for the next scene to be acted there. The existence of the inner and upper stage would seem to account for the very common alternation of public and private scenes in the plays of this period, since it made the frequent change of locale on both main and subsidiary inner or upper stages more credible.

The two side doors already mentioned, and illustrated in the Swan drawing, were the normal means of entering and leaving the main stage. They would wherever possible be used to suggest the different hinterlands behind them, thus assisting the audience in understanding where the scene was set. In Coriolanus the two main divisions are between Rome and the Volscian lands, so it would be an obvious staging practice to reserve one door for the Roman entrances, the other for those of her enemies, as in the first two scenes of the

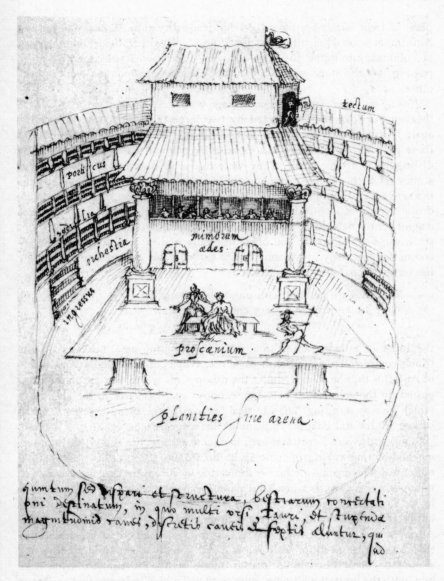

The interior of the Swan Theatre as seen in about 1596 (from a sketch by van Buchell after de Witt).
tectum – roof, *porticus* – gallery, *sedilia* – seats, *mimorum aedes* – actors' rooms, *orchestra* – seats for important patrons, *ingressus* – entrance, *proscaenium* – main stage, *planities sive arena* – arena for standing spectators.

play, or i.viii where we have the Folio stage direction, 'Enter Martius and Aufidius at several (i.e. different) doors'. In v.v, however, the triumphal entry of Volumnia into Rome, the stage direction 'Enter two Senators, with Ladies, passing over the Stage' suggests that they came in one door and went out the other.

Jutting out over part of the main stage was a roof known as the 'shadow', 'heavens' or 'canopy', supported by two large pillars, one at each corner, again clearly illustrated in The Swan drawing. An eyewitness tells us that these pillars were wooden, but so skilfully painted that they could not be distinguished from marble. They were useful in dividing up the stage for scenes in which separate groups operated, such as the patricians and plebeians in *Coriolanus*, and in providing hiding places for the many spying and eaves-dropping scenes in Elizabethan drama. The underside of the 'heavens' was magnificently painted or sculptured with representations of the sun, moon, stars, signs of the zodiac and other heavenly bodies, and this doubtless accounts for the many invitations by the actor for his audience to behold the heavens. When Julius Caesar declares

> The skies are painted with unnumbered sparks,
> They are all fire, and every one doth shine.

(Julius   Caesar, III.i.63)

the audience is being asked to admire the sparkling new 'heavens' of The Globe, completed just a few months before. When Coriolanus tells the servants of Aufidius that he dwells 'under the canopy' his words were probably suggested by the connection between 'canopy' and 'heavens' in the theatre in which he was standing. The physical features of the theatre were a fruitful source of idea and imagery in many of Shakespeare's plays.

Signboards were sometimes used to denote setting, but this crude practice, mocked by that astringent critic Sir Philip Sidney, seems to have early fallen out of use. The normal method of indicating locality is for one of the actors to tell us where we are, as when Touchstone, as he arrives in the forest of Arden in *As You Like It*, remarks 'Now am I in Arden'. Very often location is un-important and unmentioned by the dramatist. In IV.iii, the scene between Adrian and Nicanor, all we know is that they are somewhere outside Rome, since there is no need for us to know more. Usually we are told whether we are indoors or not. In v.iii Coriolanus finally invites his family to drink with him, with the invitation, 'Come, enter with us,' which indicates that the scene has been on the main stage in the open; and concludes with their exit to his tent, probably through the curtains of the inner stage. Often one scene will indicate where the next, or a subsequent scene is set. In IV.iv Coriolanus's first words, 'A goodly city is this Antium' tells us at once where we are, which we need, since his last appearance was in IV.i as he left Rome with no indication of where he was going. In IV.iv also he asks a Citizen to direct him to Aufidius's house, so that when he appears in IV.v we know without being told that the setting is Aufidius's house. Very often the dramatist's need to tell his audience where they are, what time of day it is, what time has passed, or what journey – which he cannot show on the stage itself – has been undertaken, is the occasion of much of the finest poetry in the drama of the time, though there happens to be little of this verbal scene-painting or time-setting in *Coriolanus*.

Above the upper stage, in the third and top storey of the theatre, was the musicians' gallery and sound effects room. It was from here that a trumpet would sound to indicate that a performance was about to begin – a useful service at a time when clocks were a rarity – and a flag was run up to indicate that a play was in progress. Elizabethans were great music lovers, a fact which explains the prevalence of songs in the plays, particularly the comedies. The nature of the subject makes song inappropriate in *Coriolanus*, and the most Shakespeare could do was to introduce the sound of off-stage music in IV.v where Aufidius is feasting his friends, and 'music plays'. The musicians, however, would be kept busy providing the military music demanded in the numerous battle scenes, and with an audience which included many soldiers or ex-soldiers who were critical about these things, they would have to distinguish correctly the calls for the advance, the retreat, the parley, the funeral and so on. There are also many demands for flourishes and sennets announcing the arrival of important personages. In all there are twenty-five stage directions requiring the use of cornets, trumpets and drums. The musicians had a highly important function, in producing resounding noise, in creating the necessary atmosphere of violence, turbulence and excitement. We find this, quite apart from the war, in the triumph of Volumnia's return to Rome, where the messenger tells us:

> The trumpets, sackbuts, psalteries, and fifes,
> Tabors and cymbals, and the shouting Romans,
> Make the sun dance.
>
> (v.iv.46)

Other features which extended the possibilities of Elizabethan staging were the trapdoors, of which there would be one or more on the main stage, and possibly one in the inner stage, through which devils, ghosts and other spirits from the nether world would enter, and one in the heavens from which gods and other aerial spirits might descend. No use is made of this facility in *Coriolanus*, which carefully avoids, for reasons discussed elsewhere in this *Introduction*, any suggestion of supernatural interference. It is believed that in some theatres there were windows above the two doors in the back wall.

Performances in the public theatres were in daylight, usually in the afternoons. Burning torches would be carried to suggest darkness in night scenes.

More realistic effects were obtained in the private indoor theatres where the room could be darkened or performances given after dark. *Coriolanus* has only the two scenes at Aufidius's house set at night, possibly a visual symbol of Coriolanus's moral collapse as he determines on revenge.

There was little or no use of stage scenery of the modern kind, confining the stage to a fixed location, but stage properties, that is, movable articles of stage furniture, such as tables, chairs, walls, banks of earth or flowers, gates, wells, and trees, were quite widely used. In keeping with the fast-moving active nature of *Coriolanus* in which public scenes are twice as numerous as private scenes (an unusual proportion in Shakespeare's plays), and also with the general air of spartan bleakness aimed at, there is very little use of stage properties; nothing, in fact, beyond scaling ladders, two stools, chairs and cushions for the Senators, and a throne for Coriolanus.

When Cominius in eulogizing Coriolanus in II.ii declares

> When he might act the woman in the scene,
> He proved best man i' th' field

he refers to the Elizabethan custom of boy actors taking the parts of women. Grounded at school in the art of rhetoric, in which Elizabethan acting was firmly rooted, these boys were accomplished actors, and there were a number of all-boy companies. Normally the boys' parts were short, to ease the physical and mental strain on them. *Coriolanus* requires four boys, who appear together in I.iii in the parts of Volumnia, Virgilia, Valeria and the Gentlewoman. Volumnia's part is particularly demanding, not so much in its length of 250-odd lines, since this would be about the average for the leading boy's part, but in the nature of the part itself. It is a tribute to the talents of the boy actors that Shakespeare created a part requiring such a variety of skills and emotional range, knowing that it could be convincingly performed by his acting company. The parts of Virgilia and Valeria, excellent roles for the actors, are not nearly so exacting.

The use of boy actors was short-term: as soon as their voices broke and beards began to grow they could no longer be used for women's parts. This helps to explain the almost total absence of particularized description of women in the plays, for if the dramatist described one of his heroines as tall, fair and blue-eyed, he might have a boy to fit the description one week, but not the next. The only feature of the women in *Coriolanus* which is specified is the 'dove's eyes' of Virgilia, and these, of course, could be of any colour.

Elizabethan acting companies were small. They would be lucky to have nine or ten male actors, three or four boys, and half a dozen supernumeraries to take small or mute parts, such as those of soldiers, attendants and messengers. Probably stage hands, and musicians when not required to provide music, would be pressed into service for a play with a large cast like *Coriolanus* which has thirty-eight speaking parts. The dramatist was thus severely cir-cumscribed when representing crowd scenes, and had to exploit his limited company carefully to suggest large numbers. We see the problem at the beginning of *Coriolanus* where Shakespeare deploys virtually the whole company in order to create the effect of serious and large-scale disturbance in Rome, threatening its ordered existence. Apart from the twelve speaking parts, he needs a crowd of citizens to create uproar, and a number of Senators to show the opposed power of the patrician faction. There are shouts off-stage and reference to another body of mutinous citizens on the other side of the city, thus extending the boundaries of the stage, and stressing the pervasive threat of rebellion through the whole city. Shakespeare makes possible the use of his whole cast in this vital opening scene by arranging the exit of many of them at line 250, and giving another 30 lines to the Tribunes, which allows the actors of the parts of Aufidius and the Volscian Senators in I.ii and the four boy actors required in I.iii time to change costume after appearing in I.i.

Another necessary economy device was the staging of battles representa-tionally, with small isolated encounters suggesting a larger pattern of events, as in the sally of the Volscians from the gates of Corioli and Coriolanus's later entry into the city in I.iv, the retreat of Cominius in I.vi, and the single combat of Coriolanus and Aufidius in I.viii. The main battle takes place, necessarily, off-stage, and the skirmishes that we see have to suggest the way the fighting is going. Adroit use of smoke, fireworks, trumpets and drums, all helped to create the illusion of large-scale conflict. Realism was attempted in the matter of blood-shedding, with the use of concealed pigs' bladders containing blood, property heads and limbs, even real entrails brought reeking from the nearest slaughter-house. Coriolanus is so smeared with the blood of his enemies that his friend Cominius does not at first recognize him, and this visual appearance of Coriolanus as 'a thing of blood' is closely related to his whole characteriza-tion and its impact upon us.

The structure of Elizabethan plays, the way the dramatist unfolds his story, was certainly influenced by the limited number of actors at his dis-posal. With fifteen to twenty actors and thirty-eight speaking parts, duplica-tion was necessary, and Shakespeare had to construct his play to make this possible. We find that several characters who appear early in the play, fade out and are not seen again. The Gentlewoman and Usher (I.iii), the Roman Lieutenant (I.vii) and the Herald (II.i) make only one appearance and are free to take parts introduced in the middle of the play, such as those of Adrian and Nicanor, who figure only in IV.iii, or the three servants of Aufidius in IV.v. Titus Lartius does not appear after III.i and could take one of the many parts confined to the end of the play, such as Aufidius's Lieutenant or the three Conspirators.

Frequently the text makes explicit the movement, gesture or facial expression required by the author. Examples of this are Coriolanus's question to Virgilia

> Wouldst thou have laughed had I come coffined home,
> That weep'st to see me triumph?

(II.i.165)

his 'Thus I turn my back' as he 'banishes' Rome (III.iii.133) or his description of the approach of his family, 'My wife comes foremost . . . and in her hand/ The grandchild to her blood' (v.iii.22), or Menenius's frenzied 'I am out of breath./Confusion's near. I cannot speak' (III.i.188) in the uproar when Coriolanus is accused of treason.

Where the acting directions are not built into the text in this way, they are often supplemented by stage directions. *Coriolanus* is exceptionally rich in stage directions which certainly came from Shakespeare's pen and so command our close attention, since they give not simply the bare bones of exits and entrances, but details of appearance and costume, the number and disposition of the actors on the stage, their movement and gesture, and even glimpses into their character and what Shakespeare thinks of them. In this edition most of Shakespeare's stage directions have been retained in their original form, but some have been modernized or altered to make the stage action clearer for the reader, and a number have been added for the same purpose.

The stage directions indicate his concern to create speed, noise, bustle, excitement, as the following selection shows: 'Enter a Messenger hastily' (I.i.208), 'Enter Martius cursing' (I.iv.29), 'Enter Martius bleeding, assaulted by the enemy' (I.iv.61), 'They all shout and wave their swords; take him up in their arms and cast up their caps' (I.vi.75), 'they all bustle about Coriolanus' (III.i.184), 'Coriolanus draws his sword' (III.i.222), 'In this mutiny, the Tribunes, the Aediles, and the people are beat in' (III.i.228), Coriolanus 'pushes him [Aufidius's servant] away from him' (IV.v.29), 'beats him' (IV.v.45), 'Drums and trumpets sound with great shouts of the people' (v.vi.48). In such stage directions as 'Citizens steal away' (I.i.237) and 'Draw both the Conspirators, and kill Martius, who falls, Aufidius stands on him' (v.vi.130) the moral nature of the characters concerned is strongly conveyed. By contrast with all the noise of the public scenes the quiet of the domestic scene, I.iii, is established through the stage direction 'They set them down on two low stools and sew'. Perhaps the most eloquent of all stage directions is found in v.iii after Volumnia's appeal to her son, 'Holds her by the hand, silent'. Failure to reflect on what that silence means has led to many inadequate critical responses to *Coriolanus*.

Little attempt was made at historical accuracy in costuming on the Elizabethan stage, though in the drawing attributed to Henry Peacham made about

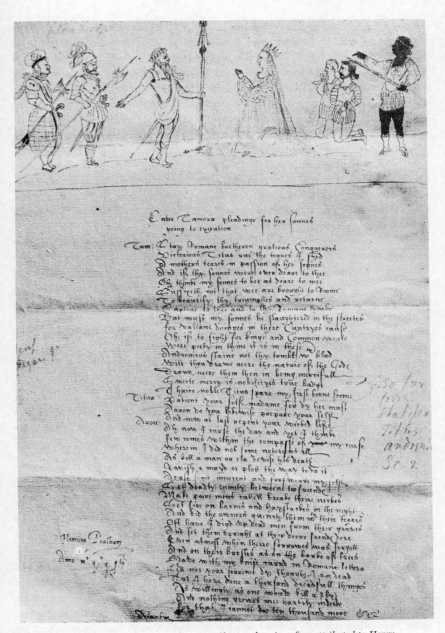

A scene from Shakespeare's Titus Andronicus *(from a drawing often attributed to Henry Peacham about 1595).*

1595 of a scene from Shakespeare's *Titus Andronicus* (see p. lxvii) there is evidence of some concessions to Roman dress. We see there an attempt to reproduce the Roman corslet which was moulded to simulate the sculpture of the human torso, the loose cloak knotted at the shoulder which probably represents the Elizabethan notion of the toga, and the oaken garland. These 'Roman' details exist side by side with the contemporary sixteenth century weapons, armour, helmets, doublets and stuffed hose visible in this interesting sketch, and we can safely assume that a similar mixture would have appeared when *Coriolanus* was staged. To some extent it is demanded by the text, which mentions the 'wolvish toga', the gown of humility and the oaken garland. The play specifies however that Coriolanus and Aufidius are bearded, the Tribunes both bald and bearded, and that Coriolanus, Menenius and the plebeians wear caps. Coriolanus waves his hat at II.iii, doublets are mentioned at I.v.6 and Volumnia refers to a bonnet in III.ii.

Very large sums were expended on costumes, which had to be the genuine article for the kings, queens, noblemen and warriors who crowded the Elizabethan stage, if they were to avoid the censure of a demanding and vocal audience who would not put up with the kind of inferior imitations that can be hidden today by distance from the stage and the use of modern lighting equipment. This lavishness was part of a general attempt to create in the theatre an exotic and splendid world which Londoners were denied in their daily lives. There are numerous contemporary tributes to the magnificence of the Elizabethan theatre.

The multiple stage of the Elizabethan theatre, with its various levels and depths – apron stage, inner stage, upper stage, trapdoors, and movable properties – was an extremely flexible instrument admirably adapted to the telling of a story swiftly and uninterruptedly, and the dramatists of the time learned to exploit it to the full.

Language and verse in the play

Shakespeare's use of language is remarkable in many ways and demands the careful attention of the reader. Firstly, he uses an enormously rich and varied vocabulary, greater than that of any other writer. Secondly, he often loads his words with more meanings than one, particularly in his verse. Whereas prose is normally straightforward, expressing one unequivocal meaning, verse often sets out deliberately to do many things at one time, and the poetic dramatist, more than other poets, is apt to use language in this way, since he is forced by the pressure of time into linguistic economy, compression and intensity. Irony, too, is one of the dramatist's major weapons, and irony is always concerned with some kind of double meaning. When Coriolanus says that if the Senate would allow it he would

> make a quarry
> With thousands of these quartered slaves
>
> (I.i.184)

he is using the image of the deer hunter cutting his prey into quarters. His hearers, however, would certainly be reminded of the Elizabethan practice of hanging, drawing and quartering traitors. Hunting images and exaggeration are Coriolanus's 'kind of speech', but the citizens of Rome would naturally take the assertion as much more sinister and savage than the hunting image would suggest. We see why Coriolanus provokes the fear and distrust of the citizens.

Shakespeare makes considerable use of dramatic irony, the device in which characters speak and act in ignorance of the true significance of what they or other characters are saying, while the audience is aware of this because it knows facts hidden from the speakers. We see this illustrated in Menenius's pessimism in v.iv where he tries to persuade Sicinius that Volumnia's mission to Coriolanus is bound to fail, since we know from the previous scene that it has succeeded. Sometimes the audience does not know more than the characters themselves, and only later sees the irony of previous speeches and actions, as is the case in I.i.168 where Coriolanus attacks the plebeians,

> With every minute you do change a mind,
> And call him noble that was now your hate,
> Him vilde that was your garland

since later we see them doing just this to him.

Often words and phrases are not to be understood simply from their literal meaning, but carry associations deriving from the context in which they occur. Coriolanus's boast

> That, like an eagle in a dovecote, I
> Fluttered your Volscians in Corioli
>
> (v.vi.114)

would lose its force and allusiveness in any prose equivalent. To begin with, the eagle was the king of birds, a type of peerlessness, and the dove a symbol of the pacific, so that the statement is at once a proud boast and a contemptuous dismissal of the fighting qualities of the Volscians, which Coriolanus makes more pointed by the use of the pronoun 'your'. 'Fluttered', together with the other alliterated 'l' sounds of the line, splendidly captures the sound and sight of the panic-stricken doves trying to escape the eagle. The lines are one of the few rhyming couplets of the play, the rhyme words stressing Coriolanus's egotism and the place where it was displayed.

The significance of words is often incomplete without reference back to earlier parts of the play. When Menenius describes the change in Coriolanus after his banishment

> There is a difference between a grub and a butterfly, yet your butterfly was a grub. This Martius is grown from man to dragon. He has wings; he's more than a creeping thing.
>
> (v.iv.10)

we are reminded of Valeria's story of how young Martius his son chased the gilded butterfly and tore it to pieces in his rage, and how Volumnia links father and son with her comment 'One on's father's moods' (I.iii.63), and also of Cominius's description of Coriolanus and his army advancing on Rome

> with no less confidence
> Than boys pursuing summer butterflies.
>
> (IV.vi.94)

The reference to the dragon carries us back to Coriolanus quitting Rome 'like to a lonely dragon' (IV.i.30) and Aufidius's report that he 'fights dragon-like' for the Volscians (IV.vii.23). The 'wings' refer to the dragon on the one hand, but also suggest the divine order since Coriolanus is said to be more than man, and this links up with many other such suggestions running through the play: Menenius, Aufidius and his soldiers and the Roman nobles all 'god' him in various ways. Thus, these three lines of Menenius are richly allusive, setting up numerous resonances and echoes, and there are many more examples of word and meaning working retrospectively in this way, in prose passages such as this speech of Menenius, as well as in the blank verse.

The staple of Shakespeare's verse is the iambic pentameter, that is, a line made up of five iambic feet (an iambic foot consisting of two syllables, the first unstressed, the second stressed, with the stress falling on those syllables which are accented in normal speech) as in the following lines:

> Nŏ púb|lĭc bén|ĕfit|whĭch yóu|rĕceíve
> Bŭt ít|prŏceéds|ŏr cómes|frŏm thém|tŏ yóu.
>
> (I.i.138)

The stressed syllables are marked ´, the unstressed ones ˘, and each foot is divided from the next by the vertical stroke |. The majority of the verse lines follow this basic pattern. In such a line as

> Wĕ háve|récŏrd|thăt vér|ў well|ĭt cán
>
> (IV.vi.50)

we have in *recòrd* an example of a word differently sounded in the sixteenth century; the stress is on the second syllable and the line is a regular iambic pentameter. Other examples are *aspéct* (v.iii.32), *instińct* (v.iii.35), *exíle* (v.iii.96), and *pretéxt* (v.vi.19). Other words, now accented on the second syllable, were then stressed on the first, such as *éndure* (I.vi.58), *plébeians* (I.ix.7, v.iv.33), *húmane* (III.i.325), *cément* (IV.vi.86).

Other examples of apparent irregularity are cases where elision, that is, the suppression of a syllable, is necessary to preserve the metrical regularity as in

I' th' end | admire; | where lad | ies shall | be fright | ed.

(I.ix.5)

The words *In the end,* properly three syllables, have had to be truncated as the spelling, taken from the First Folio, shows, to make two syllables as the metre requires. There are more elisions in *Coriolanus* than in any other Shakespearian play, producing an acceleration of the verse which is in keeping with the rapidity of the action of the play. Other examples are: *'t* (it), *on's* (on his), *'a* (he), *has* (he has), *o' th'* (of the, on the), *in's* (in his), *'em* (them), *thou'st* (thou shalt), *thou't* (thou wouldst), *shall's* (shall we), *y'are* (you are). The line quoted above also illustrates, in the extra unstressed syllable at the end of the line, another favourite method of Shakespeare in the later plays of varying his rhythmic pattern.

Another freedom open to the Elizabethan poet was to sound the final *-ed* in verbs and adjectives which would not be sounded in normal speech, as in

My grain | èd ash | an hund | red times | hath broke

(IV.v.104)

and in *crownèd* (I.i.101), *condemnèd* (I.viii.15), *renownèd* (II.i.156, III.i.289), *blearèd* (II.i.194), *deservèd* (III.i.290) and *burnèd* (IV.vi.86), where the *-ed* gives the line its ten syllables.

A common feature of Shakespeare's verse is inversion – found in most literary ages and in many languages – which may be simply the reversal of the normal prose order of, say, adjective followed by noun, as in *backs red* (I.iv.37) or *carbuncle entire* (I.iv.55), or more complicatedly, a structural inversion of the syntax, as in *most charitable care/Have the patricians of you* (I.i.53), where we have the object followed by the verb and then the subject. Inversion was a useful device for the poet, making easier his task of fitting his thought and language to the metrical demands of the iambic pentameter, and enabling him to emphasize chosen words, phrases and ideas in a way usually impossible in prose.

From time to time the dramatist will vary the metre to avoid monotony, reducing or increasing the number of syllables, a shorter line often effectively marking a pause in speech, or by running one line on to the next without a pause, or by introducing different stress patterns from the iambic. For example, in the line

Man-ént | ěred thús, | hě wáx | ěd likě | ǎ séa

(II.ii.96)

the first foot is a spondee, with two stressed syllables, so that attention is drawn, through the disruption of the normal pattern to the word *man*, stressing Coriolanus's development from boy to man. The question of Coriolanus's manhood, its existence and nature, is very much the concern of the play, and it is Aufidius's insult, 'Boy', which leads swiftly to Coriolanus's death.

Further variety and flexibility are acquired by variation in the position of the caesura, the pause which the sense of the words dictates within many lines even where there is no punctuation involved. In the following examples the caesural pause is marked by the double vertical lines ‖:

who resists
Are mocked ‖ for valiant ignorance

(IV.vi.104)

As many coxcombs
As you threw caps up ‖ will he tumble down

(IV.vi.135)

That which shall break his neck ‖ or hazard mine.

(IV.vii.25)

In using blank verse, that is, unrhymed iambic pentameters, Shakespeare was using the form handed down by his predecessors who had by trial and error discovered it to be the best medium for conveying dramatic purpose in a memorable and succinct way. Shakespeare's achievement lay in experimenting with this medium until he had made it a refined instrument of great flexibility, capable of containing multiple meanings compactly, and of communicating subtle shades and nuances. We see the compactness in such words and phrases as *cloven army* (I.iv.21), *bragged progeny* (I.viii.12), *ridges horsed with variable complexions* (II.i.200), *hear my nothings monstered* (II.ii.74), *man-entered* (II.ii.96), *hopeless restitution* (III.i.16), *tiger-footed rage* (III.i.310), *inshelled* (IV.vi.45), *so-never-needed help* (V.i.34), *grief-shot* (V.i.44), *unhearts* (V.i.49). Some, like *Triton of the minnows* (III.i.89), have passed into the common currency of the language, but all of them would require many more words in prose to convey their meanings, which would certainly be less memorable.

Images which have only a single meaning in isolation can acquire various levels of meaning when repeated or woven into a pattern running through the play. The dramatist may use reiteration of imagery to convey meaning, shape the audience's response, or create a special tone or atmosphere. The basic image of *Coriolanus* is that of the body and its functioning, and it is through this primarily that Shakespeare conducts his critique of Roman society. Almost every bodily part and function finds mention: head, hair, face, brow, lips, eyes, tongue, teeth, cheeks, chin, neck, trunk, back, front, sides, bosom, stomach, breasts, bowels, heart, lungs; arms, hands, fingers, thumb; leg, knee, foot, toe; blood, veins, sinews, sweat, digestion, breath – the list is endless and the references to the body all-pervading. Menenius's Fable of the Belly creates an elaborate correspondence between the state and the body which the First Citizen extends by comparing the king, statesman, soldier, horse and trumpeter to, respectively, the head, eye and heart, arm, leg and tongue. This analogy coming at the beginning of the play, colours all subsequent body references, so that most of them have more than just a literal significance, and function symbolically by standing for something more than themselves, revealing character, attitudes, relationships. Coriolanus's knee bent to his mother reflects visually his conception of 'nature', his sweat is his anger embodied; the 'legs' that the tribunes want from their followers symbolize their ambition; the bound brows of Coriolanus represent a concept of honour, a definable way of life; the tribunes are 'mouths' and 'tongues' for the 'hands' or plebeians; 'voices' are people and also their approval and support. Rome too is conceived of as a body, a mother and dear nurse, and Coriolanus accused of tearing out her bowels; his gesture of turning his back on her in IV.i reflects physically his spiritual regression, and so on.

These body images powerfully convey the truth that Rome and her inhabitants are so closely related as to be essentially one, and stress that the state is an organism, subject to either health or sickness, infection, suffering and cure. Ironically, the discordant members, all seeing their opponents as diseased – *scabs, itches, measles, gangrene, poison, canker* – and recommending drastic surgery, underline the general malaise that grips Rome. The city's failure to attain anything like the ideal represented in Menenius's fable leads to disaster.

Another important image-group is that centred on acting. 'Action', says Volumnia, 'is eloquence' (III.ii.76), and by 'action' she means 'acting'. The difficulty is to know the reality from the appearance, to know what the action is saying, as Shakespeare is at pains to demonstrate. All the major figures play roles, adopt poses, present appearances of themselves. Menenius is an accomplished player; the tribunes are both actors in their hypocrisy, deciding to 'seem humbler' after their display of power (IV.ii.4), and producers, rehearsing their cast, the citizens, in their parts, and feeding them with their cues (III.ii.12f). Volumnia actually gives her son a practical demonstration of acting (III.iii.72) and Cominius agrees to act as prompter (line 106). Just what the true nature of Coriolanus is forms the subject of debate between citizens at I.i.28 and II.iii.149. Coriolanus cannot wait to shed his costume, the gown of humility, and become himself again (II.iii.136). At III.ii.15 he opposes his mother's wish that he should dissemble by asking her

> would you have me
> False to my nature? Rather say I play
> The man I am.

Here he regards 'playing' as being false, and then as being true, his true self being a part he plays, which suggests the difficulty of separating the two. He is censured for over-acting by Volumnia:

> You might have been enough the man you are,
> With striving less to be so
>
> (III.ii.19)

which again raises the question, 'What is he?' without resolving it. Coriolanus plays a part in disguise at Antium. Later Cominius reports, 'He would not seem to know me' (v.i.8), while after Menenius's mission Coriolanus himself concedes he has been acting. 'Though I showed sourly to him' (v.iii.13) – and later 'like a dull actor' forgets his part (v.iii.40). These acting images impress on us the difficulty of reaching the truth about people and events, especially in this treacherous, mutable, deceptive world of Rome.

There are over a hundred animal references in the play, most of them used pejoratively of one side or the other. The citizens are labelled curs, rats, hares, geese, camels, mules, wolves, cats, crows, minnows, multiplying spawn, the herd, Hydra, 'the beast with many heads'. Coriolanus is called, on the debit side, serpent, viper, wolf, dog, sheep, cat, grub, butterfly and wild horse; and on the credit side, lion, osprey, steed and lamb. He calls himself both eagle and gosling, and a number of ambiguous terms are applied to him, such as tiger (a type of strength, but singled out here for its mercilessness) and dragon, which can be serpent or winged creature. Sicinius and Brutus are called ass, goat and fox; the patricians dogs and conies, the Coriolans, fawning grey-hounds, and all the Romans, flies.

This double-edged imagery is certainly not intended to favour one side at the expense of the other, as has been suggested. Rather it impresses on us the deplorable extremes, the 'violentest contrarieties' of the Roman social fabric. Many of the animal references occur in juxtaposed pairs of opposites, such as lions/hares (I.i.157), foxes/geese (I.i.158), mouse/cat (I.vi.44), wolf/lamb (II.i.6), Triton/minnows (III.i.89), crows/eagles (III.i.139), and 'dogs on sheep' (II.i.246). In I.i we see enough of the human qualities of the plebeians, distorted though they are by privation, to discount the animal epithets hurled at them by Coriolanus and his fellow patricians, and perceive the lack of human feeling that prompts them. Both sides, however, viewing their fellow Romans almost exclusively in animal terms, ironically proclaim their own defective humanity.

A number of fire images are found at the end of the play (at IV.vi.79, 138; v.i.14, 64; v.ii.7, 44, 68; v.iii.181) which spring from Shakespeare's decision to alter Plutarch by having Coriolanus plan to burn Rome. The projected fire becomes the objective expression of Coriolanus's burning anger and desire for revenge, inwardly consuming him as Cominius's description makes clear:

> I tell you he does sit in gold, his eye
> Red as 'twould burn Rome.
>
> (v.i.63)

Shakespeare's audience was made up of all levels of society from the monarch to the apprentice boy, combining men of learning and unlettered labourers. Dramatists like Shakespeare, writing for the public theatre, while careful to provide interest and pleasure for the latter (the 'groundlings' or 'penny stinkards'), also aimed to satisfy the well-read. A great number of literary allusions, presupposing a knowledge of ancient history and mythology (as in the allusion to Diana at I.i.243) would be beyond the knowledge and understanding of the groundlings but would capture the interest of the literate members of the audience.

Almost a quarter of the play is in prose, an unusually high proportion in the later plays and tragedies. *Antony and Cleopatra* for example has only 8% prose. Prose is used in three main ways: firstly, for the speech of characters low in the social scale; secondly, for those of higher rank in their more relaxed moments; and thirdly, for comic scenes.

Examples of the first category are those scenes in which the plebeians figure, namely the mutiny scene (I.i) and the election scene (II.iii). An interesting variation occurs in I.i when the First Citizen attempts to match Menenius in debate and begins, like him, to use blank verse; his pretentiousness however, breaks down comically into incoherence. Also in this group are the informal chat about Coriolanus by the two Senate officials (II.ii.1–33) and the meeting between Adrian and Nicanor (IV.iii) where prose fits the sordid reality of their spying.

In the second group we have I.iii in which the three high-born ladies relax and gossip over their sewing in Coriolanus's house. Their quiet prose is an effective contrast to the high-sounding rhetoric of the market-place and the battlefield in the scenes which surround it, though we should notice that for some twenty lines Volumnia switches to verse when she is imagining the epic action of her son in battle.

The third use of prose, for comic effect, is illustrated in the slanging match between Menenius and the tribunes (II.i). When Coriolanus enters Menenius

immediately reverts to blank verse, his normal medium as a senator. There is
more comic material in the conversation of Aufidius's servants in IV.v, though
servants would speak in prose whether their talk is comic or not. In v.ii
Menenius at first attempts to impress the guards with his importance and
speaks verse (lines 1–23). When he is unsuccessful he falls into their medium,
prose, and continues it after the entry of Coriolanus, who speaks verse
throughout. The contrast of forms highlights Menenius's inferior position as
humble suppliant, and also emphasizes the gap that now divides them.

While Aufidius speaks verse throughout as befits his rank, we find Coriolanus twice using prose: first, when he begs for the citizens' votes (a role that
he feels demeans him) and second when he goes disguised into Aufidius's
house, where ironically he is unaware of the base role that he is playing. In
both cases prose is cleverly apt.

Messengers, soldiers, heralds and the like speak verse while performing
their duties, and in the presence of their superiors. Examples of this are the
herald's announcement in II.i, the reports of the messengers in I.vi and I.x and
the soldiers in battle in I.iv, though an interesting variation is that when they
turn to looting in I.v they drop appropriately into prose.

Rhyme is uncommon in Shakespeare's later plays, and *Coriolanus* contains
only thirteen couplets. Six of these are found in the soliloquy of the hero when
he is left alone momentarily in the midst of his vote canvassing (II.iii.102–13).
The speech stands out from the surrounding prose, and the rhyme underlines
this first direct glimpse into his mind, accenting his internal struggle:

> Better it is to die, better to starve
> Than crave the hire which first we do deserve.

'Deserve' was pronounced 'desarve' in Shakespeare's day, making this a perfect rhyme. Another memorable use of rhyme is Volumnia's couplet after she
has been using only prose at II.i.149,

> Death, that dark spirit, in's nervy arm doth lie,
> Which being advanced, declines, and then men die.

The use of the couplet for a weighty, sententious or epigrammatic statement
of this kind was common in Elizabethan drama. It was also used to end a
scene, giving it a note of finality. This is illustrated in Aufidius's speech
closing IV.vii, where the last four lines are couplets, the first an aphorism, the
second an ominous pointer to the destruction of Coriolanus. Coriolanus's
solitary couplet at v.iii.129

> Not of a woman's tenderness to be,
> Requires nor child nor woman's face to see

marks an important moment of realization and also assures us that Volumnia
has already won her appeal. As is usual, the play ends with a couplet.

Passages of literary criticism relating to *Coriolanus*

The aim of the following selections is to present varied viewpoints on the play by distinguished critics.

(a) The following extract from John Dennis is interesting as being the earliest recorded criticism of the play, and as revealing the strongly moralistic demands made on literature by the neo-classic Augustan age in which Dennis lived.

> The Good must never fail to prosper, and the Bad must be always punished. Otherwise the Incidents, and particularly the Catastrophe which is the grand Incident, are liable to be imputed rather to Chance than to Almighty Conduct and to Sovereign Justice. The want of this impartial Distribution of Justice makes the *Coriolanus* of Shakespeare to be without Moral. 'Tis true indeed Coriolanus is kill'd by those Foreign Enemies with whom he had openly sided against his Country, which seems to be an Event worthy of Providence, and would look as if it were contriv'd by infinite Wisdom, and executed by supreme Justice, to make Coriolanus a dreadful Example to all who lead on Foreign Enemies to the Invasion of their native Country; if there were not something in the Fate of the other Characters, which gives occasion to doubt of it, and which suggests to the Sceptical Reader that this might happen by accident. For Aufidius the principal Murderer of Coriolanus, who in cold blood gets him assassinated by Ruffians, instead of leaving him to the Law of the Country, and the Justice of the Volscian Senate, and who commits so black a Crime, not by an erroneous Zeal, or a mistaken publick Spirit, but thro' Jealousy, Envy, and inveterate Malice; this Assassinator not only survives, and survives unpunished but seems to be rewarded for so detestable an Action by engrossing all those Honours to himself which Coriolanus before had shar'd with him. . . . The Good and the Bad then perishing promiscuously in the best of Shakespeare's Tragedies, there can be either none or very weak Instruction in them: For such promiscuous Events call the Government of Providence into Question, and by Scepticks and Libertines are resolv'd into Chance.
>
> John Dennis: *An Essay on the Genius and Writings of Shakespeare,* 1712

(b) In this all-too-short passage, Dr Johnson gives the play high praise for its power to hold an audience's attention, chiefly through its variety of character and situation.

> The tragedy of *Coriolanus* is one of the most amusing [i.e. entertaining or interesting] of our author's performances. The old man's merriment

in Menenius; the lofty lady's dignity in Volumnia; the bridal modesty in Virgilia; the patrician and military haughtiness in Coriolanus; the plebeian malignity and tribunitian insolence in Brutus and Sicinius, make a very pleasing and interesting variety: and the various revolutions of the hero's fortunes fill the mind with anxious curiosity. There is, perhaps, too much bustle in the first act, and too little in the last.

Samuel Johnson: *Preface to Shakespeare*, 1765

(c) Coleridge, in the few notes he left on the play, stresses Shakespeare's impartiality and patriotism, but questions some details of Shakespeare's drawing of the character of Aufidius.

The wonderful philosophic impartiality in Shakespeare's politics. His own country's history had furnished him with no *matter* but what was too recent, and he [was] devoted to *patriotism*. Besides, the dispassionate instruction of ancient history. This most remarkable in *Julius Caesar*. In all this good-humoured laugh at mobs, collate with Sir Thomas Browne.

Commenting on Aufidius's speech at I.x.12–27, 'Mine emulation' etc. he continues:

I have such deep faith in Shakespeare's heart-lore that I take for granted, this is in nature, and not as a mere anomaly, altho' I cannot in myself discover any germ of possible feeling which could wax and unfold itself into such sentiment.

On Aufidius's speech, 'All places yield to him' IV.vii.28–57 he comments:

I have always thought this in itself so beautiful speech the least explicable from the mood and full intention of the speaker of any in the whole works of Shakespeare. I cherish the hope that I am mistaken and, becoming wiser, shall discover some profound excellence in what I now appear to myself to detect an imperfection.

S. T. Coleridge: *Notes on the Tragedies of Shakespeare,* c1810

(d) A. C. Bradley, one of the most influential critics in the early part of the twentieth century, finds *Coriolanus* a play of vehement passion, power and nobility, but inferior in popular appeal to the four great tragedies, *Hamlet*, *Othello*, *King Lear* and *Macbeth*, and attributes this to the absence of mystery, inward conflict in the hero, the supernatural, and a nature which is not just background but a 'fellow actor and fellow-sufferer', all of which elements give these plays their peculiar imaginative effect, he contends.

Coriolanus's nature is large, simple, passionate; but . . . not, in any marked degree, imaginative. He feels all the rapture, but not, like Othello, all the poetry of war. He covets honour no less than Hotspur, but he has not Hotspur's vision of honour. He meets with ingratitude, like Timon, but it does not transfigure all mankind for him. He is very eloquent, but his only free eloquence is that of vituperation and scorn. It is sometimes more than eloquence, it is splendid poetry; but it is never such magical poetry as we hear in the four greatest tragedies. Then, too, it lies in his nature that his deepest and most sacred feeling, that for his mother, is almost dumb. It governs his life and leads him uncomplaining towards death, but it cannot speak. And finally his inward conflicts are veiled from us. The change that came when he found himself alone and homeless in exile is not exhibited.

The representation of the people, whatever else it may be, is part of a dramatic design. The design is based on the main facts of the story, and these imply a certain character in the people and the hero. Since the issue is tragic, the conflict between them must be felt to be unavoidable and wellnigh hopeless. The necessity for dramatic sympathy with both sides demands that on both there should be some right and some wrong, both virtues and failings; and if the hero's monstrous purpose of destroying his native city is not to extinguish our sympathy, the provocation he receives must be great. This being so, the picture of the people is, surely, no darker than it had to be. . . .

All the force and nobility of Rome's greatest man have to be thrown away and wasted. That is tragic; and it is doubly so because it is not only his faults that make him impossible. There is bound up with them a nobleness of nature in which he surpasses everyone around him. . . .

To me the scene [v.iii] is one in which the tragic feelings of fear and pity have little place. Such anxiety as I feel is not for the fate of the hero or of any one else: it is, to use religious language, for the safety of his soul. And when he yields, though I know, as he divines, that his life is lost, the emotion I feel is not pity: he is above pity and above life. And the anxiety itself is but slight: it bears no resemblance to the hopes and fears that agitate us as we approach the end in *Othello* or *King Lear*. . . .

A tragedy it is, for the passion is gigantic, and it leads to the hero's death. But the catastrophe scarcely diminishes the influence of the great scene. Since we know that his nature, though the good in it has conquered, remains unchanged, and since his rival's plan is concerted before our eyes, we wait with little suspense, almost indeed with tranquillity, the certain end. As it approaches it is felt to be the more inevitable because the steps which lead to it are made to repeat as exactly as possible the steps which led to his exile. His task, as then, is to excuse himself, a task the most repugnant to his pride. Aufidius, like the tribunes then, knows how to render its fulfilment impossible. He

hears a word of insult, the same that he heard then – 'traitor'. It is followed by a sneer at the most sacred tears he ever shed, and a lying
description of their effect on the bystanders; and his pride, and his
loathing of falsehood and meanness, explode, as before, in furious
speech. For a moment he tries to check himself and appeals to the
senators; but the effort seems only to treble his rage. Though no man,
since Aufidius spoke, has said a word against him, he defies the whole
nation, recalling the day of its shame and his own triumph, when alone,
like an eagle, he fluttered the dovecotes in Corioli. The people, who had
accompanied him to the market-place, splitting the air with the noise of
their enthusiasm, remember the kinsfolk whom he slaughtered, change
sides, and clamour for his death. As he turns on Aufidius, the conspirators rush upon him, and in a moment, before the vision of his glory has
faded from his brain, he lies dead. The instantaneous cessation of
enormous energy (which is like nothing else in Shakespeare) strikes us
with awe, but not with pity. As I said, the effect of the preceding
scene, where he conquered something stronger than all the Volscians
and escaped something worse than death, is not reversed; it is only
heightened by a renewed joy in his greatness. Roman and Volscian will
have peace now, and in his native city patrician and plebeian will move
along the way he barred. And they are in life, and he is not. But life has
suddenly shrunk and dwindled, and become a home for pygmies and
not for him.

A. C. Bradley: A Miscellany, 1929

(e) G. Wilson Knight sees a final regeneration in Coriolanus as his pride gives
way to love.

The heavens do truly open, as for the first time he realizes love's
intolerant autonomy within his own breast. Here that love, beating
equally in a gosling's 'instinct' (v.iii.35) and a Coriolanus's pride, itself
more iron-strong than any antagonist, turns delicately back the sword
of pride on the hand that wields it. Love, after all, rules this metallic
world. Coriolanus's eyes 'sweat compassion':

> Ladies, you deserve
> To have a temple built you. All the swords
> In Italy and her confederate arms
> Could not have made this peace.

(v.iii.206)

Love has proved more strong than 'swords'. Now all the past scattered
nature poetry of the play springs to our memory, newly-bright. And
Volumnia's and Coriolanus's exclusive pride is justified: justified by
failure. It has, in each, bowed to a greater than itself. Each for the first

time loves purely, but at the cost of lasting severance. So, throughout the Roman plays, the great Shakespearian value of warrior-honour is found to exist only in lieutenantry to the imperial throne of Love. . . .

Coriolanus returns to his death at Antium. He goes, rightly, to meet the death which is the wage of his long pride. First a traitor to Rome, now he is a traitor to the Volscians. So surely his 'honour' has landed him among contradictions. He is accordingly sacrificed that communities may remain in health. But he is now purified. All may be forgiven to one who loves greatly, who enthrones a love above all other values. Moreover, by bowing to love, every other value is mysteriously itself enriched and enlarged. Coriolanus first sought nobility in itself, unrooted in the soil of communal life. He has tried to live on capital, which was soon exhausted and left him only a renegade and treacherous pride: that too spent itself swiftly and became bankrupt. . . . But love draws on an infinite exchequer. Therefore Coriolanus now, as never before, enlists our sympathy. . . .

This is no easy play to enjoy. It has no rich colourings, no luxuriant emotions, no easy melodies of diction: or, if any, but little and widely scattered. But we work through the metallism of its imagery, the sickening crash and iron clangour of its contests, its grimness and its sounds of death, to so exquisite a consummation, in which the whole is suddenly aglow with heating love, that I doubt if there is any more concentrated emotion in Shakespeare than in those lines where Coriolanus's love for his mother dissolves his pride, or whether any speech gives a more exquisite thrill than his final cry of triumph at the hour of his death.

G. Wilson Knight: *The Imperial Theme*, 1931

(f) Willard Farnham takes the opposite view that Coriolanus's pride repels our sympathy or pity for him. The play, he concludes, is 'a magnificent failure'.

The pride of Coriolanus has two very contradictory faculties. It is the tragic flaw in his character and therefore has the well-known power of pride the pre-eminent deadly sin to produce other faults and destroy good in the spirit of its possessor; but it is at the same time the basis of self-respect in his character and thus has the power to produce good in his spirit. Whether destructive of good or productive of good, it is a fierce pride, accompanied by a wrath that makes it work at white heat. The wrath is like the pride it accompanies in not always having the qualities of a deadly sin; it can at times be righteous wrath, directed against human baseness. Hence both the pride and the wrath of Coriolanus can be admirable as well as detestable. . . .

That Coriolanus has thoroughly honest principles and thoroughly honest reasons for detesting the citizens, it may be hard for us of a democratic age to believe; but we are certainly meant to understand that he does have them and that they are well based according to his view of things. . . .

His mother, assuming a role of which there is no hint in Plutarch, plays the tempter and succeeds so well in confusing his judgement that he decides to go contrary to all his principles. On this occasion, as always, the principles of the individualistic Coriolanus are nothing more than his instinct. To do right seems to him only a matter of being his natural self. . . . The honesty of Coriolanus, which has regard for nothing but this precious 'nature' of his, is thus a selfish honesty . . . Coriolanus yields to Volumnia and yet is not fully corrupted by her. He retains his conscience. . . . From the dishonesty of flattery he turns to the honesty of curses and finds relief for his spirit as he cries:

> The fires i' th' lowest hell fold in the people!
> Call me their traitor?

(III.iii.68)

This is the turning point of the tragedy. Coriolanus has reached the pinnacle of his fortune and as he leaves Rome to go into banishment he begins his descent to destruction. Because we can see very well that he brings misfortune on himself by his pride, and because we can see equally well that his pride is a vicious defect, we may feel that when misfortune comes to him he thoroughly deserves it. Nevertheless, there is irony in the fact that he is banished and started on his way to ruin because his pride keeps him from being false to the truth. One of his heroic aspects is that of a martyr to honesty. . . .

Coriolanus, then, can be thought of as greatly noble, and a chorus of Volscians urges us at the end of the tragedy to remember him thus. He is probably the last of the paradoxically noble heroes of Shakespeare's last tragic world. . . . He is monstrously deficient as a human being, and his deficiency is the more unfortunate because it tends not to foster pity for him but to destroy any that we might give him. . . . Coriolanus, the fanatical lover of himself who never knows disillusionment, whose pride is so great that his spiritual self-sufficiency is never shaken, repels pity at any time, and when he does not inspire admiration, he is apt to inspire such detestation as to leave no room for pity.

Willard Farnham: Shakespeare's Tragic Frontier, 1950

(g) A. P. Rossiter, agreeing with T. S. Eliot that *Coriolanus* is 'one of Shakespeare's most assured artistic successes', insists that it is above all a political play.

There are many ways of interpreting this play, and the one that begins nearest to Jacobean times is one that is necessarily a long way from our own. Moreover, as far as I can judge, the interpretations that arise spontaneously in our own times are so violently opposed to one another, and lead so inevitably into passionate political side-tracks, that almost any line of thinking that gets us away from them gives the play a better chance as a tragic play.

'Political': there I said it. *Coriolanus* is about power: about State, or *the* State; about order in society and the forces of disorder which threaten 'that integrity which should become't' (III.i.159); about conflict, not in personal but political life; and – the aspect which catches our minds first? – about the conflict of classes. I put that last deliberately for . . . if we begin at that end, the play's tragic qualities are endangered at once: it tends to be seen as political, i.e. to be filled with imported feelings which are too partisan for the kind of contemplation which is tragedy. It also readily becomes polemical and seems to be giving *answers*, solutions to human conflicts, which tragedy does *not*. . . .

I will demonstrate that *Coriolanus* is an allegory of more than one political idealist of our time, who followed his own inner counsels, despised common humanity, betrayed his trust, to become a lonely dragon in a fen. . . .

By 'political' I do not mean the class-war, nor even narrowly the Tudor system of God-ordained order. I mean *Coriolanus* plays on political feeling, the capacity to be not only intellectually, but emotionally and purposively, engaged by the management of public affairs; the businesses of groups of men in ordered communities; the contrivance or maintenance of agreement; the establishment of a will-in-common; and all the exercises of suasion, pressure, concession and compromise which achieve that *will* (a mind to *do*) in place of a chaos of confused appetencies. . . .

The explicit political principles in the play are mainly put into the mouth of Coriolanus; and particularly in III.i where he makes what is in effect a single political utterance, though in several parts. He says that the power of the people has increased and must be diminished; the Senators have nourished the cockle of rebellion by the corn-dole: made themselves no better than plebeians to let these Tribunes play the Senator with their 'absolute "shall"'; the people think that concessions have been made through fear; no stable or ordered policy can come from direction by ignorant numbers through 'voices' (votes); and the State is ruined and disintegrated unless this power of disordering policy and vetoing wise decisions is taken away from them. No statement of policy could be more sincere: none less well-timed. It is Martius' 'tragic blunder' (the Aristotelian *hamartia*) to state these convictions when he does. Yet so far as Shakespeare tells us what is right for the State in the play, there we have it. We may dislike it: we can say it belongs to a past age; . . . we can say that we dislike the man who speaks (and there is no reason that I can see to *like* Coriolanus at any stage of the play). But the personality of Caius Martius is one thing, and the convictions of Coriolanus are quite another. The rightness of a man's ideas or convictions is not affected by his unpleasantness; *or* by his popularity, his 'popular "shall"'. Indeed, being right is rarely too conducive to popularity. What is amiss with demagogy, but that it confuses popularity (what people like hearing) with rightness (expediency)? What do Brutus and Sicinius display, but just that?

The personality of Caius Martius, his attempts to manage men everywhere but on the battlefield, are, you may say, wrong throughout. But his convictions about the State are good and right, however impolitically he may phrase or time them. There you have a tragic clash: the basis of a political tragedy, not a Tudor morality . . . *Coriolanus* is the last and greatest of the Histories. It is Shakespeare's only great political play; and it is slightly depressing, and hard to come to terms with, because it is *political tragedy*.

A. P. Rossiter: *Angel with Horns,* 1961

Bibliography

The original dates of publication are given. In many cases more recent editions have been published.

(1)   Criticism with special reference to *Coriolanus*

Bradley, A. C.: *A Miscellany*, (1929). Includes the British Academy Shakespeare Lecture of 1912 on *Coriolanus*.

Brower, R. S.: *Hero and Saint*, (1971), pp. 354–81.

Campbell, O. J.: *Shakespeare's Satire*, (1943), pp. 198–217.

Chambers, E. K.: *Shakespeare: A Survey*, (1925), pp. 258–67.

Coleridge, S. T.: *Shakespearean Criticism*, ed. T. M. Raysor, (1960), Vol. 1, pp. 79–81.

Ellis-Fermor, U.: *Shakespeare the Dramatist and Other Papers*, ed. K. Muir, (1961), pp. 48–52, 60–77, 132–8.

Enright, D. J.: *'Coriolanus:* Tragedy or Debate?' *Essays in Criticism*, (1954), Vol. 4, No. 1, pp. 1–19. Reprinted with minor revisions in *The Apothecary's Shop*, (1957), pp. 32-53.

Farnham, W.: *Shakespeare's Tragic Frontier*, (1950), pp. 207–64.

Gordon, D. J.: 'Name and Fame: Shakespeare's *Coriolanus'*, *Papers Mainly Shakespearian*, ed. G. I. Duthie, (1961), pp. 40–57.

Granville-Barker, H.: *Prefaces to Shakespeare*, Vol. 2, (1947), pp. 150–299.

Holloway, J.: *The Story of the Night*, (1961), pp. 121–34.

Knight, G. W.: *The Imperial Theme*, (1959), revised edn., (1965), pp. 154–98.

Knights, L. C.: *Some Shakespearean Themes*, (1959), pp. 143–156. *Further Explorations*, (1965).

MacCallum, M. W.: *Shakespeare's Roman Plays and their Background*, (1910).

Murry, J. M.: *Countries of the Mind*, (1922), pp. 31–50. Also found in *John Clare and Other Studies*, (1950), pp. 222–45.

Palmer, J.: *Political Characters of Shakespeare*, (1945).

Partridge, C. J.: *Coriolanus. Notes on English Literature*, (1970).

Ribner, I.: *Patterns in Shakespearean Tragedy*, (1960), pp. 168–201.

Rossiter, A. P.: *Angel with Horns*, (1961), pp. 235–52.

Stirling, B.: *The Populace in Shakespeare*, (1949).

Traversi, D.: *Shakespeare: The Roman Plays*, (1963), pp. 207–88.

Waith, E. M.: *The Herculean Hero*, (1962), pp. 121–43.

(2)   Shakespeare's Language and Imagery

Charney, M.: *Shakespeare's Roman Plays: The Function of Imagery in the Drama*, (1961), pp. 142–96.

Clemen, W.: *The Development of Shakespeare's Imagery*, (1951), pp. 154–8.
Onions, C. T.: *A Shakespeare Glossary*, (1911), revised edn., (1953).
Spurgeon, C. F. E.: *Shakespeare's Imagery and What It Tells Us*, (1935).

(3)   Sources

Bullough, G.: *Narrative and Dramatic Sources of Shakespeare*, (1964), Vol. 5.
Muir, K.: *Shakespeare's Sources*, (1957), Vol. 1, pp. 219–24.
Spencer, T. J. B.: *Shakespeare's Plutarch*, (1964).

(4)   The Age of Shakespeare

Craig, H.: *The Enchanted Glass: The Elizabethan Mind in Literature*, (1936).
Ford, B.: *The Age of Shakespeare*, (1955).
Lee, S. and Onions, C. T. (editors): *Shakespeare's England*, 2 vols., (1916).
Tillyard, E. M. W.: *The Elizabethan World Picture*, (1943).
Wilson, J. D.: *Life in Shakespeare's England*, (1944).

(5)   The Elizabethan Theatre and Acting

Beckerman, B.: *Shakespeare at the Globe 1599–1609*, (1962).
Coghill, N.: *Shakespeare's Professional Skills*, (1964).
Hodges, C. W.: *The Globe Restored*, (1953).
Joseph, B. L.: *Elizabethan Acting*, (1951).
          The Tragic Actor, (1959).
          Acting Shakespeare, (1960).
Nagler, A. M.: *Shakespeare's Stage*, (1958).
Shakespeare Survey, Vols. 10 and 12, (1957, 1959).
Watkins, R.: *On Producing Shakespeare*, (1950).

(6)   Shakespeare's Life

Alexander, P.: *Shakespeare*, (1964).
Halliday, F. E.: *The Life of Shakespeare*, (1961).
Williams, C.: *A Short Life of Shakespeare*, (1933).

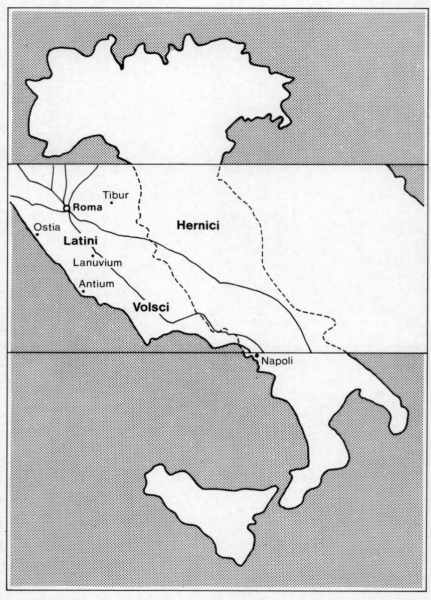

A map of the area covered by the play, showing the main roads and tribal areas, at the time of Coriolanus.

Coriolanus

Dramatis personae

CAIUS MARTIUS, *afterwards* CAIUS MARTIUS CORIOLANUS
TITUS LARTIUS,
COMINIUS, } *Roman generals*
MENENIUS AGRIPPA, *friend of Coriolanus*
SICINIUS VELUTUS,
JUNIUS BRUTUS, } *tribunes of the people*
YOUNG MARTIUS, *son of Coriolanus*
NICANOR, *a Roman spying for the Volscians*
A ROMAN HERALD
TULLUS AUFIDIUS, *Volscian general*
LIEUTENANT *to Aufidius*
CONSPIRATORS *with Aufidius*
A CITIZEN *of Antium*
TWO VOLSCIAN GUARDS
ADRIAN, *a Volscian*
VOLUMNIA, *mother of Coriolanus*
VIRGILIA, *wife of Coriolanus*
VALERIA, *friend of Virgilia*
GENTLEWOMAN *attending on Virgilia*
AN USHER *attending on Valeria*
SENATORS, PATRICIANS, AEDILES, LICTORS, CITIZENS, SOLDIERS, MESSENGERS,
ATTENDANTS, SERVANTS, DRUMMER, TRUMPETER

*The scenes are set in and around Rome and the two neighbouring cities of
Corioli and Antium about the year 491* B.C.

Volumnia (left), Valeria (centre), and Virgilia sit sewing at home, discussing Coriolanus who is away at war (Act I, Scene iii).

Coriolanus being reunited with Cominius after the seige of Corioli (Act I, Scene vi).

Coriolanus, at the height of his power, being given the title 'Coriolanus' by Cominius and Lartius (Act I, Scene ix).

I.i.   In the city of Rome, trouble which has been growing for some time now breaks out, as
          the citizens, incensed at the shortage of corn and the high prices they have to pay for it,
          at the edicts supporting usurers, and at other repressive measures, resolve to kill
          Coriolanus,* whom they regard as their chief enemy. Just as they are about to storm to the
          Capitol, the aged senator Menenius Agrippa enters and calms them by narrating the Fable
          of the Belly. Coriolanus now appears, at once displaying his contempt for these 'dissentious
          rogues', and reporting that they have been granted five tribunes to defend their interests.
          He welcomes the news that the Volscians, Rome's neighbours, are about to wage war
          on them, as he sees this as one way of employing and containing the mutinous plebeians.
          In an epilogue to the scene, Brutus and Sicinius, two of the newly-appointed tribunes
          discuss Coriolanus, condemning his pride, insolence and desire for fame.
             As in *Julius Caesar* and *Romeo and Juliet*, Shakespeare begins with an explosive, action-
          packed scene. It introduces the two major public conflicts – the enmity between the
          Romans and the Volscians, and the internal dissension in Rome between patricians and
          plebeians. The essential characteristics of Coriolanus, the tribunes and the people, whose
          relationship is to be explored and demonstrated as the play proceeds, are revealed to us.
          In addition, Shakespeare introduces a number of themes central to the play, such as the
          friendship between Coriolanus and Menenius, the suggestion of a close relationship
          between Coriolanus and his mother, the rivalry in arms between Coriolanus and Aufidius,
          and the envy of the tribunes. This vivid scene, so full of tension and the ominous promise
          of further conflict, captures audience interest from the start.

7   *know't – 't* for *it*. See the list of such forms on p. lxxi.
9   *Is't a verdict?*: Do you all agree?
10   *on't*: about it.
12   *accounted*: considered.
12   *patricians* – Romans belonging to the original citizen families or *gentes* which made up the
                  ancient Roman *populus*, hence Roman nobles.
12   *good*: wealthy. – The Second Citizen used the word in its ordinary sense (line 11). The First
                  Citizen now plays ironically on a less common meaning of the word.
13   *authority surfeits on*: those in power have in excess.
14   *superfluity while it were wholesome*: surplus while it is still in good condition. – He implies
                  that the authorities will only distribute corn when it has gone bad.
15   *guess*: think.
15   *but humanely*: only out of human sympathy.
16   *we are too dear*: the price we want (i.e. their surplus corn) is too high. – The First Citizen
                  probably intends also a sarcastic play on the word *dear*, meaning 'precious'.
17   *object*: sight.
17   *an inventory . . . abundance*: a catalogue listing in detail their abundant possessions. – The
                  First Citizen argues that the patricians choose not to relieve the poor since the
                  sight of their poverty gives them a pleasurable reminder of their own wealth.
18   *sufferance*: suffering.
19   *pikes . . . rakes* – The speaker means that they should take to arms to get revenge before
                  they grow too weak to resist. The skeletal rake is seen in his play on words as a
                  kind of harmless pike, lacking its pointed steel head. Cf. the common expres-
                  sion, 'As thin as a rake'. In lines 20–1 he plays on *hunger* and *thirst*.
20   *the gods* – the pagan gods of ancient Rome. See *Introduction*, page xxii, in connection with
                  Shakespeare's presentation of the Roman world.
23   *a very dog to the commonalty*: utterly savage in his hostility to the common people.
25   *give him good report*: praise him.
26   *pays himself* – i.e. for his services to Rome.
28   *famously*: to win fame.
28   *to that end*: with that purpose in mind.
29   *soft-conscienced*: indulgent, over-tolerant.
31   *to be partly proud*: partly to satisfy his pride.
31   *the altitude of his virtue*: the highest extent of his courage. – The First Citizen claims that
                  the pride of Martius is as great as his courage.

*For simplicity Caius Martius is referred to as Coriolanus throughout the *Introduction* and Notes
even before the change of name.

Coriolanus ACT I scene i

Rome. A street.

Enter a company of mutinous CITIZENS, *with staves, clubs, and other weapons.*

FIRST CITIZEN Before we proceed any further, hear me speak. *Crowd*

ALL Speak, speak! *easily*

FIRST CITIZEN You are all resolved rather to die than to famish? *led.*

ALL Resolved, resolved!

FIRST CITIZEN First, you know, Caius Martius is chief enemy to the 5
people.

ALL We know't, we know't!*

FIRST CITIZEN Let us kill him, and we'll have corn at our own price. Is't a
verdict?*

ALL No more talking on't!* Let it be done! Away, away! 10

SECOND CITIZEN One word, good citizens.

FIRST CITIZEN We are accounted* poor citizens, the patricians* good.*
What authority surfeits on* would relieve us. If they
would yield us but the superfluity while it were wholesome,* we might guess* they relieved us but humanely.* 15
But they think we are too dear.* The leanness that afflicts
us, the object* of our misery, is as an inventory* to
particularize their abundance; our sufferance* is a gain to
them. Let us revenge this with our pikes,* ere we become
rakes. For the gods* know, I speak this in hunger for 20
bread, not in thirst for revenge.

SECOND CITIZEN Would you proceed especially against Caius Martius?

FIRST CITIZEN Against him first. He's a very dog to the commonalty.*

SECOND CITIZEN Consider you what services he has done for his country?

FIRST CITIZEN Very well, and could be content to give him good report* 25
for't, but that he pays himself* with being proud.

SECOND CITIZEN Nay, but speak not maliciously.

FIRST CITIZEN I say unto you, what he hath done famously,* he did it to
that end.* Though soft-conscienced* men can be content to
say it was for his country, he did it to please his mother, 30
and to be partly proud,* which he is, even to the altitude of
his virtue.*

1

34	*must . . . covetous:* cannot say that he is greedy.
35	*I need . . . accusations,* i.e. there are plenty of other things I can accuse him of.
36	*faults . . . repetition:* numerous faults, tiring to list.
36	*Shouts within* – i.e. shouts are heard from off-stage, which are intended to suggest that they come from another part of the city.
38	*prating:* chattering.
38	*the Capitol,* the south-west summit of the Capitoline Hill, one of the seven hills of Rome, on which stood the temples of Jupiter, Juno and Minerva. The Senate House was on this hill, so that *Capitol* and *Senate* are often synonymous terms.
40	*Soft:* Wait a moment.
43	*honest:* honourable.
43	*Would:* I wish.
44	*in hand:* going on.
45	*bats and clubs,* i.e. cudgels, weapons commonly used by London workmen in street disturbances.
47	*inkling:* a suspicion, hint.
48	*poor suitors:* lower-class wooers – with word-play on the idea that the citizens are *suitors* in having a *suit,* or request, to bring to the Senate.
49	*strong:* offensive. – The First Citizen, with his fondness for punning, plays on this and the more common meaning of *strong* in *strong arms* in the same line.
51	*undo:* ruin.
53	*most charitable . . . of you:* the patricians have the most loving care of you. – An example of the inversion considered on page lxxi of the *Introduction.*
54	*For:* As for. – Cf. line 60.
55	*dearth:* famine.
56	*staves:* sticks.
57	*on:* go on.
58	*cracking . . . impediment:* breaking apart ten thousand restraints (*curbs*) each stronger than any that you can offer. – A *curb* was a circular framework of any kind, such as a hoop round a barrel; *in your impediment:* in any obstruction you can cause.
62	*Your knees to them,* i.e. bent in prayer.
62	*Alack:* Alas.
63	*transported:* carried away (both literally in body, and figuratively in mind).
64	*Thither where more attends you:* to where further calamity awaits you, i.e. both to the Capitol, and to a state of rebellion which will prove more dangerous.
65	*helms o' th' state* – Menenius pictures the state as a ship, its leaders as pilots.
67	*True, indeed* – The First Citizen is scornfully sarcastic.
68	*Suffer us:* They allow us.
69	*edicts for usury:* laws about moneylending.
70	*wholesome:* sound.
71	*piercing statutes:* distressing laws.

SECOND CITIZEN What he cannot help in his nature, you account a vice in
him. You must* in no way say he is covetous.

FIRST CITIZEN If I must not, I need* not be barren of accusations. He hath   35
faults,* with surplus, to tire in repetition. [*Shouts within.**]
What shouts are these? The other side o' the city is risen.
Why stay we prating* here? To the Capitol!*

ALL Come, come!

FIRST CITIZEN Soft,* who comes here?   40

Enter MENENIUS AGRIPPA.

SECOND CITIZEN Worthy Menenius Agrippa, one that hath always loved
the people.

FIRST CITIZEN He's one honest* enough. Would* all the rest were so!

MENENIUS What work's, my countrymen, in hand?* Where go you
with bats and clubs?* The matter speak, I pray you.   45

FIRST CITIZEN Our business is not unknown to the Senate; they have had
inkling* this fortnight what we intend to do, which now
we'll show 'em in deeds. They say poor suitors* have
strong* breaths; they shall know we have strong arms too.

MENENIUS Why, masters, my good friends, mine honest neighbours,   50
Will you undo* yourselves?

FIRST CITIZEN We cannot, sir; we are undone already. *Good quotation*

MENENIUS I tell you, friends, most charitable* care
Have the patricians of you. For* your wants,
Your suffering in this dearth,* you may as well   55
Strike at the heaven with your staves* as lift them
Against the Roman state, whose course will on*
The way it takes, cracking* ten thousand curbs
Of more strong link asunder than can ever
Appear in your impediment. For the dearth,   60
The gods, not the patricians, make it, and
Your knees to them,* not arms, must help. Alack,*
You are transported* by calamity
Thither where more attends you;* and you slander
The helms o' th' state,* who care for you like fathers,   65
When you curse them as enemies.

FIRST CITIZEN Care for us? True, indeed!* They ne'er cared for us yet.
Suffer us* to famish, and their storehouses crammed with
grain; make edicts for usury,* to support usurers; repeal
daily any wholesome* act established against the rich, and   70
provide more piercing statutes* daily, to chain up and

Money lending.

72	*eat us not up:* do not consume us as soldiers.
75	*wondrous:* extremely.
77	*pretty:* pleasant.
79	*stale't a little more:* make it a bit staler by telling it again.
80	*fob off our disgrace:* talk away our ill-treatment.
81	*and't please you, deliver:* tell your story if you wish.
84	*gulf:* bottomless pit.
86	*Still cupboarding the viand:* continually hoarding up the food.
86	*bearing:* enduring.
87	*Like:* similar.
87	*where:* whereas.
87	*instruments:* bodily organs.
88	*devise:* deliberate.
89	*mutually participate:* co-operating with each other.
89	*minister/Unto:* supply.
90	*affection common:* common desire.
93	*a kind . . . lungs –* i.e. a contemptuous smile, not a joyous one which came (it was thought) from the lungs.
94	*even thus –* Menenius here gives the contemptuous smile he has in mind.
96	*tauntingly:* contemptuously.
98	*his receipt:* what he received.
98	*even so most fitly:* just as aptly. – Menenius is being ironical.
99	*malign:* slander.
99	*for that:* because.
100	*Your Belly's . . .* – The First Citizen, trying to match Menenius in debate, speaks inflated verse. See *Introduction,* page lxxv.
101	*vigilant:* watchful.
102	*counsellor:* counselling.
104	*muniments:* defences.
105	*this our fabric:* this body of ours.
106	*'Fore me, this fellow speaks:* Upon my word, this fellow can talk.
107	*cormorant:* insatiably greedy, like the cormorant, a large sea-bird.
108	*sink:* sewer, cesspit.
109	*former agents:* bodily instruments, earlier mentioned.

restrain the poor. If the wars eat us not up,* they will; and
there's all the love they bear us.

MENENIUS Either you must
Confess yourselves wondrous* malicious,   75
Or be accused of folly. I shall tell you
A pretty* tale; it may be you have heard it,
But since it serves my purpose, I will venture
To stale't a little more.*

FIRST CITIZEN Well, I'll hear it, sir; yet you must not think to fob off our   80
disgrace* with a tale. But and't please you, deliver.*

MENENIUS There was a time when all the body's members
Rebelled against the Belly, thus accused it:
That only like a gulf* it did remain
I' th'midst o' th'body, idle and unactive,   85
Still cupboarding the viand,* never bearing*
Like* labour with the rest, where* th' other instruments*
Did see and hear, devise,* instruct, walk, feel,
And, mutually participate,* did minister
Unto* the appetite and affection common*   90
Of the whole body. The Belly answered –

FIRST CITIZEN Well, sir, what answer made the Belly?

MENENIUS Sir, I shall tell you. With a kind of smile,
Which ne'er came from the lungs,* but even thus* –
For, look you, I may make the Belly smile   95
As well as speak – it tauntingly* replied
To th' discontented members, the mutinous parts
That envied his receipt,* even so most fitly*
As you malign* our senators for that*
They are not such as you.

FIRST CITIZEN   Your Belly's answer?* What?   100
The kingly crownèd head, the vigilant* eye,
The counsellor* heart, the arm our soldier,
Our steed the leg, the tongue our trumpeter,
With other muniments* and petty helps
In this our fabric,* if that they –

MENENIUS   What then?   105
'Fore me, this fellow speaks!* What then? What then?

FIRST CITIZEN – Should by the cormorant* Belly be restrained,
Who is the sink* o' th' body –

MENENIUS   Well, what then?

FIRST CITIZEN – The former agents,* if they did complain,
What could the Belly answer?

111   *bestow a small:* show a small amount of.
112   *you'st:* you shall.
113   *Y'are:* you are. – This contraction is widely used throughout the play.
114   *Your most grave Belly:* this very dignified Belly we're talking about. – *Your* was used colloquially in Shakespeare's time to indicate something or someone known to all those present. Cf. v.iv.11.
114   *deliberate:* thoughtful.
116   *incorporate:* united in one body.
119   *shop:* workshop.
122   *to the court . . . brain:* to the court, which is the heart, and to the throne, which is the brain.
123   *cranks:* winding channels.
123   *offices:* workplaces. – The *offices* of a house are the inferior rooms where the more menial household work is done.
124   *nerves:* muscles, sinews.
125   *natural competency:* sufficient supply according to their nature.
126   *though that:* though.
130   *make my audit up:* prepare my statement of accounts for inspection. – The Belly insists that his statement of receipts and expenditure is impeccable.
131   *flour:* finest extract. – A play on *flower*, meaning the choicest part, is also doubtless intended.
132   *bran:* coarse husks.
132   *to't:* about this.
133   *How apply you this?:* How do you relate this to the present situation?
136   *disgest:* interpret. – An old form of *digest*.
137   *Touching . . . common:* concerning the welfare of the people.
139   *But it proceeds:* that does not proceed.
141   *great toe:* big toe (in modern English).
144   *goest foremost:* walk at the front.
145   *rascal:* (a) one of low birth, (b) an inferior deer or hound.
145   *worst in blood to run:* in poorest condition for running.
146   *vantage:* advantage.
147   *stiff:* strong.
149   *have bale:* be destroyed.

MENENIUS   I will tell you;   110
If you'll bestow a small* – of what you have little –
Patience awhile, you'st* hear the Belly's answer.

FIRST CITIZEN Y'are* long about it.

MENENIUS   Note me this, good friend;
Your most grave Belly* was deliberate,*
Not rash like his accusers, and thus answered: 115
'True is it, my incorporate* friends,' quoth he,
'That I receive the general food at first,
Which you do live upon; and fit it is,
Because I am the storehouse and the shop*
Of the whole body. But if you do remember,   120
I send it through the rivers of your blood
Even to the court,* the heart, to th' seat o' th' brain;
And, through the cranks* and offices* of man,
The strongest nerves* and small inferior veins
From me receive that natural competency*   125
Whereby they live. And though that* all at once,
You, my good friends,' – this says the Belly, mark me –

FIRST CITIZEN Ay, sir; well, well.

MENENIUS   – 'Though all at once cannot
See what I do deliver out to each,
Yet I can make my audit up,* that all   130
From me do back receive the flour* of all,
And leave me but the bran.'* What say you to't?*

FIRST CITIZEN It was an answer. How apply you this?*

MENENIUS The senators of Rome are this good Belly,
And you the mutinous members. For examine   135
Their counsels and their cares, disgest* things rightly
Touching* the weal o' th' common, you shall find   *The peop̃*
No public benefit which you receive   → *Taking, not givĩ*
But it proceeds* or comes from them to you,
And no way from yourselves. What do you think,   140
You, the great toe* of this assembly?

FIRST CITIZEN I the great toe! Why the great toe?

MENENIUS For that, being one o' th' lowest, basest, poorest,
Of this most wise rebellion, thou goest foremost.*
Thou rascal,* that are worst in blood to run,*   145
Lead'st first to win some vantage.*
But make you ready your stiff* bats and clubs.
Rome and her rats are at the point of battle;
The one side must have bale.*

150   *dissentious:* quarrelsome.
151   *That rubbing . . . scabs:* who, worrying away over your opinions, make things worse for yourselves. – *Scab* means (a) a loathsome fellow, and (b) the crust on a sore. By scratching the plebeians become scabs as in (a), and make scabs as in (b).
152   *We have ever your good word:* We always get praise from you. – This is said, of course, sarcastically.
154   *Beneath abhorring:* in so debased a way as to be beneath contempt.
155   *nor . . . nor:* neither . . . nor.
155   *The one affrights . . . proud:* War frightens you, peace makes you proud (and thus difficult to manage, like high-spirited *curs*).
158   *surer:* more reliable.
159   *the coal of fire upon the ice* – This is possibly an allusion by Shakespeare to the so-called Great Frost of January 1608, when the River Thames froze over and fairs were set up on it, with fires in braziers to warm the people.
160   *virtue:* distinguishing quality.
161   *To make him . . . did it:* to consider praiseworthy the man whose offences cause him to be punished, and to curse the magistrate who punished him.
162   *Who deserves . . . hate:* The man who deserves greatness earns your hatred.
163   *your affections . . . evil,* i.e. like a sick man you want what is bad for you. *Evil:* illness.
165   *He that . . . rushes* – i.e. Anyone who depends on you won't get very far. *Rushes:* reeds.
168   *change a mind:* change your mind.
169   *now your hate:* just recently the object of your hatred.
170   *vilde* – an old form of *vile*.
170   *your garland:* the object of your admiration. – The Romans crowned victors in war and sport with garlands.
171   *several:* different.
173   *awe, which else:* control, who otherwise.
174   *seeking:* petition.
175   *at their own rates:* at prices fixed by them.
177   *presume to know:* they have the effrontery to pretend to know.
178   *like:* likely. – In Shakespeare's time adjectives were often used adverbially, as here. Cf. *passing,* I.i.189, *bountiful,* II.iii.93, *unlike,* III.i.49, *like,* II.i.230, III.i.48, 133.
179   *side factions:* take sides in political strife.
179   *give out/Conjectural marriages:* proclaim as certain marriages which are only conjectural. – The marriages are those linking influential Roman families, intended to consolidate their political power.
180   *making parties strong:* saying that parties are strong (because they approve of them).
181   *feebling . . . cobbled shoes:* disparaging those they dislike as if they were the dirt under their patched shoes. – Coriolanus's contempt for the masses emerges in such images as that of the *cobbled shoes.*
183   *Would the nobility . . . ruth·* If the patricians would forget their pity (for the plebeians).
184   *quarry:* heap of corpses. – This term, usually used of dead animals, further conveys Coriolanus's contempt.
185   *quartered:* cut up into parts. – The Elizabethan punishment for traitors was to hang, draw and quarter them, and Shakespeare's audience would certainly perceive more than a simple hunting reference here.
186   *pick:* throw.

Enter CAIUS MARTIUS.

                                      Hail, noble Martius!

MARTIUS Thanks. What's the matter, you dissentious* rogues   150
That rubbing* the poor itch of your opinion,
Make yourselves scabs?

FIRST CITIZEN   We have ever your good word.*

MARTIUS He that will give good words to thee will flatter
Beneath abhorring.* What would you have, you curs,
That like nor* peace nor war? The one affrights* you,   155
The other makes you proud. He that trusts to you,
Where he should find you lions, finds you hares;
Where foxes, geese. You are no surer,* no,
Than is the coal of fire upon the ice,*
Or hailstone in the sun. Your virtue* is,   160
To make him* worthy whose offence subdues him,
And curse that justice did it. Who deserves* greatness
Deserves your hate; and your affections* are
A sick man's appetite, who desires most that
Which would increase his evil. He that* depends   165
Upon your favours swims with fins of lead
And hews down oaks with rushes. Hang ye! Trust ye?
With every minute you do change a mind,*
And call him noble that was now your hate,*
Him vilde* that was your garland.* What's the matter, 170
That in these several* places of the city
You cry against the noble Senate, who,
Under the gods, keep you in awe, which else*
Would feed on one another? What's their seeking?*

MENENIUS For corn at their own rates,* whereof they say   175
The city is well stored.

MARTIUS   Hang 'em! They say?
They'll sit by th'fire, and presume to know*
What's done i' th' Capitol; who's like* to rise,
Who thrives and who declines; side factions* and give out
Conjectural marriages,* making parties strong,*   180
And feebling* such as stand not in their liking
Below their cobbled shoes. They say there's grain enough?
Would the nobility* lay aside their ruth,
And let me use my sword, I'd make a quarry*
With thousands of these quartered* slaves, as high   185
As I could pick* my lance.

187   *almost thoroughly persuaded* – i.e. of their folly, by Coriolanus.
189   *passing:* extremely. – See the note to line 178.
190   *troop:* crowd of citizens.
190   *are dissolved:* have melted away.
191   *an-hungry:* hungry.
191   *sighed forth:* uttered.
192   *hunger broke stone walls* – i.e. a hungry man will break through walls and steal to satisfy his hunger.
194   *shreds:* scraps. – Coriolanus mocks their speech with its simple truisms, which they regard as profound truths.
195   *vented:* voiced.
195   *answered:* satisfied.
197   *To break the heart of generosity* – Either (a) carrying generosity too far, or (b) giving the final blow to the power of the nobility (from the Latin *generosus*, meaning 'of good birth').
198   *make bold power look pale:* frighten even the strong among those in authority.
199   *As:* as if.
200   *Shouting their emulation:* rivalling one another in shouting cheers.
201   *tribunes.* – The tribunes were magistrates of plebeian birth, elected annually and charged with the protection of the people. They could block the actions of other magistrates by their right of veto. Their persons were inviolable. They had power to summon meetings of the people to discuss public affairs and propose changes in the law.
201   *to defend their vulgar wisdoms:* to defend the wisdom of whatever the plebeians decide.
203   *I know not:* I don't know who else.
203   *'Sdeath:* By God's death, an oath.
204   *should have . . . me:* would first have had to destroy Rome before getting me to agree to this.
206   *Win upon . . . arguing:* increase their power and produce more important subjects for rebels to argue about – i.e. ever-growing demands from rebellious citizens. The abstract *insurrection* is used for the concrete 'rebels'.
208   *fragments:* incomplete men. – Coriolanus intends to convey his conviction of their human incompleteness both physically and mentally. Their rags and cobbled shoes point to the former, *shreds* (line 194) to the latter.
210   *the Volsces . . . arms* – i.e. mobilized for war. The Volsces were an Italian tribe whose territories lay to the south of Rome and north of Naples, in the Liris Valley and in the regions to the south-east of the Alban Hills. They were a military threat to Rome for two hundred years, but were totally subjugated by 304 B.C.
211   *on't:* of it.
211   *ha':* have.
211   *vent our musty superfluity:* get rid of our excess population who are going stale (*musty*) – through idleness here in Rome.
212   *best elders:* wisest leaders. – He does not, of course, include Sicinius and Brutus in this term.
213   *that:* what.
215   *put you to't:* put you to the test.
216   *sin in envying* – Envy, the sixth of the Seven Deadly Sins, figures largely in medieval and Elizabethan thought and literature.
217   *And were . . . only he:* and if I were anyone but myself, I would want to be Aufidius.

MENENIUS Nay, these are almost thoroughly persuaded;*
For though abundantly they lack discretion,
Yet are they passing* cowardly. But, I beseech you
What says the other troop?*

MARTIUS   They are dissolved.* Hang 'em!   190
They said they were an-hungry;* sighed forth* proverbs,
That hunger broke stone walls,* that dogs must eat,
That meat was made for mouths, that the gods sent not
Corn for the rich men only. With these shreds*
They vented* their complainings, which being answered,*   195
And a petition granted them – a strange one,
To break the heart of generosity*
And make bold power look pale* – they threw their caps
As* they would hang them on the horns o' th' moon,
Shouting their emulation.*

MENENIUS   What is granted them?   200

MARTIUS Five tribunes* to defend their vulgar wisdoms,*
Of their own choice. One's Junius Brutus,
Sicinius Velutus, and I know not.* 'Sdeath!*
The rabble should have* first unroofed the city
Ere so prevailed with me. It will in time   205
Win upon* power and throw forth greater themes
For insurrection's arguing.

MENENIUS   This is strange.

MARTIUS Go, get you home, you fragments!*

Enter a MESSENGER, *hastily.*

MESSENGER Where's Caius Martius?

MARTIUS   Here. What's the matter?

MESSENGER The news is, sir, the Volsces* are in arms.   210

MARTIUS I am glad on't;* then we shall ha'* means to vent
Our musty superfluity.* See, our best elders.*

Enter SICINIUS VELUTUS, JUNIUS BRUTUS, COMINIUS, TITUS
LARTIUS, *with other* SENATORS.

FIRST SENATOR Martius, 'tis true that* you have lately told us;
The Volsces are in arms.

MARTIUS   They have a leader,
Tullus Aufidius, that will put you to't.*   215
I sin in envying* his nobility;
And were* I anything but what I am,
I would wish me only he.

218 *together:* against each other.
219 *half to half . . . ears:* one half of the world fighting the other.
220 *Upon my party:* among those on my side.
220 *revolt:* change sides.
220 *make/Only my wars with him:* fight against him only.
223 *Attend upon:* accompany.
225 *I am constant:* I keep my word. – We perceive the irony of this later.
227 *stiff:* obstinate.
227 *Stand'st out?:* Are you opting out of the fight? – Coriolanus adopts a bantering tone to his old comrade-in-arms.
229 *Ere stay . . . business:* rather than miss this war.
231 *attend:* wait for.
233 *Right worthy you priority:* you fully deserve first place.
236 *their garners:* the granaries of the Volscians.
236 *Worshipful mutiners:* Most honourable rebels. – Coriolanus's sarcasm is unconcealed.
237 *puts well forth:* makes a fine show. – The image is that of a blossoming flower. Coriolanus speaks ironically as he watches the crowd melting away at his suggestion that they should take part in the war.
241 *his lip and eyes* – Coriolanus's features evidently mirrored his feelings; a hint here to the actor of the part.
242 *moved:* angered.
242 *spare to gird:* abstain from jibing at.
243 *Bemock the modest moon:* Mock at the modesty of the moon. – Diana, the moon goddess, was bashful and chaste.
244 *The present wars devour him:* May he be destroyed in the war which is about to begin.
245 *Too proud to be so valiant* – i.e. it is dangerous to the state when so brave a man grows so arrogant.
246 *Tickled:* delighted.
246 *success:* result (good or bad). Cf. I.vi.7.
246 *disdains . . . noon:* disdains even his own shadow.

COMINIUS	You have fought together.*
MARTIUS	Were half to half* the world by th' ears, and he
	Upon my party,* I'd revolt,* to make 220
	Only my wars with him.* He is a lion
	That I am proud to hunt.
FIRST SENATOR	Then, worthy Martius,
	Attend upon* Cominius to these wars.
COMINIUS	It is your former promise.
MARTIUS	Sir, it is,
	And I am constant.* Titus Lartius, thou 225
	Shalt see me once more strike at Tullus' face.
	What, art thou stiff?* Stand'st out?*
TITUS	No, Caius Martius;
	I'll lean upon one crutch and fight with t'other
	Ere stay* behind this business.
MENENIUS	O true-bred!
FIRST SENATOR	Your company to th' Capitol, where I know 230
	Our greatest friends attend* us.
TITUS	[To COMINIUS] Lead you on.
	[To MARTIUS] Follow Cominius; we must follow you;
	Right worthy you priority.*
COMINIUS	Noble Martius!
FIRST SENATOR	[To the CITIZENS] Hence to your homes, be gone!
MARTIUS	Nay, let them follow.
	The Volsces have much corn; take these rats thither 235
	To gnaw their garners.* Worshipful mutiners,*
	Your valour puts well forth.* Pray, follow.

[CITIZENS *steal away. Exeunt all except* SICINIUS
and BRUTUS

SICINIUS	Was ever man so proud as is this Martius?
BRUTUS	He has no equal.
SICINIUS	When we were chosen tribunes for the people – 240
BRUTUS	Marked you his lip and eyes?*
SICINIUS	Nay, but his taunts.
BRUTUS	Being moved,* he will not spare to gird* the gods.
SICINIUS	Bemock the modest moon.*
BRUTUS	The present wars devour him!* He is grown
	Too proud to be so valiant.*
SICINIUS	Such a nature, 245
	Tickled* with good success,* disdains* the shadow
	Which he treads on at noon. But I do wonder

248   *His insolence can brook:* one so arrogant can bear.
249   *the which:* which. – Fame is here referred to as an impersonal object, and in the next line
             as the goddess Fama, who has granted her favours to Coriolanus.
250   *well graced:* highly favoured.
250   *cannot . . . fault:* cannot be maintained better or acquired in greater measure (*more
             attained*) than in a place lower than the first, since what goes wrong (*miscarries*)
             will be considered the general's fault. – Brutus argues that if one is seeking
             fame it is best to be in a subordinate position, because people will blame the
             commander for mistakes and say that his subordinate would not have made
             them had he been in command.
253   *perform . . . of a man:* do all that anyone can.
254   *giddy censure:* unreliable public opinion.
255   *of:* about.
255   *O if . . . business:* If he had been in charge of the action, things would have been different.
257   *Opinion . . . Cominius:* public approval of Coriolanus will deprive Cominius of the high
             reputation he deserves. – *demerits:* merits (from the Latin *demerere*, to deserve).
259   *Half all . . . them not:* Coriolanus gets half the honour due to Cominius without earning it.
260   *all his faults . . . honours:* all of Coriolanus's faults are reckoned as honours.
262   *aught:* anything.
263   *dispatch . . . singularity:* arrangements have been concluded, and in what manner, apart
             from his characteristically odd behaviour.
264   *goes/Upon:* sets out on.

I.ii.   In the Volscian city of Corioli the Volscian general, Tullus Aufidius, reads to the senators
         a letter from Rome outlining the situation there and reporting that the Romans are fully
         aware of the aggressive intentions of the Volscians and prepared with an army to meet
         them.
             In this brief scene, which switches our attention to the enemy side, the uncertainty
         among the Volscians creates a strong sense of Roman superiority, which is strengthened
         by Aufidius's lament that Volscian plans, however well guarded, are always known at
         once to the Romans. The efficiency of the Romans, reflected in the competence of their
         intelligence service, is indicated also by the news that detachments of their army are
         already on the march towards Corioli, thus snatching the initiative from the Volscians.
         All this contrasts strongly with the vagueness and facile optimism of the Volscian senators.
             The Volscians, too, have their spies, as we see from Aufidius's letter and later from
         IV.iii. This spying on both sides powerfully impresses upon us a sense of the treachery
         and uncertainty at the heart of the political world of the play. Another important note is
         Aufidius's sworn rivalry to Coriolanus, which matches Coriolanus's remarks about him
         in the opening scene and sharpens another of the conflicts of the play, so that we wait
         in suspense for their confrontation.

2   *they of . . . proceed:* the Romans have knowledge of our purposes, and our plans for
             carrying them out.
4   *What:* What plans. – The subject is *counsels* (line 2), hence the plural verb *have* (line 4).
4   *on:* of.
5   *brought to bodily act:* put into action.
6   *Had circumvention:* was able to get the better of us.

They are new to their jobs
& support the people.
ACT I scene ii   15

His insolence can brook* to be commanded
Under Cominius.

cynical.

BRUTUS   Fame, at the which* he aims,
In whom already he's well graced,* cannot*   250
Better be held, nor more attained, than by
A place below the first; for what miscarries
Shall be the general's fault, though he perform*
To th' utmost of a man, and giddy censure*
Will then cry out of* Martius, 'O, if* he   255
Had borne the business!'

SICINIUS   Besides, if things go well,
Opinion,* that so sticks on Martius, shall
Of his demerits rob Cominius.

BRUTUS   Come.
Half all* Cominius' honours are to Martius,
Though Martius earned them not; and all his faults*   260
To Martius shall be honours, though indeed
In aught* he merit not.

SICINIUS   Let's hence, and hear
How the dispatch* is made, and in what fashion,
More than his singularity, he goes
Upon* this present action.

BRUTUS   Let's along.   265

[*Exeunt*

scene ii

Corioli. The Senate House.

Enter TULLUS AUFIDIUS *with* SENATORS *of Corioli.*

FIRST SENATOR So, your opinion is, Aufidius,
That they of* Rome are entered in our counsels,
And know how we proceed.

AUFIDIUS   Is it not yours?
What* ever have been thought on* in this state
That could be brought to bodily act* ere Rome   5
Had circumvention?* 'Tis not four days gone
Spies.

7   *thence:* from there, i.e. Rome.
9   *pressed a power:* conscripted an army.
13   *of Rome . . . of you:* hated more by the people of Rome than by you. – This is one of the many statements in the play whose irony is revealed by later events.
15   *preparation:* army prepared for war.
16   *Whither 'tis bent:* for wherever it is intended.
17   *Consider of it:* Think about it.
18   *made doubt but:* doubted that.
19   *answer:* fight with. – Cf. I.iv.52.
20   *great pretences veiled:* main intentions secret.
21   *in the hatching:* as soon as they were devised.
22   *appeared:* became known.
22   *discovery:* disclosure.
23   *be shortened . . . aim:* be deprived of the necessary time to carry out our plan.
24   *take in:* capture.
26   *your commission:* letter of authority entrusting the army to you.
26   *hie you:* hurry.
26   *bands:* troops.
27   *Let us alone:* Trust us.
28   *set down before's:* besiege us. – Cf. I.iii.94.
28   *for the remove:* to raise the siege.
32   *parcels of their power are forth:* detachments of their army have left.
33   *only hitherward:* coming in this direction only.
35   *'Tis . . . strike:* we have sworn to continue the fight.

Since I heard thence* – these are the words – I think
I have the letter here. Yes, here it is:
[*Reads*] *They have pressed a power,* but it is not known*
Whether for east or west. The dearth is great,   10
The people mutinous, and it is rumoured,
Cominius, Martius your old enemy
(Who is of Rome* worse hated than of you),
And Titus Lartius, a most valiant Roman,
These three lead on this preparation*   15
Whither 'tis bent;* most likely 'tis for you.
Consider of it.*

FIRST SENATOR   Our army's in the field.
We never yet made doubt but* Rome was ready
To answer* us.

AUFIDIUS   Nor did you think it folly
To keep your great pretences veiled* till when   20
They needs must show themselves; which in the hatching,*
It seemed, appeared* to Rome. By the discovery*
We shall be shortened* in our aim, which was
To take in* many towns ere, almost, Rome
Should know we were afoot.

SECOND SENATOR   Noble Aufidius,   25
Take your commission,* hie you* to your bands.*
Let us alone* to guard Corioli.
If they set down before's,* for the remove*
Bring up your army; but, I think, you'll find
They've not prepared for us.

AUFIDIUS   O, doubt not that;   30
I speak from certainties. Nay, more,
Some parcels of their power are forth* already,
And only hitherward.* I leave your honours.
If we and Caius Martius chance to meet,
'Tis* sworn between us, we shall ever strike   35
Till one can do no more.

ALL   The gods assist you.

AUFIDIUS And keep your honours safe.

FIRST SENATOR   Farewell.

SECOND SENATOR   Farewell.

[*Exeunt*

I.iii.   With Coriolanus away at the war, his mother Volumnia and his wife Virgilia sit sewing quietly at home. Volumnia tries to cheer up the anxious Virgilia with assurances of Coriolanus's success. A friend, Valeria, calls and tries to persuade Virgilia to come out, but Virgilia has resolved not to leave the house until Coriolanus returns, and Volumnia and Valeria leave without her.

Shakespeare here leaves the public affairs of Rome and Corioli to focus on the domestic scene, showing the impact of war on those left behind. All the major characters and themes have now been presented. A strong contrast is developed between Volumnia and Virgilia. Both women love Coriolanus, although their love is expressed in different ways, and this has the important effect of establishing the magnetism of the hero in the audience's mind. Valeria's report of the latest war news cleverly and economically fills in the necessary background information. This scene is Shakespeare's invention, having no counterpart in Plutarch; it therefore demands our close attention, both for what it may reveal of his purposes, and to the effects it achieves. With impressive skill he creates in little over a hundred lines the distinctive characters of the three women, whom we feel we know thoroughly at the end of the scene. A quiet contrast to the preceding and following scenes, this one is both retrospective in showing us something of Coriolanus's past, and preparative in that it establishes his relationship with the rest of his family, one which is to be so important in the later stages of the action.

2	*comfortable sort:* cheerful way.
3	*freelier:* more readily.
5	*tender-bodied:* very young.
6	*with comeliness plucked all gaze:* together with good looks attracted everyone's eyes.
7	*for a day of kings' entreaties:* even if kings should beg all day.
8	*should not . . . beholding:* would not let him out of her sight for an hour.
9	*I, considering . . . let him:* Realizing how well honour would suit such a handsome body – which without fame to animate it would be no better than a picture to hang on the wall – I willingly allowed him to.
12	*like:* likely. – See I.i.178 and note.
12	*a cruel war* – This was the Battle of Lake Regillus fought against the Tarquins.
14	*oak:* wreath of oak leaves, a symbol of valour. – The oak garland was awarded to one who had saved the life of a fellow-soldier in battle. Shakespeare appears to have thought, incorrectly, that it was an award given to the best soldier in the battle. The oak-leaf is still a decoration for gallantry in the British and German armies.
14	*I sprang . . . man–child* – This is an echo of *John* 16:21: 'A woman in labour is in pain because her time has come; but when the child is born she forgets the anguish in her joy that a man has been born into the world.'
19	*issue:* a child.
19	*profess:* declare.
20	*each . . . alike:* whom I loved equally.
22	*voluptuously . . . action:* live a life of idle self-indulgence.
25	*Beseech:* I beg.
25	*retire:* withdraw.
27	*Methinks:* I think.
27	*hither:* coming this way.
27	*drum* – i.e. drummer.
29	*As children . . . shunning him:* the Volsces avoiding him, like children running away from a bear.
30	*stamp thus* – Volumnia imitates the warlike action of Coriolanus as she imagines it.
31	*got:* begotten.

scene iii

Rome. A room in Martius' house.

Enter VOLUMNIA *and* VIRGILIA. *They sit down on two low stools and sew.*

VOLUMNIA I pray you, daughter, sing, or express yourself in a more comfortable sort.* If my son were my husband, I should freelier* rejoice in that absence wherein he won honour than in the embracements of his bed where he would show most love. When yet he was but tender-bodied,* and the 5 only son of my womb; when youth with comeliness plucked all gaze* his way; when, for a day of kings' entreaties,* a mother should not* sell him an hour from her beholding; I, considering* how honour would become such a person – that it was no better than picture-like to hang by 10 the wall, if renown made it not stir – was pleased to let him seek danger where he was like* to find fame. To a cruel war* I sent him, from whence he returned, his brows bound with oak.* I tell thee, daughter, I sprang* not more in joy at first hearing he was a man-child, than now in 15 first seeing he had proved himself a man.

VIRGILIA But had he died in the business, madam, how then?

VOLUMNIA Then his good report should have been my son; I therein would have found issue.* Hear me profess* sincerely: had I a dozen sons, each* in my love alike, and none less dear 20 than thine and my good Martius, I had rather had eleven die nobly for their country, than one voluptuously* surfeit out of action.

Enter a GENTLEWOMAN.

GENTLEWOMAN Madam, the Lady Valeria is come to visit you.

VIRGILIA Beseech* you give me leave to retire* myself. 25

VOLUMNIA Indeed you shall not.
Methinks* I hear hither* your husband's drum,*
See him pluck Aufidius down by th' hair,
As children* from a bear, the Volsces shunning him.
Methinks I see him stamp thus,* and call thus: 30
'Come on, you cowards! You were got* in fear,

32   *His . . . wiping:* Then wiping his bloody brow with his gauntlet. – A *gauntlet* of interlaced
              metal rings or overlapping plates was a contemporary sixteenth-century
              piece of armour, not a Roman one.
34   *Like . . . hire:* like a harvester employed either to mow everything or to forfeit his wages.
36   *Jupiter* – the chief Roman god, a sky deity.
37   *more becomes . . . trophy:* is more fitting to a man than gilding is to his funeral monument.
38   *Hecuba* – the wife of Priam, King of Troy, and mother of Hector who distinguished
              himself as a warrior in the war between Greece and Troy.
40   *it spit forth blood:* blood spurted from it, i.e. when wounded by the *Grecian sword.*
41   *contemning:* contemptuously.
42   *fit:* ready.
43   *bless my lord from fell Aufidius:* protect Coriolanus from the fierce Aufidius.
45   S.D. An *usher* was a male attendant employed by wealthy Elizabethans to clear their
              path in public, admit visitors at home, and announce their presence when
              visiting.
49   *How do you both:* How are you both? – Cf. *How does your little son?* (lines 50–1).
49   *manifest housekeepers:* (a) obviously housekeepers (because she sees them sewing),
              (b) real stay-at-homes.
50   *spot:* embroidered pattern (of small flowers, fruits, etc.).
55   *O':* Upon.
56   *O' my troth:* Upon my word.
57   *has:* he has.
57   *a confirmed countenance:* determined features.
58   *gilded:* golden, i.e. yellow.
59   *over and over . . . up again:* he falls over and gets up again.
60   *or whether:* and whether.
61   *how 'twas:* whatever the explanation.
61   *set his teeth* – i.e. in determination.
62   *warrant:* assure you.
62   *mammocked it:* tore it to pieces.
63   *on's:* of his.
64   *la* – an emphatic interjection, without meaning in itself. Cf. line 85 below.
65   *crack:* lively youngster.
67   *huswife:* housewife.
68   *will not out:* will not go out.

Though you were born in Rome.' His* bloody brow
With his mailed hand then wiping, forth he goes,
Like* to a harvest-man that's tasked to mow
Or all or lose his hire.   35

VIRGILIA His bloody brow? O Jupiter,* no blood!
VOLUMNIA Away, you fool! It more becomes* a man
Than gilt his trophy. The breasts of Hecuba,*
When she did suckle Hector, looked not lovelier
Than Hector's forehead when it spit forth blood*   40
At Grecian sword, contemning.* Tell Valeria
We are fit* to bid her welcome.

                             [*Exit* GENTLEWOMAN

VIRGILIA Heavens bless my lord from fell Aufidius!*
VOLUMNIA He'll beat Aufidius' head below his knee,
And tread upon his neck.   45

Enter VALERIA *with an* USHER* *and the* GENTLEWOMAN.

VALERIA My ladies both, good day to you.
VOLUMNIA Sweet madam.
VIRGILIA I am glad to see your ladyship.
VALERIA How do you both?* You are manifest housekeepers.* What
are you sewing here? A fine spot,* in good faith. How does   50
your little son?
VIRGILIA I thank your ladyship; well, good madam.
VOLUMNIA He had rather see the swords and hear a drum than look
upon his schoolmaster.
VALERIA O'* my word, the father's son. I'll swear 'tis a very pretty   55
boy. O' my troth,* I looked upon him o' Wednesday half
an hour together; has* such a confirmed countenance.*
I saw him run after a gilded* butterfly, and when he caught
it, he let it go again; and after it again, and over and over*
he comes, and up again; catched it again; or whether* his   60
fall enraged him, or how 'twas,* he did so set his teeth,*
and tear it. O, I warrant,* how he mammocked it!*
VOLUMNIA One on's* father's moods.
VALERIA Indeed, la,* 'tis a noble child.
VIRGILIA A crack,* madam.   65
VALERIA Come, lay aside your stitchery; I must have you play the
idle huswife* with me this afternoon.
VIRGILIA No, good madam, I will not out* of doors.
VALERIA Not out of doors?
VOLUMNIA She shall, she shall.   70

71   *by your patience:* if you don't mind.
71   *I'll not over:* I won't cross.
73   *Fie:* Shame on you.
74   *lies in:* is in confinement for the birth of her child.
75   *speedy strength:* a quick return to strength.
78   *'Tis not to save labour* – Virgilia means that her unwillingness to visit the lady is not because of laziness. There may be a pun on *labour* meaning 'childbirth', though the serious-minded Virgilia seems unlikely to jest.
78   *want:* lack.
79   *Penelope* was the faithful wife of Ulysses, King of Ithaca. While he was away at the Trojan War she remained at home weaving. She outwitted the many suitors who besieged her there by insisting that she must first finish the shroud she was weaving, and undoing each night what she had woven during the day, so that the work was never finished.
81   *moths:* (a) insects (b) suitors, living in Ulysses' home at his expense.
81   *cambric:* fine white linen.
81   *sensible:* capable of feeling.
82   *that:* so that.
82   *for pity:* out of pity (at the pain you were causing it).
88   *Verily:* Truly.
94   *set down:* besieging. – Cf. I.ii.28.
95   *nothing doubt prevailing:* have no doubt they will win.
95   *make it brief wars* – i.e. overcome the Volsces quickly.
98   *in everything:* in everything else but this.
100   *disease our better mirth:* spoil our enjoyment, which will be greater without her.
102   *troth:* truth.
103   *turn thy solemnness out o' door:* expel this serious mood of yours.
105   *at a word:* in short.

VIRGILIA Indeed, no, by your patience;* I'll not over* the threshold
till my lord return from the wars.

VALERIA Fie,* you confine yourself most unreasonably. Come, you
must go visit the good lady that lies in.*

VIRGILIA I will wish her speedy strength,* and visit her with my   75
prayers; but I cannot go thither.

VOLUMNIA Why, I pray you?

VIRGILIA 'Tis not to save labour,* nor that I want* love.

VALERIA You would be another Penelope;* yet, they say, all the
yarn she spun in Ulysses' absence did but fill Ithaca full of   80
moths.* Come; I would your cambric* were sensible* as
your finger, that* you might leave pricking it for pity.*
Come, you shall go with us.

VIRGILIA No, good madam, pardon me; indeed, I will not forth.

VALERIA In truth, la, go with me, and I'll tell you excellent news of   85
your husband.

VIRGILIA O good madam, there can be none yet.

VALERIA Verily,* I do not jest with you; there came news from him
last night.

VIRGILIA Indeed, madam?   90

VALERIA In earnest, it's true; I heard a senator speak it. Thus it is:
the Volsces have an army forth, against whom Cominius
the general is gone, with one part of our Roman power.
Your lord and Titus Lartius are set down* before their city
Corioli; they nothing doubt prevailing,* and to make it   95
brief wars.* This is true, on mine honour; and so, I pray,
go with us.

VIRGILIA Give me excuse, good madam; I will obey you in everything* hereafter.

VOLUMNIA Let her alone, lady; as she is now, she will but disease our   100
better mirth.*

VALERIA In troth,* I think she would. Fare you well, then. Come,
good sweet lady. Prithee, Virgilia, turn thy solemness out
o' door,* and go along with us.

VIRGILIA No, at a word,* madam. Indeed I must not. I wish you much   105
mirth.

VALERIA Well then, farewell.

                                                                                    [Exeunt

I.iv.   While Cominius is elsewhere engaging the main Volscian army under Aufidius, Coriolanus and Titus Lartius are besieging Corioli. A body of Volscians comes out of the city and beats back the Romans, whom Coriolanus curses for their cowardice. He counter-attacks, repels the Volscians, and enters the city, but his men will not follow him and the gates are closed, shutting him in. Titus Lartius concludes that Coriolanus is lost, but the gates are opened again and the Romans, led by Lartius, go to the assistance of the wounded Coriolanus in the city.

The action swings over to the battlefield, and the purpose of this and the following scenes up to I.ix is to demonstrate and build up Coriolanus as warrior-hero. Suspense is engendered through the swaying fortunes of the two armies in battle and the uncertain fate of Coriolanus in the city. Coriolanus's contempt for the conscripted citizens of Rome as soldiers now appears justified and goes a long way in making us accept his valuation of them expressed already in I.i and again later in the play. It is well to remember that these numerous short battle scenes, which tend to appear episodic and disjointed in print, formed one continuous action on the stage, accompanied by a great deal of noise, and the martial sounds of trumpet and drum, and created excitement and variety for the audience.

S.D.	*drum and colours* – i.e. a drummer and a soldier carrying a standard.
1	*A wager they have met:* I bet you they (i.e. the armies of Cominius and the Volsces) have met in battle.
2	*My horse to yours, no:* I'll bet my horse against yours that they have not.
4	*They lie in view:* They are positioned within sight of each other.
4	*spoke:* fought.
5	*of:* from.
6	*nor . . . nor:* neither . . . nor.
7	*Summon:* Call to a parley.
9	*'larum:* alarum, a call to arms.
10	*Mars* – the Roman god of war.
10	*prithee:* beg you (literally 'pray thee').
11	*with smoking swords:* with blood making our (hot) swords steam.
12	*fielded:* on the battlefield.
12	S.D. A *parley* was the trumpet call for a discussion between the two sides. For the stage setting *on the walls*, see *Introduction*, page lx.
14	*No, nor . . . little* – The Senator's expression is confused. What he means is that no one in Corioli fears Coriolanus. The Coriolans could not fear him less than Aufidius does, since his fear is so infinitesimal as to be non-existent. Shakespeare often uses *less* to intensify the negative where today we would use *more*.
16	*break . . . us up:* emerge from the city rather than let them shut us up like animals in a pound. – A *pound* is an enclosure for stray animals.
18	*but pinned with rushes:* secured only with grass reeds.
19	S.D. *Alarum* – It is probable that here and at lines 42 and 47 the word is intended to denote the sound of fighting as well as that of the martial drums and trumpets.
20	*List what . . . army:* Hark at the havoc he is causing in your army which is being cut to pieces (*cloven*).
22	*our instruction:* the signal for us to attack.
22	*Ladders, ho.* – Lartius calls for scaling ladders for his men to ascend the walls of Corioli.

scene iv

Before the city of Corioli.

Enter MARTIUS, TITUS LARTIUS, *with drum and colours,**
CAPTAINS, SOLDIERS *at one door. Enter a* MESSENGER *at the
other door.*

MARTIUS	Yonder comes news. A wager they have met.*
LARTIUS	My horse to yours, no.*
MARTIUS	'Tis done.
LARTIUS	Agreed.
MARTIUS	Say, has our general met the enemy?
MESSENGER	They lie in view,* but have not spoke* as yet.
LARTIUS	So, the good horse is mine.
MARTIUS	I'll buy him of* you.

5

LARTIUS	No, I'll nor* sell nor give him. Lend you him I will
	For half a hundred years. [*To a* TRUMPETER]
	Summon* the town.
MARTIUS	How far off lie these armies?
MESSENGER	Within this mile and half.
MARTIUS	Then shall we hear their 'larum,* and they ours.

	Now Mars,* I prithee,* make us quick in work,
	That we with smoking swords* may march from hence
	To help our fielded* friends! Come, blow thy blast.

10

*They sound a parley.** Enter two* SENATORS *with others on the
walls of Corioli.*

	Tullus Aufidius, is he within your walls?
FIRST SENATOR	No, nor* a man that fears you less than he;
	That's lesser than a little. [*Drum afar off.*] Hark, our drums

15

	Are bringing forth our youth. We'll break* our walls
	Rather than they shall pound us up. Our gates,
	Which yet seem shut, we have but pinned with rushes;*
	They'll open of themselves. [*Alarum* far off.*]
	Hark you, far off!
	There is Aufidius. List what* work he makes

20

	Amongst your cloven army.
MARTIUS	O, they are at it!
LARTIUS	Their noise be our instruction.* Ladders, ho!*

23   *forth:* out of.
25   *proof:* tested and proved impregnable.
26   *much beyond our thoughts:* more than we thought possible.
29   *edge:* sword.
30   *contagion of the south:* pestilence from the south. – It was thought that the mild, damp
               winds of the south and south-west brought disease with them.
30   *light:* descend.
31   *You herd of* – Coriolanus breaks off, speechless with anger, unable to think of an epithet
               bad enough for his cowardly troops. Characteristically he describes them in
               animal terms as a *herd*.
32   *Plaster you o'er:* cover you like plaster.
32   *abhorred/Farther than seen* – i.e. because their stinking sores can be smelt further than
               they can be seen; *abhorred:* loathed.
33   *one infect . . . mile:* infect each other for the distance of a mile, depite the fact that the wind
               bringing the disease is blowing the other way.
36   *Pluto* – the Roman god of Hades, the classical underworld, or hell.
37   *All hurt behind* – i.e. their wounds are all on their backs because they have been running
               away.
38   *agued fear:* fear which causes trembling, like a fever.
38   *Mend and charge home:* Mend your ways and charge into the heart of the enemy.
39   *the fires of heaven* – i.e. the sun, moon and stars.
40   *Look to't:* See that you do it.
42   *As they us:* As they just beat us.
42   *Follow's:* follow us, i.e. follow me. – The Folio reads *trenches followes* which makes no
               sense. Various emendations have been suggested, one of which is adopted here.
43   *ope:* open.
43   *seconds:* helpers.
44   *'Tis for . . . fliers:* Fortune has opened the gates for us, the pursuers, not for the Volsces
               who are running away.
45   *like:* same.
46   *Foolhardiness:* It would be folly.
47   *To th' pot:* to destruction (literally, cut in pieces like meat for the cooking pot).
47   *warrant him:* am sure.

The gates open. Enter the army of the Volsces from inside the city.

MARTIUS They fear us not, but issue forth* their city.
Now put your shields before your hearts, and fight
With hearts more proof* than shields. Advance, brave
                                        Titus.   25

They do disdain us much beyond our thoughts,*
Which makes me sweat with wrath. Come on, my fellows.
He that retires, I'll take him for a Volsce,
And he shall feel mine edge.*

Alarum. MARTIUS *pursues some of the Volsces offstage at one door. The main body of Volsces beat the other Romans offstage at the other door.* MARTIUS *re-enters, cursing.*

MARTIUS All the contagion of the south* light* on you,   30
You shames of Rome! You herd of* — boils and plagues
Plaster you o'er,* that you may be abhorred
Farther than seen,* and one infect* another
Against the wind a mile! You souls of geese
That bear the shapes of men, how have you run   35
From slaves that apes would beat! Pluto* and hell!
All hurt behind,* backs red, and faces pale
With flight and agued fear!* Mend and charge home,*
Or, by the fires of heaven,* I'll leave the foe,
And make my wars on you! Look to't.* Come on;   40
If you'll stand fast, we'll beat them to their wives,
As they us* to our trenches. Follow's.*

Another alarum. The Volsces withdraw into the city.
MARTIUS *follows them to the gates.*

So, now the gates are ope.* Now prove good seconds.*
'Tis for* the followers Fortune widens them,
Not for the fliers. Mark me, and do the like.*   45
          [*Exit into the city. The gates close, shutting him in*
FIRST SOLDIER Foolhardiness.* Not I.
SECOND SOLDIER   Nor I.
FIRST SOLDIER   See, they
          Have shut him in.
          ALL   To th' pot,* I warrant him.*
                                        [*Alarum continues*

48   *is become of:* has happened to.
49   *at the very heels:* close on their heels.
50   *who . . . sudden:* and suddenly they.
51   *Clapped to:* closed up.
52   *answer:* fight with. – Cf. I.ii.19.
53   *Who sensibly . . . stand'st up:* who, able to feel, is braver than his unfeeling sword, and
        stands up and fights when his sword bends.
55   *A carbuncle entire:* A perfect ruby.
56   *Were not:* would not be.
57   *Even to Cato's wish:* exactly according to Cato's idea. – In fact, Cato the Censor (234–149
        B.C.) lived some two hundred and fifty years after Coriolanus. This kind of
        anachronism is very common in Elizabethan literature in general, and par-
        ticularly in drama, reflecting their unconcern for minute historical accuracy.
        Plutarch wrote a *Life of Cato*. The Folio reads *Calues wish,* an error we are able
        to rectify by reference to Plutarch's *Life of Martius Coriolanus:* 'For he was
        even such another, as Cato would have a soldier.'
61   *feverous:* feverish.
62   *fetch him . . . alike:* rescue him, or stay with him and share his fate.

I.v.   Coriolanus and Lartius, emerging from the city gates, come upon some of their soldiers
        who have been looting in Corioli. Coriolanus is incensed and about to attack them when
        his attention is distracted by the noise of the main battle between Cominius and Aufidius.
        He quickly instructs Lartius to take enough troops to hold the city, while he hurries off
        to help Cominius, ignoring the wounds which Lartius urges him to have attended to.
            Admiration for Coriolanus is secured by his courage, his disregard for his wounds, and
        his unselfish concern for Cominius, and is given expression in Lartius's words, 'Thou
        worthiest Martius'. It is in strong contrast to the selfish cupidity and cowardice of the
        looting soldiers.

S.D.   *spoils* – i.e. booty or plunder taken from the enemy.
3   *murrain:* plague (literally, a cattle disease).

Enter TITUS LARTIUS.

LARTIUS What is become of* Martius?

ALL   Slain, sir, doubtless.

FIRST SOLDIER Following the fliers at the very heels,*

With them he enters; who,* upon the sudden   50

Clapped to* their gates. He is himself alone,

To answer* all the city.

LARTIUS   O noble fellow!

Who sensibly* outdares his senseless sword,

And when it bows stand'st up! Thou art lost, Martius!

A carbuncle entire,* as big as thou art,   55

Were not* so rich a jewel. Thou wast a soldier

Even to Cato's wish,* not fierce and terrible

Only in strokes, but with thy grim looks and

The thunder-like percussion of thy sounds

Thou mad'st thine enemies shake, as if the world   60

Were feverous* and did tremble.

The gates open. Enter MARTIUS *bleeding, assaulted by the enemy.*

FIRST SOLDIER   Look, sir.

LARTIUS   O, 'tis Martius!

Let's fetch him* off, or make remain alike.

            [*They fight, and all enter the city*

scene v

Before Corioli.

*Enter Roman soldiers with spoils.**

FIRST ROMAN This will I carry to Rome.

SECOND ROMAN And I this.

THIRD ROMAN A murrain* on't! I took this for silver.

                                            [*Exeunt*

4   *movers:* active creatures. – Coriolanus is being sarcastic. The men are busy looting, not getting on with the battle.

4   *prize . . . drachma:* value their time by how much money they can make. – A *drachma* was a Greek coin of little value, worthless when cracked.

6   *Irons of a doit:* swords worth a mere trifle. – A *doit* was an old Dutch coin of very little value.

6   *doublets . . . wore them* – i.e. because they were so ragged as to be worthless. The doublet was a contemporary sixteenth century jacket, close fitting with a short skirt, and with or without sleeves. Traditionally the hangman had the right to take the clothes of those he executed.

9   *To him:* Let us join him.

11   *Piercing:* wounding.

12   *Convenient:* sufficient.

12   *make good:* secure.

16   *course of fight:* bout of fighting.

18   *physical:* like physic, or medicine, hence beneficial. – Bloodletting was a common medical treatment in Shakespeare's day.

20   *Now . . . Fall:* May the beautiful goddess, Fortune, fall.

21   *charms:* magic spells.

22   *Misguide:* misdirect, i.e. direct them away from harming you.

23   *Prosperity be thy page:* may success attend you (like a *page*, a young attendant).

23   *Thy friend . . . Than:* May she favour you as much as.

28   *know our mind:* learn our intentions.

Alarum continues still afar off.
Enter MARTIUS *and* TITUS LARTIUS *with a* TRUMPETER.

MARTIUS   See here these movers* that do prize* their hours
At a cracked drachma! Cushions, leaden spoons,   5
Irons of a doit,* doublets* that hangmen would
Bury with those that wore them, these base slaves,
Ere yet the fight be done, pack up. Down with them!
And hark, what noise the general makes! To him!*
There is the man of my soul's hate, Aufidius,   10
Piercing* our Romans. Then, valiant Titus, take
Convenient* numbers to make good* the city,
Whilst I, with those that have the spirit, will haste
To help Cominius.
LARTIUS   Worthy sir, thou bleed'st;
Thy exercise hath been too violent   15
For a second course of fight.*
MARTIUS   Sir, praise me not.
My work hath not yet warmed me. Fare you well.
The blood I drop is rather physical*
Than dangerous to me. To Aufidius thus,
I will appear and fight.
LARTIUS   Now* the fair goddess, Fortune,   20
Fall deep in love with thee, and her great charms*
Misguide* the opposers' swords. Bold gentleman,
Prosperity be thy page.*
MARTIUS   Thy friend* no less
Than those she placeth highest. So farewell.
LARTIUS   Thou worthiest Martius!   25
                                        [*Exit* MARTIUS

Go sound thy trumpet in the market-place;
Call thither all the officers o' th' town,
Where they shall know our mind.* Away!
                                        [*Exeunt*

I.vi.   Cominius having retreated with his forces is dismayed by the messenger's report that the
Volscians have beaten back Coriolanus and Lartius. At this point Coriolanus enters and is
joyously reunited with Cominius. He begs to be allowed to attack directly Aufidius who
leads the Antiates, the best of the enemy troops. This is granted by Cominius, and
Coriolanus selects followers from those who volunteer to accompany him.

The suspense of the battle continues. The cautious, prudent generalship of Cominius
sets off the dashing heroism of Coriolanus.

1	*Breathe you:* Have a rest.
1	*are come off:* have acquitted ourselves.
2	*our stands:* the occasions when we refused to yield.
3	*retire:* retreat.
4	*struck:* been fighting.
5	*By interims and conveying gusts:* at intervals and through gusts of wind carrying the sound.
6	*charges:* attacks.
6	*The Roman gods* – A vocative use, meaning 'O Roman gods' or 'You Roman gods'.
7	*Lead . . . sacrifice:* give them the good fortune that we wish for ourselves so that both our armies may meet, and with smiles [of triumph] may offer sacrifices to you in gratitude.
10	*issued:* come out.
16	*briefly:* a short time ago.
17	*confound:* spend.
19	*Held me in chase:* pursued me.
19	*that . . . wheel:* so that I was forced to take a roundabout route.
20	*about:* out of my way.
20	*else:* otherwise.
21	*since:* ago.
22	*as:* as if. – Cf. I.i.199.
22	*flayed:* bloody (like a skinned carcase in a butcher's shop).
23	*stamp:* image.
24	*Before-time:* on former occasions.
25	*knows not . . . man:* cannot distinguish the sound of thunder from a drum better than I can distinguish Coriolanus's voice from every inferior man's. – A *tabor* is a small drum.

scene vi

Near the Roman camp.

Enter COMINIUS *with* SOLDIERS *in retreat.*

COMINIUS Breathe you,* my friends. Well fought. We are come off*
Like Romans, neither foolish in our stands*
Nor cowardly in retire.* Believe me, sirs,
We shall be charged again. Whiles we have struck,*
By interims and conveying gusts* we have heard   5
The charges* of our friends. The Roman gods,*
Lead* their successes as we wish our own,
That both our powers, with smiling fronts encountering,
May give you thankful sacrifice.

Enter a MESSENGER.

                                        Thy news?
MESSENGER The citizens of Corioli have issued,*   10
And given to Lartius and to Martius battle.
I saw our party to their trenches driven,
And then I came away.
COMINIUS   Though thou speakest truth,
Methinks thou speak'st not well. How long is't since?
MESSENGER Above an hour, my lord.   15
COMINIUS 'Tis not a mile; briefly* we heard their drums.
How couldst thou in a mile confound* an hour,
And bring thy news so late?
MESSENGER   Spies of the Volsces
Held me in chase,* that* I was forced to wheel
Three or four miles about;* else* had I, sir,   20
Half an hour since* brought my report.

Enter MARTIUS.

COMINIUS   Who's yonder
That does appear as* he were flayed?* O gods!
He has the stamp* of Martius, and I have
Before-time* seen him thus.
MARTIUS   Come I too late?
COMINIUS The shepherd knows not* thunder from a tabor   25
More than I know the sound of Martius' tongue
From every meaner man.
MARTIUS   Come I too late?

28   *Ay, if . . . own:* Yes, if it is your own blood and not that of others that you are covered in.
    – *Mantled:* covered as with a cloak.

29   *clip:* embrace.

31   *nuptial day was done:* wedding day was ended.

32   *tapers burned to bedward:* lights showed the way to bed.

32   *Flower:* Perfection, quintessence.

34   *busied about decrees:* busily engaged in giving orders.

36   *Ransoming him, or pitying:* fixing a ransom for someone or remitting it out of pity.

38   *like a fawning greyhound* – The simile suggests the servile, wheedling demeanour of the
    captive Coriolans.

39   *let him slip at will:* unleash him when he wishes. – To *let slip* was a common term in
    hunting.

42   *inform:* tell.

42   *But for . . . common file:* As for our gentlemen, the rank and file of our army. – Coriolanus
    is scornful about his plebeian troops who ran away. As at I.iv.31, the very
    thought of them makes him so angry that he cannot finish his sentence.

43   *Tribunes for them!:* And we grant them tribunes!

44   *budge:* run away.

45   *rascals:* rabble. – See note to I.i.145.

46   *Will the time serve to tell:* Is there enough time to tell you?

46   *think:* think so.

50   *to win our purpose:* in order to be able to gain our objective.

51   *How lies their battle?:* How is their army deployed?

52   *men of trust:* most reliable troops.

53   *bands i' th' vaward:* troops in the vanguard.

53   *the Antiates* – i.e. the men of Antium, the Volscian capital. The word is trisyllabic.

55   *Their very heart of hope:* the centre of their hopes.

58   *éndure:* always remain.

60   *not delay the present:* do not put off the present opportunity.

61   *advanced:* raised.

61   *darts:* spears.

*He compares
his passion of
marriage with
that of battle.*

COMINIUS   Ay, if* you come not in the blood of others,
            But mantled in your own.

MARTIUS   O, let me clip* ye
            In arms as sound as when I wooed; in heart   30
            As merry as when our nuptial day was done,*
            And tapers burned to bedward.*

COMINIUS   Flower* of warriors!
            How is't with Titus Lartius?

MARTIUS   As with a man busied about decrees:*
            Condemning some to death and some to exile;   35
            Ransoming him, or pitying,* threat'ning th'other;
            Holding Corioli in the name of Rome,
            Even like a fawning greyhound* in the leash,
            To let him slip at will.*

COMINIUS   Where is that slave
            Which told me they had beat you to your trenches?   40
            Where is he? Call him hither.

MARTIUS   Let him alone;
            He did inform* the truth. But for* our gentlemen,
            The common file – a plague! Tribunes for them!* –
            The mouse ne'er shunned the cat as they did budge*
            From rascals* worse than they.

COMINIUS   But how prevailed you?   45

MARTIUS   Will the time serve to tell?* I do not think.*
            Where is the enemy? Are you lords o' th' field?
            If not, why cease you till you are so?

COMINIUS   Martius,
            We have at disadvantage fought, and did
            Retire to win our purpose.*   50

MARTIUS   How lies their battle?* Know you on which side
            They have placed their men of trust?*

COMINIUS   As I guess, Martius,
            Their bands i' th' vaward* are the Antiates,*
            Of their best trust; o'er them Aufidius,
            Their very heart of hope.*

MARTIUS   I do beseech you,   55
            By all the battles wherein we have fought,
            By th' blood we've shed together, by th' vows
            We've made to endure* friends, that you directly
            Set me against Aufidius and his Antiates;
            And that you not delay the present,* but,   60
            Filling the air with swords advanced* and darts,*

62   *prove:* put to the proof.
64   *balms:* healing ointments.
68   *were:* would be.
68   *this painting* – i.e. blood.
69   *any fear . . . report:* anyone is less afraid of danger to himself than of a bad reputation.
73   *so many so minded:* as many as are of the same mind.
74   *disposition:* state of mind.
76   *O, me alone* – Coriolanus modestly disclaims the idea that he alone deserves this praise.
          They have lifted him up like one of the *swords advanced* spoken of at line 61.
77   *shows be not outward:* actions are not just external flourishes (and therefore insincere).
78   *But is:* is not the equal of.
81   *Though thanks to all:* though I thank all of you.
82   *bear the business:* manage the action.
83   *As cause will be obeyed:* where and when they are needed.
84   *four shall . . . command:* four subordinate officers shall select those men whom I will
          command in this action.
86   *Make good this ostentation:* Make this show of courage a reality in battle.
87   *Divide in all:* share the spoils.

We prove* this very hour.

COMINIUS   Though I could wish
You were conducted to a gentle bath,
And balms* applied to you, yet dare I never
Deny your asking. Take your choice of those   65
That best can aid your action.

MARTIUS   Those are they
That most are willing. If any such be here –
As it were* sin to doubt – that love this painting*
Wherein you see me smeared; if any fear*
Lesser his person than an ill report;.   70
If any think brave death outweighs bad life,
And that his country's dearer than himself,
Let him alone, or so many so minded,*
Wave thus, to express his disposition,*
And follow Martius.   75

*They all shout and wave their swords, take him up in their
arms, and cast up their caps.*

O, me alone?* Make you a sword of me?
If these shows be not outward,* which of you
But is* four Volsces? None of you but is
Able to bear against the great Aufidius
A shield as hard as his. A certain number,   80
Though thanks to all,* must I select from all. The rest
Shall bear the business* in some other fight,
As cause will be obeyed.* Please you to march,
And four shall* quickly draw out my command,
Which men are best inclined.

COMINIUS   March on, my fellows.   85
Make good this ostentation,* and you shall
Divide in all* with us.

                                                    [*Exeunt*

I.vii.   Lartius leaves a skeleton force under a Lieutenant to hold Corioli and hastens to join Cominius and Coriolanus.
         Urgency and suspense are maintained in such words as those of Lartius, 'If we lose the field,/We cannot keep the town.'

1   *ports*: gates.
3   *centuries*: companies – These were originally of one hundred men.
4   *For a short holding*: to hold the town for a short time.
4   *field*: battle.
5   *Fear not our care*: Do not doubt our diligence.
6   *Hence* – i.e. go inside the city.
7   *guider*: guide.

I.viii.   Coriolanus and Aufidius confront one another in single combat. Despite the arrival of some Volscians who help Aufidius, Coriolanus overcomes them all and drives them off.
         This is the climax of the battle scenes. Coriolanus's victory over the redoubtable Aufidius is the highest point of his growth to epic stature. Aufidius's shame at his defeat is an important explanatory cause of his later treachery towards Coriolanus.

3   *Not Afric owns*: In the whole of Africa there is not.
4   *thy fame and envy*: your fame and the envy you arouse.
4   *Fix thy foot*: Stand and fight it out.
5   *the first budger*: the one who gives way first.
6   *doom*: judge.
7   *Hollow me like a hare*: pursue me, shouting like huntsmen after the hare. – The hare was the type of extreme cowardice. See the contrast of lions and hares at I.i.157.
9   *made what work*: did as much destruction as.
10   *Wherein . . . masked*: which you see me covered with, like a mask.
11   *Wrench . . . th' highest* – i.e. summon up all your strength. – The image is that of a soldier drawing back the string of the crossbow to its tightest extent.
11   *Hector . . . bragged progeny*: Hector, the champion of the Trojan warriors, from whom you boast that you are descended. – Rome was reputedly founded by the Trojan Aeneas. Hector is described here as the *whip* or scourge of the Greeks.

scene vii

Before Corioli.

Enter TITUS LARTIUS *with a* LIEUTENANT, SOLDIERS, *a* SCOUT, DRUMMER *and* TRUMPETER.

LARTIUS   So, let the ports* be guarded; keep your duties
As I have set them down. If I do send, dispatch
Those centuries* to our aid; the rest will serve
For a short holding.* If we lose the field,*
We cannot keep the town.

LIEUTENANT   Fear not our care,* sir.   5

LARTIUS   Hence,* and shut your gates upon's.
Our guider,* come; to th' Roman camp conduct us.

                                                  [*Exeunt*

scene viii

A battlefield near the Roman camp.

Enter MARTIUS *at one door,* AUFIDIUS *at the other.*

MARTIUS   I'll fight with none but thee, for I do hate thee
Worse than a promise-breaker.

AUFIDIUS   We hate alike.
Not Afric owns* a serpent I abhor
More than thy fame and envy.* Fix thy foot.*

MARTIUS   Let the first budger* die the other's slave,   5
And the gods doom* him after.

AUFIDIUS   If I fly, Martius,
Hollow me like a hare.*

MARTIUS   Within these three hours, Tullus,
Alone I fought in your Corioli walls,
And made what work* I pleased. 'Tis not my blood
Wherein* thou seest me masked. For thy revenge   10
Wrench* up thy power to th' highest.

AUFIDIUS   Wert thou the Hector*

13   *scape:* escape.
14   *Officious:* Interfering, i.e. in giving him help he does not want.
15   *In your condemnèd seconds:* by your damnable help. – Aufidius tries to put the blame for
       his defeat upon the Volsces who came to help him.

I.ix.   The Romans, mainly due to the efforts of Coriolanus, are victorious. He tries to silence
          the praises of Cominius and Lartius, and refuses to take the tenth of the spoils which
          Cominius awards him, preferring an equal share with everyone else. Cominius awards
          him his horse, the title of Coriolanus and the oaken garland. Coriolanus requests freedom
          for one of the prisoners, a poor man from Corioli who had formerly shown him hospitality,
          but when Lartius asks his name so that he may be freed, Coriolanus cannot remember it.
             Coriolanus is at his height. He shows modesty when acclaimed by his general and the
          army, proves true what the Second Citizen had said of him in I.i 'You must in no way
          say he is covetous', and disproves the suspicions of the tribunes in the same scene that he
          was motivated by a selfish love of fame and was unwilling to serve under Cominius.

S.D.   *Flourish* – a trumpet-blast like a bugle call.
         retreat – the trumpet-call signalling the recall of troops.
         scarf: sling.
1   *tell thee o'er:* describe to you in detail.
2   *Thou't:* you would (a contraction of *thou wouldst*).
4   *attend:* listen.
4   *shrug* – i.e. in disbelief.
5   *admire:* wonder at it.
6   *gladly quaked:* willingly made to tremble.
6   *dull:* stupid.
7   *fusty:* stale-smelling.
7   *plébeians:* common people.
8   *against their hearts:* unwillingly.
10   *cam'st thou . . . before* – Cominius is saying that Coriolanus, when coming to his aid, had
                already done a full day's fighting. The battle on Cominius's front was a morsel
                compared with the full meal of the earlier part in Corioli.
12   *Here is . . . caparison:* Coriolanus (*the steed*) did all the work, we were mere accessories. –
                caparison: a horse's trappings, equipment.
14   *a charter to extol her blood:* licence to praise her own flesh and blood. – A *charter* is a
                written grant of rights and privileges to an individual or a group, conferred
                by a sovereign or a legislature.
16   *that's what I can:* that is, as much as I could.
17   *Induced:* led on.

That was the whip of your bragged progeny,
Thou shouldst not scape* me here.

They fight and some Volsces come to the aid of AUFIDIUS.
MARTIUS *fights till they are driven off breathless.*

Officious,* and not valiant, you have shamed me
In your condemnèd seconds.*   15

                                        [*Exeunt*

scene ix

The Roman camp.

Flourish.* Alarum. A retreat* is sounded.
Enter at one door COMINIUS *with the Romans; at the other,*
MARTIUS *with his arm in a scarf.**

COMINIUS   If I should tell thee o'er* this day's work,
Thou't* not believe thy deeds. But I'll report it
Where senators shall mingle tears with smiles;
Where great patricians shall attend,* and shrug,*
I' th' end admire;* where ladies shall be frighted,   5
And, gladly quaked,* hear more; where the dull* tribunes,
That with the fusty* plébeians* hate thine honours,
Shall say against their hearts,* 'We thank the gods
Our Rome hath such a soldier.'
Yet cam'st thou* to a morsel of this feast,   10
Having fully dined before.

Enter TITUS LARTIUS *with his* SOLDIERS *from the pursuit.*

LARTIUS   O general,
Here is* the steed, we the caparison!
Hadst thou beheld—
MARTIUS   Pray now, no more. My mother,
Who has a charter to extol her blood,*
When she does praise me, grieves me. I have done   15
As you have done, that's what I can;*
Induced* as you have been, that's for my country.

18   *but effected his good will:* only carried out his good intentions.
19   *overta'en mine act:* surpassed my performance.
19   *You shall . . . deserving:* You cannot be allowed to bury your praiseworthy actions in silence.
21   *own:* own sons.
21   *'Twere:* It would be.
22   *traducement:* defamation.
24   *to the spire . . . modest:* even if the praise were worded in the highest possible terms it would seem only moderate.
26   *In sign . . . hear me:* you must listen to what I am going to say about you in front of our army, which is not to reward what you have done, but simply to record what you are.
28   *smart . . . remembered:* hurt when you remind me of them. – Coriolanus is modestly trying to stop Cominius from talking of his exploits by suggesting that this causes him physical pain. In fact, it is mental torture to Coriolanus to hear his praises sung; see *Introduction*, page xxviii.
29   *Should they . . . with death:* If your wounds were not remembered they ought to fester at our ingratitude and cure themselves by killing you, i.e. your wounds deserve praise. – To *tent* a wound is to probe and clean it with lint. Cominius exaggerates in arguing that remembrance and praise of Coriolanus's wounds are necessary to his life.
32   *ta'en good and good store:* captured good horses and plenty of them.
33   *in this field achieved and city:* won on the battlefield and in the city.
34   *we render . . . choice* – Coriolanus is being offered a tenth of the spoils at his choice before they are divided among the whole army (*the common distribution*) as promised by Cominius himself at I.vi.86.
39   *stand upon . . . doing:* insist on an equal share with all the rest who were present in the action.
40   *S.D. bareheaded* – This is a sign of respect for Coriolanus. In Shakespeare's time caps were taken off in the presence of one's superiors.
41   *May these . . . wars* – This difficult passage has provoked much discussion. The general sense seems to be, 'I would rather that these trumpets which you misuse (by using them in my honour) were silent. When drums and trumpets are used for flattery on the battlefield, let courts and cities be wholly given up to deceitfulness. When armour grows as soft as the parasite's silk, let him be offered the job of fighting the wars.' Coriolanus means that when flattery, a common phenomenon in courts and cities, is found on the battlefield it is time for the soldier to resign his function to the courtier. Some editors emend *overture* (offer) to *coverture*.
47   *For that:* Because.
48   *Or foiled . . . wretch:* or because I have got the better of some feeble fellow.
48   *without note . . . done:* many others have done unnoticed.
49   *you shout . . . with lies:* you acclaim me in exaggerated terms as if I wanted my small efforts (*my little*) to be fed (*dieted*) with praises made more appetizing (*sauced*) by lies.

He that has but effected his good will*
Hath overta'en mine act.*

COMINIUS   You shall* not be
The grave of your deserving; Rome must know   20
The value of her own.* 'Twere* a concealment
Worse than a theft, no less than a traducement,*
To hide your doings, and to silence that
Which, to the spire* and top of praises vouched,
Would seem but modest. Therefore I beseech you,   25
In sign* of what you are, not to reward
What you have done, before our army hear me.

MARTIUS   I have some wounds upon me, and they smart*
To hear themselves remembered.

COMINIUS   Should they* not,
Well might they fester 'gainst ingratitude,   30
And tent themselves with death. Of all the horses,
Whereof we have ta'en good and good store,* of all
The treasure in this field achieved and city,*
We render* you the tenth, to be ta'en forth
Before the common distribution,   35
At your only choice.

MARTIUS   I thank you, general,
But cannot make my heart consent to take
A bribe to pay my sword. I do refuse it,
And stand upon* my common part with those
That have beheld the doing.   40

*A long flourish. They all cry 'Martius! Martius!' cast up
their caps and lances. COMINIUS and LARTIUS stand bare-
headed.**

May these* same instruments, which you profane,
Never sound more. When drums and trumpets shall
I' th' field prove flatterers, let courts and cities be
Made all of false-faced soothing. When steel grows
Soft as the parasite's silk, let him be made   45
An overture for the wars. No more I say!
For that* I have not washed my nose that bled,
Or foiled* some debile wretch, which without note*
Here's many else have done, you shout* me forth
In acclamations hyperbolical,   50
As if I loved my little should be dieted
In praises sauced with lies.

54   *give:* report.
54   *By your patience:* With your permission.
56   *means his proper harm:* intends to injure himself.
59   *garland:* the oak wreath. – See note to I.i.170 and I.iii.14.
59   *the which:* which.
61   *his trim belonging:* either (a) the equipment that goes with it, or (b) its fine trappings.
63   *host:* army.
64   *Caius Martius Coriolanus – Caius* is the *praenomen,* peculiar to the individual, similar to the modern Christian name; *Martius* is the *nomen gentilicium* or family name; Coriolanus (meaning 'of Corioli') the *agnomen* or honorary title. As Plutarch tells us, 'The third [name] was some addition given, either for some act or notable service . . . or else for some special virtue they had.'
65   *addition:* title.
68   *fair:* clean.
68   *you shall . . . no –* He means that he *is* blushing.
69   *Howbeit:* However.
70   *stride:* bestride.
71   *undercrest . . . my power:* take as my crest the honourable title you have given me and live up to it to the best of my ability. – *Undercrest,* a word not found elsewhere, probably means 'support', as one would a crest or heraldic device on one's coat-of-arms or helmet.
72   *to our tent:* let us go to my tent.
73   *ere we do repose us:* before we sleep.
76   *The best –* i.e. the leading citizens of Corioli.
76   *articulate:* negotiate articles of peace.
78   *now:* just now.
81   *sometime lay:* once stayed.
82   *used:* treated.
83   *cried to me:* begged me for help.
83   *saw him prisoner:* saw him taken prisoner.
87   *were he the butcher of:* even if he had killed.
88   *Deliver him:* Set him free.

COMINIUS   Too modest are you;
          More cruel to your good report than grateful
          To us that give* you truly. By your patience,*
          If 'gainst yourself you be incensed, we'll put you,   55
          Like one that means his proper harm,* in manacles,
          Then reason safely with you. Therefore be it known,
          As to us, to all the world, that Caius Martius
          Wears this war's garland;* in token of the which,*
          My noble steed, known to the camp, I give him,   60
          With all his trim belonging;* and from this time,
          For what he did before Corioli, call him,
          With all th' applause and clamour of the host,*
          Caius Martius Coriolanus.*
          Bear the addition* nobly ever!   65
                              [*Flourish. Trumpets and drums sound*
ALL   Caius Martius Coriolanus!
CORIOLANUS I will go wash.
          And when my face is fair,* you shall* perceive
          Whether I blush or no. Howbeit,* I thank you.
          I mean to stride* your steed, and at all times   70
          To undercrest* your good addition
          To th' fairness of my power.
COMINIUS   So, to our tent,*
          Where, ere we do repose us,* we will write
          To Rome of our success. You, Titus Lartius,
          Must to Corioli back. Send us to Rome   75
          The best* with whom we may articulate*
          For their own good and ours.
LARTIUS   I shall, my lord.
CORIOLANUS The gods begin to mock me. I, that now*
          Refused most princely gifts, am bound to beg
          Of my lord general.
COMINIUS   Take't, 'tis yours. What is't?   80
CORIOLANUS I sometime lay* here in Corioli
          At a poor man's house; he used* me kindly.
          He cried to me;* I saw him prisoner,*
          But then Aufidius was within my view,
          And wrath o'erwhelmed my pity. I request you   85
          To give my poor host freedom.
COMINIUS   O, well begged!
          Were he the butcher of* my son he should
          Be free as is the wind. Deliver him,* Titus.

89   *forgot:* I have forgotten it.
92   *visage:* face.
93   *looked to:* attended to.

I.x.   Aufidius is embittered by his fifth defeat at the hands of Coriolanus and vows to get
        revenge by fair means or foul.
        Aufidius's reaction here is a careful preparation by the dramatist for his later behaviour,
        and is introduced at the very moment of Coriolanus's triumph, sounding a note of fore-
        boding.

S.D.   *Cornets* – trumpet-like wind instruments.
2   *delivered back on good condition:* given back to us on favourable terms.
3   *Condition:* State. – In his bitterness Aufidius goes on to play with other meanings of the
        word at line 5 where it means 'quality' and line 6 where it means both 'quality'
        and 'terms'.
4   *I cannot . . . I am* – i.e. being a Volscian, and thus a defeated man, he cannot be what
        he feels he is, an unconquerable spirit.
6   *can a treaty . . . mercy:* can a treaty discover in the losing side, i.e. one who is beaten, in
        Aufidius's view, is dishonoured.
8   *so often:* just as often.
10   *th' elements* – i.e. the four elements which were thought to make up the physical universe,
        namely, earth, water, air and fire. Aufidius is swearing by all that there is.
11   *e'er:* ever.
12   *He's mine, or I am his:* we will fight to the death of one or the other of us.
12   *Mine emulation . . . it had:* My rivalry with Coriolanus is less honourable than it was. –
        Aufidius is aware of a deterioration in his character.
13   *where/I thought . . . force:* whereas I intended to overcome him on equal terms.
15   *potch:* poke, stab at. – The mean, unheroic verb reflects the deterioration in Aufidius.
16   *Or wrath or craft:* so that either anger or cunning.
17   *subtle:* crafty.
18   *With only . . . him:* merely through being eclipsed.
18   *for him . . . itself:* will change its true nature because of him, i.e. become debased.
19   *Nor . . . nor:* neither . . . nor.
19   *sanctuary:* the protection offered by a church or other sacred place.
20   *naked:* unarmed.
20   *fane:* temple.

LARTIUS   Martius, his name?
CORIOLANUS   By Jupiter, forgot!*
     I am weary; yea, my memory is tired.   90
     Have we no wine here?
COMINIUS   Go we to our tent.
     The blood upon your visage* dries; 'tis time
     It should be looked to.* Come.

                                                          [*Exeunt*

scene x

The camp of the Volsces.

A flourish. Cornets. *Enter* TULLUS AUFIDIUS, *bloody, with
two or three* SOLDIERS.

AUFIDIUS   The town is ta'en.
FIRST SOLDIER   'Twill be delivered back on good condition.*
AUFIDIUS   Condition?*
     I would I were a Roman, for I cannot,*
     Being a Volsce, be that I am. Condition?   5
     What good condition can a treaty* find
     I' th' part that is at mercy? Five times, Martius,
     I have fought with thee; so often* hast thou beat me,
     And wouldst do so, I think, should we encounter
     As often as we eat. By th' elements,*   10
     If e'er* again I meet him beard to beard,
     He's mine, or I am his.* Mine emulation*
     Hath not that honour in't it had, for where
     I thought* to crush him in an equal force,
     True sword to sword, I'll potch* at him some way,   15
     Or wrath or craft* may get him.
FIRST SOLDIER   He's the devil.
AUFIDIUS   Bolder, though not so subtle.* My valour's poisoned
     With only* suffering stain by him; for him*
     Shall fly out of itself. Nor* sleep, nor sanctuary,*
     Being naked,* sick, nor fane,* nor Capitol,   20
     The prayers of priests, nor times of sacrifice,

[handwritten margin note beside lines 10–15] Aufidius has decided that he can't beat Coriolanus in a fair fight, so he'll kill Coriolanus any way possible.

22   *Embarquements all of fury:* all things which prohibit anger.
22   *lift up:* support, exert.
23   *rotten:* worn out through age. – That Aufidius should describe things which normal men
              regard as humane restraints as *rotten privileges* is a telling indication of his
              moral corruption at this point in the play.
24   *were it:* even if it were.
25   *upon my brother's guard:* under my brother's protection.
26   *the hospitable canon:* the law of hospitality (which forbids the ill-treatment of guests).
27   *Wash . . . in's heart* – i.e. dip it in Coriolanus's heart's-blood.
28   *how:* with how great a force.
28   *what:* who.
30   *attended:* awaited.
31   *south:* south of.
32   *How the world . . . journey:* what is going on so that I may adapt my action accordingly.

Embarquements all of fury,* shall lift up*
Their rotten* privilege and custom 'gainst
My hate to Martius. Where I find him, were it*
At home, upon my brother's guard,* even there,   25
See notes.   ← Against the hospitable canon,* would I
Wash* my fierce hand in's heart. Go you to th' city,
Learn how* 'tis held, and what* they are that must
Be hostages for Rome.

FIRST SOLDIER   Will not you go?

AUFIDIUS I am attended* at the cypress grove. I pray you –   30
'Tis south* the city mills – bring me word thither
How the world* goes, that to the pace of it
I may spur on my journey.

FIRST SOLDIER   I shall, sir.
                                                    [*Exeunt*

The Senators of Rome offering Coriolanus the Consulship (Act II, Scene ii).

Coriolanus trying to obtain support from a citizen for his Consulship (Act II, Scene iii).

II.i.   The scene opens with a conversation between Menenius and the tribunes which rapidly
         becomes an exchange of insults. Menenius accuses them of the same vice of pride for
         which they censure Coriolanus. Volumnia, entering with Virgilia and Valeria, announces
         the imminent return of her son, and she and Menenius discuss his former exploits until
         he arrives, preceded by a herald who proclaims his new title, 'Coriolanus'. Coriolanus
         tries to silence the acclamations of the Romans, greets his women folk, and leaves with
         them to pay his respects to the patricians. The tribunes, alone on-stage, describe the
         joyous welcome which the Romans have given him. They are aware that their power will
         be threatened if he becomes Consul, but they believe that his intemperate nature will
         arouse the hostility of the plebeians, and resolve to do all they can to kindle this
         antagonism.

         With the war scenes now over, the play moves into its second phase, that of the struggle
         for political power. Coriolanus, whose epic dimensions have been enhanced by the
         narration of his past deeds of heroism and by the tumultuous welcome given him by the
         whole of Rome, appears triumphant. Ironically, however, at this very moment of glory
         there are signs of trouble. We are made slightly uneasy by the tears of Virgilia at his
         return and by Menenius's confession, 'I am light and heavy', but much more so by
         Coriolanus's assertion that he would rather be Rome's servant in his own way than her
         master in anyone else's, and in the implacable envy of the tribunes, ready to exploit the
         slightest opportunity to turn the people against him. The exchanges between Menenius
         and the tribunes introduce a comic note, but this is muted and restrained, as we are
         uneasily aware that Menenius's mockery of them, although amusing, is the expression of
         a profound difference of outlook which is fundamentally serious and tragic in its implica-
         tions. The splendidly graphic description by Brutus of Coriolanus's triumphal entry into
         Rome serves the useful double function of conveying events which Shakespeare could
         not convincingly display on the Elizabethan stage, and of revealing the envy at the root
         of Brutus's character.

1   *The augurer* was a Roman religious official who by observing and interpreting natural
                  phenomena such as the actions of birds and the entrails of animals claimed to
                  foretell events.
5   *Nature . . . The lamb* – Shakespeare appears to have derived this passage from the Bible:
                  'Every beast loveth his like [other beasts of the same kind] . . . What fellowship
                  hath [friendship has] the wolf with the lamb?' *Ecclesiasticus* (Apocrypha)
                  13:15–17.
8   *Ay:* Yes.
10   *baas like a bear* – Brutus ironically dismisses Menenius's comparison of Coriolanus to a
                  lamb. In Brutus's view he is more like a bear.
14   *In what . . . abundance:* What fault is there in a small amount in Martius that is not present
                  in your two selves in a very large amount?
16   *stored with all:* has all faults in abundance.
18   *topping:* surpassing.
20   *censured:* considered. – Cf. I.i.254.
20   *of us o' the right-hand file:* by us of the upper class. – The term is a military one. When a
                  body of troops is drawn up in line, the right-hand file, which leads the column
                  on the march, is composed of the tallest and smartest soldiers.
24   *Well, well* – i.e. Well, let us hear what you have to say.
25   *'tis no great . . . patience:* it doesn't matter much if I do make you angry; I might as well
                  speak plainly since it takes very little to make you lose your patience.
26   *Give your dispositions the reins:* Let your inclinations have free play, i.e. react how you
                  wish.
27   *at your pleasures:* if you wish.
32   *grow wondrous single:* be remarkably (a) weak (b) solitary.
33   *infant-like:* feeble.

ACT II scene i

A street in Rome.

Enter MENENIUS *with the two* TRIBUNES *of the people,* SICINIUS *and* BRUTUS.

MENENIUS The augurer* tells me we shall have news tonight.
BRUTUS Good or bad?
MENENIUS Not according to the prayer of the people, for they love not Martius.
SICINIUS Nature* teaches beasts to know their friends.   5
MENENIUS Pray you, who does the wolf love?
SICINIUS The lamb.
MENENIUS Ay,* to devour him, as the hungry plebeians would the noble Martius.
BRUTUS He's a lamb indeed, that baas like a bear.*   10
MENENIUS He's a bear indeed, that lives like a lamb. You two are old men: tell me one thing that I shall ask you.
BOTH Well, sir?
MENENIUS In what enormity is Martius poor in, that you two have not in abundance?*   15
BRUTUS He's poor in no one fault, but stored with all.*
SICINIUS Especially in pride.
BRUTUS And topping* all others in boasting.
MENENIUS This is strange now. Do you two know how you are censured* here in the city – I mean of us o' the right-hand   20
file?* Do you?
BOTH Why, how are we censured?
MENENIUS Because you talk of pride now. Will you not be angry?
BOTH Well, well,* sir, well.
MENENIUS Why 'tis no great* matter; for a very little thief of occasion   25
will rob you of a great deal of patience. Give your dispositions the reins,* and be angry at your pleasures;* at the least, if you take it as a pleasure to you in being so. You blame Martius for being proud?
BRUTUS We do it not alone, sir.   30
MENENIUS I know you can do very little alone, for your helps are many, or else your actions would grow wondrous single.* Your abilities are too infant-like* for doing much

53

34   *turn your eyes . . . necks* – i.e. look at yourselves objectively.

38   *brace:* couple.

38   *unmeriting:* undeserving.

39   *testy:* bad-tempered.

39   *alias fools:* in other words, fools. – Magistrates in Shakespeare's plays are frequently represented as foolish men, which may reflect either a social reality of his day, or simply his personal prejudice.

41   *known well enough:* notorious.

42   *humorous:* whimsical. – Elizabethans believed man to be composed of the four elements (see note to I.x.10). If these were disproportionately mixed a *humorous* man resulted – either sanguine, choleric, melancholic or phlegmatic; if well mixed the result was a balanced personality. The modern meaning of *humorous* as 'amusing' is a later development.

43   *hot wine* – This was a favourite drink in Shakespeare's time, commonly known as mulled wine. It was spiced with various seasonings.

43   *a drop of allaying Tiber:* any water from the Tiber diluting it. – Water was often added to wine to weaken it. The Tiber is the river on which Rome stands.

44   *something imperfect . . . complaint:* somewhat at fault in favouring the complainant (or plaintiff) in legal cases, i.e. ignoring or neglecting the case of the defendant, presumably in order to get the hearing over quickly.

45   *tinder-like . . . motion:* apt to flare up without sufficient reason.

46   *one that converses . . . morning:* one who sees more of the latter part (*buttock:* backside) of the night than of the first part (*forehead:* forehead) of the day. – Menenius means that he is more accustomed to going to bed late than getting up early.

48   *spend my malice in my breath:* when I have spoken, my ill-will is at an end. – Menenius does not bear grudges.

49   *wealsmen:* men devoted to the common good. – Menenius, of course, speaks ironically.

50   *Lycurguses* – i.e. wise legislators. Lycurgus was the traditional founder of the constitution, social and military systems of ancient Sparta. Plutarch praises his wisdom as a lawgiver.

50   *touch . . . adversely:* tastes nasty, I screw up my face – i.e. if I don't like what you say, my face shows it.

52   *delivered:* stated your case (against Coriolanus).

53   *ass in compound . . . syllables:* most of what you say is foolish.

54   *bear with:* put up with.

55   *reverend grave:* worthy of respect and serious. – Cf. II.ii.39.

55   *deadly:* grievously.

56   *tell:* say.

56   *see this . . . microcosm:* discern all these thoughts in my face. – His face is to his body (*microcosm*) what a map is to the world, or *macrocosm*. Just as a map of the world (or *macrocosm*) gives its details in miniature, so the face reflects the thoughts of the whole man (*microcosm*).

58   *bisson conspectuities:* blind insights. – Menenius is trying to blind them with high-sounding but self-contradictory terms. *Conspectuities* is a word he coins himself.

59   *glean out of this character:* deduce from this character-sketch.

63   *ambitious for . . . legs:* anxious to have poor men take off their caps and kneel out of respect for you. – Both actions were customary in the presence of a superior. Cf. I.ix.40 and II.ii.24. In this whole speech (lines 65–76) Shakespeare presents a satirical picture of the incompetent magistrate so common in his day, a picture which, if we are to judge by the frequency of such attacks in the drama of the time, the audience evidently enjoyed.

64   *wear out . . . forenoon:* waste a perfectly good morning.

64   *cause:* legal case.

65   *an orange-wife and a faucet-seller:* a woman orange-seller and a seller of taps for barrels. – Such occupations, which brought in a very small income, ranked very low on the social scale.

65   *rejourn the controversy of threepence:* adjourn a quarrel over threepence.

66   *audience:* hearing.

67   *party and party:* two disputing parties.

     alone. You talk of pride. O that you could turn your eyes*
     toward the napes of your necks, and make but an interior 35
     survey of your good selves! O that you could!
BOTH What then, sir?
MENENIUS Why then you should discover a brace* of unmeriting,*
     proud, violent, testy* magistrates, alias fools,* as any in
     Rome. 40
SICINIUS Menenius, you are known well enough* too.
MENENIUS I am known to be a humorous* patrician, and one that
     loves a cup of hot wine,* with not a drop of allaying
     Tiber* in't; said to be something imperfect* in favouring
     the first complaint, hasty and tinder-like* upon too trivial 45
     motion; one that converses* more with the buttock of the
     night than with the forehead of the morning. What I
     think, I utter, and spend my malice in my breath.* Meet-
     ing two such wealsmen* as you are – I cannot call you
     Lycurguses* – if the drink you give me touch* my palate 50
     adversely, I make a crooked face at it. I cannot say your
     worships have delivered* the matter well, when I find
     the ass in compound* with the major part of your syl-
     lables. And though I must be content to bear with* those
     that say you are reverend grave* men, yet they lie deadly* 55
     that tell* you you have good faces. If you see this* in the
     map of my microcosm, follows it that I am known well
     enough too? What harm can your bisson conspectuities*
     glean out of this character,* if I be known well enough
     too? 60
BRUTUS Come, sir, come, we know you well enough.
MENENIUS You know neither me, yourselves, nor anything. You are
     ambitious for* poor knaves' caps and legs. You wear out* a
     good wholesome forenoon in hearing a cause* between an
     orange-wife and a faucet-seller,* and then rejourn the 65
     controversy of threepence* to a second day of audience.*
     When you are hearing a matter between party and party,*

68   *pinched with the colic:* gripped by stomach-ache.

68   *faces like mummers* – Mummers, who mimed or acted in dumb show, had to convey their meaning largely by facial expressions.

69   *set up . . . patience* – i.e. declare war on patience. A red flag was the standard of war in Elizabethan times.

71   *bleeding* – i.e. without curing the *controversy.*

71   *the more entangled by your hearing:* made more complicated by your handling of the case.

74   *a perfecter giber . . . Capitol:* better as a witty conversationalist at a meal than an indispensable member of the Senate.

77   *Our very priests:* Our priests themselves.

77   *become mockers:* stop being serious (as befits priests) and start mocking.

78   *subjects:* (a) citizens (b) subjects for discussion.

78   *When . . . purpose:* Even when you are talking most sense.

81   *a grave:* an end.

81   *a botcher's cushion:* the cushion on which a mender of old clothes sat.

82   *must be saying:* keep saying.

83   *in a cheap estimation:* even at a low valuation.

84   *since Deucalion:* since the Flood. – Deucalion, forewarned by his father, Prometheus, escaped a world-wide flood sent by the angry Jupiter to punish man, by building a boat which landed on Mount Parnassus when the waters subsided. He repeopled the earth by throwing on the ground stones which turned into men.

85   *peradventure:* probably.

85   *hereditary hangmen* – The office of hangman in Shakespeare's day (as down to the present century) was frequently handed on from father to son.

86   *God-den* – a contraction of 'God give you good evening'. It was used any time after midday.

87   *being:* since you are.

88   *beastly:* cattle-like.

90   *How now:* Hallo. – This phrase, common in Shakespeare's day, had no very precise meaning.

90   *the moon:* i.e. Diana. See note to I.i.243.

91   *follow your eyes so fast:* Either (a) look so eagerly, or (b) move so quickly.

94   *Juno* – wife of Jupiter. She was the protectress of women and also a moon goddess, so that Volumnia's mention of her might have been suggested by Menenius's reference to the *moon* at line 90.

96   *most prosperous approbation:* the greatest success, which has been confirmed.

98   *Jupiter* was, among other things, the god of the sky. Menenius aptly names him here after Volumnia's *Juno* (line 94), throwing his cap into Jupiter's element, the air.

98   *Hoo:* Hooray.

100   *Nay:* Indeed.

101   *the state* – i.e. the Senate.

103   *reel:* go round. – Menenius intends to get drunk in celebration of Coriolanus's return.

if you chance to be pinched with the colic,* you make faces
like mummers,* set up* the bloody flag against all patience,
and in roaring for a chamber-pot, dismiss the controversy   70
bleeding,* the more entangled by your hearing.* All the
peace you make in their cause is calling both the parties
knave. You are a pair of strange ones.

BRUTUS   Come, come, you are well understood to be a perfecter
           giber* for the table than a necessary bencher in the   75
           Capitol.

MENENIUS   Our very priests* must become mockers* if they shall
           encounter such ridiculous subjects* as you are. When*
           you speak best unto the purpose, it is not worth the
           wagging of your beards, and your beards deserve not so   80
           honourable a grave* as to stuff a botcher's cushion,* or to
           be entombed in an ass's pack-saddle. Yet you must be
           saying* Martius is proud; who, in a cheap estimation,* is
           worth all your predecessors since Deucalion,* though
           peradventure* some of the best of 'em were hereditary   85
           hangmen.* God-den* to your worships. More of your
           conversation would infect my brain, being* the herdsmen
           of the beastly* plebeians. I will be bold to take my leave of
           you.

                              [BRUTUS *and* SICINIUS *move to one side*

           Enter VOLUMNIA, VIRGILIA, *and* VALERIA.

           How now,* my as fair as noble ladies – and the moon,*   90
           were she earthly, no nobler – whither do you follow your
           eyes so fast?*

VOLUMNIA   Honourable Menenius, my boy Martius approaches. For
           the love of Juno,* let's go.

MENENIUS   Ha? Martius coming home?   95

VOLUMNIA   Ay, worthy Menenius, and with most prosperous
           approbation.*

MENENIUS   Take my cap, Jupiter,* and I thank thee. Hoo!* Martius
           coming home!

VIRGILIA ⎫
  and   ⎬ Nay,* 'tis true.   100
VALERIA ⎭

VOLUMNIA   Look, here's a letter from him; the state* hath another, his
           wife another, and, I think, there's one at home for you.

MENENIUS   I will make my very house reel* tonight. A letter for me?

VIRGILIA   Yes, certain, there's a letter for you; I saw't.

105	*gives me an estate of:* endows me with an extra lease of life.
106	*make a lip at the physician:* sneer at the doctor, i.e. have nothing to do with him.
107	*sovereign:* excellent.
107	*Galen* (A.D. 129–199) was a famous Greek physician and prolific writer on medicine. He lived for a time in Rome, but several centuries later than the events of the play.
108	*empiricutic:* empirical, i.e. based on observation rather than on principle, and hence unreliable, quackish. – This is another of Menenius's coinages.
108	*to this preservative:* compared to this preservative of life and health, i.e. the news of Coriolanus's success and return.
108	*of no better . . . drench:* of as little value as a dose of medicine for a horse.
109	*wont:* accustomed. – Menenius's gallantry gives way to tactlessness as he mentions Coriolanus's wounds in Virgilia's presence.
113	*Brings:* Does he bring.
114	*become:* suit, are fitting for.
115	*On's brows:* On his brows. – Volumnia answers Menenius's question about Coriolanus bringing *a victory in his pocket*. Rather, she replies, he brings one marked by the garland of oak leaves on his head.
117	*disciplined:* thrashed.
119	*got off:* escaped.
120	*warrant him:* assure him of.
120	*And:* If.
121	*fidiused* – i.e. treated as Aufidius was by Coriolanus. – Menenius coins another word, playing on Aufidius's name.
123	*possessed:* informed.
125	*the whole name of the war:* all the credit for victory.
128	*troth:* truth.
128	*wondrous:* wonderful.
128	*spoke:* spoken.
129	*true purchasing:* really earning them.
132	*Pow waw* – equivalent to the modern 'pooh-pooh'. Volumnia scornfully dismisses the idea that the reports of Coriolanus's exploits are untrue.
135	*more cause to be proud* – Menenius taunts the tribunes by alluding to their earlier complaints about Coriolanus's pride (lines 17f above).
138	*cicatrices . . . people:* scars to show the people. – This is the first mention of this Roman custom which is to play such an important part in the development of the action.
139	*stand for his place:* stand for election as consul.
139	*Tarquin* – Tarquinius Superbus, the last of the seven kings of Rome, who murdered his predecessor in 534 B.C. and abolished the rights conferred on the plebeians. He was expelled and defeated at Lake Regillus in 496 B.C., and the monarchy was abolished.
145	*Every gash was an enemy's grave:* Every wound he received cost the life of one of the enemy.

MENENIUS   A letter for me? It gives me an estate of* seven years'   105
            health; in which time I will make a lip at the physician.*
            The most sovereign* prescription in Galen* is but empiri-
            cutic,* and, to this preservative,* of no better* report than
            a horse-drench. Is he not wounded? He was wont* to
            come home wounded. *wants* *His mother, volun.*   110

VIRGILIA   O no, no, no.   *of glory, live to leave with*

VOLUMNIA   O, he is wounded; I thank the gods for't.

MENENIUS   So do I too, if it be not too much. Brings* a victory in his
            pocket? The wounds become* him.

VOLUMNIA   On's brows,* Menenius. He comes the third time home   115
            with the oaken garland.

MENENIUS   Has he disciplined* Aufidius soundly?

VOLUMNIA   Titus Lartius writes they fought together, but Aufidius
            got off.*

MENENIUS   And 'twas time for him too, I'll warrant him* that. And* he   120
            had stayed by him, I would not have been so fidiused* for
            all the chests in Corioli, and the gold that's in them. Is the
            Senate possessed* of this?

VOLUMNIA   Good ladies, let's go. Yes, yes, yes. The Senate has letters
            from the general, wherein he gives my son the whole name   125
            of the war.* He hath in this action outdone his former
            deeds doubly.

VALERIA   In troth,* there's wondrous* things spoke* of him.

MENENIUS   Wondrous? Ay, I warrant you, and not without his true
            purchasing.*   130

VIRGILIA   The gods grant them true.

VOLUMNIA   True? Pow waw!*

MENENIUS   True? I'll be sworn they are true. Where is he wounded?
            [*To the* TRIBUNES] God save your good worships! Martius
            is coming home. He has more cause to be proud.* – Where   135
            is he wounded?

VOLUMNIA   I' the shoulder, and i' the left arm. There will be large
            cicatrices* to show the people, when he shall stand for his
            place.* He received in the repulse of Tarquin* seven hurts
            i' the body.   140

MENENIUS   One i' the neck, and two i' the thigh – there's nine that I
            know.

VOLUMNIA   He had, before this last expedition, twenty-five wounds
            upon him.

MENENIUS   Now it's twenty-seven. Every gash was an enemy's grave.*   145
            [*A shout and flourish*

147	*ushers:* heralds, announcers. – See note to I.iii.45.
147	*Before him he carries noise:* He brings music (noise) in front of him.
148	*tears* – i.e. those of the Volsces and inhabitants of Corioli.
149	*in's:* in his.
149	*nervy:* muscular.
150	*being advanced, declines:* having been raised, descends.
150	S.D. *A sennet* was a set of notes for trumpet or cornet to herald the processional entrance or exit of persons of high rank, differing from a flourish or fanfare.

        In having Titus Lartius enter here, Shakespeare apparently made a mistake since he was ordered to return to Corioli at I.ix.75 and is still there at II.ii.35 when Menenius suggests that he be sent for.

153	*With fame, a name to:* along with fame, a name in addition to.
153	*these/In honour follows Coriolanus:* the name of Coriolanus comes after these names as a title of honour. See note to I.ix.64.
159	*petitioned . . . prosperity:* prayed to all the gods for my success.
160	S.D. *Kneels* – It was the custom in Shakespeare's time for a son to kneel and receive his parents' blessing when greeting or leaving them.
162	*deed-achieving honour:* honour acquired by great deeds.
164	*My gracious silence* – He refers to Virgilia who is silent and weeping.
168	*lack sons* – i.e. have lost them in battle.
168	*crown:* reward.
169	*live you yet:* are you still living. – This is said jocularly.
169	*pardon* – Coriolanus begs Valeria's pardon for not noticing her before.
170	*I know not where to turn* – a sign of Volumnia's joy.
171	*y'are:* you are.
173	*light and heavy* – i.e. joyful and sad.
174	*on's:* of his.
175	*three* – i.e. Coriolanus, Cominius and Titus Lartius.
176	*dote on:* worship.
177	*old crab-trees* – He refers to the aged tribunes, Sicinius and Brutus. The fruit of the crab-apple tree is notoriously sour.

Hark, the trumpets!

VOLUMNIA These are the ushers* of Martius. Before him he carries
noise,* and behind him he leaves tears.*
Death, that dark spirit, in's* nervy* arm doth lie,
Which being advanced, declines,* and then men die.   150

A sennet. Trumpets sound. Enter* COMINIUS *and* LARTIUS,
and between them CORIOLANUS, *crowned with an oaken
garland, with* CAPTAINS, SOLDIERS *and a* HERALD.

HERALD Know, Rome, that all alone Martius did fight
Within Corioli gates, where he hath won,
With fame, a name to* Caius Martius; these
In honour follows Coriolanus.*
Welcome to Rome, renownèd Coriolanus!   155

[*Flourish*

ALL Welcome to Rome, renownèd Coriolanus!
CORIOLANUS No more of this, it does offend my heart.
Pray now, no more.
COMINIUS   Look, sir, your mother.
CORIOLANUS   O,
You have, I know, petitioned* all the gods
For my prosperity.   [*Kneels*
VOLUMNIA   Nay, my good soldier, up.   160
My gentle Martius, worthy Caius, and
By deed-achieving honour* newly named –
What is it? – Coriolanus must I call thee? –
But, O, thy wife!
CORIOLANUS   My gracious silence,* hail!
Wouldst thou have laughed had I come coffined home,   165
That weep'st to see me triumph? Ay, my dear,
Such eyes the widows in Corioli wear,
And mothers that lack sons.*
MENENIUS   Now the gods crown* thee!
CORIOLANUS And live you yet?* [*To* VALERIA] O my sweet lady, pardon.*
VOLUMNIA I know not where to turn.* O, welcome home!   170
And welcome, general; and y'are* welcome all.
MENENIUS A hundred thousand welcomes. I could weep,
And I could laugh: I am light and heavy.* Welcome.
A curse begin at very root on's* heart
That is not glad to see thee! You are three*   175
That Rome should dote on.* Yet, by the faith of men,
We've some old crab-trees* here at home that will not

178 *grafted to your relish*: improved so as to bear fruit to your taste. – Grafting is the process of inserting into a fruit tree a shoot from another stock to produce a new variety.

179 *We call . . . but folly* – This is Menenius's way of saying that the tribunes can't help being troublesome fools.

180 *Ever right*: Right as always.

181 *Menenius, ever, ever*: The same old Menenius.

182 *Give way there* – The Herald orders the crowd to make way for the procession to move on.

184 *shade my head*: take shelter, i.e. enter.

187 *change of honours*: fresh honours.

188 *inherited*: in your possession. – Coriolanus, she says, has inherited all she has wished him to be endowed with.

188 *very*: exact..

189 *buildings of my fancy*: completion of what I have imagined. – *Buildings* continues the metaphor of the inheritance of property.

190 *one thing* – i.e. the consulship.

191 *cast*: confer.

192 *their servant in my way* – i.e. as a soldier, in my own fashion.

193 *sway with them in theirs*: rule as consul over them in the way they want.

194 *bleared sights/Are spectacled*: people with poor eyesight have put on spectacles. – Another anachronism, since spectacles date from the thirteenth century.

195 *Your prattling nurse*: The talkative nurse.

196 *rapture*: fit, paroxysm.

197 *chats him*: gossips about Coriolanus.

197 *malkin*: wench.

198 *Her richest . . . neck*: her best linen around her dirty neck. – *Lockram* was a loosely-woven hempen fabric used by the lower classes.

199 *bulks* – flat projecting frameworks or counters in front of shops.

200 *smothered up*: filled with people.

200 *leads*: roofs covered with lead.

200 *ridges horsed . . . complexions*: people of all types sit astride the tops of the roofs (as if on horseback).

201 *agreeing/In earnestness*: equally keen.

202 *Seld-shown flamens*: Priests rarely seen in public. – A *flamen* was a Roman priest attached to a temple and devoted to the service of a particular god. One of his tasks was to blow the flames of offerings to the gods, hence the name from the Latin *flamen*, a blowing.

203 *popular throngs*: crowds of people.

203 *puff . . . vulgar station*: get out of breath trying to obtain a good place among the commoners. – Flamens were usually patricians and lived a life withdrawn from society.

204 *Our veiled . . . kisses*: Our ladies, who normally protect themselves with veils, abandon their skilfully made-up (*nicely gauded*) cheeks to the unrestrained ravages (*wanton spoils*) of the burning sun (*Phoebus*). – *Damask*: red (from the Damascus rose). They are so eager to get a good look at Coriolanus that they remove their veils. Elizabethan ladies considered it a blemish to be sunburnt.

207 *pother*: commotion.

208 *As if . . . graceful posture*: as if Coriolanus's guardian deity had stealthily inhabited his body and given him a divine bearing.

210 *On the sudden . . . consul*: I guarantee he will quickly be made consul.

Be grafted to your relish.* Yet welcome, warriors.
We call* a nettle but a nettle, and
The faults of fools but folly.

COMINIUS   Ever right.*   180
CORIOLANUS Menenius, ever, ever.*
HERALD Give way there,* and go on.
CORIOLANUS [To VOLUMNIA and VIRGILIA] Your hand, and yours.
Ere in our own house I do shade my head,*
The good patricians must be visited,   185
From whom I have received not only greetings,
But with them change of honours.*

VOLUMNIA   I have lived
To see inherited* my very* wishes
And the buildings of my fancy.* Only
There's one thing* wanting, which I doubt not but   190
Our Rome will cast* upon thee.

CORIOLANUS   Know, good mother,
I had rather be their servant in my way*
Than sway with them in theirs.*

COMINIUS   On, to the Capitol.
[Flourish. Cornets. Exeunt in state

BRUTUS and SICINIUS come forward.

BRUTUS All tongues speak of him, and the blearèd sights
Are spectacled* to see him. Your prattling nurse*   195
Into a rapture* lets her baby cry
While she chats him;* the kitchen malkin* pins
Her richest* lockram 'bout her reechy neck,
Clamb'ring the walls to eye him. Stalls, bulks,* windows,
Are smothered up,* leads* filled and ridges horsed*   200
With variable complexions, all agreeing
In earnestness* to see him. Seld-shown flamens*
Do press among the popular throngs,* and puff*
To win a vulgar station. Our veiled* dames
Commit the war of white and damask in   205
Their nicely gauded cheeks to th'wanton spoil
Of Phoebus' burning kisses. Such a pother,*
As if* that whatsoever god who leads him
Were slyly crept into his human powers,
And gave him graceful posture.

SICINIUS   On the sudden*.   210
I warrant him consul.

211   *Then our office . . . sleep* – Brutus foresees that if Coriolanus is made consul, the tribunes will become powerless.

213   *temp'rately transport . . . end:* sustain his honours in a moderate, self-controlled way. – The tribunes are comforted by the thought that Coriolanus's extremism will undermine him.

215   *Doubt not . . . but they:* Do not doubt that the commoners whom we represent.

217   *Upon their ancient malice:* because of their long-standing dislike of him.

218   *which/That . . . do it:* I have no doubt that he will be only too glad to give them cause to forget his recent honours. – *Which* refers to *the least cause. As:* as that. – They turn even Coriolanus's modesty into pride.

223   *napless vesture of humility:* threadbare, humble toga.

225   *beg their stinking breaths:* ask for the support of their voices. – Coriolanus's language, as reported by the tribunes, sounds authentic.

226   *he would . . . to him:* he would prefer not to have it rather than win it except (*but*) by the request of the patricians.

229   *hold that purpose . . . execution:* stick to that intention and act upon it.

230   *like:* likely. – Cf. note to I.i.178.

231   *as our good wills:* as our interest demands.

232   *So it must . . . end* – i.e. He must be destroyed, or our authority will be.

234   *suggest the people:* insinuate into the people's minds.

235   *still:* always.

235   *to's power . . . mules:* to increase his power he would have treated them like beasts of burden.

236   *their pleaders:* those who plead for them, i.e. the tribunes themselves.

237   *Dispropertied their freedoms:* dispossessed them of their rights.

237   *holding:* considering.

239   *soul:* intellectual power.

240   *in their war:* in a war.

240   *have their provand:* receive their food.

241   *sore:* severe.

243   *soaring insolence:* ambitious pride.

244   *touch:* inflame. – The Folio here has *teach* which most editors emend to *touch*, variously interpreting the word to mean 'touch to the quick', 'wound', 'irritate'. An established Elizabethan meaning of the word is 'to set light to', which fits well with *fire, kindle* and *blaze*, which follow. The image is a biblical echo from *Obadiah*, v.18, 'The house of Jacob will be a fire, and the house of Joseph a flame, and the house of Esau stubble; they shall burn them and consume them, and there shall be no survivor to the house of Esau.'

244   *which time shall not want:* and that time will come. – *Want:* be lacking.

BRUTUS   Then our office* may,
During his power, go sleep.

SICINIUS He cannot temp'rately transport* his honours
From where he should begin and end, but will
Lose those he hath won.

BRUTUS   In that there's comfort.

SICINIUS   Doubt not*   215
The commoners, for whom we stand, but they
Upon their ancient malice* will forget
With the least cause these his new honours, which
That* he will give them make I as little question
As he is proud to do it.

BRUTUS   I heard him swear,   220
Were he to stand for consul, never would he
Appear i' th' market-place, nor on him put
The napless vesture of humility,*
Nor, showing, as the manner is, his wounds
To th' people, beg their stinking breaths.*

SICINIUS   'Tis right.   225

BRUTUS It was his word. O, he would* miss it rather
Than carry it, but by the suit of the gentry to him,
And the desire of the nobles.

SICINIUS   I wish no better
Than have him hold that purpose* and to put it
In execution.

BRUTUS   'Tis most like* he will.   230

SICINIUS It shall be to him then as our good wills,*
A sure destruction.

BRUTUS   So it must* fall out
To him, or our authority's for an end.
We must suggest the people* in what hatred
Always ⟶ He still* hath held them; that to's power* he would   235
Have made them mules, silenced their pleaders* and
Dispropertied their freedoms;* holding* them,
In human action and capacity,
Of no more soul* nor fitness for the world
Than camels in their war,* who have their provand*   240
Only for bearing burdens, and sore* blows
For sinking under them.

SICINIUS   This, as you say, suggested
At some time when his soaring insolence*
Shall touch* the people – which time shall not want,*

245   *put upon't:* provoked to it.
245   *as easy . . . sheep* – Dogs are notorious sheep-worriers.
246   *will be* – i.e. *This* (line 249) will be.
247   *kindle:* set fire to. – The plebeians are seen as highly inflammable. When they burst into
         flame they will permanently eclipse (*darken*) Coriolanus. *Stubble:* stumps of
         grain left sticking up after harvesting.
248   *darken:* eclipse.
253   *scarfs:* neck ornaments.
253   *handkerchers:* handkerchiefs.
254   *bended:* bowed.
255   *Jove* – i.e. Jupiter, *Jove's* – i.e. Jupiter's. See note to I.iii.36.
256   *shower* – The messenger compares the mass of caps, thrown up and then descending, to a
         shower of rain, the shouts to thunder.
258   *carry with . . . event:* keep our ears and eyes open to what is happening now, but our
         minds fixed on our plans for the future.
259   *Have with you:* Let's go.

II.ii.   Two officials preparing the Senate House for the election of the consul analyse the
         character of Coriolanus. The senators enter, but Coriolanus who is unwilling to hear his
         praises sung leaves before Cominius begins his formal eulogy which spans the whole of
         Coriolanus's military career. He is recalled and offered the consulship, but pleads in vain
         to be excused the customary wearing of the toga of humility, the exhibition of his wounds
         and the request for the people's votes. When the senators have left the tribunes end the
         scene with their comments.
            The two Senate officials as neutral observers belonging to neither the patrician nor
         plebeian groups have the important dramatic function of providing an impartial assess-
         ment of Coriolanus for the guidance of the audience, somewhat in the manner of the
         Chorus in Greek tragedy. Shakespeare distinguishes the two individuals – the First
         Official being more critical of Coriolanus, the Second Official more admiring – but together
         their testimony is complete and authoritative. Coriolanus is characterized by them as
         worthy, brave and deserving honour from his country. He is approved for his hatred of
         flattery and his awareness of the mob's fickleness, but censured for his pride and his
         habit of going out of his way to incur the dislike of the plebeians, a 'noble carelessness'
         which is heading for trouble. The reliability of their diagnosis is immediately seen in his
         reaction to the customs mentioned above, which, he says, 'might well/Be taken from the
         people', a statement which the tribunes are only too ready to report to the people and
         use to overthrow his nomination for the consulship.

1   S.D. *to lay cushions* – i.e. for the Senators to sit on. This was an Elizabethan, not a Roman,
         custom. See note to III.i.101.
3   *of:* by.
4   *carry it:* win.
5   *vengeance:* excessively. – Cf. the modern phrase 'with a vengeance'.
7   *Faith:* Indeed.
7   *hath* – This use of the verb in the singular before a plural subject was common in the
         sixteenth century.
8   *who* – i.e. the *great men* (line 7).
9   *they* – i.e. the people (5 times in this sentence).
9   *wherefore:* why.
10   *they know . . . ground:* without knowing why, they will hate with no better reason.

If he be put upon't,* and that's as easy*   245
As to set dogs on sheep – will be* his fire
To kindle* their dry stubble; and their blaze
Shall darken* him for ever.

Enter a MESSENGER.

BRUTUS   What's the matter?
MESSENGER You are sent for to the Capitol. 'Tis thought
That Martius shall be consul.   250
I have seen the dumb men throng to see him, and
The blind to hear him speak. Matrons flung gloves,
Ladies and maids their scarfs* and handkerchers,*
Upon him as he passed. The nobles bended,*
As to Jove's* statue, and the commons made   255
A shower* and thunder with their caps and shouts.
I never saw the like.
BRUTUS   Let's to the Capitol,
And carry with* us ears and eyes for th' time,
But hearts for the event.
SICINIUS   Have with you.
                                                        [*Exeunt*

scene ii

Rome. The Senate House on the Capitol.

Enter two OFFICERS *to lay cushions.**

FIRST OFFICER Come, come, they are almost here. How many stand for
consulships?
SECOND OFFICER Three, they say; but 'tis thought of* everyone that
Coriolanus will carry it.*
FIRST OFFICER That's a brave fellow, but he's vengeance* proud, and   5
loves not the common people.
SECOND OFFICER Faith,* there hath* been many great men that have
flattered the people, who* ne'er loved them; and there be
many that they* have loved, they know not wherefore:*
so that if they love they know* not why, they hate upon   10
no better a ground. Therefore, for Coriolanus neither to

13	*in their disposition:* of their character.
14	*carelessness:* indifference (to their opinion).
16	*waved indifferently 'twixt:* he would waver neutrally between.
17	*devotion:* enthusiasm.
18	*render it him:* give it to him.
19	*discover him their opposite:* reveal that he is their opponent.
19	*seem to affect the malice:* appear to desire the ill-will.
22	*ascent is not:* rise to power has not been.
23	*degrees as those:* steps as that of those.
24	*supple:* compliant.
24	*bonneted:* took off their caps. – This custom used by power-seekers towards inferiors is one form of flattery which Coriolanus dislikes. Cf. note to II.i.63.
24	*without any . . . report:* without doing anything else at all to worm their way into (*have them*) the people's (*their*) esteem (*estimation*) and commendation.
28	*confess . . . injury:* admit it (his worthiness) would be (*were*) a kind of insult showing ingratitude.
29	*a malice:* an act of ill-will.
30	*giving itself the lie:* showing itself to be untrue.
30	*pluck reproof . . . heard it:* evoke the disagreement and censure of everyone who heard it.
33	S.D. *Sennet.* See note to II.i.150 S.D.
	Lictors – Roman officials who announced the approach of the magistrates, kept the streets clear for them, and carried out their punishments.
34	*determined of:* decided about.
36	*after-meeting:* follow-up to the main meeting.
37	*gratify:* reward.
37	*that:* who.
38	*stood for:* defended.
38	*please you:* may it please you. – Cf. line 58.
39	*reverend and grave* – Menenius used the phrase ironically when speaking to Sicinius and Brutus (II.i.55). He uses it now without irony.
40	*last general:* general in the last action, i.e. Cominius, who is also the *present consul* (line 40).
41	*well-found:* well-deserved.
44	*remember/With . . . himself:* distinguish with honours befitting his noble nature.
46	*for length:* because you think it would be too long to include.
47	*Rather . . . it out:* rather that Rome lacks the means to reward him than that we lack the will to make the reward greater.

care whether they love or hate him manifests the true
knowledge he has in their disposition,* and out of his
noble carelessness* lets them plainly see't.

FIRST OFFICER If he did not care whether he had their love or no, he   15
waved indifferently 'twixt* doing them neither good nor
harm. But he seeks their hate with greater devotion* than
they can render it him,* and leaves nothing undone that
may fully discover him their opposite.* Now, to seem to
affect the malice* and displeasure of the people is as bad as   20
that which he dislikes, to flatter them for their love.

SECOND OFFICER He hath deserved worthily of his country, and his ascent
is not* by such easy degrees as those* who, having been
supple* and courteous to the people, bonneted,* without
any* further deed to have them at all into their estimation   25
and report. But he hath so planted his honours in their
eyes, and his actions in their hearts, that for their tongues
to be silent and not confess* so much were* a kind of
ingrateful injury; to report otherwise were a malice* that,
giving itself the lie,* would pluck reproof* and rebuke   30
from every ear that heard it.

FIRST OFFICER No more of him; he's a worthy man. Make way, they are
coming.

Sennet. Enter the* PATRICIANS *and the* TRIBUNES, *with*
LICTORS* *before them,* CORIOLANUS, MENENIUS *and* COMI-
NIUS. SICINIUS *and* BRUTUS *stand apart.*

MENENIUS Having determined of* the Volsces, and
To send for Titus Lartius, it remains,   35
As the main point of this our after-meeting,*
To gratify* his noble service that*
Hath thus stood for* his country. Therefore, please you*
Most reverend and grave* elders, to desire
The present consul and last general*   40
In our well-found* successes to report
A little of that worthy work performed
By Caius Martius Coriolanus, whom
We met here both to thank and to remember
With* honours like himself.

FIRST SENATOR   Speak, good Cominius.   45
Leave nothing out for length,* and make us think
Rather* our state's defective for requital,
Than we to stretch it out.

49	*kindest ears:* very kind attention.
50	*loving motion toward:* kind influence with.
51	*yield what passes here:* approve what happens here (namely the nomination of Coriolanus to the consulship).
51	*are convented . . . treaty:* have come together to discuss a proposal pleasing to us.
53	*advance . . . assembly:* further the business for which we have met.
55	*blessed:* happy.
55	*remember/A kinder value of:* maintain a better opinion of.
57	*hereto prized:* previously valued.
57	*off:* off the point, irrelevant.
60	*pertinent:* to the point.
62	*tie him . . . bedfellow:* do not bind him to be their close friend.
64	*never shame:* do not be ashamed.
66	*have my wounds to heal again:* have to endure the pain of having my wounds heal again.
67	*hear say:* hear someone tell.
68	*disbenched you not:* did not cause you to leave your seat.
70	*soothed:* flattered.
71	*as they weigh:* according to their worth. – He means they are light, and thus worthless.
71	*Pray now, sit down* – Menenius hurriedly interrupts Coriolanus to prevent some tactless remark from him which will further alienate the tribunes.
72	*one scratch . . . sun* – Coriolanus paints a picture of what, for him, is extreme idleness.
73	*When the alarum were struck:* when the drums were sounded summoning men to battle.
74	*my nothings monstered:* my insignificant actions described as marvels.
75	*Your multiplying . . . flatter:* How can he flatter the rapidly multiplying plebeians you represent.
76	*That's . . . good one:* among whom there is only one good one in a thousand.

[*To the* TRIBUNES] Masters o' th' people,
We do request your kindest ears;* and, after,
Your loving motion toward* the common body,   50
To yield what passes here.*

SICINIUS   We are convented*
Upon a pleasing treaty, and have hearts
Inclinable to honour and advance*
The theme of our assembly.

BRUTUS   Which the rather
We shall be blessed* to do, if he remember   55
A kinder value of* the people than
He hath hereto prized* them at.

MENENIUS   That's off,* that's off.
I would you rather had been silent. Please you
To hear Cominius speak?

BRUTUS   Most willingly.
But yet my caution was more pertinent*   60
Than the rebuke you gave it.

MENENIUS   He loves your people,
But tie him* not to be their bedfellow.
Worthy Cominius, speak.
                    [CORIOLANUS *rises and attempts to leave*
                    Nay, keep your place.

FIRST SENATOR Sit, Coriolanus; never shame* to hear
What you have nobly done.

CORIOLANUS   Your honours' pardon.   65
I had rather have my wounds to heal again*
Than hear say* how I got them.

BRUTUS   Sir, I hope
My words disbenched you not.*

CORIOLANUS   No, sir. Yet oft,
When blows have made me stay, I fled from words.
You soothed* not, therefore hurt not; but your people,   70
I love them as they weigh* –

MENENIUS   Pray now, sit down.*

CORIOLANUS I had rather have one scratch* my head i' th' sun
When the alarum were struck,* than idly sit
To hear my nothings monstered.* ~~*gariously*~~
embarrassed by this
                                            [*Exit*

MENENIUS   Masters of the people,
Your multiplying* spawn how can he flatter –   75
That's* thousand to one good one – when you now see

77	*venture:* risk.
78	*Than . . . hear it:* than that one of his ears should hear his honour praised.
79	*I shall lack voice:* My voice will not be strong enough.
81	*virtue:* manly quality.
82	*haver:* possessor.
83	*in the world . . . counterpoised:* be equalled by any single man in the world.
85	*made a head for:* raised an army against.
86	*mark:* power, capacity.
86	*Our then dictator:* Our dictator at that time. – Plutarch does not name him.
87	*point at:* allude to.
88	*Amazonian* – i.e. beardless, because of his youth. The Amazons were the celebrated women warriors who lived near the Euxine Sea in ancient Greek times.
89	*bristled lips:* bearded men.
89	*bestrid/An o'erpressed Roman:* stood astride, defending a R. man who had been overwhelmed by the enemy.
90	*view:* sight.
91	*Tarquin's self:* Tarquin himself.
92	*struck him on his knee:* beat him to his knees, i.e. killed him.
93	*might act the woman in the scene:* might (being a boy) have played the part of the woman. – Shakespeare alludes to the custom in the Elizabethan theatre of boys taking the female parts. It is interesting that a boy of sixteen could still apparently play these parts. See *Introduction*, page lxiv.
94	*meed:* reward.
95	*brow-bound with the oak:* decorated with the garland of oak leaves. – See note to I.iii.14.
95	*His pupil . . . thus:* Having shown himself a man in this way while still a boy in years. – This alludes to the Elizabethan custom of apprenticing boys to a trade for a number of years before they became tradesmen. While still an apprentice warrior in age, Coriolanus is a qualified tradesman in war.
96	*waxèd like a sea* – The image is that of the swelling tide.
97	*brunt:* violence.
98	*lurched . . . the garland:* stole the crown of glory from everyone else.
98	*last:* latest action.
100	*speak him home:* find adequate words to describe him.
100	*fliers* – i.e. Romans who were running away.
102	*terror into sport:* flight into pursuit. – *Sport* here refers to the chase in hunting.
102	*weeds:* reeds (in a river).
104	*stem:* prow, bows of a ship.
104	*stamp:* tool or die for stamping an impression on a softer material.
105	*it took, from face to foot:* made its impression on whatever part of the body it struck, i.e. it killed.
106	*a thing of blood:* a creature shedding blood.
106	*motion/Was timed with:* movement was accompanied by.
108	*mortal:* (apparently) deadly.
108	*which* – i.e. the city.
108	*painted/With shunless destiny:* covered with the blood of men who could not avoid their destined fates.
109	*aidless came off:* fought his way out unaided.
111	*struck/Corioli like a planet:* blasted Corioli. – Planets, it was thought then, had the power to infect the earth with disease, or 'strike'. Possibly Shakespeare intends us to think of the planet Mars here.
111	*Now all's his:* He was now completely victorious.
112	*gan pierce:* penetrated.
113	*ready sense:* acute senses.
113	*straight . . . was fatigate:* at once his spirit, twice as strong as before, revived his weary body.
116	*Run reeking . . . men:* run like a smoking stream of blood, drowning men.
117	*perpetual spoil:* never-ending slaughter (of animals hunted in the chase)
118	*field:* the battle.

He had rather venture* all his limbs for honour
Than* one on's ears to hear it? Proceed, Cominius.
COMINIUS I shall lack voice:* the deeds of Coriolanus
Should not be uttered feebly. It is held   80
That valour is the chiefest virtue,* and
Most dignifies the haver.* If it be,
The man I speak of cannot in the world*
Be singly counterpoised. At sixteen years,
When Tarquin made a head for* Rome, he fought   85
Beyond the mark* of others. Our then dictator,*
Whom with all praise I point at,* saw him fight,
When with his Amazonian* chin he drove
The bristled lips* before him. He bestrid
An o'erpressed Roman,* and i' th' consul's view*   90
Slew three opposers. Tarquin's self* he met,
And struck him on his knee.* In that day's feats,
When he might act the woman in the scene,*
He proved best man i' th' field, and for his meed*
Was brow-bound with the oak.* His pupil* age   95
Man-entered thus, he waxèd like a sea,*
And in the brunt* of seventeen battles since,
He lurched* all swords of the garland. For this last,*
Before and in Corioli, let me say,
I cannot speak him home.* He stopped the fliers,*   100
And by his rare example made the coward
Turn terror into sport.* As weeds* before
A vessel under sail, so men obeyed,
And fell below his stem.* His sword, death's stamp,*
Where it did mark, it took, from face to foot.*   105
He was a thing of blood,* whose every motion
Was timed with* dying cries. Alone he entered
The mortal* gate of th' city, which* he painted
With shunless destiny;* aidless came off,*
And with a sudden reinforcement struck   110
Corioli like a planet.* Now all's his,*
When by and by the din of war gan pierce*
His ready sense;* then straight* his doubled spirit
Re-quickened what in flesh was fatigate,
And to the battle came he, where he did   115
Run reeking* o'er the lives of men, as if
'Twere a perpetual spoil;* and till we called
Both field* and city ours, he never stood

119   *with panting:* by getting his breath back.
119   *Worthy:* Heroic.
120   *with measure fit:* adequately measure up to.
121   *devise:* plan for.
121   *spoils he kicked at:* spurned our booty.
122   *as:* as if.
123   *He covets . . . give:* He wants less for himself than one who is miserliness personified
                would give away. *Misery:* miserliness.
124   *rewards . . . end it:* for him action is sufficient reward for his deeds, and he is only too
                happy killing time in action.
126   *right:* altogether.
130   *still:* always.
132   *That you do:* for you to.
133   *o'erleap:* avoid.
134   *gown:* toga, the vesture of humility, a long flowing robe.
134   *naked:* exposed.
135   *suffrage:* vote.
136   *pass this doing:* by-pass this action.
137   *have their voices:* be allowed to use their votes.
137   *bate . . . ceremony:* reduce the customary ritual in the slightest degree.
138   *Put them not to't:* Do not force them to do it.
139   *Pray you:* I beg you.
139   *fit you:* adapt yourself to.
140   *Take to you:* accept.
141   *Your honour with your form:* the honour that belongs to you, together with the ceremony
                it imposes on you.
141   *It is . . . acting* – This is one of the many references to the actor's profession in Shakespeare's
                plays. See *Introduction*, pages lxxiii–iv.
142   *might well . . . people:* the people could well do without this custom.
145   *unaching:* healed and no longer painful.
146   *hire/Of their breath only:* only for the reward (*hire*) of their expressions of approval
                (*breath*).

To ease his breast with panting.*

MENENIUS   Worthy* man!

FIRST SENATOR He cannot but with measure fit* the honours   120
Which we devise* him.

COMINIUS   Our spoils he kicked at,*
And looked upon things precious as* they were
The common muck of the world. He covets* less
Than misery itself would give, rewards*
His deeds with doing them, and is content   125
To spend the time to end it.

MENENIUS   He's right* noble.
Let him be called for.

FIRST SENATOR   Call Coriolanus.

OFFICER He doth appear.

Enter CORIOLANUS.

MENENIUS The Senate, Coriolanus, are well pleased
To make thee consul.

CORIOLANUS   I do owe them still*   130
My life and services.

MENENIUS   It then remains
That you do* speak to the people.

CORIOLANUS   I do beseech you
Let me o'erleap* that custom, for I cannot
Put on the gown,* stand naked,* and entreat them
For my wounds' sake to give their suffrage.* Please you   135
That I may pass this doing.*

SICINIUS   Sir, the people
Must have their voices;* neither will they bate*
One jot of ceremony.

MENENIUS   Put them not to't.*
Pray you,* go fit you* to the custom, and
Take to you,* as your predecessors have,   140
Your honour with your form.*

CORIOLANUS   It is* a part
That I shall blush in acting, and might well*
Be taken from the people.

BRUTUS   [*To* SICINIUS] Mark you that.

CORIOLANUS To brag unto them, thus I did, and thus,
Show them th' unaching* scars which I should hide,   145
As if I had received them for the hire
Of their breath only!*

147   *stand upon't:* insist upon it.
148   *recommend:* commit.
149   *purpose:* proposal.
152   *use:* treat.
153   *perceive's intent:* perceive his intention.
153   *require:* request.
154   *contemn what:* despise the fact that what.
155   *in them:* in their power.
156   *On:* In.
157   *do attend:* are waiting for.

II.iii.   The crowd are discussing Coriolanus and displaying a goodwill towards him providing he will 'incline to the people'. They leave, and Menenius enters with Coriolanus, unwillingly wearing the gown of humility. Menenius instructs Coriolanus on how to behave towards the people, but is uneasily aware that Coriolanus is likely to 'mar all' by his pride and contempt for them. He goes out and the citizens re-enter in small groups as they have been instructed. Coriolanus asks for and receives their vocal support. Menenius and the tribunes now appear, and Coriolanus goes off with Menenius to the Senate. The tribunes, learning from the citizens how Coriolanus has mocked them in his request for their votes and refused to show his wounds, skilfully work on them and persuade them to gather all their number together and rush to the Capitol to revoke their election.

    The political action gathers momentum as the tribunes decide to stake everything on an immediate confrontation with Coriolanus. The scene confirms, through Coriolanus's tactless and uncompromising nature, his incapacity for political life. By contrast we see in the wily and unscrupulous manoeuvres of the tribunes in manipulating the crowd, those qualities that succeed in the political world. In this intriguing and complex scene Shakespeare skilfully retains a balance of sympathy. While we respect Coriolanus's honesty, which shows to advantage by contrast with the blatant dishonesty of the tribunes, and sympathize with his mental torture at having to act a part alien to his nature, we censure the gratuitous insults he deals out to the crowd when all they require is a moderate degree of politeness from him to give him their full support. We share their resentment at his mockery and feel that he has deserved their *volte-face* over the election. We have to concede also that the tribunes, mean-spirited and cunning as they are, are justified in their fear that Coriolanus will deprive the plebeians of their liberties.

S.D.   The Forum Romanum, a large open space between the Palatine and Capitoline Hills surrounded by the chief civic buildings and temples of Rome, was the centre of the political, religious and commercial life of the city and the general meeting place of its citizens.
1   *Once if . . . voices:* If he once asks for our votes.
3   *will:* want to.
4   *We have power . . . power to do:* We have the right to deny him our votes, but it is a right we could never exercise (since it would show monstrous ingratitude). – The Third Citizen's good nature comes across despite his confused expression. Shakespeare seems to have looked on ingratitude with particular severity, judging by the numerous denunciations of it in his plays and sonnets.
6   *put our tongues . . . them* – Wounds are frequently described as dumb mouths in Shakespeare's plays. The Third Citizen says they must lend their tongues to those mouths and speak in praise of them.
9   *ingrateful:* ungrateful.
13   *And to make . . . serve:* Very little help from us will be enough to make Coriolanus think us no better than monsters.
14   *once:* when.
14   *stood up:* made a stand.
15   *stuck not:* did not hesitate.
15   *the many-headed* – i.e. like the monstrous Hydra, a poisonous water-snake. When one of its heads was cut off, others grew in its place. Its destruction was one of the twelve labours of Hercules. Cf. III.i.93.

MENENIUS   Do not stand upon't.*
          We recommend* to you, tribunes of the people,
          Our purpose* to them, and to our noble consul
          Wish we all joy and honour.   150
SENATORS To Coriolanus come all joy and honour!

          Flourish of cornets. Exeunt all except SICINIUS *and* BRUTUS.

BRUTUS   You see how he intends to use* the people.
SICINIUS May they perceive's intent.* He will require* them
          As if he did contemn what* he requested
          Should be in them* to give.
BRUTUS   Come, we'll inform them   155
          Of our proceedings here. On* th' market-place
          I know they do attend* us.
                                                              [*Exeunt*

scene iii

*Rome. The Forum.**

Enter seven or eight CITIZENS.

FIRST CITIZEN Once if* he do require our voices, we ought not to deny
          him.
SECOND CITIZEN We may, sir, if we will.*
THIRD CITIZEN We have power* in ourselves to do it, but it is a power that
          we have no power to do. For if he show us his wounds and   5
          tell us his deeds, we are to put our tongues* into those
          wounds and speak for them. So if he tell us his noble
          deeds, we must also tell him our noble acceptance of them.
          Ingratitude is monstrous, and for the multitude to be in-
          grateful* were to make a monster of the multitude; of the   10
          which we, being members, should bring ourselves to be
          monstrous members.
FIRST CITIZEN And to make* us no better thought of, a little help will
          serve; for once* we stood up about the corn, he himself
          stuck not* to call us the many-headed* multitude.   15

16   *of:* by.
16   *not that . . . brown:* not because some of our heads are brown.
17   *abram:* dark brown.
18   *wits:* intellects.
18   *diversely coloured* – i.e. varied.
20   *consent of one direct way:* agreement to follow one straight course. – The Third Citizen is
            talking elaborate nonsense. His own wits are flying in all directions.
26   *wedged up:* jammed.
27   *'twould sure:* it would certainly go.
30   *rotten dews:* unhealthy damp. – See note to I.iv.30.
31   *for conscience sake:* because of a guilty conscience.
31   *to get thee a wife* – The phrase is obscure. Possibly, as one editor suggests, because of the
            bastards he has fathered, or as another conjectures, it may be indicating a
            contempt for courtship and marriage, since these require only a quarter of a
            man's wit; in other words, one must be rather witless to marry.
32   *tricks:* jokes.
32   *You may, you may:* All right, have your little joke.
34   *the greater part carries it:* a majority will be enough to win (even if they don't all vote for
            Coriolanus).
35   S.D. *a gown of humility* – This was a threadbare toga. See note to II.ii.134.
37   *are not to:* must not. – The expression suggests that he has had these instructions from the
            tribunes. Cf. 1.166 below.
38   *by him:* near him.
39   *He's to:* He must.
39   *by particulars:* one by one, to each one in turn.
43   *Content:* Agreed.
44   *you are not right* – Coriolanus has obviously been arguing with Menenius, still trying to
            avoid the ceremony.
44   *Have you not known:* Don't you know.
46   *Plague upon't:* Confound it.
47   *a pace:* a step. – The image, from horsemanship, comes aptly from Coriolanus.
49   *roared:* cried out with fear.
52   *think upon:* think favourably.

THIRD CITIZEN   We have been called so of* many; not that* our heads are
some brown, some black, some abram,* some bald, but
that our wits* are so diversely coloured.* And truly, I
think, if all our wits were to issue out of one skull, they
would fly east, west, north, south, and their consent of   20
one direct way* should be at once to all the points o' the
compass.

SECOND CITIZEN   Think you so? Which way do you judge my wit would
fly?

THIRD CITIZEN   Nay, your wit will not so soon out as another man's will;   25
'tis strongly wedged up* in a blockhead; but if it were at
liberty, 'twould sure* southward.

SECOND CITIZEN   Why that way?

THIRD CITIZEN   To lose itself in a fog, where being three parts melted
away with rotten dews,* the fourth would return for   30
conscience sake,* to help to get thee a wife.*

SECOND CITIZEN   You are never without your tricks.* You may, you may.*

THIRD CITIZEN   Are you all resolved to give your voices? But that's no
matter, the greater part carries it,* I say. <u>If he would incline
to the people, there was never a worthier man.</u>   35

Enter CORIOLANUS *in a gown of humility,* with* MENENIUS.

Here he comes, and in the gown of humility. Mark his
behaviour. We are not to* stay all together, but to come by
him* where he stands, by ones, by twos, and by threes.
He's to* make his requests by particulars,* wherein
every one of us has a single honour, in giving him our own   40
voices with our own tongues. Therefore follow me, and
I'll direct you how you shall go by him.

ALL   Content,* content.

[*Exeunt* CITIZENS

MENENIUS   O sir, you are not right.* Have you not known*
The worthiest men have done't.

CORIOLANUS   What must I say? —   45
'I pray, sir' — Plague upon't!* I cannot bring
My tongue to such a pace.* 'Look, sir, my wounds.
I got them in my country's service, when
Some certain of your brethren roared* and ran
From th' noise of our own drums.'

MENENIUS   O me, the gods!   50
You must not speak of that. You must desire them
To think upon* you.

*He hates the
plebs, because
they ran a-
way*

from battle.

53   *I would they would:* I wish they would.
53   *like the virtues . . . 'em:* as they forget the virtues which our priests preach to them in vain.
54   *mar all:* spoil everything.
56   *wholesome:* reasonable. – Coriolanus takes up Menenius's word in another sense, that of 'salutary' or 'sanitary'.
57   *brace:* couple. – The term is commonly used of a pair of dogs, deriving from the strap or brace holding them together, and the connotations of the word are in keeping with Coriolanus's habit of describing the plebeians in animal terms. Many readers have found the word *brace* here confusing, since the Folio stage direction at line 56 reads *Enter three of the Citizens*. It is clear, however, that the Citizens are obeying their instruction at line 37 to approach Coriolanus in ones and twos, and that he catches sight of two of them together, ahead of the third.
58   *sir* – Coriolanus has to speak to each one separately.
59   *what hath brought you to't:* why you are standing for the consulship.
60   *desert:* merit.
63   *How?:* What?
66   *think:* reflect that.
68   *your price o':* what price are you asking for.
70   *ha't:* have it. – See also line 73.
71   *shall be yours:* I shall show you.
71   *Your good voice:* Your vote in my favour. – Coriolanus turns to address this to the Second Citizen.
74   *A match:* A bargain.
74   *There's in all:* Altogether that is. – Coriolanus sustains his idea that he is a begger soliciting charity (*alms*).
74   *two worthy voices begged* – Like the term *brace* discussed above (line 57) this line has given trouble, since Coriolanus has been talking to three citizens. We should remember, however, that Menenius has reminded him that he must address each voter individually, and this is what he has done, soliciting the First Citizen at line 70, and the Second Citizen at line 73. There is thus no need to alter the Folio reading in any way as many editors do.
75   *alms:* charity.
75   *Adieu:* Goodbye.
76   *something:* somewhat.
77   *And 'twere to give again:* If I had my vote to give over again. – The Second Citizen is already wishing he had not given Coriolanus his vote.
78   *stand:* agree.
79   *customary gown:* toga, as prescribed by custom.
82   *Your enigma:* Explain your riddle.
83   *a scourge to:* a whip to chastise.
84   *a rod to:* a stick to beat.

CORIOLANUS	Think upon me? Hang 'em!
	I would they would* forget me, like the virtues
	Which our divines lose by 'em.*
MENENIUS	You'll mar all.*
	I'll leave you. Pray you, speak to 'em, I pray you,
	In wholesome* manner.

[Exit MENENIUS

Enter three of the CITIZENS.

CORIOLANUS	Bid them wash their faces,
	And keep their teeth clean. So, here comes a brace.*
	You know the cause, sir,* of my standing here.
THIRD CITIZEN	We do, sir; tell us what hath brought you to't.*
CORIOLANUS	Mine own desert.*
SECOND CITIZEN	Your own desert?
CORIOLANUS	Ay, not mine own desire.
THIRD CITIZEN	How?* Not your own desire?
CORIOLANUS	No sir, 'twas never my desire yet to trouble the poor with begging.
THIRD CITIZEN	You must think,* if we give you anything, we hope to gain by you.
CORIOLANUS	Well then, I pray, your price o'* the consulship?
FIRST CITIZEN	The price is, to ask it kindly.
CORIOLANUS	Kindly, sir, I pray let me ha't.* I have wounds to show you, which shall be yours* in private. Your good voice,* sir. What say you?
SECOND CITIZEN	You shall ha't, worthy sir.
CORIOLANUS	A match,* sir. There's in all* two worthy voices begged.* I have your alms.* Adieu.*
THIRD CITIZEN	But this is something* odd.
SECOND CITIZEN	And 'twere to give again* – but 'tis no matter.

[Exeunt the three CITIZENS

Enter two other CITIZENS.

CORIOLANUS	Pray you now, if it may stand* with the tune of your voices that I may be consul, I have here the customary gown.*
FIRST CITIZEN	You have deserved nobly of your country, and you have not deserved nobly.
CORIOLANUS	Your enigma?*
FIRST CITIZEN	You have been a scourge to* her enemies, you have been a rod to* her friends. You have not indeed loved the common people.

55

60

65

70

75

80

85

86   *account:* consider.

87   *been common in my love:* given my love to everyone.

88   *sworn brother:* most intimate friend, one with whom one takes an oath to share fortunes.

88   *a dearer estimation of:* a higher opinion from. – The citizens fail to perceive Coriolanus's irony.

89   *condition:* mode of behaviour.

89   *account gentle:* consider gentlemanly.

89   *the wisdom of their choice is:* they choose in their wisdom. – This is said ironically.

90   *have my hat:* have me raise my hat to them (a token of respect).

91   *insinuating:* ingratiating.

91   *be off:* take off my hat.

92   *counterfeitly:* hypocritically.

92   *counterfeit . . . popular man:* imitate the bewitching manners of some demagogue.

93   *bountiful:* bountifully, in full measure. – See note to I.i.178.

94   *beseech you:* I beg that.

98   *seal your knowledge:* confirm what you already know. – A seal, usually of wax, was attached to a document to make it legally authentic.

99   *make much of:* value highly.

102   *starve:* die a lingering death. – The next 12 lines are a soliloquy, marked off from the rest of the scene by the couplet form.

103   *crave the hire:* beg for the reward.

103   *first:* already.

104   *wolvish toga:* hypocritical toga. – The reference here is to the *toga candida,* worn by those canvassing for office. The Folio here reads *tongue,* presumably a misreading of *toge* (a common Elizabethan spelling of *toga*). A similar error, *tongued Consuls,* is found in the Folio version of *Othello,* which can be corrected by the earlier Quarto reading, *toged Consuls.* The meaning here is that Coriolanus the warrior deplores his pretence of a humility he does not feel. Menenius has earlier described him as *a bear . . . that lives like a lamb* (II.i.11). Coriolanus among the cowardly citizens sees himself as a wolf in sheep's clothing, as in the well-known fable. Shakespeare was doubtless familiar with the story of Romulus and Remus, the founders of Rome, who were nurtured by a wolf, which thus had a special significance for Romans.

105   *Hob and Dick* – i.e. every man, or in the modern phrase, 'every Tom, Dick and Harry'. Hob was the countryman's nickname for Robert, and hence becomes a generic name for a rustic, clownish fellow. The phrase conveys yet again Coriolanus's contempt for the mob.

105   *that does appear:* as they appear, one by one.

106   *needless vouches:* unnecessary testimonials of support. – This is wishful thinking on Coriolanus's part, since their *vouches* are necessary to him. Possibly he thinks they are unnecessary because he has already been appointed by the Senate but, ironically, he is mistaken. As line 34 makes clear, he needs a majority of the citizens' votes to confirm his election.

106   *calls me to't:* demands that I do it.

107   *What custom . . . do't:* If we did all that custom demands.

108   *The dust . . . to o'erpeer:* we would be buried in the customs of the past, and truth would be submerged under a mountain of errors. – *O'erpeer:* see over the top. – Coriolanus argues that by perpetuating the customs of the past instead of questioningly examining them, we obscure what is best in it, and truth suffers. Shakespeare seems to have in mind an old neglected tomb or monument. Cf. Sonnet 55, where he speaks of a monumental tomb as 'unswept stone, besmeared with sluttish time'.

110   *fool it so:* play the fool in this way. – Another theatrical allusion, to the stock part of the Fool. This role, Coriolanus feels, demeans him; the hero's part is the one to his taste.

112   *do thus* – i.e. obey custom. – Coriolanus contemplates giving up his quest for the consulship.

113   *The one part suffered:* I have endured half of it. – He changes his mind, feeling that having come so far, he might as well push on to the end. The word *part* no doubt was suggested by the theatrical image at line 110.

114   *moe:* more.

116   *Watched:* kept watch, through the night as a soldier.

CORIOLANUS You should account* me the more virtuous, that I have
not been common in my love.* I will, sir, flatter my sworn
brother,* the people, to earn a dearer estimation of* them;
'tis a condition* they account gentle.* And since the wisdom of their choice is* rather to have my hat* than my 90
heart, I will practise the insinuating* nod, and be off* to
them most counterfeitly;* that is, sir, I will counterfeit* the
bewitchment of some popular man, and give it bountiful*
to the desirers. Therefore, beseech you* I may be consul.

SECOND CITIZEN We hope to find you our friend, and therefore give you 95
our voices heartily.

FIRST CITIZEN You have received many wounds for your country.

CORIOLANUS I will not seal your knowledge* with showing them. I will
make much of* your voices and so trouble you no farther.

BOTH CITIZENS The gods give you joy, sir, heartily! 100

[*Exeunt* CITIZENS

CORIOLANUS Most sweet voices!
Better it is to die, better to starve,*
Than crave the hire* which first* we do deserve.
Why in this wolvish toga* should I stand here
To beg of Hob and Dick* that does appear* 105
Their needless vouches?* Custom calls me to't.*
What custom* wills, in all things should we do't,
The dust* on antique time would lie unswept,
And mountainous error be too highly heaped
For truth to o'erpeer. Rather than fool it so,* 110
Let high office and the honour go
To one that would do thus.* I am half through;
The one part suffered,* the other will I do.

Enter three more CITIZENS.

Here come moe* voices.
Your voices! For your voices I have fought, 115
Watched* for your voices; for your voices bear
Of wounds two dozen odd; battles thrice six
I have seen and heard of; for your voices have
Done many things, some less, some more.* Your voices!
Indeed, I would* be consul. 120

— —

119 *some less, some more:* some of lesser importance, some greater.
120 *would:* want to. – Coriolanus mocks the plebeians by adopting a mock-epic mode of
speech, with its inversions, repetition and hyperbole, but they do not notice it.

127	*stood your limitation:* completed the time laid down for requesting votes.
128	*Endue:* endow.
128	*Remains:* It only remains.
129	*in th'official marks invested:* robed in the insignia of office.
130	*Anon:* shortly.
130	*done:* usually done.
131	*discharged:* carried out.
132	*admit:* accept.
133	*anon, upon your approbation:* at once about the ratification of your appointment (as consul).
136	*straight do:* do at once.
136	*knowing myself again* – Having shed his costume and his part, Coriolanus feels he will be himself again. As actor in this playing of *the custom of request* he has shed his own personality.
137	*Repair:* make my way.
138	*Will you along?:* Will you come with us? – The question is addressed to Brutus and Sicinius.
141	*'Tis warm at's heart:* The consulship warms his heart, delights him; *at's:* at his.
142	*humble weeds:* humble garments, i.e. the gown of humility.
143	*chose:* chosen. – This was a common Elizabethan form of the past participle. Cf. line 203 below.
146	*notice:* observation.
148	*flouted us downright:* expressed his thorough contempt for us.
149	*his kind of speech:* just his way of speaking.
150	*Not one . . . but:* Everyone, except you.

FIRST CITIZEN   He has done nobly, and cannot go without any honest
                 man's voice.
SECOND CITIZEN   Therefore let him be consul. The gods give him joy, and
                 make him good friend to the people!
ALL   Amen, amen. God save thee, noble consul!   125
                                                      [Exeunt CITIZENS
CORIOLANUS   Worthy voices!

                 Enter MENENIUS *with* BRUTUS *and* SICINIUS.

MENENIUS   You have stood your limitation,* and the tribunes
                 Endue* you with the people's voice. Remains*
                 That in th' official marks invested,* you
                 Anon* do meet the Senate.
CORIOLANUS   Is this done?*   130
SICINIUS   The custom of request you have discharged.*
                 The people do admit* you and are summoned
                 To meet anon, upon your approbation.*
CORIOLANUS   Where? At the Senate House?
SICINIUS   There, Coriolanus.
CORIOLANUS   May I change these garments?
SICINIUS   You may, sir.   135
CORIOLANUS   That I'll straight do,* and knowing myself again,*
                 Repair* to the Senate House.
MENENIUS   I'll keep you company. Will you along?*
BRUTUS   We stay here for the people.
SICINIUS   Fare you well.
                                  [Exeunt CORIOLANUS *and* MENENIUS
                 He has it now; and by his looks, methinks,   140
                 'Tis warm at's heart.*
BRUTUS   With a proud heart he wore
                 His humble weeds.* Will you dismiss the people?

                 Enter the PLEBEIANS.

SICINIUS   How now, my masters, have you chose* this man?
FIRST CITIZEN   He has our voices, sir.
BRUTUS   We pray the gods he may deserve your loves.   145
SECOND CITIZEN   Amen, sir. To my poor unworthy notice,*
                 He mocked us when he begged our voices.
THIRD CITIZEN   Certainly;
                 He flouted us downright.*
FIRST CITIZEN   No, 'tis his kind of speech;* he did not mock us.
SECOND CITIZEN   Not one* amongst us, save yourself, but says   150

Help ?

151   *used:* treated.

156   The Third Citizen's report indicates how the actor of Coriolanus's part has to play the action he is recounting.

157   *Aged:* Ancient.

158   *But by your voices:* except with your votes.

160   *Here was:* his next speech was.

161   *left* – i.e. with me, hence, given me.

162   *no further with you:* no more to do with you.

163   *ignorant to see't:* too stupid to see it.

165   *To yield:* as to give.

166   *lessoned:* instructed (i.e. by the tribunes themselves). – Brutus scolds the plebeians for forgetting the instructions the tribunes had given them. They should have extracted a promise of love and support from Coriolanus before giving him their votes. Without it their position will be worse later than it is now.

168   *He was:* that he was.

168   *ever spake:* always spoke.

169   *charters . . . weal:* privileges that belong to you in the commonwealth.

170   *arriving . . . sway o':* reaching a position of power and authority in.

172   *malignantly:* maliciously.

173   *Fast foe:* determined enemy.

173   *plebeii* – Latin for 'plebeians'.

173   *your voices . . . yourselves:* in giving him your votes you may turn out to have been cursing yourselves.

176   *what he stood for:* the office he stood for, i.e. the consulship.

177   *think upon you:* think well of you. – Cf. line 52 above.

178   *Translate:* transform.

179   *Standing your friendly lord:* remaining a lord friendly to you.

180   *fore-advised:* advised beforehand.

180   *had touched:* would have tested (like a touchstone which tested the quality of precious metals).

181   *tried his inclination:* put his disposition to the test.

183   *As cause had called you up:* when some occasion had roused you.

184   *galled:* irritated (literally 'made sore by rubbing'). – The image is that of a high-spirited horse.

185   *Which easily . . . aught:* which does not easily endure any condition (*article*) binding him to anything. – The horse metaphor is continued in the image of *tying*.

186   *So putting him to rage:* Forcing him to anger in this way (*so*).

187   *You should . . . unelected:* you would have taken advantage of his anger and passed him over without electing him.

189   *did solicit . . . contempt:* sought your help with unconcealed contempt.

He used* us scornfully. He should have showed us
His marks of merit, wounds received for's country.

SICINIUS Why, so he did, I am sure. *→ Sarcasm, siring up
ALL No, no. No man saw 'em. *the crowd. He knows that
THIRD CITIZEN He said he had wounds which he could show in private;   155
*consul didn't
And with his hat, thus waving it in scorn,
'I would be consul,' says he. 'Aged* custom,
But by your voices,* will not so permit me.
Your voices, therefore.' When we granted that
Here was,* 'I thank you for your voices. Thank you,   160
Your most sweet voices. Now you have left* your voices,
I have no further with you.*' Was not this mockery?

SICINIUS Why either were you ignorant to see't,*
Or seeing it, of such childish friendliness
To yield* your voices?

BRUTUS   Could you not have told him,   165
As you were lessoned,* when he had no power,
But was a petty servant to the state,
He was* your enemy, ever spake* against
Your liberties and the charters* that you bear
I' th' body of the weal; and now, arriving*   170
A place of potency and sway o' th' state,
If he should still malignantly* remain
Fast foe* to the plebeii,* your voices* might
Be curses to yourselves? You should have said
That as his worthy deeds did claim no less   175
Than what he stood for,* so his gracious nature
Would think upon you* for your voices, and
Translate* his malice towards you into love,
Standing your friendly lord.*

SICINIUS   Thus to have said,
As you were fore-advised,* had touched* his spirit   180
And tried his inclination;* from him plucked
Either his gracious promise, which you might,
As cause had called you up,* have held him to;
Or else it would have galled* his surly nature,
Which easily* endures not article   185
Tying him to aught. So putting him to rage,*
You should* have ta'en th' advantage of his choler,
And passed him unelected.

BRUTUS   Did you perceive
He did solicit* you in free contempt

191 *bruising . . . crush:* damaging to you once he has the power to oppress you.
192 *had your bodies . . . among you:* was there no one with any spirit among the lot of you.
193 *had you tongues . . . judgement:* what made your tongues speak against the dictates of your judgement. – *rectorship:* government, rule.
195 *Ere now . . . tongues:* previously refused one who asked, but now give your support, which men are anxious to get, to one who did not ask but mocked you. – *Of:* on.
198 *confirmed:* installed in office.
198 *deny him yet:* still reject him.
200 *of that sound:* of the same sound, i.e. all agreeing to refuse the consulship to Coriolanus.
201 *piece 'em:* add to them.
204 *of no more . . . do so:* as silent as dogs which have often been beaten for barking although they are kept as watchdogs (which ought to bark).
207 *safer:* sounder.
207 *revoke/Your ignorant election:* cancel your choice which was made in ignorance.
208 *Enforce:* Emphasize.
209 *old:* long-continued.
210 *weed:* garment.
211 *suit:* request.
211 *but:* but say that.
213 *apprehension of:* power to understand.
213 *portance:* behaviour.
214 *gibingly, ungravely:* mockingly, in an undignified manner.
215 *After the inveterate hate:* in accordance with the long-established hatred.
215 *Lay/A fault on us:* Put the blame on us.
216 *that we laboured . . . on him:* saying that we worked hard, putting no obstacle in your way, to make you elect him.
219 *after:* following.
221 *affections:* desires.
222 *against the grain . . . consul:* against your wishes make him consul by your votes.
224 *read lectures to:* instructed.
225 *How youngly:* at what a tender age.
226 *How long continued:* how long he has served his country.
226 *stock he springs of:* family he is descended from.

When he did need your loves? And do you think   190
That his contempt shall not be bruising* to you
When he hath power to crush? Why, had your bodies*
No heart among you? Or had you tongues* to cry
Against the rectorship of judgement?

SICINIUS   Have you
Ere now* denied the asker, and now again,   195
Of him that did not ask but mock, bestow
Your sued-for tongues?

THIRD CITIZEN He's not confirmed;* we may deny him yet.*

SECOND CITIZEN And will deny him.

I'll have five hundred voices of that sound.*   200

FIRST CITIZEN I twice five hundred, and their friends to piece 'em.*

BRUTUS Get you hence instantly, and tell those friends
They have chose a consul that will from them take
Their liberties, make them of no more* voice
Than dogs that are as often beat for barking   205
As therefore kept to do so.

SICINIUS   Let them assemble;
And on a safer* judgement, all revoke
Your ignorant election.* Enforce* his pride
And his old* hate unto you. Besides, forget not
With what contempt he wore the humble weed,*   210
How in his suit* he scorned you; but* your loves,
Thinking upon his services, took from you
Th' apprehension of* his present portance,* which
Most gibingly, ungravely,* he did fashion
After the inveterate hate* he bears you.

Corio. hates you.

BRUTUS   Lay   215
A fault on us,* your tribunes, that we laboured,*
No impediment between, but that you must
Cast your election on him.

SICINIUS   Say you chose him
More after* our commandment than as guided
By your own true affections,* and that your minds,   220
Preoccupied with what you rather must do
Than what you should, made you against the grain*
To voice him consul. Lay the fault on us.

BRUTUS Ay, spare us not. Say we read lectures to* you,
How youngly* he began to serve his country,   225
How long continued,* and what stock he springs of,*
The noble house of the Martians, from whence came

228   *Ancus Martius* – the fourth of the Roman kings.
228   *Numa* – the second of the seven kings of Rome, successor to Romulus, the traditional
                founder of the city.
229   *Hostilius* – a legendary king of Rome.
230   *house:* family. – Plutarch mentions Publius and Quintus, but nothing further is known of
                them than is reported here.
231   *conduits:* channels or pipes.
232   *And Censorinus . . . surnamed* – This line is not in the Folio. It is clear that something has
                been omitted by the compositor, probably a whole line. This has been supplied
                here from the passage in Plutarch from which these lines derive.
233   *censor* – Two censors were elected every five years in Rome to take the census of the
                people and to supervise the general conduct of the citizens.
235   *well in his person wrought:* worked well personally.
237   *To your remembrances:* for you to remember (when you were casting your votes).
238   *Scaling:* putting in the scales, hence, weighing.
239   *fixèd:* unchanging.
239   *revoke/Your sudden approbation:* withdraw your hasty approval.
240   *ne'er . . . putting on:* would never have done it (keep stressing that point) if we had not
                urged you to it.
242   *presently:* immediately.
242   *drawn your number:* gathered your supporters.
243   *Repair:* make your way.
244   *in:* of.
245   *This mutiny . . . greater:* It is better to risk (*put in hazard*) the failure of this disturbance
                (*mutiny*) than to wait (*stay*) for a more serious (*greater*) one, whose success
                would be certain (*past doubt*) to occur. – The tribunes want civic disorder at
                any price in order to oust Coriolanus, and are prepared to risk failure now
                rather than wait for future certainty.
247   *fall in rage:* falls into a rage.
249   *answer/The vantage of his anger:* take advantage of the opportunity his anger offers us.
252   *goaded onward:* incited.

That Ancus Martius,* Numa's* daughter's son,
Who after great Hostilius* here was king;
Of the same house* Publius and Quintus were,   230
That our best water brought by conduits* hither,
And Censorinus* that was so surnamed,
And nobly naměd so, twice being censor,*
Was his great ancestor.

SICINIUS   One thus descended,
That hath beside well in his person wrought*   235
To be set high in place, we did commend
To your remembrances;* but you have found,
Scaling* his present bearing with his past,
That he's your fixěd* enemy, and revoke
Your sudden approbation.*

BRUTUS   Say you ne'er had* done't   240
(Harp on that still) but by our putting on.
And presently,* when you have drawn your number,*
Repair* to th' Capitol.

ALL   We will so. Almost all
Repent in* their election.

                                        [*Exeunt* PLEBEIANS

BRUTUS   Let them go on.
This mutiny* were better put in hazard,   245
Than stay, past doubt, for greater.
If, as his nature is, he fall in rage*
With their refusal, both observe and answer
The vantage of his anger.*

SICINIUS   To th' Capitol, come.
We will be there before the stream o' th' people;   250
And this shall seem, as partly 'tis, their own,
Which we have goaded onward.*

                                            [*Exeunt*

Coriolanus, with the Senators, attacking the hostile citizens (Act III, Scene i).

Volumnia arguing with Coriolanus about his conduct towards the citizens (Act III, Scene ii).

Brutus and Sicinius planning their strategy to destroy Coriolanus (Act III, Scene iii).

III.i.   As the senators make their way through the streets of Rome they are stopped by the tribunes who announce that the people have changed their mind and that it is dangerous for them to proceed. This check provokes an angry speech from Coriolanus in which he recommends the dissolution of the tribunate. At this the tribunes order his arrest and summon the citizens. Sicinius commands the aediles to throw Coriolanus to his death from the Tarpeian rock. Coriolanus and his friends attack the mob and drive them off, and Coriolanus is persuaded against his will to leave the scene with Cominius. When the tribunes and the people return Menenius persuades them, in order to avoid civil war, to accept his plan to bring Coriolanus to answer any charges against him by due legal process.

The dramatic tempo rises to a climax as Coriolanus's anger, deliberately provoked by the tribunes, breaks out and causes the situation that they had hoped for. With breath-taking swiftness, Shakespeare reverses Coriolanus's fortunes: from being virtual consul he becomes a branded traitor whose life hangs in the balance. We should not overlook the important news at the start of the scene that Aufidius has rearmed against Rome, since he is to be the agent of the final crisis of the play and Shakespeare must keep his existence and this threat in our minds.

1   *had made new head:* had raised a new army. – From the tense we infer that Titus Lartius has just spoken (before their entry) of the situation in Volscian territory from which he has recently arrived.

3   *Our swifter composition:* our coming to terms with them more quickly than we would otherwise have done.

5   *time shall prompt them:* the time is ripe for them.

5   *make road/Upon's:* invade us.

6   *worn . . . so:* so exhausted.

7   *ages:* lifetime.

9   *On safeguard:* Under safe conduct, i.e. his visit was made by permission of Titus Lartius and with a promise that he would not be molested.

10   *for:* because.

10   *vilely/Yielded:* basely surrendered.

11   *is retired:* has retreated.

12   *Spoke . . . What?* – Coriolanus's eagerness to discover Aufidius's opinion of him is un-expected after his earlier demonstrations of indifference to public opinion. Like renaissance warriors, however, Coriolanus highly valued his honour and reputation as reflected in the opinion of people he respected, in this case a man of outstanding military ability.

15   *pawn his fortunes . . . vanquisher:* pawn his fortunes without any hope of redeeming them provided he could beat you. – Aufidius is willing to endure any misfortune provided he can once beat Coriolanus in battle.

20   *To oppose . . . fully:* to show him that my hatred for him is as great as his for me. – The following *Welcome home* is addressed to Titus Lartius, not to the tribunes who are just coming on stage.

23   *prank them:* dress themselves up.

24   *Against all noble sufferance:* in a way no noble can endure.

ACT III scene i

Rome. A street.

Cornets. Enter CORIOLANUS, MENENIUS, COMINIUS, TITUS
LARTIUS *and other* SENATORS.

CORIOLANUS Tullus Aufidius then had made new head?*
LARTIUS He had, my lord, and that it was which caused
 Our swifter composition.*
CORIOLANUS So then the Volsces stand but as at first,
 Ready, when time shall prompt them,* to make road   5
 Upon's* again.
COMINIUS   They are worn,* lord consul, so,
 That we shall hardly in our ages* see
 Their banners wave again.
CORIOLANUS   Saw you Aufidius?
LARTIUS On safeguard* he came to me, and did curse
 Against the Volsces, for* they had so vilely   10
 Yielded* the town. He is retired* to Antium.
CORIOLANUS Spoke* he of me?
LARTIUS   He did, my lord.
CORIOLANUS   How? what?
LARTIUS How often he had met you, sword to sword;
 That of all things upon the earth he hated
 Your person most; that he would pawn his fortunes* 15
 To hopeless restitution, so he might
 Be called your vanquisher.
CORIOLANUS   At Antium lives he?
LARTIUS At Antium.
CORIOLANUS I wish I had a cause to seek him there,
 To oppose* his hatred fully. Welcome home.   20

Enter SICINIUS *and* BRUTUS.

[*Aside to his friends*] Behold, these are the tribunes of the
            people,
 The tongues o' th' common mouth. I do despise them,
 For they do prank them* in authority,
 Against all noble sufferance.*
SICINIUS   Pass no further.

95

28   *The matter?:* What is wrong?
29   *passed the noble and the common:* been accepted by patricians and plebeians.
30   *Have . . . voices?* – Coriolanus means that the votes he has had were from men of Rome,
          not from children who cannot be expected to know their own minds.
31   *shall to:* must go to.
33   *fall in broil:* degenerate into a fight.
34   *Must . . . tongues:* Is it right for people to have votes if they can give their approval one
          minute and repudiate it the next?
35   *offices:* duties.
36   *You being . . . teeth?:* Since you are their mouths (i.e. spokesmen), why don't you stop
          them from biting? – Having just described them as a *herd*, he now sees them as
          a pack of dogs.
37   *set them on:* incited them (as dogs were incited to attack bears and bulls for sport in
          Shakespeare's time).
38   *a purposed . . . plot:* a premeditated thing, growing bigger by (deliberate) plotting.
40   *Suffer't, and live:* If you allow it you will have to live.
42   *cry:* complain.
43   *gratis:* free.
43   *repined:* disapproved.
44   *Scandalled the suppliants:* slandered those who petitioned.
45   *Time-pleasers:* time-servers, men acting out of self-interest.
47   *sithence:* since.
47   *How:* What.
48   *like:* likely. – Some editions, like the First Folio, attribute this speech to Cominius.
49   *Not unlike . . . yours:* Likely in every way to do your business (i.e. rule) better than you
          will. – See note to I.i.178.
50   *yond:* yonder.
51   *so ill:* as badly.
52   *that/For which:* that spirit (i.e. pride) on account of which.
53   *stir:* are disturbed.
54   *where you are bound:* the place you are heading for, i.e. the consulship.
55   *are out of:* have lost.
56   *be so noble as a consul:* reach as noble a position as that of consul.
57   *yoke with him for tribune:* be associated with him as a tribune.

CORIOLANUS Ha? What is that?   25
BRUTUS It will be dangerous to go on. No further.
CORIOLANUS What makes this change?
MENENIUS The matter?*
COMINIUS Hath he not passed the noble and the common?*
BRUTUS Cominius, no.
CORIOLANUS   Have* I had children's voices?   30
FIRST SENATOR Tribunes, give way; he shall to* th' market-place.
BRUTUS The people are incensed against him.
SICINIUS   Stop,
        Or all will fall in broil.*
CORIOLANUS   Are these your herd?
        Must* these have voices, that can yield them now,
        And straight disclaim their tongues? What are your offices?* 35
        You being* their mouths, why rule you not their teeth?
        Have you not set them on?*
MENENIUS   Be calm, be calm.
CORIOLANUS It is a purposed* thing, and grows by plot,
        To curb the will of the nobility.
        Suffer't, and live* with such as cannot rule,   40
        Nor ever will be ruled.
BRUTUS   Call't not a plot.
        The people cry* you mocked them; and of late,
        When corn was given them gratis,* you repined,*
        Scandalled the suppliants* for the people, called them
        Time-pleasers,* flatterers, foes to nobleness.   45
CORIOLANUS Why, this was known before.
BRUTUS   Not to them all.
CORIOLANUS Have you informed them sithence?*
BRUTUS   How!* I inform them?
CORIOLANUS You are like* to do such business.
BRUTUS   Not unlike*
        Each way to better yours.
CORIOLANUS Why then should I be consul? By yond* clouds,   50
        Let me deserve so ill* as you, and make me
        Your fellow tribune.
SICINIUS   You show too much of that
        For which* the people stir.* If you will pass
        To where you are bound,* you must inquire your way,
        Which you are out of,* with a gentler spirit,   55
        Or never be so noble as a consul,*
        Nor yoke with him for tribune.*

58 *abused, set on:* deceived, incited.
58 *palt'ring:* trickery.
59 *Becomes not:* is unfitting for.
60 *this so dishonoured rub:* such a dishonourable obstacle as this. – A *rub* is a term used in the
        game of bowls to denote an impediment or obstacle hindering or diverting
        the bowl from its proper course (the *plain way* of the following line).
60 *laid falsely:* treacherously placed.
61 *Tell . . . corn:* Are you talking to me about corn? – Coriolanus refers to the allegations of
        lines 43–5. This mention of *corn* leads him to the line of imagery connected with
        corn and weeds (*cockle;* see line 70 below and note).
63 *heat:* angry state.
65 *My:* As for my.
66 *For the mutable . . . meiny:* As for the changeable, foul-smelling mob.
67 *Regard me . . . flatter:* pay attention to me as one who does not flatter.
68 *Therein behold themselves:* see themselves reflected in what I say about them.
69 *soothing:* flattering.
70 *cockle:* weed (often found in corn). – Shakespeare took the word from North's Plutarch,
        where Coriolanus speaks of the 'seed and cockle of insolence and sedition'.
        He then associated it with the biblical parable of the wheat and the tares
        (*Matthew* 13 : 24–30), making Coriolanus see the patricians as the good seed,
        the plebeians as the bad.
71 *scattered* – The image is that of the sower who walked along the furrows scattering seed
        as he went. Coriolanus accuses his fellow patricians of helping to propagate
        rebellion and sedition by their own former actions.
72 *By mingling . . . beggars:* by allowing them (the lower classes represented by their tribunes)
        to mix with ourselves, the patricians; we (*Who*) certainly have manly qualities
        (*virtue*), and even power, except for the power that we have given away to
        beggars.
75 *How?:* What?
76 *As:* Just as.
78 *Coin:* mint, turn out.
78 *their decay . . . catch them:* they are destroyed by the disease whose scabby eruption in us
        we deplore (*disdain*), while we are doing the very thing to ensure we catch it. –
        tetter: cover with scabs.
82 *of their infirmity:* having faults like them.
82 *'Twere . . . let:* We ought to let.
83 *choler:* anger.
85 *patient:* calm.
86 *'twould be my mind:* I should think the same.
88 *Not . . . further:* and not be in a position to spread – i.e. if Coriolanus is to be consul
        he will be able to make his poisonous opinions felt.
88 *'Shall remain'* – Coriolanus sarcastically echoes the words of Sicinius.

MENENIUS   Let's be calm.

COMINIUS The people are abused, set on.* This palt'ring*
Becomes not* Rome; nor has Coriolanus
Deserved this so dishonoured rub,* laid falsely*   60
I' th' plain way of his merit.

CORIOLANUS   Tell* me of corn!
This was my speech, and I will speak't again —

MENENIUS Not now, not now.

FIRST SENATOR   Not in this heat,* sir, now.

CORIOLANUS Now, as I live, I will.
My* nobler friends, I crave their pardons.   65
For the mutable,* rank-scented meiny, let them
Regard me* as I do not flatter, and
Therein behold themselves.* I say again,
In soothing* them we nourish 'gainst our Senate
The cockle* of rebellion, insolence, sedition,   70
Which we ourselves have ploughed for, sowed, and
                                    scattered,*
By mingling* them with us, the honoured number,
Who lack not virtue, no, nor power but that
Which they have given to beggars.

MENENIUS   Well, no more.

FIRST SENATOR No more words, we beseech you.

CORIOLANUS   How?* no more?   75
As* for my country I have shed my blood,
Not fearing outward force, so shall my lungs
Coin* words till their decay* against those measles
Which we disdain should tetter us, yet sought
The very way to catch them.

BRUTUS   You speak o' the people   80
As if you were a god to punish, not
A man of their infirmity.*

SICINIUS   'Twere* well
We let the people know't.

MENENIUS   What, what? His choler?*

CORIOLANUS Choler?
Were I as patient* as the midnight sleep,   85
By Jove, 'twould be my mind!*

SICINIUS   It is a mind
That shall remain a poison where it is,
Not* poison any further.

CORIOLANUS   'Shall remain'?*

89 *Triton of the minnows:* giant of the little fishes. – In Greek mythology, Triton was a fish-shaped god, Neptune's trumpeter, who blew on a conch-shell.

90 *His absolute 'shall':* his positive, unconditional word, 'shall'. – Coriolanus mocks Sicinius's dictatorial habit of laying down the law.

90 *from the canon:* against the law. – Sicinius is exceeding his authority, having no power to silence a senator or anyone else.

92 *grave:* reverend.

93 *Given Hydra here:* allowed this Hydra (i.e. the Roman mob). – The Hydra was a poisonous water-snake with many heads. See note to II.iii.15.

94 *That with . . . channel his:* who with his dictatorial (*péremptory*) 'shall', although he is really supposed only to voice the plebeians' thoughts, does not hesitate to express his intention of diverting your power and taking it over for himself. – Coriolanus sees power as a current of water flowing along a channel. Sicinius, he says, will empty the patricians' current of power into a ditch and use their channel to convey his own power. Shakespeare makes Coriolanus a polished orator. His use of the rhetorical question, the sequence of balanced 'if' clauses, the antithetically poised adjectives and clauses all leading to a concluding climax show his skill in the art of persuasion.

95 *the horn and noise* – Coriolanus carries through the association with Triton, Neptune's trumpeter, from line 89.

95 *o' th' monster's* – i.e. of the mob. The double use of the possessive case is frequent in Elizabethan English.

97 *If he have . . . none:* If he really has power, then let those of you who out of ignorance gave him the power bow down (*vail*) before him; if he has no power (i.e. if it is a bluff).

99 *lenity:* mildness.

99 *learned:* wise.

101 *have cushions by you:* sit as senators beside you. – The cushion was invented by Shakespeare as a symbol of senatorial rank. See II.ii.1 S.D.

101 *plébeians* – accented on the first syllable, as nearly always, Cf. V.iv.35.

102 *no less* – i.e. than senators.

103 *both your voices . . . theirs:* with your voices and theirs blended, the predominant note is theirs, i.e. they will have most power because they will be in the majority. – Coriolanus's image of *voices* (doubtless prompted by his humiliating memory of the vital part they have just played in his canvassing for the consulship), now *blended*, as he visualizes a Senate with plebeians outnumbering patricians, leads him on to the associated image of *taste* (since both originate in the same part of the body). Just as in food and drink which is blended the most powerful ingredient prevails most strongly in the taste, so the 'taste' (or will) of this mingled Senate will be its most powerful element, the plebeians.

105, 106 *'shall'* – Coriolanus believes that Sicinius uses the word *shall* not simply as an indication of future events, but as a command: 'It shall be so.'

106 *popular:* vulgar, plebeian.

106 *a graver . . . Greece:* a more dignified authority (i.e. the Senate) than even a Greek ruling body.

107 *Jove* – Jupiter; see note to I.iii.36.

109 *up:* opposed in action.

110 *confusion:* ruin.

111 *'twixt the gap of both:* through the gap between the two.

111 *take/The one by th'other:* destroy one by means of the other.

113 *give forth:* distribute.

114 *gratis:* free.

114 *'twas used/Sometime:* was formerly the custom.

116 *absolute:* unrestricted.

117 *they* – i.e. the Romans who ordered the distribution of corn.

120 *More worthier* – The double comparative, often used to add emphasis, was permissible in Shakespeare's day. Cf. *more proudlier* (IV.vii.8).

121 *our recompense:* a reward by us for their services.

121 *resting well assured:* knowing very well.

122 *pressed:* conscripted.

Quote

Hear you this Triton of the minnows?* Mark you
His absolute 'shall'?*

COMINIUS   'Twas from the canon.*

CORIOLANUS   'Shall'!   90
O good, but most unwise patricians, why,
You grave* but reckless senators, have you thus
Given Hydra here* to choose an officer,
That with* his péremptory 'shall', being but
The horn and noise* o' th' monster's,* wants not spirit   95
To say he'll turn your current in a ditch,
And make your channel his? If he have* power,
Then vail your ignorance; if none, awake
Your dangerous lenity.* If you are learned,*
Be not as common fools; if you are not,   100
Let them have cushions by you.* You are plébeians,*
If they be senators; and they are no less,*
When, both your voices* blended, the great'st taste
Most palates theirs. They choose their magistrate,
And such a one as he, who puts his 'shall',*   105
His popular* 'shall', against a graver* bench
Than ever frowned in Greece. By Jove* himself,
It makes the consuls base, and my soul aches
To know, when two authorities are up,*
Neither supreme, how soon confusion*
May enter 'twixt the gap of both,* and take   110
The one by th' other.*

COMINIUS   Well, on to th' market-place.

CORIOLANUS   Whoever gave the counsel to give forth*
The corn o' th' storehouse gratis,* as 'twas used
Sometime* in Greece –

MENENIUS   Well, well, no more of that.   115

CORIOLANUS   – Though there the people had more absolute* power,
I say they* nourished disobedience, fed
The ruin of the state.

BRUTUS   Why shall the people give
One that speaks thus their voice?

CORIOLANUS   I'll give my reasons,
More worthier* than their voices. They know the corn   120
Was not our recompense,* resting well assured*
They ne'er did service for't. Being pressed* to th' war,

123   *navel:* vital centre. – Cf. Menenius's defence of the belly as the controlling centre of the
            body in I.i.
123   *touched:* threatened.
124   *thread:* pass through, i.e. on their way to defend Rome in battle.
127   *spoke not for them:* gave no evidence in their favour.
127   *Th'accusation* – i.e. that the Senate never cared for the people; see, for example, I.i.68. –
            Coriolanus argues that the groundless complaint by the people that the Senate
            never cared for them was certainly not the reason for the Senate's gift of corn
            to them.
129   *All cause unborn:* without any cause.
129   *native:* origin, cause.
130   *our so frank donation:* our gift given so freely.
131   *How . . . digest:* How must we expect these many minds to understand. – This is an
            extension of the Hydra metaphor at line 93 and of the pervading image of the
            belly.
132   *Let deeds . . . words:* Let their (the plebeians') behaviour show us what their words are
            likely to be.
134   *poll:* number of heads.
134   *true:* genuine.
136   *seats* – i.e. in the Senate.
137   *cares:* solicitude (for the state).
137   *which* – i.e. their belief that our *cares* are really *fears,* that we are afraid of them.
138   *ope:* open.
139   *crows to peck the eagles* – Coriolanus sees the plebeians as scavenging carrion eaters,
            crows; the senators as kingly *eagles.*
140   *over-measure:* excess.
141   *What may be sworn by:* Whatever I can take an oath on.
142   *Seal what I end withal:* confirm the truth of my final remark. – *withal:* with.
142   *double worship* – i.e. paying simultaneous respect to the *two authorities* of line 109.
143   *one part does disdain with cause:* one side (the patricians) is justifiably contemptuous.
143   *the other* – i.e. the plebeians.
144   *without:* beyond.
144   *gentry:* high birth.
145   *Cannot conclude . . . ignorance:* can only make decisions with the approval of the ignorant
            mob.
146   *omit:* neglect.
147   *give way the while:* give up the whole of its time.
148   *unstable slightness:* wayward trivialities. – Coriolanus says that when those who could
            (in their wisdom) see the true essentials (for the welfare of the state) are
            obliged to take notice of the will of the rabble, they have to devote their time
            to ever-changing trivialities and so can give no attention to the essentials.
148   *Purpose so . . . purpose:* When government is obstructed in this way it follows that nothing
            effective is done.
149   *beseech:* I beg.
150   *less fearful than discreet:* more prudent (*discreet*) than afraid.
151   *fundamental part of state:* basic constitution of the commonwealth.
152   *doubt:* fear.
152   *on't:* of it.
153   *a long* – i.e. a long life.
154   *jump . . . without it:* risk giving a dangerous medicine to a body that would certainly
            die without it.
156   *the multitudinous tongue:* the voice of the multitude, i.e. the tribunes.
156   *lick . . . poison* – i.e. enjoy their office whose power corrupts them.
157   *Your dishonour . . . judgement:* Your degradation as senators impairs the true administration
            of justice.
158   *bereaves:* deprives.
159   *integrity:* unity.
159   *should become't:* ought to dignify it.
160   *would:* wants to.
161   *For th'ill . . . control't:* because of the evil which overpowers it.
161   *Has:* He has.

Even when the navel* of the state was touched,*
They would not thread* the gates. This kind of service
Did not deserve corn gratis. Being i' th' war,   125
Their mutinies and revolts, wherein they showed
Most valour, spoke not for them.* Th' accusation*
Which they have often made against the Senate,
All cause unborn,* could never be the native*
Of our so frank donation.* Well, what then?   130
How* shall this bosom multiplied digest
The Senate's courtesy? Let deeds* express
What's like to be their words: 'We did request it.
We are the greater poll,* and in true* fear
They gave us our demands.' Thus we debase   135
The nature of our seats,* and make the rabble
Call our cares* fears, which* will in time
Break ope* the locks o' th' Senate and bring in
The crows to peck the eagles.*

MENENIUS   Come, enough.
BRUTUS   Enough, with over-measure.*
CORIOLANUS   No, take more.   140
What may be sworn by,* both divine and human,
Seal what I end withal.* This double worship,*
Where one part does disdain with cause,* the other*
Insult without* all reason; where gentry,* title, wisdom,
Cannot conclude* but by the yea and no   145
Of general ignorance, it must omit*
Real necessities, and give way the while*
To unstable slightness.* Purpose so* barred, it follows,
Nothing is done to purpose. Therefore beseech* you,
You that will be less fearful than discreet;*   150
That love the fundamental part of state*
More than you doubt* the change on't;* that prefer
A noble life before a long,* and wish
To jump* a body with a dangerous physic
That's sure of death without it, at once pluck out   155
The multitudinous tongue;* let them not lick*
The sweet which is their poison. Your dishonour*
Mangles true judgement, and bereaves* the state
Of that integrity* which should become't,*
Not having the power to do the good it would,*   160
For th' ill* which doth control't.

BRUTUS   Has* said enough.

162   *answer* – i.e. answer the charge.
163   *despite o'erwhelm thee:* Either (a) may contempt wither you, or (b) may injury destroy you.
164   *bald:* (a) trivial (b) hairless.
165   *On whom . . . bench* – i.e. in depending on the tribunes the people fail in their obedience
          to the higher authority, the Senate.
166   *In a rebellion . . . chosen:* They were appointed in a time of rebellion, when what was
          expedient (*what must be*) and not what was right (*meet*) became the law.
168   *In a better hour:* At a more favourable time (than that of rebellion).
169   *Let what . . . be meet:* let it be said (by you) that what is right must be done.
172   *The aediles* – Each tribune had two aediles assigned to him to carry out police duties
          under his orders for the maintenance of public order.
172   *apprehended:* arrested.
173   *myself/Attach:* I arrest.
174   *innovator:* revolutionary.
175   *weal:* welfare.
176   *to thine answer:* to answer the charges against you.
176   *old goat* – Sicinius and Brutus are bearded as well as bald. Cf. II.i.80.
177   *surety him:* go bail for him.
180   *more respect:* show more consideration.
187   *Peace:* Be quiet. – There are similar cries for silence at lines 191, 192 etc.
189   *Confusion's near:* Ruin is imminent.
189   *You* – i.e. You speak. – Menenius, out of breath and unable to pacify the mob, begs the
          tribunes to do so.

SICINIUS Has spoken like a traitor, and shall answer*
    As traitors do.
CORIOLANUS   Thou wretch, despite o'erwhelm thee!*
    What should the people do with these bald* tribunes,
    On whom* depending, their obedience fails   165
    To th' greater bench. In a rebellion,*
    When what's not meet, but what must be, was law,
    Then were they chosen. In a better hour*
    Let what* is meet be said it must be meet,
    And throw their power i' th' dust.   170
BRUTUS Manifest treason!
SICINIUS   This is a consul? No.
BRUTUS The aediles,* ho!

Enter an AEDILE.

           Let him be apprehended.*
SICINIUS Go call the people [*exit* AEDILE], in whose name myself
    Attach* thee as a traitorous innovator,*
    A foe to th' public weal.* [*He attempts to seize*
          CORIOLANUS] Obey, I charge thee,   175
    And follow to thine answer.*
CORIOLANUS   Hence, old goat!*
SENATORS We'll surety him.*
COMINIUS   Aged sir, hands off!
CORIOLANUS Hence, rotten thing, or I shall shake thy bones
    Out of thy garments.
SICINIUS   Help, ye citizens!

Enter a rabble of PLEBEIANS *with the* AEDILES.

MENENIUS On both sides more respect.*   180
SICINIUS Here's he that would take from you all your power.
BRUTUS Seize him, aediles!
CITIZENS Down with him, down with him!
FIRST SENATOR Weapons, weapons, weapons!
          [*They all bustle about* CORIOLANUS
ALL Tribunes! Patricians! Citizens! What ho!   185
    Sicinius! Brutus! Coriolanus! Citizens!
    Peace,* peace, peace! Stay, hold, peace!
MENENIUS What is about to be? I am out of breath.
    Confusion's near.* I cannot speak. You,* Tribunes
    To the people! Coriolanus, patience!   190
    Speak, good Sicinius.

193   *at point to lose:* on the point of losing.
194   *Martius* – Here and at line 210 the Tribunes pointedly refer to Coriolanus by his *praenomen* Martius, and not by his *agnomen* or honorary title.
195   *late . . . named for:* you have just chosen as.
195   *Fie:* Shame on you.
196   *kindle, not to quench:* start a fire, not to put it out, i.e. to make the people riot, not to pacify them.
202   *so are like to do:* are likely to do so.
205   *yet distinctly ranges:* still stands, separate and distinct. – Shakespeare is apparently thinking of the outspread buildings of a city, each distinct in appearance, which will be levelled to an indistinguishable heap of rubble if anarchy prevails, the architectural ruin symbolizing the destruction of the commonwealth.
206   *This deserves death* – Sicinius refers to the earlier speeches of Coriolanus which reached a climax in line 170, not to what Cominius has just said.
207   *Or . . . Or:* Either . . . or.
207   *stand to:* maintain.
209   *Upon the part o':* on behalf of.
209   *in whose . . . theirs:* by whose authority we were elected to represent their power. – The authority of the tribunes has been questioned; Brutus insists that it is absolute, giving the tribunes power to execute Coriolanus without trial.
211   *present:* immediate.
212   *th' rock Tarpeian* – a precipitous rock-face on the Capitoline Hill in Rome, from which criminals were hurled to their death.
215   *Beseech:* I beg.
215   *but a:* just one.
217   *that:* what.
218   *temp'rately . . . redress:* take moderate measures to put right (*redress*) the things that you are trying to deal with by violence.
219   *cold ways:* dispassionate methods.
220   *prudent helps:* wise ways of improving the situation.

SICINIUS	Hear me, people, peace!
CITIZENS	Let's hear our tribune. Peace! – Speak, speak, speak.
SICINIUS	You are at point to lose* your liberties.
	Martius* would have them all from you; Martius,
	Whom late* you have named for consul.

MENENIUS   Fie,* fie, fie!   195

This is the way to kindle, not to quench.*

FIRST SENATOR To unbuild the city, and to lay all flat.

SICINIUS What is the city but the people?

CITIZENS   True,

The people are the city.

BRUTUS By the consent of all, we were established   200

The people's magistrates.

CITIZENS   You so remain.

MENENIUS And so are like to do.*

COMINIUS That is the way to lay the city flat,

To bring the roof to the foundation,

And bury all which yet distinctly ranges*   205

In heaps and piles of ruin.

SICINIUS   This deserves death.*

BRUTUS Or* let us stand to* our authority,

Or let us lose it. We do here pronounce,

Upon the part o'* th' people, in whose* power

We were elected theirs, Martius is worthy   210

Of present* death.

SICINIUS   Therefore lay hold of him;

Bear him to th' rock Tarpeian,* and from thence

Into destruction cast him.

BRUTUS   Aediles, seize him!

CITIZENS Yield, Martius, yield!

MENENIUS   Hear me one word.

Beseech* you, tribunes, hear me but a* word.   215

AEDILES Peace, peace!

MENENIUS [To BRUTUS] Be that* you seem, truly your country's friend,

And temp'rately* proceed to what you would

Thus violently redress.

BRUTUS   Sir, those cold ways,*

That seem like prudent helps,* are very poisonous   220

Where the disease is violent. – Lay hands upon him,

And bear him to the rock.

                          [CORIOLANUS *draws his sword*

CORIOLANUS   No, I'll die here.

224   *try . . . seen me* – He invites those who (as soldiers) have seen him in action to experience what it is like to be 'on the receiving end'.

229   *get you to your house* – This is addressed to Coriolanus, as is the Second Senator's *Get you gone* (line 230).

230   *naught else:* ruined if you do not.

232   *put to that:* put to that extreme test, i.e. of a civil war.

233   *home:* go home.

234   *cause:* disease.

235   *tent:* treat. – See note to I.ix.29.

235   *beseech:* I beg.

237   *barbarians:* uncivilized foreigners. – The Romans considered all those outside Roman jurisdiction to be barbarians. Coriolanus means that, although Roman citizens, they behave like savages.

238   *littered:* born. – The term is normally used of the birth of certain animals; its application to the people here is contemptuous.

238   *not Romans:* I wish they were not Romans.

239   *Though . . . Capitol:* although they were born in the portico of Jupiter's temple on the Capitoline Hill. – Coriolanus continues the derisive animal imagery begun with *littered* (line 238).

240   *Put not . . . tongue:* Do not express your justifiable anger.

241   *One time will owe another:* We will get even for the present disturbance at some future time.

241   *fair:* even.

243   *Take up a brace:* fight a couple. – Menenius is an old man, well past his fighting days.

244   *'tis odds beyond arithmetic:* they are infinitely more numerous than us.

245   *manhood . . . falling fabric:* it is not brave but foolish to stand near a collapsing building.

247   *tag:* rabble.

247   *doth rend . . . to bear:* tears things apart like an obstructed current and overwhelms what they normally endure. – The image seems to be that of a river bursting its banks, a favourite with Shakespeare.

250   *wit:* intellect.

250   *be in request/With:* is wanted by.

251   *This must . . . any colour* – i.e. We must use whatever means we can to restore order.

There's some among you have beheld me fighting;
Come try* upon yourselves what you have seen me.
MENENIUS Down with that sword! Tribunes withdraw awhile.   225
BRUTUS Lay hands upon him.
MENENIUS   Help Martius, help!
You that be noble, help him, young and old!
CITIZENS Down with him, down with him!

[*The* TRIBUNES, *the* AEDILES *and the* CITIZENS *are beaten off-stage*

MENENIUS Go, get you to your house.* Be gone, away!
All will be naught else.*
SECOND SENATOR   Get you gone.
CORIOLANUS   Stand fast.   230
We have as many friends as enemies.
MENENIUS Shall it be put to that?*
FIRST SENATOR   The gods forbid!
I prithee, noble friend, home* to thy house.
Leave us to cure this cause.*
MENENIUS   For 'tis a sore upon us
You cannot tent* yourself. Be gone, beseech* you.   235
COMINIUS Come, sir, along with us.
CORIOLANUS I would they were barbarians,* as they are,
Though in Rome littered;* not Romans,* as they are not,
Though* calved i' th' porch o' th' Capitol.
MENENIUS   Be gone.
Put not* your worthy rage into your tongue.   240
One time will owe another.*
CORIOLANUS   On fair* ground
I could beat forty of them.
MENENIUS   I could myself
Take up a brace* o' th' best of them; yea, the two
                                        tribunes.
COMINIUS But now 'tis odds beyond arithmetic,*
And manhood* is called foolery when it stands   245
Against a falling fabric. Will you hence
Before the tag* return, whose rage doth rend*
Like interrupted waters, and o'erbear
What they are used to bear.
MENENIUS   Pray you, be gone.
I'll try whether my old wit* be in request   250
With* those that have but little. This must* be patched
With cloth of any colour.

253   *marred his fortune* – i.e. destroyed his hopes of becoming consul.
255   *for his trident:* in order to get his trident. – Neptune, the Roman god of the sea, carried a
              trident, or three-pronged spear, as a symbol of his rule over the seas.
256   *for's:* for his.
256   *His heart's his mouth:* He says what he feels.
257   *What his breast forges:* Whatever idea his mind shapes.
257   *vent:* express.
258   *does forget . . . death* – i.e. he fears nothing.
260   *would:* wish.
260   *abed:* in bed.
261   *What the vengeance!* – An emphatic expletive. Cf. the modern 'What the devil!'
262   *speak 'em fair:* speak politely to them.
262   *viper,* a poisonous snake. – Sicinius in his turn, now speaks of Coriolanus in animal terms.
              The viper was used as the type of the unnatural traitor, since it was erroneously
              believed that young vipers gnawed their way through the bowels of their
              mother.
264   *Be every man himself:* act as if he were the whole city.
266   *With rigorous hands:* by men of inflexible minds.
267   *scorn . . . trial/Than:* contemptuously refuse to let him have any trial except.
268   *public power:* power derived from the people.
269   *so sets at nought:* sets no value on in this way.
269   *well know:* learn thoroughly.
271   *sure on't:* certainly.
273   *Do not . . . warrant:* Do not authorize a merciless slaughter which exceeds your limited
              power. – To *cry havoc,* a term taken from warfare, was to authorize general
              destruction and plunder. Menenius is warning the tribunes that they are
              exceeding their authority.
274   *how comes't:* how does it come about that, i.e. why is it.
275   *holp* – an old form of *helped.*
275   *make this rescue* – a legal term for the unlawful action of releasing a man by force from
              the custody of the law.

COMINIUS   Nay, come away.

               [*Exeunt* CORIOLANUS *and* COMINIUS

PATRICIAN This man has marred his fortune.*

MENENIUS His nature is too noble for the world.

He would not flatter Neptune for his trident,*   255
Or Jove for's* power to thunder. His heart's his mouth.*
What his breast forges,* that his tongue must vent,*
And being angry, does forget* that ever
He heard the name of death.

                       [*A noise within*

Here's goodly work!

PATRICIAN   I would* they were abed!*   260

MENENIUS I would they were in Tiber! What the vengeance!*
Could he not speak 'em fair?*

Enter BRUTUS *and* SICINIUS *with the rabble again.*

SICINIUS   Where is this viper*
That would depopulate the city and
Be every man himself?*

MENENIUS   You worthy tribunes —

SICINIUS He shall be thrown down the Tarpeian rock   265
With rigorous hands.* He hath resisted law,
And therefore law shall scorn* him further trial
Than the severity of the public power,*
Which he so sets at nought.*

FIRST CITIZEN   He shall well know*
The noble tribunes are the people's mouths,   270
And we their hands.

ALL   He shall, sure on't.*

MENENIUS   Sir, sir —

SICINIUS Peace!

MENENIUS Do not* cry havoc where you should but hunt
With modest warrant.

SICINIUS   Sir, how comes't* that you
Have holp* to make this rescue?*

MENENIUS   Hear me speak.   275
As I do know the consul's worthiness,
So can I name his faults.

SICINIUS   Consul? What consul?

MENENIUS The consul Coriolanus.

BRUTUS   He consul?

ALL No, no, no, no, no.

280   *leave:* permission.
282   *The which . . . time:* which will not cause you to lose anything except the time spent listening to me.
284   *peremptory to dispatch:* determined to kill. – *Peremptory* is stressed on the first and third syllables.
285   *viperous traitor* – See note to line 262 above.
285   *To eject . . . danger:* To drive him away (out of the city into banishment) would simply be a continual danger.
290   *deservèd:* deserving.
290   *enrolled . . . book* – i.e. well known to the gods. The idea is probably derived from the biblical 'book of life' mentioned in *Revelation* xx.12, in which men's deeds are recorded.
291   *dam:* mother.
292   *own:* own offspring.
295   *Mortal:* (it would be) fatal.
296   *worthy:* worthy of.
298   *vouch:* affirm.
300   *And what . . . world:* and for him to lose what is left (of his blood) at the hands of his own countrymen (*by his country*) would be (*were*) for all of us who cause it or allow it, an everlasting mark of shame (*brand*).
302   *clean kam:* quite wrong. – *Kam* is probably from the Welsh *cam* meaning 'crooked', 'false'.
303   *Merely awry:* Completely distorted.
304   *The service . . . it was* – Menenius is answering the assertion of Sicinius that Coriolanus is *a disease that must be cut away* (line 293), and arguing that this is monstrous ingratitude. It is like ignoring the good service a diseased foot performed before it became infected.
307   *pluck him thence:* remove him from it.
310   *tiger-footed* – i.e. swift and fierce.
311   *unscanned swiftness:* thoughtless haste.
312   *Tie leaden pounds to's heels:* tie heavy pound-weights to its heels, i.e. to slow down the rage. – Menenius argues that when they discover the harm their rashness has caused it will be too late to remedy it.
312   *process:* the normal process of law.
313   *Lest . . . Romans:* in case, since he has loyal admirers, factions (*parties*) begin fighting, and cause the destruction of this great city of Rome by (*with*) Romans. – Menenius fears civil war.

MENENIUS If by the tribunes' leave,* and yours, good people,   280
                I may be heard, I would crave a word or two,
                The which* shall turn you to no further harm
                Than so much loss of time.

SICINIUS   Speak briefly then,
                For we are peremptory to dispatch*
                This viperous traitor.* To eject* him hence   285
                Were but one danger, and to keep him here
                Our certain death. Therefore it is decreed
                He dies tonight.

MENENIUS   Now the good gods forbid
                That our renownèd Rome, whose gratitude
                Towards her deservèd* children is enrolled*   290
                In Jove's own book, like an unnatural dam*
                Should now eat up her own!*

SICINIUS He's a disease that must be cut away.

MENENIUS O, he's a limb that has but a disease;
                Mortal,* to cut it off: to cure it, easy.   295
                What has he done to Rome that's worthy* death?
                Killing our enemies, the blood he hath lost –
                Which I dare vouch* is more than that he hath
                By many an ounce – he dropped it for his country;
                And what* is left, to lose it by his country   300
                Were to us all that do't and suffer it
                A brand to th' end o' th' world.

SICINIUS   This is clean kam.*

BRUTUS Merely awry.* When he did love his country
                It honoured him.

MENENIUS   The service* of the foot
                Being once gangrened, is not then respected   305
                For what before it was.

BRUTUS   We'll hear no more.
                Pursue him to his house and pluck him thence,*
                Lest his infection, being of catching nature,
                Spread further.

MENENIUS   One word more, one word!
                This tiger-footed* rage, when it shall find   310
                The harm of unscanned swiftness,* will, too late,
                Tie leaden pounds to's heels.* Proceed by process,*
                Lest* parties – as he is beloved – break out,
                And sack great Rome with Romans.

BRUTUS   If it were so –

315   *What do ye talk?:* What are you talking about?
317   *smote:* have been struck.
319   *'a:* he.
319   *ill-schooled/In bolted language:* not well-trained in the use of refined language. — To 'bolt'
meal was to sieve it, separating the flour from the bran. The metaphor is
continued in the next sentence. Coriolanus, says Menenius, speaks straight-
forwardly, the rough with the smooth, without careful premeditation or
choice of words.
323   *answer . . . utmost peril:* answer the charges against him peacefully and in the way the law
requires, even though his life is at stake.
325   *húmane way:* civilized way of proceeding.
326   *the end . . . beginning* — i.e. we do not know how it will end. — He too fears civil war.
329   *Masters* — Sicinius addresses the people by this flattering term.
330   *on:* in.
330   *attend:* wait for.
332   *our first way:* as we first decided to, i.e. to put him to death.
334   *to:* go to.

III.ii.   Back at home, Coriolanus, infuriated by the charge of treason, swears he will never change
in his attitude to the people and their leaders. He is deeply disturbed by his mother's
disapproval of his conduct. She tells him he has been trying to wield power before he has
it, and that he must dissemble his true feelings and apologize to the people. His friends
second her argument, stressing the danger to the whole city, and finally Coriolanus agrees
to act this part so repugnant to his nature.
A new tragic note is introduced with this development of the relationship between
mother and son. Volumnia, who has formed Coriolanus's character and who has led him
in his contempt for the plebeians, is the last person from whom he would expect censure;
but now she urges upon him a policy of expediency which seems hateful to him and
opposed to all he values most. At the same time she argues that it is a course of action he
has supported in his war-making, which is for him a shattering revelation. He finds
himself in the dilemma of having to choose between his hitherto unquestioned loyalty
to her and his duty to save Rome from civil war on the one hand, and all his deepest
convictions and sense of honour on the other. Volumnia and Rome prove the stronger,
with disastrous results for Coriolanus. We feel his predicament acutely, and admire the
effort which this proud man makes to follow the advice of others which he finds abhorrent
and demeaning.

1   *pull all about mine ears:* bring everything down to destruction.
1   *present me:* prescribe for me.
2   *Death on the wheel* — i.e. by being tied to a wheel and flogged to death.
2   *at wild horses' heels* — i.e. tied to horses and torn apart. Both forms of punishment were
Elizabethan; neither was practised by the Romans.
4   *That the precipitation . . . sight:* so that the drop should be so deep that no one could see
to the bottom.
6   *thus* — i.e. infuriated, adamant.

SICINIUS   What do ye talk?*   315
             Have we not had a taste of his obedience?
             Our Aediles smote,* ourselves resisted? Come!
MENENIUS   Consider this. He has been bred i' th' wars
             Since 'a* could draw a sword, and is ill-schooled
             In bolted language.* Meal and bran together   320
             He throws without distinction. Give me leave;
             I'll go to him, and undertake to bring him
             Where he shall answer,* by a lawful form,
             In peace, to his utmost peril.
FIRST SENATOR   Noble tribunes,
             It is the húmane way.* The other course   325
             Will prove too bloody, and the end* of it
             Unknown to the beginning.
SICINIUS   Noble Menenius,
             Be you then as the people's officer.
             Masters,* lay down your weapons.
BRUTUS   Go not home.
             Meet on* the market-place. We'll attend* you there, 330
             Where, if you bring not Martius, we'll proceed
             In our first way.*
SICINIUS   I'll bring him to you.
             [To the SENATORS] Let me desire your company. He must
                      come,
             Or what is worst will follow.
FIRST SENATOR   Pray you, let's to* him.
                                                    [Exeunt

scene ii

Rome. The house of CORIOLANUS.

Enter CORIOLANUS *with* PATRICIANS.

CORIOLANUS   Let them pull all about mine ears,* present me*
             Death on the wheel,* or at wild horses' heels,*
             Or pile ten hills on the Tarpeian rock,
             That the precipitation* might down stretch
             Below the beam of sight; yet will I still   5
             Be thus* to them.

6   *do the nobler:* in this way act all the more nobly. – *Nobler* is pronounced as a trisyllable here.

7   *muse . . . further:* cannot understand why my mother no longer approves of my actions.

8   *was wont:* used.

9   *woollen vassals:* coarse slaves. – A reference to the coarse woollen cloth worn by the poorer classes in Elizabethan England.

9   *things created . . . groats:* men created only to be petty tradesmen. – A *groat* was an English coin of low value.

10   *to show bare heads/In congregations:* to show respect by removing their hats in company. – The reference to congregations and yawning make it probable that Shakespeare had a boring church sermon in mind here. See note to II.i.63.

12   *When one but of my ordinance:* whenever someone of my rank.

15   *I play/The man I am:* I am acting as I really am, i.e. he is not 'acting' at all, but being himself.

17   *put your power . . . out* – Volumnia speaks as if the consulship were a garment which Coriolanus has rashly worn out before he has had time to put it on, i.e. she censures him for throwing away power before he has secured it.

18   *Let go:* Enough of that.

19   *You might . . . be so:* You could have been sufficiently yourself even if you had been less determined to be so.

20   *Lesser . . . dispositions:* Your desires would have been less opposed.

21   *crossings.* – The Folio reads *things* here, which makes no sense and gives a metrically defective line. The metre requires a two-syllable word, and the sense demands some such word as *crossings* (thwarting), which Shakespeare uses in this sense in other plays. Other emendations such as *taxations, thwartings,* have been suggested by various editors. *Crossings* is attractive because it ties up with *cross* (line 23 – thwart) just as *dispositions* (line 21) ties up with *disposed* (line 22).

23   *Ere they lacked power:* before they lost the power, i.e. after you had been elected consul.

25   *something:* rather.

26   *mend it:* repair the damage.

26   *There's no remedy . . . perish:* There is no help for it; otherwise, if you do not do so, Rome will be divided into two factions and destroyed.

28   *Pray be counselled:* I beg you to take this advice.

29   *as little apt:* as unwilling.

30   *leads my use . . . vantage:* shows me how to use my anger to better advantage.

32   *Before he . . . physic:* Before allowing him to humble himself completely (*stoop to th' heart*), if it were not for the fact that the present violent madness (*fit*) demands it as a cure (*physic*).

35   *can scarcely bear:* hardly have the strength to support – because of his age.

FIRST PATRICIAN   You do the nobler.*

Enter VOLUMNIA.

CORIOLANUS [*To the* PATRICIANS] I muse* my mother
Does not approve me further, who was wont*
To call them woollen vassals,* things created*
To buy and sell with groats, to show bare heads   10
In congregations,* to yawn, be still and wonder,
When one but of my ordinance* stood up
To speak of peace or war. [*To* VOLUMNIA] I talk of you.
Why did you wish me milder? Would you have me
False to my nature? Rather say I play   15
The man I am.*

VOLUMNIA   O sir, sir, sir,
I would have had you put your power* well on
Before you had worn it out.

CORIOLANUS   Let go.*
VOLUMNIA You might* have been enough the man you are,
With striving less to be so. Lesser* had been   20
The crossings* of your dispositions, if
You had not showed them how ye were disposed
Ere they lacked power* to cross you.

CORIOLANUS   Let them hang.
VOLUMNIA Ay, and burn too.

Enter MENENIUS *with* SENATORS.

MENENIUS Come, come, you have been too rough, something* too
                rough.   25
You must return and mend it.*

SENATOR   There's no remedy,*
Unless, by not so doing, our good city
Cleave in the midst and perish.

VOLUMNIA   Pray be counselled.*
I have a heart as little apt* as yours,
But yet a brain that leads my use* of anger   30
To better vantage.

MENENIUS   Well said, noble woman.
Before he* should thus stoop to th' heart, but that
The violent fit o' th' time craves it as physic
For the whole state, I would put mine armour on,
Which I can scarcely bear.*

CORIOLANUS   What must I do?   35

37	*spoke:* spoken.
39	*absolute:* uncompromising.
40	*therein . . . extremities speak:* in being uncompromising you can never be too noble, except when extreme situations demand compromise.
42	*Honour . . . together:* in wartime honour and political expediency go hand in hand, like inseparable friends. – *Policy* usually connoted cunning, or underhand stratagems, at this time.
43	*Grant that . . . not there* – Volumnia asks why the same should not be true in peacetime. *That* (line 45) . . . *there:* that prevents them from working together then (in peacetime).
45	*That:* so that.
45	*Tush* – an exclamation of impatience.
45	*demand:* question.
46	*to seem/The same:* to appear to be what.
48	*adopt as.* adopt as.
49	*That it shall hold companionship:* if your policy (of deception) go hand in hand with.
51	*It stands in like request:* it is equally necessary.
51	*force:* urge.
52	*lies you on:* it is your duty.
53	*by your own instruction:* according to your own knowledge.
54	*by the matter . . . prompts you:* following your deepest feelings.
55	*roted in . . . bosom's truth:* learned by heart and spoken, which are spurious words in no way reflecting what you know in your heart to be the truth.
59	*take in:* capture.
60	*Which else . . . much blood:* which, without the gentle words, would force you to run the risk of defeat and serious bloodshed.
62	*dissemble with my nature:* disguise my true feelings.
64	*I am in this:* In this matter I represent.
66	*will rather show . . . ruin:* prefer to show common fellows your frowns than expend a little flattery on them to obtain their love and safeguard what might be destroyed for the lack of their love. – *inheritance:* possession.
70	*fair:* politely.
70	*salve, so:* heal, in this way.
71	*Not:* not only. – Cf. III.iii.97.

MENENIUS   Return to th' tribunes.

CORIOLANUS   Well, what then? What then?

MENENIUS   Repent what you have spoke.*

CORIOLANUS   For them? I cannot do it to the gods;
Must I then do't to them?

VOLUMNIA   You are too absolute,*
Though therein* you can never be too noble   40
But when extremities speak. I have heard you say,
Honour* and policy, like unsevered friends,
I' th' war do grow together. Grant that,* and tell me
In peace what each of them by th' other lose
That* they combine not there.

CORIOLANUS   Tush,* tush!

MENENIUS   A good demand.*   45

VOLUMNIA   If it be honour in your wars to seem
The same* you are not, which for the best ends
You adopt* your policy, how is it less or worse
That it shall hold companionship* in peace
With honour as in war, since that to both   50
It stands in like request?*

CORIOLANUS   Why force* you this?

VOLUMNIA   Because that now it lies you on* to speak
To th' people, not by your own instruction,*
Nor by the matter* which your heart prompts you,
But with such words that are but roted in*   55
Your tongue, though but bastards, and syllables
Of no allowance to your bosom's truth.
Now, this no more dishonours you at all
Than to take in* a town with gentle words,
Which else* would put you to your fortune and   60
The hazard of much blood.
I would dissemble with my nature,* where
My fortunes and my friends at stake required
I should do so in honour. I am in this*
Your wife, your son, these senators, the nobles;   65
And you will rather show* our general louts
How you can frown than spend a fawn upon 'em
For the inheritance of their loves, and safeguard
Of what that want might ruin.

MENENIUS   Noble lady!
Come, go with us. Speak fair.* You may salve, so,*   70
Not* what is dangerous present, but the loss

73	*this bonnet:* this hat of yours. – Possibly Volumnia takes off Coriolanus's hat, or perhaps just points to it.

73   *this bonnet:* this hat of yours. – Possibly Volumnia takes off Coriolanus's hat, or perhaps just points to it.

74   *stretched it:* held it out.

74   *here be with them:* go along with (i.e. humour) them, i.e. to get what you want from them.

75   *bussing:* kissing. – Volumnia curtsies to show Coriolanus how to do it.

76   *Action is eloquence . . . ears* – Actions, or gestures, says Volumnia, speak louder than words as far as the mob is concerned. Action, which in rhetoric comprised all the possible uses of the body – head, trunk, limbs, hands and fingers – including the use of the voice, was an essential part of the orator's art.

77   *waving:* bowing up and down.

78   *Which often . . . heart:* which (i.e. the head) often chastising your proud feelings in this way, i.e. by being bowed and moved up and down in apparent humility and repentance.

79   *Now humble as* – i.e. make as humble as.

80   *That will . . . handling* – i.e. too ripe to bear much handling. The image is one of a very ripe fruit, hanging heavy and passive. The grammar of lines 74–80 is loose, and some editors to improve it emend *Which* (line 78) to *With,* and omit *or* in line 80. These emendations, however, do not perfect the grammar, and it may well be that the imperfect syntax was intended by the dramatist to show the urgency and force of Volumnia's attempt to sway her son.

80   *say . . . person* (line 86): tell them that you are their soldier and, having had much of your education on the battlefield (*in broils*), you have not the gentle (*soft*) manner which, you admit, you ought to have and they have a right to expect (*claim*) when you ask them for their kind regard (*good loves*); but (say to them) that you will certainly (*forsooth*) act according to their wishes in the future to the best of your ability.

86   *This but done:* If only this were done.

87   *were:* would be.

88   *they have pardons . . . purpose:* they are as ready to forgive as they are to talk nonsense.

91   *in a fiery gulf:* into a flaming abyss, i.e. to hell.

92   *bower:* garden, or perhaps bedroom. – *Bower* often meant an unlocalized, idealized place.

94   *make strong party:* gather a strong body of supporters around you.

94   *or defend yourself/By calmness:* either protect yourself against your enemies by keeping your anger under control.

95   *All's in anger:* Everyone is angry.

96   *fair:* polite. – Cf. 1.70 above.

97   *thereto frame his spirit:* make up his mind to do that – i.e. to speak courteously, as Menenius suggests.

99   *unbarbed sconce:* unarmed (i.e. bare) head. – See note to II.i.63 and III.ii.10.

100   *noble* – i.e. belonging to one of Rome's noble families. As Coriolanus sees it, to lie is to betray his noble blood. *Noble* is contrasted with *base* in this same line.

102   *were there . . . Martius:* if the danger was to my own body alone, to this single member of the family of Martius. – *plot:* piece of earth, and so his body; *mould:* (a) form, (b) clay.

Of what is past.

VOLUMNIA   I prithee now, my son,
Go to them with this bonnet* in thy hand,
And thus far having stretched it* – here be with them* –
Thy knee bussing* the stones (for in such business   75
Action is eloquence,* and the eyes of th' ignorant
More learned than the ears), waving* thy head,
Which often* thus correcting thy stout heart,
Now humble as* the ripest mulberry
That will* not hold the handling; or say* to them   80
Thou art their soldier, and being bred in broils
Hast not the soft way which, thou dost confess,
Were fit for thee to use, as they to claim,
In asking their good loves, but thou wilt frame
Thyself, forsooth, hereafter theirs, so far   85
As thou hast power and person.

MENENIUS   This but done,*
Even as she speaks, why, their hearts were* yours,
For they have pardons,* being asked, as free
As words to little purpose.

VOLUMNIA   Prithee now,
Go, and be ruled, although I know thou hadst rather   90
Follow thine enemy in a fiery gulf*
Than flatter him in a bower.*

Enter COMINIUS.

                              Here is Cominius.

COMINIUS I have been i' th' market-place; and, sir, 'tis fit
You make strong party,* or defend yourself
By calmness,* or by absence. All's in anger.*   95

MENENIUS Only fair* speech.

COMINIUS   I think 'twill serve, if he
Can thereto frame his spirit.*

VOLUMNIA   He must, and will.
Prithee now, say you will, and go about it.

CORIOLANUS Must I go show them my unbarbed sconce?* Must I
With my base tongue give to my noble* heart   100
A lie that it must bear? Well, I will do't.
Yet were there* but this single plot to lose,
This mould of Martius, they to dust should grind it,
And throw't against the wind. To th' market-place!

105   *put me . . . th'life:* forced on me such a difficult part to play that I shall not be able to perform it convincingly. – This a further example of Shakespeare's use of the actor's art for his imagery, possibly suggested by the word *plot* (line 102). Cominius continues the metaphor by promising to act as prompter if Coriolanus forgets his lines, and Volumnia exhorts him to a superlative performance.

111   *Away, my disposition . . . spirit:* May I forget my natural inclinations and be possessed by the spirit of some wretch. – Coriolanus feels that he will have to be possessed by a devil to act this part. *Harlot*, meaning 'base creature', was a term used of both men and women in Shakespeare's day, and frequently applied to actors, who in his early days were despised as inferior members of society. Cf. *1 Henry IV*, II.iv.442: 'these harlotry players'. Coriolanus thus continues the acting metaphor he began at line 105.

112   *My throat . . . drum:* Let my soldier's voice, which was in tune (as in a *choir*) with my drum, be changed.

113   *a pipe . . . eunuch:* a voice as high-pitched as a eunuch's.

114   *virgin:* girlish.

115   *babies lulls:* lulls dolls.

116   *Tent:* pitch their tents, i.e. lodge.

116   *take up:* occupy – i.e. so that he will be unable to see what he is doing.

117   *glasses of my sight:* my eyeballs.

119   *Who bowed but:* which bent only.

119   *his/That . . . alms* – i.e. a beggar's.

121   *surcease . . . own truth:* stop respecting my devotion to truth.

123   *inherent:* permanent.

124   *To beg . . . of them:* It is a greater dishonour for me to beg from you, than for you to beg from the mob. – The Romans held their parents in such honour that for a mother to have to beg a favour from her son would have seemed improper to them, contrary to their sense of *pietas* or dutiful family conduct.

125   *Come all to ruin:* Let everything be ruined.

125   *Let/Thy mother . . . stoutness:* Let me rather experience the disaster which your pride will cause than live in fear of the danger which your obstinacy threatens. – *stoutness:* obstinacy. Volumnia would prefer Rome's ruin and even her own death to a life of fear.

128   *list:* please.

130   *owe:* own, possess. – Volumnia boasts that he imbibes his courage from her, as a baby takes milk from its mother; his obstinacy is his own, she avers.

132   *mountebank their loves:* win their love through trickery, like a quack. – The *mountebank* (from the Italian *monta in banco* – to mount on a bench) got up on a bench to sell his wares. His dishonesty was notorious. He appealed to his audience by means of stories, tricks, juggling etc.

133   *Cog:* cheat.

133   *beloved/Of:* loved by.

134   *trades:* tradesmen.

137   *Do your will* – The irony is striking. Coriolanus is doing her will, certainly not his own.

138   *do attend:* are waiting for.

138   *Arm:* Prepare.

             You have put me* now to such a part which never   105
             I shall discharge to th' life.

COMINIUS   Come, come, we'll prompt you.

VOLUMNIA I prithee now, sweet son, as thou hast said
             My praises made thee first a soldier, so,
             To have my praise for this, perform a part
             Thou hast not done before.

CORIOLANUS   Well, I must do't.   110
             Away, my disposition,* and possess me
             Some harlot's spirit! My throat* of war be turned,
             Which choired with my drum, into a pipe*
             Small as an eunuch, or the virgin* voice
             That babies lulls* asleep. The smiles of knaves   115
             Tent* in my cheeks, and schoolboys' tears take up*
             The glasses of my sight.* A beggar's tongue
             Make motion through my lips, and my armed knees,
             Who bowed but* in my stirrup bend like his
             That* hath received an alms. I will not do't,   120
             Lest I surcease* to honour mine own truth,
             And by my body's action teach my mind
             A most inherent* baseness.

VOLUMNIA   At thy choice then.
             To beg* of thee, it is my more dishonour
             Than thou of them. Come all to ruin.* Let   125
             Thy mother* rather feel thy pride than fear
             Thy dangerous stoutness, for I mock at death
             With as big heart as thou. Do as thou list.*
             Thy valiantness was mine, thou suck'st it from me;
             But owe* thy pride thyself.

CORIOLANUS   Pray, be content.   130
             Mother, I am going to the market-place.
             Chide me no more. I'll mountebank their loves,*
             Cog* their hearts from them, and come home beloved
             Of* all the trades* in Rome. Look, I am going.
             Commend me to my wife. I'll return consul,   135
             Or never trust to what my tongue can do
             I' th' way of flattery further.

VOLUMNIA   Do your will.*
                       [*Exit* VOLUMNIA

COMINIUS Away, the tribunes do attend* you. Arm* yourself
             To answer mildly, for they are prepared
             With accusations, as I hear, more strong   140

141   *are upon:* have been made against.
142   *word:* password. – Coriolanus characteristically uses military language.
143   *accuse me by invention:* invent charges against me.
144   *in mine honour:* in a manner consistent with my honour.

III.iii.   Brutus and Sicinius plan their strategy for the destruction of Coriolanus, rehearsing the
cues and responses for the people. From one side Coriolanus and the patricians enter,
from the other the citizens, presenting in visual terms the opponents in the political
struggle, a confrontation full of menace. Coriolanus agrees to abide by the judicial
process of the tribunes provided that he is tried only on the charge that he 'affects/
Tyrannical power'. They then accuse him of treason, knowing from III.i how this incenses
him. Coriolanus swallows the bait, refusing to be calmed and they find it an easy matter
to banish him on pain of death if he returns. Coriolanus leaves them, declaring that it is
he who is banishing them.

   This is the last round of the struggle for power round Rome, and the tribunes win it. It is
their moment of triumph. More important dramatically speaking, however, is the effect
of the action on the audience. As always, Shakespeare contrives to swing sympathy
strongly towards his protagonist at the moment when his fortunes are at their lowest.
While we may admire the efficiency and thoroughness of the tribunes' campaign against
Coriolanus, we are alienated by the farcical pretence of a trial in which no attempt is
made to prove the charge of tyranny and Cominius is silenced when he tries to speak.
Their meanness of spirit as they order the people to pursue Coriolanus to the gates with
insults contrasts unfavourably with the honest rashness of Coriolanus which makes him
so vulnerable to their wiles.

1   *charge him home:* press your charges against him as hard as you can.
1   *affects:* desires.
2   *evade us there:* sidesteps this charge.
3   *Enforce him with:* insist strongly upon.
3   *envy:* malice.
4   *spoil got on:* plunder won from.
5   *ne'er distributed:* not divided (among the Roman citizens).
5   *What . . . come:* Well, is he going to come?
9   *voices* – i.e. those who will give vocal support.
10   *by th' poll:* by counting heads, i.e. naming each voter.
11   *tribes* – The normal voting procedure in Rome was by centuries, or *hundreds*. Since the
patricians controlled 98 of the 193 centuries such a vote would certainly have
gone against the tribunes. They therefore arranged voting by tribes of which
there were 21 at this time. In most tribes the poorer members were in the
majority so that the tribal vote was almost certain to be against Coriolanus,
and in fact the vote was 9 tribes for and 12 against. This was the first time that
a tribal vote was taken in Rome.
12   *presently:* immediately.
14   *I' th' right and strength:* according to the rights and by the power.
17   *old prerogative:* long-established right. – Sicinius uses deliberately vague language to
fool the people into believing that they have an ancient right to pass the death
sentence without trial.

                       Than are upon* you yet.
CORIOLANUS The word* is 'mildly'. Pray you, let us go.
                       Let them accuse me by invention,* I
                       Will answer in mine honour.*
MENENIUS   Ay, but mildly.
CORIOLANUS Well, mildly be it then, mildly.   145

                                                    [*Exeunt*

scene iii

Rome. The Forum.

Enter SICINIUS *and* BRUTUS.

BRUTUS In this point charge him home,* that he affects*
              Tyrannical power. If he evade us there,*
              Enforce him with* his envy* to the people,
              And that the spoil got on* the Antiates
              Was ne'er distributed.*

              Enter an AEDILE.

                                    What,* will he come?   5
AEDILE He's coming.
BRUTUS   How accompanied?
AEDILE With old Menenius and those senators
              That always favoured him.
SICINIUS   Have you a catalogue
              Of all the voices* that we have procured,
              Set down by th' poll?*
AEDILE   I have; 'tis ready.   10
SICINIUS Have you collected them by tribes?*
AEDILE   I have.
SICINIUS Assemble presently* the people hither,
              And when they hear me say, 'It shall be so
              I' th' right and strength* o' th' commons,' be it either
              For death, for fine, or banishment, then let them,   15
              If I say 'Fine', cry 'Fine!' if 'Death', cry 'Death!'
              Insisting on the old prerogative*

18	*i' th' truth o' th' cause:* in the justice of the case.
18	*inform:* instruct.
19	*when such time:* when once.
19	*cry:* shout.
21	*Enforce the present execution:* urge the immediate carrying out.
22	*chance to sentence:* happen to decree.
23	*hint:* opportunity.
24	*hap:* happen.
25	*Put him to choler straight:* Make him angry straight away.
26	*Ever:* always.
26	*have his worth/Of contradiction:* Either (a) be as contrary as he likes (*worth:* pennyworth, full value), or (b) acquire his reputation from opposition (which he overcomes). *worth:* reputation.
27	*chafed:* roused to anger.
28	*reined again to temperance:* brought back again to a restrained and self-controlled state. – Brutus speaks of Coriolanus as an angry war-horse.
29	*that is there . . . us:* there is that there (*in his heart*) which promises (*looks*) as we desire.
32	*ostler:* stableman at an inn.
32	*poorest piece:* smallest coin.
33	*bear . . . volume:* endure any amount of being called a rascal.
33	*The honoured gods:* May the honoured gods.
36	*Throng:* Fill.
36	*shows:* ceremonies.
40	*List:* listen.
40	*Audience:* Pay attention.
42	*Shall I . . . present?:* Am I going to be charged only with this present matter?
43	*Must all determine here?:* Shall everything be settled here, once and for all?
43	*demand:* demand to know.
44	*submit you:* submit yourself.
45	*Allow:* accept.

And power i' th' truth o' th' cause.*

AEDILE   I shall inform* them.

BRUTUS   And when such time* they have begun to cry,*
Let them not cease, but with a din confused   20
Enforce the present execution*
Of what we chance to sentence.*

AEDILE   Very well.

SICINIUS   Make them be strong, and ready for this hint*
When we shall hap* to give't them.

BRUTUS   Go about it.

[*Exit* AEDILE

Put him to choler straight.* He hath been used   25
Ever* to conquer and to have his worth
Of contradiction.* Being once chafed,* he cannot
Be reined again to temperance;* then he speaks
What's in his heart, and that is there* which looks
With us to break his neck.

Enter CORIOLANUS, MENENIUS, COMINIUS *and* SENATORS.

SICINIUS   Well, here he comes.   30

MENENIUS   Calmly, I do beseech you.

CORIOLANUS   [*To* MENENIUS] Ay, as an ostler,* that for th' poorest
piece*
Will bear* the knave by the volume.
[*To the* TRIBUNES] The honoured gods*
Keep Rome in safety, and the chairs of justice
Supplied with worthy men! Plant love among's!   35
Throng* our large temples with the shows* of peace,
And not our streets with war!

FIRST SENATOR   Amen, amen.

MENENIUS   A noble wish.

Enter the AEDILE *with the* PLEBEIANS.

SICINIUS   Draw near, ye people.

AEDILE   List* to your tribunes. Audience!* Peace, I say!   40

CORIOLANUS   First hear me speak.

BOTH TRIBUNES   Well, say. Peace, ho!

CORIOLANUS   Shall I* be charged no further than this present?
Must all determine here?*

SICINIUS   I do demand*
If you submit you* to the people's voices,
Allow* their officers, and are content   45

46	*censure:* punishment.
47	*upon:* against.
51	*Like graves . . . churchyard* – It is not clear just what points of similarity between Coriolanus's wounds and churchyard graves Shakespeare had in mind, though several are possible. The mounds of graves could be compared to the scars and cicatrices on the body; the scattered headstones and tombs could look like blemishes in the churchyard, just as wounds are on the body. Menenius may also have had in mind the multiplicity of Coriolanus's wounds. His use of the adjective *holy* suggests his reverence for Coriolanus's Roman piety as a warrior.
51	*briars:* prickly bushes.
52	*move laughter:* provoke laughter (at the insignificance of the wounds). – Coriolanus characteristically shrugs off Menenius's compliments.
54	*Do not . . . envy you:* Do not consider his gruff words (*rougher accents*) as having any malice in them, but accept them as a soldier's speech, not as showing enmity (*envy*) towards you.
58	*the matter:* the reason.
59	*full voice:* everyone's support.
60	*the very hour . . . off:* at the very same moment you withdraw your support.
61	*Answer to us:* You must answer our charges. – Coriolanus has asked a question but Sicinius insists that he is not there to ask questions but to answer them.
62	*Say:* Speak.
62	*I ought so* – i.e. I ought to answer you. – Coriolanus is trying hard to be polite.
63	*contrived:* plotted.
64	*seasoned:* (a) long-established, mature (b) moderate. – Sicinius may be deliberately ambiguous here, hoping to persuade the dim-witted plebeians that Coriolanus is attempting to overthrow one of their ancient privileges. The tribunes, far from being long-established, had only recently been instituted.
64	*wind:* wriggle, insinuate. – This carefully-chosen word, with its suggestion of 'twisting', so inapplicable to Coriolanus's methods, is just the sort of word to rouse him to fury.
68	*i' th' lowest hell* – Both the Roman Hades and the Christian Hell are imagined as having various levels, the lowest reserved for the greatest sinners.
68	*fold in:* enfold.
69	*their traitor:* traitor to them.
69	*injurious:* insulting.
70	*Within* – i.e. If within. – i.e. If you held (the power to order) twenty thousand deaths (for me) in your eyes, twenty million in your hands, and twenty million in your lying tongue . . .
73	*free:* frank, unrestrained.
76	*put new matter to his charge:* charge him with new offences.

	To suffer lawful censure* for such faults	
	As shall be proved upon* you.	
CORIOLANUS	I am content.	
MENENIUS	Lo, citizens, he says he is content.	
	The warlike service he has done, consider. Think	
	Upon the wounds his body bears, which show	50
	Like graves* i' th' holy churchyard.	
CORIOLANUS	Scratches with briars,*	
	Scars to move laughter* only.	
MENENIUS	Consider further,	
	That when he speaks not like a citizen,	
	You find him like a soldier. Do not* take	
	His rougher accents for malicious sounds,	55
	But, as I say, such as become a soldier	
	Rather than envy you.	
COMINIUS	Well, well, no more.	
CORIOLANUS	What is the matter,*	
	That being passed for consul with full voice,*	
	I am so dishonoured, that the very hour*	60
	You take it off again?	
SICINIUS	Answer to us.*	
CORIOLANUS	Say,* then. 'Tis true I ought so.*	
SICINIUS	We charge you, that you have contrived* to take	
	From Rome all seasoned* office, and to wind*	
	Yourself into a power tyrannical,	65
	For which you are a traitor to the people.	
CORIOLANUS	How! Traitor?	
MENENIUS	Nay, temperately. Your promise.	
CORIOLANUS	The fires i' th' lowest hell* fold in* the people!	
	Call me their traitor,* thou injurious* tribune?	
	Within* thine eyes sat twenty thousand deaths,	70
	In thy hands clutched as many millions, in	
	Thy lying tongue both numbers, I would say	
	'Thou liest' unto thee with a voice as free*	
	As I do pray the gods.	
SICINIUS	Mark you this, people?	
CITIZENS	To th' rock, to th' rock with him!	
SICINIUS	Peace!	75
	We need not put new matter to his charge.*	
	What you have seen him do and heard him speak,	
	Beating your officers, cursing yourselves,	
	Opposing laws with strokes, and here defying	

81	*in such capital kind:* of such a serious nature that it deserves death.
82	*extremest:* most violent.
83	*What do you prate of service?:* What are you saying about service?
84	*that that:* that because I.
85	*You?* – Coriolanus, who recognizes fighting as the only form of *service*, is incredulous at Brutus's claim.
88	*Let . . . death:* If they condemn me to be thrown to death from the precipitous Tarpeian rock.
89	*Vagabond exile:* (sentence me to) homeless exile.
89	*flaying:* having my skin stripped off.
89	*pent . . . a day:* imprisoned, with life sustained on a mere daily grain (of corn).
91	*fair:* polite.
92	*check my courage:* restrain my spirit.
93	*have't with:* obtain it by.
93	*morrow:* morning.
93	*For that:* Because.
94	*As much as in him lies:* as far as he had power.
95	*Envied against:* shown malice towards.
96	*as now at last:* and has now finally.
97	*not:* not only. – Cf. III.ii.71.
99	*distribute:* administer.
102	*In peril of precipitation:* on penalty of being thrown.
110	*marks* – i.e. his wounds.
113	*estimate:* reputation.
113	*womb's increase:* offspring.
114	*treasure of my loins:* my treasured children.

Those whose great power must try him; even this,   80
So criminal and in such capital kind,*
Deserves th' extremest* death.

BRUTUS   But since he hath
Served well for Rome –

CORIOLANUS   What do you prate of service?*

BRUTUS   I talk of that that* know it.

CORIOLANUS   You?*   85

MENENIUS   Is this the promise that you made your mother?

COMINIUS   Know, I pray you –

CORIOLANUS   I'll know no further.
Let* them pronounce the steep Tarpeian death,
Vagabond exile,* flaying,* pent* to linger
But with a grain a day, I would not buy   90
Their mercy at the price of one fair* word,
Nor check my courage* for what they can give,
To have't with* saying 'Good morrow'.*

SICINIUS   For that* he has,
As much as in him lies,* from time to time
Envied against* the people, seeking means   95
To pluck away their power, as now at last*
Given hostile strokes, and that not* in the presence
Of dreaded justice, but on the ministers
That do distribute* it – in the name o' th' people,
And in the power of us the tribunes, we,   100
Even from this instant, banish him our city,
In peril of precipitation*
From off the rock Tarpeian, never more
To enter our Rome gates. I' th' people's name,
I say it shall be so.

CITIZENS   It shall be so, it shall be so!   105
Let him away! He's banished, and it shall be so!

COMINIUS   Hear me, my masters, and my common friends –

SICINIUS   He's sentenced. No more hearing.

COMINIUS   Let me speak.
I have been consul, and can show for Rome
Her enemies' marks* upon me. I do love   110
My country's good, with a respect more tender,
More holy and profound, than mine own life,
My dear wife's estimate,* her womb's increase*
And treasure of my loins.* Then if I would
Speak that –

115   *drift:* aim.
119   *cry:* pack.
120   *As reek o' th' rotten fens:* like the smelly fog in unhealthy marshes.
123   *uncertainty:* fickleness.
125   *their plumes:* the feathers of their helmets.
126   *Fan you into despair:* make you cold with terror.
128   *finds not till it feels:* understands nothing till it experiences it.
129   *Making but . . . foes:* leaving in Rome only yourselves who are always your own worst
            enemies.
130   *deliver you:* gives you up.
131   *Abated:* humbled.
132   *without blows* – As Coriolanus sees it, they will surrender without a fight.
133   *For you:* because of you.
137   *out at gates:* out of the gates.
138   *all despite:* all the contempt you can.
139   *deserved vexation:* the torment he deserves.

SICINIUS   We know your drift.* Speak what? 115
BRUTUS There's no more to be said, but he is banished
        As enemy to the people and his country.
        It shall be so.
CITIZENS   It shall be so, it shall be so.
CORIOLANUS You common cry* of curs, whose breath I hate
        As reek o' th' rotten fens,* whose loves I prize 120
        As the dead carcases of unburied men
        That do corrupt my air, I banish you.
        And here remain with your uncertainty!*
        Let every feeble rumour shake your hearts,
        Your enemies with nodding of their plumes,* 125
        Fan you into despair!* Have the power still
        To banish your defenders, till at length
        Your ignorance (which finds not till it feels,*
        Making but* reservation of yourselves,
        Still your own foes) deliver you* as most 130
        Abated* captives to some nation
        That won you without blows.* Despising
        For you* the city, thus I turn my back.
        There is a world elsewhere.
        [*Exeunt* CORIOLANUS, COMINIUS, MENENIUS *and* SENATORS
AEDILE The people's enemy is gone, is gone! 135
CITIZENS Our enemy is banished, he is gone! Hoo-oo!
                    [*They all shout and throw up their caps*
SICINIUS Go see him out at gates,* and follow him,
        As he hath followed you, with all despite.*
        Give him deserved vexation.* Let a guard
        Attend us through the city. 140
CITIZENS Come, come, let's see him out at gates. Come.
        The gods preserve our noble tribunes! Come.
                                    [*Exeunt*

Aufidius welcoming Coriolanus to his house at Antium, and offering him command of half his army (Act IV, Scene v).

Aufidius planning Coriolanus' downfall with his Lieutenant and a Volscian soldier (Act IV, Scene vii).

IV.i.   Coriolanus is seen off at the gates of Rome by his weeping womenfolk and friends.
          In this moving scene a new and attractive gentleness is evident in Coriolanus. The
pathos of the parting is built up by his quiet demeanour, in which, for once, he is advising
and comforting others, by the fact that so many show their love for him in their sorrow at
his going, and by the fact that he leaves, not with three or four friends, as in Plutarch,
but quite alone. He leaves with no thought of joining the Volscians against Rome.

1	*The beast/With many heads* – i.e. the Hydra, or multitude. See note to II.iii.15.
3	*ancient* – i.e. which you used to show.
3	*You were used:* You used.
4	*extremities was . . . spirits:* great difficulties were a test of character. – The use of a plural subject with a singular verb, as here, was permissible in the sixteenth century. Cf. *hath* (IV.iii.12), *seems* (IV.iv.13), *hath* (IV.v.72), *hath* (IV.vi.51), *doth* (V.vi.77).
5	*common chances . . . bear:* ordinary men could bear ordinary mishaps.
7	*mastership:* similar skill.
7	*fortune's blows . . . cunning:* that when fortune's blows strike hardest, to act like a gentleman, though injured, demands a noble mind. – *Cunning:* wisdom, knowledge.
10	*precepts . . . conned them:* moral instructions which would make invulnerable anyone who took them to heart. – *conned:* studied, learnt.
12	*I prithee, woman* – Coriolanus is about to beg Virgilia to control her grief. – His use of *woman* is an endearment.
13	*the red pestilence* – i.e. a contemporary Elizabethan reference to the plague, of which red spots were a symptom.
13	*trades:* tradesmen.
14	*occupations:* manual labour.
15	*I shall . . . lacked:* After I have left the Romans will miss me and want me again.
16	*Resume . . . say:* return to the mood in which you used (*were wont*) to say (that if . . .).
18	*Six of his labours* – An allusion to the twelve labours of Hercules, imposed on him by Eurystheus. Had Volumnia been Hercules's wife she would have taken on half his *sweat*. One of the labours of Hercules, the slaying of the Hydra has earlier been mentioned. See note to II.iii.14. Another, the eleventh, is referred to at IV.vi.100.
20	*Droop not:* do not be dejected.
23	*venomous:* stinging.
23	*sometime:* former.
26	*fond:* as foolish.
27	*wot:* know.
28	*My hazards . . . solace:* the dangers I have undergone have always given you pleasure.
29	*Believe't not lightly:* be assured of this.
30	*that his fen/Makes:* Either (a) that makes his marshy lair, or (b) whose marshy lair makes it.

ACT IV scene i

Rome. The city gates.

Enter CORIOLANUS, VOLUMNIA, VIRGILIA, MENENIUS, COMI-
NIUS *and* PATRICIANS.

CORIOLANUS   Come, leave your tears. A brief farewell. The beast
With many heads* butts me away. Nay, mother,
Where is your ancient* courage? You were used*
To say extremities was* the trier of spirits;
That common chances* common men could bear;   5
That when the sea was calm all boats alike
Showed mastership* in floating; fortune's blows,*
When most struck home, being gentle wounded, craves
A noble cunning. You were used to load me
With precepts* that would make invincible   10
The heart that conned them.
VIRGILIA   O heavens! O heavens!
CORIOLANUS   Nay, I prithee, woman* –
VOLUMNIA   Now the red pestilence* strike all trades* in Rome,
And occupations* perish!
CORIOLANUS   What, what, what?
I shall* be loved when I am lacked. Nay, mother,   15
Resume* that spirit, when you were wont to say
If you had been the wife of Hercules,
Six of his labours* you'd have done, and saved
Your husband so much sweat. Cominius,
Droop not.* Adieu. Farewell, my wife, my mother.   20
I'll do well yet. Thou old and true Menenius,
Thy tears are salter than a younger man's,
And venomous* to thine eyes. My sometime* general,
I have seen thee stern, and thou hast oft beheld
Heart-hard'ning spectacles. Tell these sad women   25
'Tis fond* to wail inevitable strokes,
As 'tis to laugh at 'em. My mother, you wot* well
My hazards* still have been your solace, and
Believe't not lightly* (though I go alone,
Like to a lonely dragon, that his fen   30
Makes* feared and talked of more than seen) your son

137

32   *or exceed . . . practice:* either do something extraordinary or be caught with crafty (*cautelous*) snares and treachery (*practice*).

33   *first* – i.e. firstborn, but not implying that Volumnia had other sons. She tells us at v.iii.162 that she has *no second brood*.

35   *Determine:* Decide.

36   *wild exposture:* rash exposure.

37   *starts i' th' way before thee:* presents itself in your path. – She urges him to follow a reasoned plan of action, not an unplanned course at the mercy of every chance event.

37   *O the gods!* – Coriolanus's tone here, in keeping with his demeanour throughout the scene, is one of sorrow at the forced parting from his family and friends, not one of anger at the gods.

38   *devise:* plan.

39   *rest:* stay.

39, 40 *of:* from.

40   *thrust forth:* present.

41   *for thy repeal:* to recall you.

41   *send:* have to send.

43   *advantage:* the opportune moment.

44   *the needer* – i.e. the one who needs the opportunity.

45   *hast years upon thee:* are advanced in years.

46   *the wars' surfeits:* the excessive hardships of war. – Coriolanus may be thinking specifically of wounds, in which case his claim that he is *yet unbruised* (line 47) would be a characteristic understatement.

47   *Bring . . . gate:* Just accompany me to the gate (of the city).

49   *noble touch:* tested nobility. – The touchstone, of quartz or jasper, was used to test the quality of gold. *Noble* was the alchemist's name for gold. Cf. note to II.iii.180.

49   *am forth:* am outside.

52   *still:* continually.

52   *aught . . . formerly:* anything that is not in keeping with my past reputation.

53   *That's worthily . . . hear* – i.e. We shall hear news of you which will be as honourable as can be.

55   *one seven years* – i.e. the burden of seven of his years. Cf. II.i.105, where he felt seven years younger at the news of Coriolanus's return.

57   *I'd with:* I would go with.

               Will or exceed* the common, or be caught
               With cautelous baits and practice.

VOLUMNIA   My first* son,
               Whither wilt thou go? Take good Cominius
               With thee awhile. Determine* on some course   35
               More than a wild expousture* to each chance
               That starts i' th' way before thee.*

CORIOLANUS   O the gods!*

COMINIUS I'll follow thee a month, devise* with thee
               Where thou shalt rest,* that thou mayst hear of* us,
               And we of thee. So if the time thrust forth*   40
               A cause for thy repeal,* we shall not send*
               O'er the vast world to seek a single man,
               And lose advantage,* which doth ever cool
               I' th' absence of the needer.*

CORIOLANUS   Fare ye well.
               Thou hast years upon thee,* and thou art too full   45
               Of the wars' surfeits* to go rove with one
               That's yet unbruised. Bring* me but out at gate.
               Come, my sweet wife, my dearest mother, and
               My friends of noble touch;* when I am forth,*
               Bid me farewell, and smile. I pray you, come.   50
               While I remain above the ground you shall
               Hear from me still,* and never of me aught*
               But what is like me formerly.

MENENIUS   That's worthily*
               As any ear can hear. Come, let's not weep.
               If I could shake off but one seven years*   55
               From these old arms and legs, by the good gods,
               I'd with* thee every foot.

CORIOLANUS   Give me thy hand.
               Come.

                                            [*Exeunt*

IV.ii.   On her return from seeing off her son, Volumnia comes upon the tribunes. 'In anger, Juno-like' she gives them such a tongue-lashing that they are forced to make a quick and rather undignified exit. There is a release of tension in her outburst – necessary before the build-up to the final climax of Act V – and we applaud their discomfiture, a diminution of their recent triumph.

1	*all* – i.e. the plebeians.
1	*home:* go home.
5	*a-doing:* being done.
10	*ta'en note of:* observed.
11	*y'are well met:* I am glad we met you.
11	*hoarded:* stored up (for punishment).
12	*Requite:* repay.
12	*your love* – i.e. the love they may profess for the gods.
13	*If that I could for weeping:* If I were not prevented by my weeping.
14	*Will you be gone:* Are you sneaking away? – She wants him to stay and hear her opinion of him.
15	*would:* wish. – Cf. line 30.
16	*mankind:* mad. – Volumnia chooses to take the word in its usual sense, 'belonging to the human race'.
18	*foxship:* cunning.
21	*Moe:* more.
22	*Yet go?:* Are you still trying to go?

scene ii

Rome. A street near the gate.

Enter SICINIUS *and* BRUTUS *with an* AEDILE.

SICINIUS [*To the* AEDILE] Bid them all* home.* [*To* BRUTUS] He's
        gone, and we'll no further.
    The nobility are vexed, whom we see have sided
        In his behalf.

BRUTUS [*To* SICINIUS] Now we have shown our power,
    Let us seem humbler after it is done
    Than when it was a-doing.*

SICINIUS   [*To the* AEDILE] Bid them home. 5
    Say their great enemy is gone, and they
    Stand in their ancient strength.

BRUTUS   Dismiss them home.
                       [*Exit* AEDILE

    Here comes his mother.

Enter VOLUMNIA, VIRGILIA, *and* MENENIUS.

SICINIUS   Let's not meet her.

BRUTUS   Why?

SICINIUS They say she's mad.

BRUTUS They have ta'en note of* us. Keep on your way. 10

VOLUMNIA O, y'are well met.* Th' hoarded* plague o' th' gods
    Requite* your love!*

MENENIUS   Peace, peace, be not so loud.

VOLUMNIA If that I could for weeping,* you should hear –
    Nay, and you shall hear some. [*To* BRUTUS] Will you be
    gone?*

VIRGILIA [*To* SICINIUS] You shall stay too. I would* I had the power 15
    To say so to my husband.

SICINIUS   Are you mankind?*

VOLUMNIA Ay, fool. Is that a shame? Note but this, fool.
    Was not a man my father? Hadst thou foxship*
    To banish him that struck more blows for Rome
    Than thou hast spoken words?

SICINIUS   O blessed heavens! 20

VOLUMNIA Moe* noble blows than ever thou wise words,
    And for Rome's good. I'll tell thee what – Yet go?*

24   *in Arabia* – Volumnia presumably means 'in a desert', or place outside Roman jurisdiction, where the tribunes would not be protected by their office.
24   *thy tribe before him:* your whole family in front of him.
26   *make an end of thy posterity:* put an end to your family (by killing them).
27   *Bastards and all:* (Killing) all your illegitimate children as well.
28   *Good man* – She refers to Coriolanus.
30   *to:* in his service to.
31   *unknit . . . made:* undone the noble bond that tied him to Rome through his heroic deeds and her gratitude.
33   *'I would he had'* – Volumnia sarcastically echoes his words which she regards as hypocritical. A similar trait is found in her son, one of Shakespeare's ways of showing her powerful influence over him. Cf. note to III.i.88.
34   *Cats* – Her son, equally derisive, had called them *curs*. She goes on to say that they are no more able to judge Coriolanus than she is to understand mysteries hidden by the gods from man's comprehension.
43   *baited/With:* annoyed by.
44   *wants:* lacks.
44   *Take . . . with you* – This was a conventional expression to those going away, but Volumnia's prayers would be for the tribunes' *bad* fortune, as line 46 makes clear.
46   *confirm:* support, i.e. make them take effect.
46   *Could I:* If I could.
47   *unclog:* relieve.
48   *to't:* on it.
48   *told them home:* told them off, or scolded them, thoroughly.
49   *by my troth* – a common Elizabethan asseveration, meaning 'in truth', 'in faith'.
51   *starve with feeding* – Paradoxically, although feeding, she will die, because she is consuming herself in grief.
52   *Leave . . . anger:* Stop this feeble whining and, like me, express your sorrow (*lament*) in anger.
53   *Juno-like* – Juno was celebrated for her anger. See note to II.i.94.
54   *Fie:* Shame. – Menenius is not commenting on the behaviour of the two women, but on the present situation in Rome now that Coriolanus has left.

Nay, but thou shalt stay too. I would my son
Were in Arabia,* and thy tribe before him,*
His good sword in his hand.

SICINIUS   What then?

VIRGILIA   What then?   25

He'd make an end of thy posterity.*

VOLUMNIA Bastards and all.*
Good man,* the wounds that he does bear for Rome!

MENENIUS Come, come, peace.

SICINIUS I would he had continued to* his country   30
As he began, and not unknit* himself
The noble knot he made.

BRUTUS   I would he had.

VOLUMNIA 'I would he had!'* 'Twas you incensed the rabble;
Cats,* that can judge as fitly of his worth
As I can of those mysteries which heaven   35
Will not have earth to know.

BRUTUS   [To SICINIUS] Pray, let's go.

VOLUMNIA Now pray, sir, get you gone.
You have done a brave deed. Ere you go, hear this:
As far as doth the Capitol exceed
The meanest house in Rome, so far my son   40
(This lady's husband here, do you see,
Whom you have banished) does exceed you all.

BRUTUS Well, well, we'll leave you.

SICINIUS   Why stay we to be baited
With* one that wants* her wits?

                                        [Exeunt TRIBUNES

VOLUMNIA   Take my prayers with you.*
I would the gods had nothing else to do   45
But to confirm* my curses. Could I* meet 'em
But once a day, it would unclog* my heart
Of what lies heavy to't.*

MENENIUS   You have told them home,*
And by my troth* you have cause. You'll sup with me?

VOLUMNIA Anger's my meat. I sup upon myself,   50
And so shall starve with feeding.* Come, let's go.
Leave* this faint puling, and lament as I do,
In anger, Juno-like.* Come, come, come.

                    [Exeunt VOLUMNIA and VIRGILIA

MENENIUS Fie,* fie, fie!

                                        [Exit

IV.iii.   Adrian, a Volscian on his way to meet Nicanor, a Roman spying for the Volscians, meets him by chance on the road. He learns that Coriolanus has been banished, which is good news for the Volscians, who are now ready for another attack on Rome.

Ọ The main function of this scene is to serve as a bridge between Coriolanus's departure from Rome and his arrival in Antium, giving him time, as it were, to perform the journey off-stage. The fact that Adrian does not at first recognize someone he knows well suggests the uncertainty and deceptive appearances of the world of the play. Nicanor's geniality should not mislead us into overlooking the fact that he is a traitor to his country. Against a general background of treachery and duplicity Coriolanus stands out through his honesty and directness. Ironically, we learn that Rome's troubles have increased since Coriolanus's banishment, and that the patricians are on the point of seizing power from the people and expelling the tribunes.

4   *against 'em* – i.e. the Romans. Nicanor is a spy in the pay of the Volscians.
8   *favour is well appeared:* identity is certainly revealed. – Adrian recognizes Nicanor not by his face but by his voice.
10   *a note:* written instructions.
12   *insurrections:* disorders.
15   *they* – i.e. the Volscians. In line 16, *them* and *their* refer to the Romans.
15   *come upon:* attack.
18   *receive:* take.
20   *in a ripe aptness:* quite ready.
22   *mature:* ripe. – There are two images in this sentence: (1) *glowing – breaking out* (bursting into flame; from *heat – blaze – flame* above) and (2) *mature* (from *ripe – pluck*).
26   *intelligence:* news.
27   *The day serves well for them:* The time is favourable for them (i.e. the Volscians).
31   *in no request of:* unwanted by.
32   *He cannot choose:* He (Aufidius) is bound to [succeed (*appear well*)].
35   *this:* this time, now.

scene iii

A road between Rome and Antium.

Enter NICANOR *and* ADRIAN.

NICANOR I know you well, sir, and you know me. Your name, I
think, is Adrian.

ADRIAN It is so, sir. Truly, I have forgot you.

NICANOR I am a Roman, and my services are, as you are, against 'em.*
Know you me yet?   5

ADRIAN Nicanor, no?

NICANOR The same, sir.

ADRIAN You had more beard when I last saw you, but your favour
is well appeared* by your tongue. What's the news in
Rome? I have a note* from the Volscian state to find you   10
out there. You have well saved me a day's journey.

NICANOR There hath been in Rome strange insurrections:* the
people against the senators, patricians and nobles.

ADRIAN Hath been? Is it ended then? Our state thinks not so;
they* are in a most warlike preparation, and hope to come   15
upon* them in the heat of their division.

NICANOR The main blaze of it is past, but a small thing would make
it flame again, for the nobles receive* so to heart the
banishment of that worthy Coriolanus, that they are in a
ripe aptness* to take all power from the people, and to   20
pluck from them their tribunes for ever. This lies glowing,
I can tell you, and is almost mature* for the violent breaking out.

ADRIAN Coriolanus banished?

NICANOR Banished, sir.   25

ADRIAN You will be welcome with this intelligence,* Nicanor.

NICANOR The day serves well for them* now. I have heard it said,
the fittest time to corrupt a man's wife is when she's
fallen out with her husband. Your noble Tullus Aufidius
will appear well in these wars, his great opposer Coriolanus 30
being now in no request of* his country.

ADRIAN He cannot choose.* I am most fortunate thus accidentally
to encounter you. You have ended my business, and I will
merrily accompany you home.

NICANOR I shall between this* and supper tell you most strange   35

38   *royal:* splendid.
38   *centurions* – officers commanding a century or troop of one hundred soldiers.
38   *charges* – i.e. the troops under their command.
39   *distinctly billeted:* Either (a) separately enrolled on a list detailing each man by name, or
       (b) assigned to particular quarters.
39   *in the entertainment:* mustered, mobilized.
41   *am the man . . . action* – Nicanor is sure that when he reports the divisions in Rome to the
       Volscians, their army will set out at once to attack Rome; *present:* immediate.
43   *heartily well met:* I am delighted to have met you.
44   *You take my part from me:* You take the words out of my mouth. – *Part* is another allusion
       to the acting profession, namely the lines to be spoken by the actor.

IV.iv.   The disguised Coriolanus arrives in Antium and asks the way to Aufidius's house. In a
         soliloquy he declares that he is filled with hatred of his birthplace, Rome, and love for the
         enemy city, Antium, and that he will offer his services to Aufidius.
            In this soliloquy of Coriolanus we get a glimpse into his mind. His hatred of Rome has
         been induced by his strong sense of betrayal, which he extends to include even those
         closest to him. There is tragic irony in his attack on the 'slippery turns' of the world,
         where friends become enemies and enemies friends: firstly because while he is thinking
         only of the Romans as defectors we see that the charge applies also to him in his decision
         to revenge himself on Rome, which will obviously involve his family and friends in
         suffering; and secondly in his belief that bitterest enemies can become friends, a fatal
         delusion as he will discover from Aufidius's behaviour. Coriolanus's mental processes
         revealed briefly here show tragically how profoundly the behaviour of his mother, his
         friends and the Romans generally have undermined his whole moral nature. The danger
         to Coriolanus's life, stressed here, generates suspense as to the outcome of the following
         scene, his meeting with Aufidius. The fact that this scene and the following one inside
         Aufidius's house are the first and only night scenes in the play may be seen as a symbolic
         visual reflection of his moral collapse.

1   S.D. *mean:* poor.
2   *made thy widows* – i.e. by killing their husbands in battle.
2   *heir . . . edifices:* men who would have inherited these fine buildings.
3   *'fore my wars:* in the face of my attacks.
4   *know me not:* do not recognize me.
5   *Lest . . . wives:* so that your wives do not.
5   *spits:* large metal skewers on which meat was roasted.
6   *Save you:* May God save you.
8   *lies:* lives.
10   *beseech:* I beg.
12   *slippery turns:* fickle changes.

things from Rome, all tending to the good of their adversaries. Have you an army ready, say you?

ADRIAN A most royal* one. The centurions* and their charges*
distinctly billeted,* already in the entertainment,* and
to be on foot at an hour's warning.   40

NICANOR I am joyful to hear of their readiness, and am the man,* I
think, that shall set them in present* action.* So, sir,
heartily well met,* and most glad of your company.

ADRIAN You take my part from me,* sir. I have the most cause to be
glad of yours.   45

NICANOR Well, let us go together.

[*Exeunt*

scene iv

Antium. In front of Aufidius's house.

Enter CORIOLANUS *in mean* apparel, disguised and muffled.*

CORIOLANUS A goodly city is this Antium. City,
'Tis I that made thy widows.* Many an heir*
Of these fair edifices 'fore my wars*
Have I heard groan and drop. Then know me not,*
Lest* that thy wives with spits,* and boys with stones,   5
In puny battle slay me.

Enter a CITIZEN.

                                      Save you,* sir.

CITIZEN And you.

CORIOLANUS   Direct me, if it be your will,
Where great Aufidius lies.* Is he in Antium?

CITIZEN He is, and feasts the nobles of the state
At his house this night.

CORIOLANUS   Which is his house, beseech* you?   10

CITIZEN This here before you.

CORIOLANUS   Thank you, sir. Farewell.

[*Exit* CITIZEN

O world, thy slippery turns!* Friends now fast sworn,

13   *double bosoms . . . heart:* separate breasts seem to have only one heart – i.e. though separate
              individuals they share the same feelings.
15   *still:* always.
17   *a dissension of a doit:* a dispute about a trifle. – See note to I.v.6.
18   *fellest:* fiercest.
19   *broke . . . the other:* kept them awake thinking about how to destroy each other.
21   *trick:* trifle.
21   *grow:* become.
22   *interjoin their issues:* Either (a) join together for action, or (b) unite their children in
              marriage.
25   *give me way:* grant my request.

IV.v.   Aufidius is feasting his friends when Coriolanus arrives at his door. The servants,
observing his ragged appearance, try to eject him. Aufidius is fetched and Coriolanus
reveals himself. Aufidius, deeply moved, tells him of the imminent attack on Roman
territory and offers him command of half his army. They go in to the feast leaving the
servants to discuss them in a comic postscript.

The scene is full of deftly-managed irony. Aufidius, who in I.x had vowed that if he
found him, 'were it/At home' he would 'Wash my fierce hand in's heart', now welcomes
him warmly. This seems to substantiate Coriolanus's recent remark that bitter enemies
will grow dear friends – but this is just one more appearance that belies reality in a world
where very little is what it seems to be. As the First Servant says, it is 'a strange alteration',
and there is comic irony in the fact that the servants cannot see that their own claim to
have seen Coriolanus's worth from the beginning, although a moment before they were
trying to throw him out, is itself a 'strange alteration'.

As often in Shakespeare, the comedy serves more purposes than simply to amuse us.
In the first place, the foolish inconsistency of the servants parallels the behaviour of the
Roman plebeians. Shakespeare seems to be stressing the general unfitness of the plebeians
to rule themselves. More significantly they are used to make some shrewd comments on
their superiors which have a corrective effect. The Third Servant's report, 'Our general
himself makes a mistress of him; sanctifies himself with's hand, and turns up the white o'
th' eye to his discourse', stresses a ludicrousness in Aufidius's behaviour which qualifies
our admiration of his epic qualities. Similarly his observation that 'our general is cut i' th'
middle and but one half of what he was yesterday' is shrewd and ominous; when Aufidius
sees this truth, friendship turns to enmity. In such ways comedy serves ironic and satiric
purposes.

1   *What service is here?:* What sort of service is this?
2   *fellows:* fellow-servants.
4   *goodly:* imposing.
5   *Appear not:* am not dressed.
6   *What . . . have?:* What do you want?
6   *Whence are you?:* Where do you come from?
7   *go to the door:* get out.

Whose double bosoms* seems to wear one heart,
Whose hours, whose bed, whose meal and exercise,
Are still* together; who twin, as 'twere, in love   15
Unseparable, shall within this hour,
On a dissension of a doit,* break out
To bitterest enmity. So fellest* foes,
Whose passions and whose plots have broke* their sleep
To take the one the other, by some chance,   20
Some trick* not worth an egg, shall grow* dear friends
And interjoin their issues.* So with me.
My birthplace hate I, and my love's upon
This enemy town. I'll enter. If he slay me,
He does fair justice; if he give me way,*   25
I'll do his country service.

                                                    [*Exit*

scene v

Antium. Inside Aufidius's house.

Music plays. Enter a SERVANT.

FIRST SERVANT Wine, wine, wine! What service is here?* I think our
fellows* are asleep.

                                                    [*Exit*

Enter another SERVANT.

SECOND SERVANT Where's Cotus? My master calls for him. Cotus!

                                                    [*Exit*

Enter CORIOLANUS.

CORIOLANUS A goodly* house. The feast smells well; but I
Appear not* like a guest.   5

Enter FIRST SERVANT.

FIRST SERVANT What* would you have, friend? Whence are you?*
Here's no place for you. Pray go to the door.*

                                                    [*Exit*

8	*I have deserved . . . Coriolanus* – Since Coriolanus is the enemy of the Volscians he does not deserve, he says, a friendly welcome.
11	*companions:* rascals.
16	*brave:* insolent.
16	*anon:* at once.
20	*What have you to do:* What business have you.
20	*avoid:* leave.
25	*marvellous:* extremely. – See note to I.i.178.
27	*station:* place to stand.
29	*Follow your function:* Go and do your job – i.e. serve.
29	*batten on cold bits:* get fat on the cold scraps.
34	*canopy:* sky. – The *canopy* was also the name of the roof overhanging part of the stage. See *Introduction*, page lxii.
38	*the city of kites and crows* – i.e. the sky. Coriolanus is also thinking of Rome, as his derogatory reference to *kites* (birds of prey and scavengers) and *crows* (notoriously ugly and rapacious birds) makes clear.
40	*daws:* jackdaws. – These were thought to be foolish birds, so that *daw* is synonymous with 'fool'.
41	*I serve not thy master* – Coriolanus ripostes to the Third Servant's insult. If he served Aufidius, he would dwell with daws, i.e. with the servants to whom he is speaking.
42	*meddle with:* interfere with. – In the following line Coriolanus uses the phrase to mean 'have intercourse with'.

CORIOLANUS I have deserved* no better entertainment,
In being Coriolanus.

Enter SECOND SERVANT.

SECOND SERVANT Whence are you, sir? Has the porter his eyes in his head,   10
that he gives entrance to such companions?* Pray get you
out.

CORIOLANUS Away!

SECOND SERVANT Away? Get you away!

CORIOLANUS Now th'art troublesome.   15

SECOND SERVANT Are you so brave?* I'll have you talked with anon.*

Enter FIRST SERVANT *at one door,* THIRD SERVANT *at the
other.*

THIRD SERVANT What fellow's this?

FIRST SERVANT A strange one as ever I looked on. I cannot get him out o'
the house. Prithee call my master to him.

THIRD SERVANT What have you to do* here, fellow? Pray you, avoid* the   20
house.

CORIOLANUS Let me but stand. I will not hurt your hearth.

THIRD SERVANT What are you?

CORIOLANUS A gentleman.

THIRD SERVANT A marvellous* poor one.   25

CORIOLANUS True, so I am.

THIRD SERVANT Pray you, poor gentleman, take up some other station.*
Here's no place for you. Pray you, avoid. Come.

CORIOLANUS Follow your function.* Go and batten on cold bits.*
                              [*He pushes the* SERVANT *away*

THIRD SERVANT What, you will not? Prithee, tell my master what a strange   30
guest he has here.

SECOND SERVANT And I shall.
                              [*Exit* SECOND SERVANT

THIRD SERVANT Where dwell'st thou?

CORIOLANUS Under the canopy.*

THIRD SERVANT Under the canopy?   35

CORIOLANUS Ay.

THIRD SERVANT Where's that?

CORIOLANUS I' the city of kites and crows.*

THIRD SERVANT I' the city of kites and crows? What an ass it is! Then thou
dwell'st with daws* too?   40

CORIOLANUS No, I serve not thy master.*

THIRD SERVANT How, sir! Do you meddle with* my master?

44	*prat'st:* talk foolishly.
45	*trencher:* wooden plate.
49	*Whence . . . wouldst thou:* Where have you come from? What do you want?
51	*Not yet thou know'st me:* You do not yet recognize me.
51	*seeing . . . am.* because of my appearance [you] cannot believe that I am a man of importance.
54	*unmusical:* of an unpleasing sound.
57	*Bears a command in't:* has a look of authority about it.
57	*tackle* – a ship's sails, rigging etc. – Aufidius means Coriolanus's dress.
58	*show'st:* appear.
58	*vessel:* (a) ship (b) body (as a vessel containing the soul). – Aufidius continues the nautical metaphor begun with *tackle*, line 57.
63	*mischief:* harm.
63	*thereto witness may/My surname:* my added name, Coriolanus, can support the truth of that.
64	*painful:* arduous.
66	*requited/But:* repaid only.
67	*memory:* memorial.
70	*envy:* ill-will.
71	*dastard:* cowardly.
72	*forsook:* forsaken, failed to support.
72	*the rest:* all my other qualities and services.
73	*suffered:* allowed.
74	*Hooped out of:* driven out with derisive shouts from.
74	*extremity:* extreme adversity.

CORIOLANUS   Ay. 'Tis an honester service than to meddle with thy
              mistress. Thou prat'st,* and prat'st. Serve with thy
              trencher.* Hence!   45

                                    [*He beats the* SERVANT

                        Enter AUFIDIUS *with* SECOND SERVANT.

AUFIDIUS   Where is this fellow?
SECOND SERVANT   Here, sir. I'd have beaten him like a dog, but for disturbing
              the lords within.

                                              [*Exeunt* SERVANTS
AUFIDIUS   Whence* com'st thou? What wouldst thou? Thy name?
              Why speak'st not? Speak man. What's thy name?
CORIOLANUS   [*Unmuffling*]   If, Tullus,   50
              Not yet thou know'st me,* and seeing* me dost not
              Think me for the man I am, necessity
              Commands me name myself.
AUFIDIUS   What is thy name?
CORIOLANUS   A name unmusical* to the Volscians' ears,
              And harsh in sound to thine.
AUFIDIUS   Say, what's thy name?   55
              Thou hast a grim appearance, and thy face
              Bears a command in't.* Though thy tackle's* torn,
              Thou show'st* a noble vessel.* What's thy name?
CORIOLANUS   Prepare thy brow to frown. Know'st thou me yet?
AUFIDIUS   I know thee not. Thy name?   60
CORIOLANUS   My name is Caius Martius, who hath done
              To thee particularly, and to all the Volsces,
              Great hurt and mischief;* thereto witness may
              My surname,* Coriolanus. The painful* service,
              The extreme dangers, and the drops of blood   65
              Shed for my thankless country, are requited
              But* with that surname – a good memory*
              And witness of the malice and displeasure
              Which thou shouldst bear me. Only that name remains.
              The cruelty and envy* of the people,   70
              Permitted by our dastard* nobles, who
              Have all forsook* me, hath devoured the rest,*
              And suffered* me by th' voice of slaves to be
              Hooped out of* Rome. Now, this extremity*
              Hath brought me to thy hearth; not out of hope   75
              (Mistake me not) to save my life; for if
              I had feared death, of all the men i' th' world

78   *voided:* avoided.
78   *mere:* pure.
79   *full quit of:* completely revenged on.
80   *Then . . . turn* (line 84): Then if you have a heart ready to revenge (*of wreak*) so that you want to revenge the wrongs done to you personally and heal those shameful wounds (*stop those maims*) visible throughout your country (e.g. the occupation of Corioli and the devastation of Volscian territory) hurry at once and use my wretchedness to your own advantage (*serve thy turn*).
84   *So use it:* Use it (i.e. Coriolanus's *misery*) in such a way.
87   *cankered:* diseased.
87   *spleen:* rage.
88   *under fiends:* infernal devils.
88   *But if . . . tired:* But if you dare not do it [trust me to fight on your side], or if you are too tired to put your fortune to the test once more (*prove more fortunes*).
90   *I also . . . weary:* I too am tired of life.
92   *thy ancient malice:* your long-standing enmity.
95   *tuns:* barrels.
99   *envy:* enmity.
99   *Jupiter . . . 'Tis true'* – Aufidius refers to the thunder thought by the Romans to be an omen signifying Jupiter's assent. – Line 100 has only eight syllables. *Dívine* is stressed on the first syllable.
103   *where against:* against which.
104   *grainèd ash:* tough ash spear. – *grained:* either 'close-grained' or 'straight-grained', hence 'strong'.
105   *clip:* embrace.
106   *The anvil of my sword* – Aufidius means Coriolanus, whose body he has often struck with his sword, like a blacksmith hammering his anvil.
106   *contest . . . love:* match your love as warmly and nobly.
110   *never man/Sighed truer breath:* No man was ever a truer lover. – An allusion to the traditional sighing lover.
111   *that:* the fact that.
112   *more dances my rapt heart:* makes my enraptured heart dance for joy more.
113   *my wedded . . . Bestride:* saw my newly married bride crossing.
114   *thou Mars* – In addressing Coriolanus by the name of the god of war, Aufidius reveals the strength of his admiration for him as a warrior.
115   *a power on foot:* an army mobilized.
116   *target:* shield.
116   *brawn:* strong arm.
117   *for't:* in the attempt.
117   *out:* completely.
118   *several:* separate. – Aufidius has earlier mentioned only five encounters with Coriolanus (I.x.7). The figure *twelve* here is a piece of epic exaggeration in keeping with the whole speech.

I would have voided* thee; but in mere* spite,
To be full quit of* those my banishers,
Stand I before thee. Then* if thou hast   80
A heart of wreak in thee, that wilt revenge
Thine own particular wrongs, and stop those maims
Of shame seen through thy country, speed thee straight
And make my misery serve thy turn. So use it*
That my revengeful services may prove   85
As benefits to thee. For I will fight
Against my cankered* country with the spleen*
Of all the under fiends.* But if* so be
Thou dar'st not this, and that to prove more fortunes
Th'art tired, then, in a word, I also* am   90
Longer to live most weary, and present
My throat to thee and to thy ancient malice;*
Which not to cut would show thee but a fool,
Since I have ever followed thee with hate,
Drawn tuns* of blood out of thy country's breast,   95
And cannot live but to thy shame, unless
It be to do thee service.

AUFIDIUS   O Martius, Martius!
Each word thou hast spoke hath weeded from my heart
A root of ancient envy.* If Jupiter*
Should from yond cloud speak dívine things,   100
And say ' 'Tis true', I'd not believe them more
Than thee, all-noble Martius, Let me twine
Mine arms about that body, where against*
My grainèd ash* an hundred times hath broke
And scarred the moon with splinters. Here I clip*   105
The anvil of my sword,* and do contest*
As hotly and as nobly with thy love,
As ever in ambitious strength I did
Contend against thy valour. Know thou first,
I loved the maid I married: never man   110
Sighed truer breath.* But that* I see thee here,
Thou noble thing, more dances my rapt heart*
Than when I first my wedded mistress saw
Bestride* my threshold. Why, thou Mars,* I tell thee,
We have a power on foot,* and I had purpose   115
Once more to hew thy target* from thy brawn,*
Or lose mine arm for't.* Thou hast beat me out*
Twelve several* times, and I have nightly since

120   *down:* on the ground.
121   *helms:* helmets.
121   *fisting:* seizing with our hands.
122   *waked:* I have waked.
123   *Had . . . that* – i.e. if our only quarrel with Rome was that.
127   *o'erbeat:* overcome.
130   *prepared against:* ready (with an army) to attack.
132   *absolute:* complete, perfect.
134   *my commission:* the troops under my command.
134   *set down:* determine.
135   *As best thou art:* since you are best.
136   *thine own ways:* how you will proceed.
138   *rudely:* violently.
139   *fright them ere destroy:* frighten them before destroying them.
140   *commend:* recommend.
143   *that was much* – i.e. you were a great enemy.
144   *a strange alteration.* – The servant had expected Coriolanus to be thrown out. He is
          therefore surprised on entering to find him being welcomed by Aufidius.
145   *I had . . . strucken:* I intended to strike.
146   *my mind gave me:* I suspected.
146   *made a false report of him:* did not truly reflect his rank.
149   *set up:* spin.
151   *methought:* it seemed to me.
153   *would . . . thought:* I'll be hanged if I did not think. – The servants are both unwittingly
          talking nonsense, of course. See the scene synopsis.
155   *rarest:* finest.

Dreamt of encounters 'twixt thyself and me.
We have been down* together in my sleep,   120
Unbuckling helms,* fisting* each other's throat
And waked* half dead with nothing. Worthy Martius,
Had* we no other quarrel else to Rome but that
Thou art thence banished, we would muster all
From twelve to seventy, and pouring war   125
Into the bowels of ungrateful Rome,
Like a bold flood o'erbeat.* O, come, go in,
And take our friendly senators by th' hands,
Who now are here, taking their leaves of me,
Who am prepared against* your territories,   130
Though not for Rome itself.

CORIOLANUS   You bless me, gods.

AUFIDIUS Therefore, most absolute* sir, if thou wilt have
The leading of thine own revenges, take
Th' one half of my commission,* and set down*
(As best thou art* experienced, since thou know'st   135
Thy country's strength and weakness) thine own ways:*
Whether to knock against the gates of Rome,
Or rudely* visit them in parts remote,
To fright them, ere destroy.* But come in.
Let me commend* thee first to those that shall   140
Say yea to thy desires. A thousand welcomes,
And more a friend than e'er an enemy;
Yet, Martius, that was much.* Your hand. Most welcome.

Enter two SERVANTS.

[*Exeunt* AUFIDIUS *and* CORIOLANUS

FIRST SERVANT Here's a strange alteration!*

SECOND SERVANT By my hand, I had* thought to have strucken him with a   145
cudgel, and yet my mind gave me* his clothes made a false
report of him.*

FIRST SERVANT What an arm he has! He turned me about with his finger
and his thumb as one would set up* a top.

SECOND SERVANT Nay, I knew by his face that there was something in him.   150
He had, sir, a kind of face methought* – I cannot tell how to
term it.

FIRST SERVANT He had so, looking as it were – would* I were hanged, but I
thought there was more in him than I could think.

SECOND SERVANT So did I, I'll be sworn. He is simply the rarest* man i' the   155
world.

157   *wot on:* know of. – He refers to Aufidius.
159   *it's no matter for that:* it doesn't matter who I'm talking about. – He means Aufidius but is too scared to name him.
160   *on him:* of him – i.e. Aufidius.
161   *not so neither* – Coriolanus, although superior to Aufidius, is not, in the opinion of the First Servant, six times as good.
161   *him* – i.e. Coriolanus.
163   *one cannot . . . that:* you can't really say that. – The Second Servant praises Aufidius as a good defensive general.
168   *had as lief:* would as soon.
171   *thwack:* thrash.
176   *fellows:* fellow-servants. – He means that, being friends, they should be able to speak openly to each other.
176   *He* – i.e. Coriolanus.
177   *him* – i.e. Aufidius.
178   *directly:* face to face, in single combat.
178   *troth:* truth.
179   *scotched him . . . carbonado:* slashed him and cut notches in him like meat ready for grilling. – The servant uses a simile from his occupation.
181   *And he had been cannibally given:* If he had been inclined to cannibalism.
184   *so made on:* made so much of.
185   *upper end:* one of the seats of honour at the top.
186   *but they stand bald:* without them taking off their hats. – *bald:* bare-headed. See note to II.iii.90, 91.
187   *makes a mistress of him:* acts as if he were in love with him.
188   *sanctifies himself with's hand:* touches Coriolanus's hand as if it were something sacred.
188   *turns up . . . discourse:* looks up in admiration at his speech.
189   *bottom:* essence.
191   *the other* – i.e. Coriolanus.
192   *sowl:* drag.
194   *passage polled:* path cleared. – To *poll* is to cut the hair.

FIRST SERVANT I think he is. But a greater soldier than he you wot on.*
SECOND SERVANT Who, my master?
FIRST SERVANT Nay, it's no matter for that.*
SECOND SERVANT Worth six on him.*   160
FIRST SERVANT Nay, not so neither;* but I take him* to be the greater
soldier.
SECOND SERVANT Faith, look you, one cannot* tell how to say that. For the
defence of a town our general is excellent.
FIRST SERVANT Ay, and for an assault too.   165

Enter THIRD SERVANT.

THIRD SERVANT O slaves, I can tell you news. News, you rascals!
FIRST *and*
SECOND SERVANTS } What, what, what? Let's partake.
THIRD SERVANT I would not be a Roman, of all nations. I had as lief* be a
condemned man.
FIRST *and*
SECOND SERVANTS } Wherefore? Wherefore?   170
THIRD SERVANT Why, here's he that was wont to thwack* our general,
Caius Martius.
FIRST SERVANT Why do you say 'thwack our general'?
THIRD SERVANT I do not say 'thwack our general', but he was always good
enough for him.   175
SECOND SERVANT Come, we are fellows* and friends. He* was ever too hard
for him;* I have heard him say so himself.
FIRST SERVANT He was too hard for him directly,* to say the troth* on't.
Before Corioli he scotched him* and notched him like a
carbonado.   180
SECOND SERVANT And he had been cannibally given,* he might have boiled
and eaten him too.
FIRST SERVANT But more of thy news.
THIRD SERVANT Why, he is so made on* here within as if he were son and
heir to Mars; set at upper end* o' the table. No question   185
asked him by any of the senators but they stand bald*
before him. Our general himself makes a mistress of him,*
sanctifies himself with's hand,* and turns up* the white o'
the eye to his discourse, But the bottom* of the news is, our
general is cut i' the middle, and but one half of what he   190
was yesterday; for the other* has half, by the entreaty and
grant of the whole table. He'll go, he says, and sowl* the
porter of Rome gate by the ears. He will mow all down
before him, and leave his passage polled.*

195   *like:* likely. See note to I.i.178.

199   *directitude* – A malapropism, possibly for *discredit*. The Third Servant is trying to impress his fellow-servants with his vocabulary and parenthetic phrases, incompetently aping his superiors. He is referring to Coriolanus's patrician friends in Rome.

201   *crest up* – This could refer literally to Coriolanus with his plumed or decorated helmet on, or metaphorically to him roused in spirit, like a bird with raised feathers or an animal with its fur raised.

202   *in blood:* full of life.

202   *conies:* rabbits.

203   *revel all:* all rejoice.

204   *goes this forward:* is this going to happen.

205   *presently:* immediately.

205   *the drum* – i.e. calling them to arms.

206   *parcel:* part.

209   *iron* – i.e. swords. Cf. I.v.6.

209   *increase tailors:* makes tailors grow wealthy.

209   *breed ballad-makers:* spawn poets. – Ballads, or printed verses set to music, were an important element of Elizabethan popular culture, not a feature of Roman life. Mostly anonymous, and of little literary merit, they dealt with a wide variety of subjects – love, war, historical personalities and events, and topical happenings of a sensational nature such as earthquakes, floods, murders and prodigious births. They were often indecent and libellous, attacking prominent people of the time, and sometimes seditious in attacking social abuses, thus earning the censure of the moralists. Ballads were sold all over the country, mainly by wandering pedlars like Autolycus in *The Winter's Tale*. The First Servant believes (though there is no evidence to support him) that ballads are less numerous in wartime, presumably because so many ballad-makers and singers would be away fighting.

212   *It's sprightly . . . lethargy* – The First Servant, in his long-winded and muddled way, is saying that war means action (*sprightly walking*), noise (is *audible*), plenty of outlets for energy (*full of vent*), whereas peace by contrast means paralysis (*a very apoplexy*) and sluggishness (*lethargy*).

213   *mulled:* dulled – like ale or wine which is heated, sweetened and thickened.

214   *a getter . . . of men* – i.e. more illegitimate children are born in time of peace than men are destroyed in time of war.

216   *in some sort:* to some extent.

218   *cuckolds* – men whose wives have been unfaithful to them.

220   *Reason:* And the reason is.

220   *The wars for my money:* Give me war [for preference].

221   *Romans as cheap as Volscians* – The Third Servant wants the Romans brought down a peg or two by being beaten in war.

222   *They are rising.* – The guests are getting up from the table.

SECOND SERVANT And he's as like* to do't as any man I can imagine.   195
THIRD SERVANT Do't? He will do't, for look you, sir, he has as many
friends as enemies; which friends, sir, as it were, durst
not, look you, sir, show themselves, as we term it, his
friends, whilst he's in directitude.*
FIRST SERVANT Directitude? What's that?   200
THIRD SERVANT But when they shall see, sir, his crest up* again, and the
man in blood,* they will out of their burrows, like conies*
after rain, and revel all* with him.
FIRST SERVANT But when goes this forward?*
THIRD SERVANT Tomorrow, today, presently.* You shall have the drum*   205
struck up this afternoon. 'Tis as it were a parcel* of their
feast, and to be executed ere they wipe their lips.
SECOND SERVANT Why, then we shall have a stirring world again. This peace
is nothing but to rust iron,* increase tailors,* and breed
ballad-makers.*   210
FIRST SERVANT Let me have war, say I. It exceeds peace as far as day does
night. It's sprightly* walking, audible, and full of vent.
Peace is a very apoplexy, lethargy; mulled,* deaf, sleepy,
insensible; a getter* of more bastard children than war's a
destroyer of men.   215
SECOND SERVANT 'Tis so; and as wars in some sort* may be said to be a
ravisher, so it cannot be denied but peace is a great maker
of cuckolds.*
FIRST SERVANT Ay, and it makes men hate one another.
THIRD SERVANT Reason:* because they then less need one another. The   220
wars for my money.* I hope to see Romans as cheap as
Volscians.* They are rising,* they are rising.
FIRST *and*
SECOND SERVANTS } In, in, in, in!

IV.vi.   In Rome Brutus and Sicinius are rejoicing at the peacefulness of life since the expulsion of Coriolanus, when an aedile reports that the Volscians have invaded Roman territory. The tribunes refuse to believe it, but it is confirmed as further news arrives reporting that Coriolanus has joined with Aufidius in the attack. Rome's destruction now seems certain, and Menenius and Cominius put the blame for this situation on the tribunes.

After the lowered tempo of the previous three scenes tension begins to mount as rumours and news pour into Rome. This is achieved by Shakespeare's technique of introducing a succession of messengers – first the aedile, then two messengers following quickly upon each other, and finally Cominius to confirm it all and add his graphic vision of the destruction that will ensue in Rome. This cumulative process creates the effect of growing panic, helplessness and suspense. Having witnessed the reconciliation of Aufidius and Coriolanus in the previous scene we perceive the irony of the self-deceiving complacency of the tribunes. Their triumph has been as short-lived as that of Coriolanus. The hypocrisy of the terrified citizens echoes that of the three servants in the previous scene.

2	*His remedies are tame:* The things which cured him are now calm. – It was the anger of the people and the civic dissension and threat to peace which led to Coriolanus's fall.
3	*which:* who.
4	*wild hurry:* commotion.
5	*Blush –* i.e. with anger.
5	*rather . . . see:* would prefer to see quarrelsome (*dissentious*) crowds infesting the streets, even if it meant inconvenience for themselves, rather than see.
9	*friendly:* in a friendly manner.
10	*stood to't in good time:* stood up to (resisted) him just when it was needed.
11	*kind:* friendly.
14	*But with:* except by.
15	*And so . . . at it:* and would continue to stand even if he were much angrier at it than he is. – Ironically they see no danger from Coriolanus.
17	*temporized:* made concessions to the needs of the time.
20	*God-den:* Good evening. – See note to II.i.86.
23	*bound:* under an obligation.
24	*wished:* wish. – The perfect tense of the verb is still used in some midland dialects to indicate a wish in the present that cannot be fulfilled.
25	*keep:* protect.

scene vi

Rome. A public place.

Enter SICINIUS *and* BRUTUS.

SICINIUS   We hear not of him, neither need we fear him.
His remedies are tame,* the present peace
And quietness of the people, which* before
Were in wild hurry.* Here do we make his friends
Blush* that the world goes well; who rather* had,   5
Though they themselves did suffer by't, behold
Dissentious numbers pest'ring streets, than see
Our tradesmen singing in their shops and going
About their functions friendly.*
BRUTUS   We stood to't in good time.*

Enter MENENIUS.

                              Is this Menenius?   10
SICINIUS   'Tis he, 'tis he. O, he is grown most kind*
Of late. Hail, sir!
MENENIUS   Hail to you both!
SICINIUS   Your Coriolanus is not much missed
But with* his friends. The commonwealth doth stand,
And so* would do, were he more angry at it.   15
MENENIUS   All's well, and might have been much better, if
He could have temporized.*
SICINIUS   Where is he, hear you?
MENENIUS   Nay, I hear nothing. His mother and his wife
Hear nothing from him.

Enter three or four CITIZENS.

CITIZENS   The gods preserve you both.
SICINIUS   God-den,* our neighbours.   20
BRUTUS   God-den to you all, god-den to you all.
FIRST CITIZEN   Ourselves, our wives and children, on our knees
Are bound* to pray for you both.
SICINIUS   Live, and thrive.
BRUTUS   Farewell, kind neighbours. We wished* Coriolanus
Had loved you as we did.
CITIZENS   Now the gods keep* you!   25

27	*comely:* agreeable.
29	*Crying confusion:* threatening destruction.
32	*affecting . . . assistance:* aiming at dictatorial power without any partners.
34	*should by this:* should by this time have. – The syntax is imperfect.
34	*all our lamentation:* the regret of all of us.
35	*gone forth:* become.
37	*still:* peaceful.
39	*several powers:* separate armies.
41	*with the deepest . . . war:* with greater enmity than has yet been seen in the war. – The Aedile sees the latest Volscian attack as part of the war which began in I.i.
45	*inshelled:* drawn into the shell. – Menenius speaks of Aufidius as a snail.
45	*stood for:* fought for.
46	*what:* why.
48	*rumourer:* rumour-monger. – Whipping was a common punishment for many minor offences in Shakespeare's time.
49	*break:* break their agreement.
52	*age:* lifetime.
52	*reason with:* question.
54	*information:* source of information.
55	*bids beware:* bids you to beware.

BRUTUS *and* ⎱
SICINIUS ⎰ Farewell, farewell.

                                       [*Exeunt* CITIZENS

SICINIUS This is a happier and more comely* time
Than when these fellows ran about the streets
Crying confusion.*

BRUTUS   Caius Martius was
A worthy officer i' th' war, but insolent,   30
O'ercome with pride, ambitious past all thinking,
Self-loving –

SICINIUS   And affecting* one sole throne
Without assistance.

MENENIUS   I think not so.

SICINIUS We should by this,* to all our lamentation,*
If he had gone forth* consul, found it so.   35

BRUTUS The gods have well prevented it, and Rome
Sits safe and still* without him.

    Enter an AEDILE.

AEDILE   Worthy tribunes,
There is a slave whom we have put in prison
Reports the Volsces with two several powers*
Are entered in the Roman territories,   40
And with the deepest* malice of the war
Destroy what lies before 'em.

MENENIUS   'Tis Aufidius,
Who, hearing of our Martius' banishment,
Thrusts forth his horns again into the world,
Which were inshelled* when Martius stood for* Rome,   45
And durst not once peep out.

SICINIUS   Come, what* talk you
Of Martius?

BRUTUS Go see this rumourer* whipped. It cannot be
The Volsces dare break* with us.

MENENIUS   Cannot be?
We have recórd that very well it can,   50
And three examples of the like hath been
Within my age.* But reason with* the fellow,
Before you punish him, where he heard this,
Lest you shall chance to whip your information,*
And beat the messenger who bids beware*   55
Of what is to be dreaded.

56   *Tell not me:* Don't talk nonsense.
59   *coming:* coming in.
60   *turns their countenances:* makes them turn pale with fear.
61   *His raising* – i.e. It is he who originated this rumour.
63   *seconded:* backed up by others.
63   *more:* more news.
64   *delivered:* reported.
66   *probable:* credible.
68   *as spacious . . . thing:* wide enough to include the youngest and the oldest. – According to
         the messenger, Coriolanus seeks revenge on every Roman.
69   *This is most likely* – Sicinius says this ironically; he does not believe the messenger.
70   *Raised only that:* Propagated only so that.
70   *sort:* kind of people.
71   *The very trick on't:* You have explained this trick exactly.
72   *This* – i.e. the Messenger's report of the rumour that Coriolanus has joined Aufidius
         against Rome.
73   *atone:* be at one, unite.
74   *violentest contrariety:* extreme opposites.
77   *Associated:* joined.
78   *have:* they have.
79   *O'erborne their way:* overcome everything in their way.
79   *took:* taken.
82   *holp:* helped.
83   *leads:* roofs (often covered with lead in Shakespeare's time). Cf. II.i.200.
83   *pates:* heads.
84   *to:* before.

SICINIUS   Tell not me.*
          I know this cannot be.
BRUTUS   Not possible.

Enter a MESSENGER.

MESSENGER The nobles in great earnestness are going
          All to the Senate House. Some news is coming*
          That turns their countenances.*
SICINIUS   'Tis this slave.   60
          Go whip him 'fore the people's eyes. His raising,*
          Nothing but his report.
MESSENGER   Yes, worthy sir,
          The slave's report is seconded,* and more,*
          More fearful, is delivered.*
SICINIUS   What more fearful?
MESSENGER It is spoke freely out of many mouths,   65
          How probable* I do not know, that Martius,
          Joined with Aufidius, leads a power 'gainst Rome,
          And vows revenge as spacious* as between
          The young'st and oldest thing.
SICINIUS   This is most likely!*
BRUTUS Raised only that* the weaker sort* may wish   70
          Good Martius home again.
SICINIUS   The very trick on't.*
MENENIUS This* is unlikely.
          He and Aufidius can no more atone*
          Than violentest contrariety.*

Enter a SECOND MESSENGER.

MESSENGER You are sent for to the Senate.   75
          A fearful army, led by Caius Martius,
          Associated* with Aufidius, rages
          Upon our territories, and have* already
          O'erborne their way,* consumed with fire, and took*
          What lay before them.   80

Enter COMINIUS.

COMINIUS O, you have made good work!
MENENIUS   What news? What news?
COMINIUS You've holp* to ravish your own daughters, and
          To melt the city leads* upon your pates,*
          To see your wives dishonoured to* your noses —

86   *in their cément:* to their foundations.

87   *franchises . . . bore:* rights which you insisted on reduced to insignificance. – *An auger's bore:* the tiny hole made by an auger.

89   *fair:* fine. – Said sarcastically. Menenius's politeness to the tribunes at the beginning of the scene appears hypocritical as he later follows the lead of Cominius who is angrily contemptuous of them. See *Introduction,* page xxxvi.

91   *He is their god* – i.e. They treat him like a god.

94   *brats:* children – a term used contemptuously implying insignificance.

97   *apron-men:* artisans who wear leather aprons.

97   *stood . . . occupation:* insisted so much on the votes of tradesmen.

99   *garlic-eaters* – Garlic seems to have been more popular with the poorer people in Shakespeare's London than it is today.

99   *shake/Your Rome about your ears:* bring your city, Rome, crashing down around you.

100   *As Hercules . . . fruit* – The eleventh labour of Hercules was to obtain the golden apples from the Garden of the Hesperides, guarded by the dragon Ladon. Another version of the story relates that Hercules persuaded Atlas to pick the fruit while he, Hercules, took over Atlas's role of supporting the vault of the heavens on his shoulders. See notes to II.iii.15, IV.i.18; *mellow:* juicy, ripe.

103   *other:* otherwise.

104   *smilingly revolt* – i.e. willingly revolt against Rome and go over to the side of Coriolanus.

104   *who resists/Are:* those who resist are. – The 's' ending of the verb was a common plural form in Shakespeare's day.

105   *for valiant ignorance:* for their brave stupidity.

106   *perish constant fools:* die foolishly loyal to Rome. – Cominius is here reporting the attitude of others to those who resist Coriolanus. As a Roman patriot he would not share the opinion that such men are *fools.*

107   *Your enemies . . . in him:* Both Volscians and Romans find something to respect in him.

111   *such pity . . . shepherds* – i.e. none.

112   *For:* As for.

113   *charged:* would be urging.

115   *therein showed:* would, in doing so, look.

116   *brand:* flaming torch.

117   *consume it:* burn it down.

117   *have not:* would not have.

118   *made fair hands:* made a good job of it. – Another piece of sarcasm.

MENENIUS What's the news? What's the news?   85
COMINIUS — Your temples burnèd in their cément,* and
          Your franchises,* whereon you stood, confined
          Into an auger's bore.
MENENIUS   Pray now, your news? —
          You've made fair* work, I fear me — Pray, your news?
          If Martius should be joined with Volscians —
COMINIUS   If?   90
          He is their god.* He leads them like a thing
          Made by some other deity than Nature,
          That shapes man better, and they follow him
          Against us brats* with no less confidence
          Than boys pursuing summer butterflies,   95
          Or butchers killing flies.
MENENIUS   You've made good work,
          You and your apron-men;* you that stood*
          So much upon the voice of occupation,
          And the breath of garlic-eaters.*
COMINIUS   He'll shake
          Your Rome about your ears.*
MENENIUS   As Hercules*   100
          Did shake down mellow* fruit. You've made fair work!
BRUTUS But is this true, sir?
COMINIUS   Ay, and you'll look pale
          Before you find it other.* All the regions
          Do smilingly revolt,* and who resists
          Are* mocked for valiant ignorance,*   105
          And perish constant fools.* Who is't can blame him?
          Your enemies* and his find something in him.
MENENIUS We are all undone unless
          The noble man have mercy.
COMINIUS   Who shall ask it?
          The tribunes cannot do't for shame; the people   110
          Deserve such pity* of him as the wolf
          Does of the shepherds. For* his best friends, if they
          Should say, 'Be good to Rome', they charged* him even
          As those should do that had deserved his hate,
          And therein showed* like enemies.
MENENIUS   'Tis true.   115
          If he were putting to my house the brand*
          That should consume it,* I have not* the face
          To say, 'Beseech you, cease.' You've made fair hands,*

119   *crafts:* craftsmen, i.e. the Roman artisans.
119   *crafted fair:* (a) carried out your work well (b) intrigued beautifully.
121   *incapable of help:* unable to get help.
122   *How!:* What do you mean!
123   *gave way unto:* surrendered to.
123   *clusters:* crowds.
125   *roar him in:* cry out in fear when he comes back to Rome.
126   *second name of men:* second in reputation (after Coriolanus).
126   *obeys his points:* obeys him in every point.
127   *Desperation . . . against them* – i.e. all that Rome can do now is despair.
131   *cast:* threw up.
134   *not a hair . . . whip:* there will not be a hair on Coriolanus's soldiers' heads that he will
         not use as a whip to punish you.
135   *coxcombs:* fools' heads. – The coxcomb, resembling a cock's comb in shape and colour,
         was the traditional headdress of the domestic fool.
137   *pay you for your voices:* repay you for your votes against him.
138   *coal:* cinder.
144   *That:* The things that.
146   *goodly things:* fine creatures.
147   *cry:* pack of hounds.
147   *Shall's:* Shall we go.

You and your crafts.* You've crafted fair!*

COMINIUS   You've brought
A trembling upon Rome, such as was never   120
So incapable of help.*

SICINIUS *and* ⎫
    BRUTUS ⎰   Say not we brought it.

MENENIUS How!* Was't we? We loved him, but like beasts
And cowardly nobles gave way unto* your clusters,*
Who did hoot him out o' th' city.

COMINIUS   But I fear
They'll roar him in* again. Tullus Aufidius,   125
The second name of men,* obeys his points*
As if he were his officer. Desperation*
Is all the policy, strength, and defence
That Rome can make against them.

        Enter CITIZENS.

MENENIUS   Here come the clusters.
[*To* COMINIUS] And is Aufidius with him?
                    [*To the* CITIZENS] You are they   130
That made the air unwholesome when you cast*
Your stinking greasy caps in hooting at
Coriolanus' exile. Now he's coming,
And not a hair* upon a soldier's head
Which will not prove a whip. As many coxcombs*   135
As you threw caps up will he tumble down,
And pay you for your voices.* 'Tis no matter;
If he could burn us all into one coal,*
We have deserved it.

CITIZENS Faith, we hear fearful news.

FIRST CITIZEN   For mine own part,   140
When I said banish him, I said 'twas pity.

SECOND CITIZEN And so did I.

THIRD CITIZEN And so did I. And to say the truth, so did very many of us.
That* we did, we did for the best, and though we willingly
consented to his banishment, yet it was against our will.   145

COMINIUS Y'are goodly things,* you voices.

MENENIUS   You have made
Good work, you and your cry.* Shall's* to the Capitol?

COMINIUS O, ay, what else?
                    [*Exeunt* COMINIUS *and* MENENIUS

SICINIUS Go, masters, get you home, be not dismayed.

150   *a side . . . fear:* members of a party who would really like this thing to happen although
              they pretend to be afraid of it.
158   *Would half . . . lie:* I would give half my fortune if it could prove this a lie. – There seems to
              be a suggestion here that Brutus has made a fortune out of his office as tribune.

IV.vii.   Aufidius reveals in this conversation with his Lieutenant that Coriolanus's pride and his
           own loss of face with his troops have turned friendship to envy and a desire for revenge.
           Whatever success Coriolanus may have against Rome, Aufidius is bent on his destruction,
           and hints mysteriously at some omission on Coriolanus's part which will be enough to
           effect this.
               The scene serves two main purposes. Firstly, it prepares us for the hero's fall. Our
           knowledge of Aufidius's intentions throws an ironic light over the subsequent scenes, for
           we see Coriolanus acting under a virtual sentence of death of which he is unaware.
           Secondly, it presents us with a character sketch of Coriolanus. On the one hand this is part
           of the characterization of Aufidius himself. His puzzled analysis of Coriolanus reflects
           his split-mindedness: he admires Coriolanus's nobility and soldiership but is simultane-
           ously envious of those very qualities which attract him so much. On the other hand this
           portrait is Shakespeare's method of putting before us three possible reasons for
           Coriolanus's downfall – pride, defective judgement, inherent nature. Aufidius comes to
           no conclusion, and this surely is what our reaction is intended to be. It is important to
           our response to the scenes which follow, however, that we should have these possibilities
           clearly in our minds, as well as the impossibility of being dogmatic about the degree to
           which each is responsible for the catastrophe.

S.D.   his *Lieutenant* – i.e. his second-in-command.
3   *use him . . . at end* – i.e. talk about him incessantly. The allusion is to conversation at a
              meal, which in Shakespeare's England began with a prayer for blessing
              (*grace* before *meat*) and ended with thanks to God for the food. *'fore:* before.
5   *darkened:* eclipsed.
5   *action:* military campaign.
6   *your own:* Either (a) in the eyes of your own men, or (b) as a result of your own action
              (in sharing your command with Coriolanus).
7   *using means . . . design:* taking steps to right the situation I cripple our proposed action
              against Rome.
8   *more proudlier* – See the note to III.i.120 on the use of the double comparative.
9   *my person:* me personally.
11   *In that's no changeling:* in his pride he is the same as he always was. – *changeling:* fickle
              or inconstant person.
13   *your particular:* as far as you personally are concerned.
14   *Joined in commission:* shared your command.
15   *Have borne the action of yourself:* had conducted the campaign by yourself.

These are a side* that would be glad to have   150
This true which they so seem to fear. Go home,
And show no sign of fear.
FIRST CITIZEN The gods be good to us! Come, masters, let's home. I ever
said we were i' the wrong when we banished him.
SECOND CITIZEN So did we all. But come, let's home.   155

                                             [*Exeunt* CITIZENS

BRUTUS I do not like this news.
SICINIUS Nor I.
BRUTUS Let's to the Capitol. Would half* my wealth
Would buy this for a lie!
SICINIUS   Pray, let's go.

                                             [*Exeunt*

scene vii

A camp near Rome.

Enter AUFIDIUS *with his* LIEUTENANT.*

AUFIDIUS Do they still fly to the Roman?
LIEUTENANT I do not know what witchcraft's in him, but
Your soldiers use him* as the grace 'fore meat,
Their talk at table and their thanks at end,
And you are darkened* in this action,* sir,   5
Even by your own.*
AUFIDIUS   I cannot help it now,
Unless by using means* I lame the foot
Of our design. He bears himself more proudlier,*
Even to my person,* than I thought he would
When first I did embrace him. Yet his nature   10
In that's no changeling,* and I must excuse
What cannot be amended.
LIEUTENANT   Yet I wish, sir,
(I mean for your particular*) you had not
Joined in commission* with him, but either
Have borne the action of yourself,* or else   15
To him had left it solely.

18   *come to his account:* explain his conduct of the war.

19   *What I can urge:* what charges I can bring.

21   *To the vulgar eye:* in the popular view.

21   *bears all things fairly:* manages everything well.

22   *husbandry:* management.

23   *achieve:* accomplish his purpose.

24   *he hath . . . account:* there is something that he has failed to do, and that failure will lead to his death, or perhaps to mine, when we have to explain our actions. – We never learn just what it is that Coriolanus has 'left undone'. At v.vi.2 Aufidius sends a letter with charges against him to the Volscian Senate, which they do not consider serious apart from his making peace with Rome. The dramatic effect of Aufidius's statement here is to create suspense and make us feel that Coriolanus's life is threatened.

27   *carry:* conquer.

28   *yields* – An old northern English plural form.

28   *sits down:* lays siege.

29   *his:* on his side.

32   *rash . . . hasty:* as eager to call him back as they were quick.

34   *the osprey to the fish* – The osprey, or fish-hawk, was thought to fascinate fish so that they turned up the whites of their bellies, allowing him to seize them more easily.

35   *sovereignty of nature:* natural superiority. – The phrase illustrates the medieval and renaissance belief in a hierarchy of creation. The hawk was superior in kind to the fish.

37   *Carry his honours even* – i.e. the honours he received unbalanced him. See II.i.213 and note.

38   *out of daily . . . man:* as a result of continued good fortune, always corrupts the lucky man.

40   *To fail . . . lord of:* in failing to use properly the chances which presented themselves to him.

42   *Not to . . . thing:* to maintain its unity and consistency. – Aufidius holds that man cannot change his essential nature. Coriolanus is a soldier through and through.

43   *th' casque to th' cushion* – i.e. the military to the civil life; *casque:* helmet; *cushion:* the senatorial seat. See note to III.i.101.

44   *austerity and garb:* austere fashion.

45   *but one . . . banished* – i.e. out of these reasons he has just mentioned (pride, defective judgement, nature – Coriolanus has a flavour, *spices*, of all of them) one, but not all three of them (Aufidius is ready to acquit him to that extent, *so far free him*), caused Coriolanus to be feared, and therefore to be hated, and therefore to be banished.

48   *a merit . . . utterance:* a virtue which stifles criticism of his fault before it can be uttered. – Aufidius is explaining his own attitude towards Coriolanus.

49   *So our virtues . . . time:* In the same way our virtues are at the mercy of people's interpretation of them at the time.

51   *And power . . . hath done* – A much disputed passage, but the general sense seems to be that however virtuous a man might be, public opinion will tarnish his reputation. To paraphrase, 'The reputation of a man of power, who has exercised it commendably, will inevitably be dead and buried as soon as anyone passes judgement and praises his deeds', i.e. the praise of his greatness arouses envy in those who hear it, who then defame him; *chair:* seat of judgement; *evident:* inevitable.

54   *One fire . . . do fail* – Aufidius compresses four proverbs into these two lines, all stressing the inevitability of change, one thing giving way to another of similar kind and force; *founder* – The Folio reads *fouler* which most editors reject as a printer's error, making no sense. Of the many emendations proposed (such as *falter, foiled, foul, fail* etc.), *founder* seems the most acceptable.

57   *shortly . . . mine:* soon after that I will have you in my power.

AUFIDIUS   I understand thee well, and be thou sure,
           When he shall come to his account,* he knows not
           What I can urge* against him. Although it seems,
           And so he thinks, and is no less apparent   20
           To the vulgar eye,* that he bears all things fairly,*
           And shows good husbandry* for the Volscian state,
           Fights dragon-like, and does achieve* as soon
           As draw his sword, yet he hath* left undone
           That which shall break his neck or hazard mine,   25
           Whene'er we come to our account.
LIEUTENANT Sir, I beseech you, think you he'll carry* Rome?
AUFIDIUS   All places yields* to him ere he sits down,*
           And the nobility of Rome are his.*
           The senators and patricians love him too.   30
           The tribunes are no soldiers, and their people
           Will be as rash in the repeal as hasty*
           To expel him thence. I think he'll be to Rome
           As is the osprey to the fish,* who takes it
           By sovereignty of nature.* First he was   35
           A noble servant to them, but he could not
           Carry his honours even.* Whether 'twas pride,
           Which out of daily* fortune ever taints
           The happy man; whether defect of judgement,
           To fail* in the disposing of those chances   40
           Which he was lord of; or whether nature,
           Not to* be other than one thing, not moving
           From th' casque to th' cushion,* but commanding peace
           Even with the same austerity and garb*
           As he controlled the war; but one* of these   45
           (As he hath spices of them all), not all
           (For I dare so far free him), made him feared,
           So hated, and so banished. But he has a merit*
           To choke it in the utt'rance. So our virtues*
           Lie in the interpretation of the time,   50
           And power,* unto itself most cómmendable,
           Hath not a tomb so evident as a chair
           T'extol what it hath done.
           One fire* drives out one fire; one nail, one nail;
           Rights by rights founder, strengths by strengths do fail.   55
           Come, let's away. When, Caius, Rome is thine,
           Thou'rt poor'st of all; then shortly* art thou mine.
                                                          [*Exeunt*

Menenius pleading with Coriolanus for mercy for Rome, with Aufidius looking on (Act V, Scene ii).

Volumnia begging Coriolanus to return to Rome (Act V, Scene iii).

The Senators welcoming the triumphant Volumnia back to Rome (Act V, Scene v).

Aufidius contemplating the body of Coriolanus, whose death he has brought about (Act V, Scene vi).

v.i.   Back in Rome the tribunes have been urging Menenius to go to Coriolanus and beg mercy
        for Rome. At first he refuses, citing the failure of Cominius's similar mission, but is finally
        persuaded. After his departure, Cominius expresses his conviction that Coriolanus will
        not listen to him and that Rome's only hope lies in an appeal by Volumnia and Virgilia.

        Suspense is sustained as we await the result of Menenius's mission. Menenius is
        unaware of the real change in Coriolanus revealed in Cominius's description of him,
        'his eye/Red as 'twould burn Rome, and his injury/The gaoler to his pity' (line 63), and his
        optimistic hope that Coriolanus will be more sympathetic after a good meal gives us little
        comfort.

1   *he* – i.e. Cominius.
2   *Which was sometime:* who was formerly.
3   *In a most dear particular:* with a very close personal affection.
3   *He* – i.e. Coriolanus.
5   *A mile . . . mercy:* fall down (on your knees) while you are still a mile from his tent, and
        make your way on your knees to obtain his mercy. – Shakespeare alludes to
        the practice of approaching great rulers, shrines, and other holy places on the
        knees.
6   *coyed:* was unwilling.
8   *He would . . . me:* He acted as if he did not know me.
9   *Yet . . . my name:* Yet formerly he would call me by my first name.
13   *He was . . . Rome* – Cominius is here reporting what Coriolanus said to him. Just as he had
        obtained the name Coriolanus for his exploits at Corioli, so he would obtain a
        new name after he had destroyed Rome. Coriolanus's image of himself hammer-
        ing out a new name at the forge of Rome is one of several fire images used to
        express his resentment and desire for revenge. See *Introduction*, page lxxv.
        titleless: nameless.
15   *Why so:* Just so, exactly. – Coriolanus's behaviour is just what Menenius would have
        expected.
16   *wracked:* worked hard with disastrous results. – Menenius, who is being ironic, creates
        a new word out of two existing words (a) *wrack:* destroy, shipwreck, and
        (b) *rack:* strain, work hard.
17   *To make coals cheap* – i.e. when Rome is burning no one will need to buy coal and its
        price will drop.
17   *A noble memory:* A fine thing to be remembered for.
18   *minded:* reminded.
20   *bare petition:* worthless request.
21   *Very well:* That was well said.
23   *offered:* attempted.
24   *For's:* for his.
25   *pick them . . . chaff:* pick them out individually like grains of corn from a heap of smelly,
        mouldy husks. – Another of Coriolanus's many references to the offensive
        smell of the plebeians.
28   *still to nose the offence:* go on smelling the offensive matter.

ACT V scene i

Rome. A public place.

Enter MENENIUS, COMINIUS, SICINIUS, BRUTUS *and others.*

MENENIUS No, I'll not go. You hear what he* hath said
Which was sometime* his general, who loved him
In a most dear particular.* He* called me father;
But what o' that? Go you that banished him;
A mile* before his tent fall down, and knee   5
The way into his mercy. Nay, if he coyed*
To hear Cominius speak, I'll keep at home.

COMINIUS He would* not seem to know me.

MENENIUS   Do you hear?

COMINIUS Yet* one time he did call me by my name.
I urged our old acquaintance, and the drops   10
That we have bled together. 'Coriolanus'
He would not answer to; forebade all names;
He was* a kind of nothing, titleless,
Till he had forged himself a name o' th' fire
Of burning Rome.

MENENIUS   Why so!* You have made good work.   15
A pair of tribunes that have wracked* for Rome
To make coals cheap.* A noble memory!*

COMINIUS I minded* him how royal 'twas to pardon
When it was less expected. He replied,
It was a bare petition* of a state   20
To one whom they had punished.

MENENIUS   Very well.*
Could he say less?

COMINIUS I offered* to awaken his regard
For's* private friends. His answer to me was,
He could not stay to pick them* in a pile   25
Of noisome musty chaff. He said 'twas folly,
For one poor grain or two, to leave unburnt
And still to nose th' offence.*

MENENIUS   For one poor grain or two!
I am one of those; his mother, wife, his child,
And this brave fellow too, we are the grains;   30
You are the musty chaff, and you are smelt

179

32   *Above the moon* – i.e. to high heaven.
34   *so-never-needed help:* help which was never needed so much.
35   *Upbraid's:* upbraid us.
35   *sure:* certainly.
37   *instant army we can make:* the army we could raise at this moment. – Sicinius is saying
      that it is now too late to raise an effective army.
41   *towards:* in dealing with.
42   *Return me:* sends me back.
44   *But:* simply.
44   *grief-shot:* stricken with grief.
46   *that thanks . . . well:* thanks from Rome in proportion to your good intentions.
48   *to bite his lip/and hum at:* the fact that he showed restrained anger and disagreement with.
      – *hum:* to make a sound signifying dissent.
49   *much unhearts me:* strongly discourages me.
50   *taken well:* approached at the right moment.
51   *The veins unfilled* – Shakespeare shared the erroneous physiological belief of his time that
      food was digested and turned directly into blood which was conveyed by the
      veins into all parts of the body. The discovery of the circulation of the blood
      was made by William Harvey a few months before Shakespeare's death in
      1616. Cf. Menenius's Fable of the Belly (I.i.118–27).
52   *pout upon:* look sulkily at.
52   *unapt:* unwilling.
54   *conveyances:* channels.
55   *suppler:* more flexible, compliant.
56   *priest-like fasts* – Shakespeare is alluding to the priest's observance of a fast from midnight
      until after he had celebrated morning Mass.
57   *dieted to my request:* prepared, by a good meal, for my request.
60   *prove:* try.
61   *Speed how it will:* however it may turn out.
61   *I shall . . . my success:* I shall soon know the result, one way or the other.
63   *in gold:* in a golden chair.
64   *Red as 'twould:* fiery, as if it wanted to.
64   *his injury . . . pity:* his sense of the wrong done him locking up his pity.

Above the moon.* We must be burnt for you.
SICINIUS Nay, pray be patient. If you refuse your aid
In this so-never-needed help,* yet do not
Upbraid's* with our distress. But sure* if you   35
Would be your country's pleader, your good tongue,
More than the instant army we can make,*
Might stop our countryman.
MENENIUS   No. I'll not meddle.
SICINIUS Pray you, go to him.
MENENIUS   What should I do?
BRUTUS Only make trial what your love can do,   40
For Rome, towards* Martius.
MENENIUS   Well, and say that Martius
Return me,* as Cominius is returned,
Unheard? What then?
But* as a discontented friend, grief-shot*
With his unkindness? Say't be so?
SICINIUS   Yet your good will   45
Must have that thanks* from Rome, after the measure
As you intended well.
MENENIUS   I'll undertake't.
I think he'll hear me. Yet to bite his lip .
And hum at* good Cominius, much unhearts me.*
He was not taken well;* he had not dined.   50
The veins unfilled,* our blood is cold, and then
We pout upon* the morning, are unapt*
To give or to forgive; but when we have stuffed
These pipes and conveyances* of our blood
With wine and feeding, we have suppler* souls   55
Than in our priest-like fasts.* Therefore I'll watch him
Till he be dieted to my request,*
And then I'll set upon him.
BRUTUS You know the very road into his kindness,
And cannot lose your way.
MENENIUS   Good faith, I'll prove* him,   60
Speed how it will.* I shall* ere long have knowledge
Of my success.   → of the outcome.
                              [Exit MENENIUS
COMINIUS   He'll never hear him.
SICINIUS   Not?
COMINIUS I tell you, he does sit in gold,* his eye
Red as 'twould* burn Rome, and his injury*

67   *Thus . . . hand:* with his hand, like this, and without speaking.
67   *What he . . . conditions:* He sent a letter after me saying what he would agree to and what
            he would not agree to, swearing an oath that we must accept his conditions. –
            Some editors believe that the text is corrupt here and have proposed various
            emendations.
71   *Unless:* except.
74   *fair:* polite.

v.ii.   At the Volscian camp Menenius is denied access to Coriolanus by the guards. Coriolanus,
however, happens to be passing at that moment and Menenius makes his plea for mercy
for Rome. Coriolanus ignores it and dismisses him, and as he leaves 'grief-shot', he is
mocked by the guards.
     The main dramatic interest of the scene lies in the testing of Coriolanus's resolve.
Having now rejected his country, in the person of Cominius, his former general, he now
rejects his friend Menenius, watched closely by Aufidius whose praise of his constancy
has an ironic ring, as do the guard's words which close the scene, 'he's the rock, the oak
not to be wind-shaken', for Coriolanus has already changed once and will again. There
are signs too, in his refusal to let Menenius speak fully and the letter he gives him, that
his resolution is not as inflexible as he would like it to be. Menenius, who had teased
and mocked the tribunes in II.i, is now baited in his turn by the guards.

1   *Stand:* Halt.
2   *by your leave:* allow me (to tell you).
10   *lots to blanks* – or as we would say, 'ten to one'. *Lots* were tickets which won prizes in a
            lottery, *blanks* those which did not. This allusion to a lottery may derive from
            The Great Frost which mentions 'A familiar talk between a Countryman and
            a Citizen touching this terrible Frost, and the great Lottery, and the effects of
            them', in which the Citizen says, 'to every prize there are put in forty blanks
            . . . There are 7,600 prizes and 42,000 blanks.' This popular lottery took place
            at the same time as the Great Frost, and the allusion strengthens the argument
            for 1608 as the year of composition of the play. See note to I.i.159, p. 8.
11   *touched:* reached.
12   *The virtue . . . passable:* Your name has no power to allow you to enter here. – Menenius,
            that is, must give the password. A pun is possibly intended on *passable*
            meaning (a) current, valid (used of money) and (b) acceptable, allowing you to
            pass.
14   *lover:* dear friend.
15   *book:* record, chronicle.

The gaoler to his pity. I kneeled before him;   65
'Twas very faintly he said, 'Rise'; dismissed me
Thus* with his speechless hand. What he would do
He sent in writing after me, what he would not,
Bound with an oath to yield to his conditions;*
So that all hope is vain,   70
<u>Unless</u>* his noble mother and his wife,
<u>Who, as I hear, mean to solicit him</u>
For mercy to his country. Therefore, let's hence,
And with our fair* entreaties haste them on.

                                                    [*Exeunt*

scene ii

The Volscian camp near Rome.

Two SENTRIES *are on guard.* MENENIUS *enters.*

FIRST SENTRY Stay. Whence are you?
SECOND SENTRY   Stand,* and go back.
MENENIUS You guard like men. 'Tis well; but by your leave,*
    I am an officer of state, and come
    To speak with Coriolanus.
FIRST SENTRY   From whence?
MENENIUS   From Rome.
FIRST SENTRY You may not pass. You must return. Our general   5
    Will no more hear from thence.
SECOND SENTRY You'll see your Rome embraced with fire before
    You'll speak with Coriolanus.
MENENIUS   Good my friends,
    If you have heard your general talk of Rome,
    And of his friends there, it is lots to blanks*   10
    My name hath touched* your ears: it is Menenius.
FIRST SENTRY Be it so; go back. The virtue* of your name
    Is not here passable.
MENENIUS   I tell thee, fellow,
    The general is my lover.* I have been
    The book* of his good acts, whence men have read   15

16   *haply amplified:* perhaps exaggerated.
17   *ever verified:* always told the truth about. – There is humorous irony in Menenius, the
        verifying witness, confessing to exaggeration of the truth.
18   *with all . . . suffer:* to the utmost extent that truth would allow without collapsing.
20   *Like to . . . throw:* as with a bowl on a deceptive bowling green, I have rolled too far. –
        Judging by the frequency of Shakespeare's references to bowls, it seems to
        have been one of his favourite games. The object of the game was to make one's
        bowl stop as near as possible to the jack, or *throw*, a small ball thrown to act
        as a mark.
22   *stamped the leasing:* authenticated a falsehood. – The image is drawn either from the
        impressing of coins, which are then passed into currency, or from the sealing
        of documents to ratify them.
29   *factionary on the party:* an active supporter on the side.
30   *Howsoever you have been his liar:* Although you have lied on his behalf.
31   *true:* truth.
38   *out:* out of.
40   *front:* oppose.
41   *easy:* requiring little effort. – He implies that the *groans* are insincere.
41   *virginal palms* – i.e. the hands of virgins raised in supplication.
42   *palsied intercession:* trembling entreaty.
43   *dotant:* feeble-minded old fellow.
47   *out of:* beyond.
49   *Sirrah* – a term used to a social inferior. – Menenius is doubtless annoyed by the sentry's
        outspokenness.
49   *use me with estimation:* treat me with respect.
51   *captain* – Menenius had used the word in the common sense of 'general', 'leader', meaning
        Coriolanus. The sentry, no doubt deliberately, maddeningly insists on taking
        the word to refer literally to his company commander.
54   *the utmost of your having:* as much as you will get.

His fame unparalleled, haply amplified;*
For I have ever verified* my friends,
Of whom he's chief, with all* the size that verity
Would without lapsing suffer. Nay, sometimes,
Like to* a bowl upon a subtle ground,   20
I have tumbled past the throw, and in his praise
Have almost stamped the leasing.* Therefore, fellow,
I must have leave to pass.

FIRST SENTRY   Faith, sir, if you had told as many lies in his behalf as you
have uttered words in your own, you should not pass   25
here; no, though it were as virtuous to lie as to live
chastely. Therefore go back.

MENENIUS   Prithee, fellow, remember my name is Menenius, always
factionary on the party* of your general.

SECOND SENTRY   Howsoever you have been his liar,* as you say you have,   30
I am one that, telling true* under him, must say you cannot
pass. Therefore go back.

MENENIUS   Has he dined, canst thou tell? For I would not speak with
him till after dinner.

FIRST SENTRY   You are a Roman, are you?   35

MENENIUS   I am, as thy general is.

FIRST SENTRY   Then you should hate Rome, as he does. Can you, when
you have pushed out* your gates the very defender of
them, and in a violent popular ignorance, given your
enemy your shield, think to front* his revenges with the   40
easy* groans of old women, the virginal palms* of your
daughters, or with the palsied intercession* of such a
decayed dotant* as you seem to be? Can you think to blow
out the intended fire your city is ready to flame in, with
such weak breath as this? No, you are deceived, therefore   45
back to Rome, and prepare for your execution. You are
condemned; our general has sworn you out of* reprieve
and pardon.

MENENIUS   Sirrah,* if thy captain knew I were here, he would use me
with estimation.*   50

FIRST SENTRY   Come, my captain* knows you not.

MENENIUS   I mean thy general.

FIRST SENTRY   My general cares not for you. Back, I say. Go, lest I let
forth your half-pint of blood. Back, that's the utmost of
your having.* Back.   55

MENENIUS   Nay, but fellow, fellow —

58   *companion:* rascally fellow. – The word could be used as a term of contempt. See note to
              IV.v.11.
58   *say an errand for you:* deliver the message instead of you.
59   *in estimation:* held in respect.
60   *Jack guardant:* an officious sentry.
60   *office me:* keep me by virtue of his function (*office*). – Cf. the modern phrase 'Jack in
              office'.
61   *but by . . . with him:* only by the way he receives me.
61   *if thou . . . hanging:* whether you are not likely to end up stiff on the gallows. – *Stand:*
              remain stiff, obstinate. Menenius who was told to *stand* (halt) by the sentry
              is playing on the word in another sense, and getting his own back, as he thinks.
62   *more long in spectatorship:* which lasts longer for the spectators.
64   *presently:* immediately.
64   *swound:* swoon.
65   *The glorious:* May the glorious . . . – i.e. it is a prayer. The alliterative phrases (*glorious
              gods, sit in . . . synod, particular prosperity, good gods*) and the rather laboured
              images of fire, water and sighs suggest that this is a carefully rehearsed piece
              of rhetoric by Menenius, designed to move Coriolanus and make Menenius
              the saviour of Rome.
65   *hourly synod:* assembly every hour.
68   *here's water* – He refers to his tears.
69   *hardly moved:* persuaded with difficulty.
70   *I have been . . . sighs* – Menenius suggests through this image the widespread grief of the
              Romans, their sighs so powerful that they have blown him out, and subtly
              reminds Coriolanus, through the phrase *your gates*, that he is a Roman about
              to attack his own city.
71   *conjure:* implore. – But (as the guard takes it in line 93), it means also 'to effect by magic'.
72   *petitionary countrymen:* fellow-Romans begging for mercy.
73   *assuage:* calm.
74   *varlet:* rascal.
74   *block:* (a) blockhead (b) obstruction.
77   *How?:* What?
79   *servanted:* put at the service of, subordinated.
79   *Though I . . . properly:* Although my revenge is mine alone. – *owe:* own.
80   *remission:* power to forgive. – This, says Coriolanus, belongs to the Volscians, not to him.
81   *That we . . . how much:* The ungrateful forgetfulness of Rome will destroy the memory of
              our friendship, sooner than my pity will force me to remember how close it was.
84   *suits:* petitions.
85   *for:* because.
89   *thou behold'st* – i.e. you see how I treat him.
90   *a constant temper:* (a) an unwavering mind (b) a loyal mind.
92   *a spell* – The sentry mocks the 'magic' of Menenius who has *conjured* (line 71) to no effect.
94   *shent:* rebuked. – The sentry refers to the threats of Menenius, lines 61–3.

Enter CORIOLANUS *with* AUFIDIUS.

CORIOLANUS   What's the matter?

MENENIUS   Now you companion,* I'll say an errand for you.* You shall
know now that I am in estimation.* You shall perceive that
a Jack guardant* cannot office me* from my son Corio-   60
lanus. Guess but by* my entertainment with him if thou*
stand'st not i' the state of hanging, or of some death more
long in spectatorship,* and crueller in suffering. Behold
now presently,* and swound* for what's to come upon
thee. [*To* CORIOLANUS] The glorious* gods sit in hourly   65
synod* about thy particular prosperity, and love thee no
worse than thy old father Menenius does. O my son, my
son! Thou art preparing fire for us; look thee, here's
water* to quench it. I was hardly moved* to come to thee,
but being assured none but myself could move thee, I   70
have been* blown out of your gates with sighs, and con-
jure* thee to pardon Rome and thy petitionary countrymen.* The good gods assuage* thy wrath, and turn the
dregs of it upon this varlet* here; this, who like a block*
hath denied my access to thee.   75

CORIOLANUS   Away!

MENENIUS   How?* Away?

CORIOLANUS   Wife, mother, child, I know not. My affairs
Are servanted* to others. Though I* owe
My revenge properly, my remission* lies   80
In Volscian breasts. That we* have been familiar,
Ingrate forgetfulness shall poison rather
Than pity note how much. Therefore be gone.
Mine ears against your suits* are stronger than
Your gates against my force. Yet, for* I loved thee,   85
Take this along. [*He gives him a letter*] I writ it for thy sake,
And would have sent it. Another word, Menenius,
I will not hear thee speak. This man, Aufidius,
Was my beloved in Rome; yet thou behold'st.*

AUFIDIUS   You keep a constant temper.*   90

[*Exeunt* CORIOLANUS *and* AUFIDIUS

FIRST SENTRY   Now, sir, is your name Menenius?

SECOND SENTRY   'Tis a spell,* you see, of much power. You know the way
home again.

FIRST SENTRY   Do you hear how we are shent* for keeping your greatness
back?   95

99   *slight:* insignificant.
99   *die by himself:* kill himself.
100   *For:* as for.
101   *that you are, long:* what you are now (i.e. an unpleasant fellow) for a long time.
102   *say to . . . said to:* I say to you, as Coriolanus said to me.

v.iii.   Just as Coriolanus is announcing his intention of attacking Rome the following day and
          refusing to receive any more ambassadors of peace, his family enter to beg him to spare
          Rome. He greets them and is compelled to listen to Volumnia who gradually persuades
          him to abandon the attack. He agrees to peace with Rome on whatever terms Aufidius
          may advise. Aufidius is exultant at Coriolanus's betrayal of the Volscian cause since it
          gives him a pretext to destroy him.
              This powerful and moving scene marks the climax of the play. Love of country and
          love of friends, as we have seen, have proved too weak to deflect Coriolanus from his
          revenge; love of family proves too much for him. In his soliloquy (lines 20–37) before
          Volumnia speaks, his repeated assertions that he will not weaken convince us of the
          contrary. Volumnia on her knees, a posture which horrifies him by its unnaturalness,
          makes every possible kind of appeal to him; reminding him that she moulded him both
          physically and mentally; pointing to his family's wretchedness as evidenced in their
          miserable appearance and to their impossible position whether he wins or loses; threaten-
          ing suicide; observing that posterity will curse him as a traitor; arguing that it is dis-
          honourable to nurse wrongs; and, subtlest stroke of all, accusing him of unfilial discourtesy
          towards her; and finally turning away as if to return to Rome. The whole splendid
          performance is too much for him; the bond of nature drives him to tears and capitulation
          to her. This is the second time she has put him on the rack, and this time his torture is
          much greater, evoking our total sympathy. There is deep tragic irony in the fact that his
          mother and wife apparently do not realize that his decision is an act of self-destruction.

2   *Set down our host:* deploy our army for a siege.
2   *My partner* – This is the vocative case: You, my partner.
3   *plainly:* honestly.
4   *borne this business:* conducted this action.
4   *Only their ends:* No other purpose but theirs.
6   *general suit of Rome:* petition of all Rome.
8   *That thought them sure of you:* as thought themselves certain to win you over.
9   *cracked:* broken.
10   *measure:* extent.
11   *godded:* made a god of, worshipped.
11   *latest refuge:* last resource.
12   *for whose old love:* for the sake of his long-continued love.
13   *showed sourly:* behaved disagreeably.
14   *The first conditions:* the terms originally offered.
15   *And cannot now accept* – It is not clear why the Romans cannot accept Coriolanus's terms.
              Possibly pride, or shame, prevents it.
15   *to grace . . . more:* only to do a favour to him who thought he would be more successful.
16   *a very . . . yielded to* – Coriolanus refers to the fact that he has given them one more chance
              to accept his original conditions.

SECOND SENTRY What cause do you think I have to swoon?

MENENIUS I neither care for the world, nor your general. For such
things as you, I can scarce think there's any, y'are so
slight.* He that hath a will to die by himself* fears it not
from another. Let your general do his worst. For* you, be   100
that you are, long,* and your misery increase with your
age. I say to* you, as I was said to, 'Away!'

[*Exit*

FIRST SENTRY A noble fellow, I warrant him.

SECOND SENTRY The worthy fellow is our general. He's the rock, the oak
not to be wind-shaken.   105

[*Exeunt*

scene iii

The same.

Enter CORIOLANUS, AUFIDIUS *and others.*

CORIOLANUS We will before the walls of Rome tomorrow
Set down our host.* My partner* in this action,
You must report to the Volscian lords how plainly*
I have borne this business.*

AUFIDIUS   Only their ends*
You have respected, stopped your ears against   5
The general suit of Rome,* never admitted
A private whisper, no, not with such friends
That thought them sure of you.*

CORIOLANUS   This last old man,
Whom with a cracked* heart I have sent to Rome,
Loved me above the measure* of a father,   10
Nay, godded* me indeed. Their latest refuge*
Was to send him; for whose old love* I have
(Though I showed sourly* to him) once more offered
The first conditions,* which they did refuse
And cannot now accept,* to grace* him only   15
That thought he could do more; a very* little

17	*Fresh . . . ear to:* From now on, I will not listen to new deputations and pleas, either from the [Roman] state or from my personal friends.
21	*In the same time:* at the very moment that.
22	*the honoured . . . framed:* the honoured form in which my own body (*trunk*) was shaped (*framed*) – i.e. his mother.
24	*out:* away with you.
25	*All bond and privilege of nature:* All natural ties and claims of human affection.
26	*obstinate:* hard-hearted.
27	*that curtsy . . . dove's eyes* – These lines give an indication of the stage business at this point. Virgilia is curtsying and looking imploringly at Coriolanus. The *dove* was a symbol of innocence and gentleness. The phrase *dove's eyes* is found several times in the biblical *Song of Solomon*. At line 29 he turns his eyes from Virgilia to his mother and son.
28	*make gods forsworn:* cause even gods to break their word.
29	*earth:* clay.
30	*Olympus to a molehill* – Coriolanus compares his mother to Mount Olympus, the home of the gods in Greek mythology, proverbial for its height, and himself to a molehill – a revealing insight into his view of their relationship.
31	*In supplication nod:* bow in humble entreaty.
32	*aspéct of intercession:* pleading look.
33	*Great . . . not* – i.e. all that is natural forbids him to refuse.
34	*Plough Rome and harrow Italy* – i.e. cut through and break up Rome and Italy, crush them completely. – There is a play on *harrow* meaning (a) break up, and (b) plunder, spoil.
35	*gosling to obey instinct:* a fool as to do what my nature prompts me to. – *gosling:* a foolish, inexperienced person.
35	*stand:* stand firm.
36	*were author of himself:* begot himself (and thus had no forebears).
38	*These eyes . . . Rome:* I see things differently from when I was in Rome.
39	*delivers . . . changed:* causes us to appear in such a changed condition. – Plutarch makes Volumnia refer to 'the state of our poor bodies and present sight of our raiment' as indications of the sorrowful life Coriolanus's family have led since he left Rome. In the play this is echoed at lines 94–6.
41	*out:* out of words (having forgotten his lines).
42	*Even to a full disgrace:* so badly as to be completely disgraced.
42	*Best of my flesh:* My better half. – He addresses Virgilia, echoing *Matthew* xix.5: 'they two shall be one flesh'.
43	*tyranny:* cruelty.
44	*For:* because of.
46	*the jealous queen of heaven* – i.e. Juno, guardian of marriage and protectress of women.
46	*that kiss . . . thee* – i.e. the kiss he is giving her is the one she had given him when he left Rome.
47	*true:* faithful.
48	*virgined it:* remained chaste.
48	*prate:* (a) boast (b) chatter.
51	*Of thy deep . . . show:* show a deeper impression (i.e. in the earth) of your profound respect.

I have yielded to. Fresh* embassies and suits,
Nor from the state nor private friends, hereafter
Will I lend ear to. [*Shout within*] Ha, what shout is this?
[*Aside*] Shall I be tempted to infringe my vow   20
In the same time* 'tis made? I will not.

Enter VIRGILIA, VOLUMNIA *leading* MARTIUS *her grandson*,
VALERIA *and* ATTENDANTS.

[*Still aside*] My wife comes foremost, then the honoured*
                                   mould
Wherein this trunk was framed, and in her hand
The grandchild to her blood. But out,* affection!
All bond and privilege of nature,* break!   25
Let it be virtuous to be obstinate.*
What is that curtsy* worth? Or those dove's eyes,
Which can make gods forsworn?* I melt, and am not
Of stronger earth* than others. My mother bows,
As if Olympus to a molehill* should   30
In supplication nod,* and my young boy
Hath an aspéct of intercession* which
Great* Nature cries 'Deny not.' Let the Volsces
Plough Rome and harrow Italy!* I'll never
Be such a gosling to obey instínct,* but stand*   35
As if a man were author of himself*
And knew no other kin.

VIRGILIA   My lord and husband!
CORIOLANUS These eyes* are not the same I wore in Rome.
VIRGILIA   The sorrow that delivers* us thus changed
Makes you think so.
CORIOLANUS   [*Aside*] Like a dull actor now,   40
I have forgot my part, and I am out,*
Even to a full disgrace.* – [*To* VIRGILIA] Best of my flesh,*
Forgive my tyranny,* but do not say,
For* that, 'Forgive our Romans.' O, a kiss
Long as my exile, sweet as my revenge!   45
Now, by the jealous queen of heaven,* that kiss*
I carried from thee, dear, and my true* lip
Hath virgined it* e'er since. [*He turns to* VOLUMNIA]
                              You gods, I prate,*
And the most noble mother of the world
Leave unsaluted. Sink, my knee, i' th' earth. [*He kneels*]   50
Of thy deep* duty more impression show

52   *blest*: lucky, fortunate.
54   *unproperly*: contrary to propriety, unbecomingly.
55   *Show duty . . . parent*: show the child's customary respect for the parent to have been all
           wrong. – Volumnia is being ironical. She certainly does not believe that it is
           proper for a mother to kneel to her son.
57   *your corrected son*: the son whom you have rebuked.
58   *hungry* – Possibly 'empty', 'barren', or perhaps 'hungry for shipwrecks'. This strange
           metaphor has never been satisfactorily explained. There is no apparent
           connection between the hunger of the beach and the striking of the stars.
           The beach he visualizes is the shingle beach, made up of a multitude of small
           rounded pebbles.
59   *Fillip*: strike (literally to 'flick the finger with the thumb'). – Coriolanus means that it is
           as unnatural for his mother to kneel to him as for the insignificant pebble to
           strike the stars – another revelation of his adulation of her.
60   *cedars* were celebrated for their great height.
61   *Murd'ring impossibility* – i.e. making the impossible possible.
62   *slight*: easy.
63   *holp to frame*: helped to form.
64   *Publicola* was one of the first Roman consuls, appointed in 509 B.C.
66   *curdied*: congealed.
67   *Dian's temple* was situated on the Arentine Hill in Rome. Diana was, among other things,
           the goddess of chastity and the *moon*.
68   *epitome*: miniature version.
69   *by th' interpretation . . . yourself*: in the fulness of time may look like you in every respect.
70   *The god of soldiers* – i.e. Mars, and an apt deity for Coriolanus to invoke.
71   *inform*: inspire.
73   *To shame invulnerable*: unable to be hurt by disgrace. – Coriolanus's prayer for his son
           underlines his own vulnerability to disgrace.
73   *stick*: stand out.
74   *sea-mark* – a marker or beacon on land or sea, to guide ships.
74   *standing every flaw*: withstanding every gale.
75   *eye thee*: look to you for guidance (as sailors do the *sea-mark*).
75   *Your knee, sirrah*: Kneel down, boy! – Volumnia uses the word *sirrah* affectionately
           (Cf. v.ii.49).
76   *That's . . . boy* – Coriolanus affectionately commends his son who dutifully kneels to him.
78   *suitors* – i.e. people with a petition or request.
78   *peace* – i.e. no more on that subject.
80   *forsworn to grant*: sworn not to grant.
81   *Be held by you denials*: be taken by you as a rejection of what you ask. – He uses *denials*
           in the plural because he is addressing all of them.
82   *capitulate*: draw up articles of agreement under various headings, hence, come to terms.
83   *mechanics*: manual labourers.
85   *T'allay*: to diminish.

Than that of common sons.

VOLUMNIA   O stand up blest!*
Whilst with no softer cushion than the flint
I kneel before thee, and unproperly*
Show duty* as mistaken all this while   55
Between the child and parent. [*She kneels*]

CORIOLANUS   What's this?
Your knees to me? To your corrected son?*
Then let the pebbles on the hungry* beach
Fillip* the stars. Then let the mutinous winds
Strike the proud cedars* 'gainst the fiery sun,   60
Murd'ring impossibility,* to make
What cannot be, slight* work.

VOLUMNIA   Thou art my warrior;
I holp to frame* thee. Do you know this lady? [*She
indicates* VALERIA]

CORIOLANUS The noble sister of Publicola,*
The moon of Rome, chaste as the icicle   65
That's curdied* by the frost from purest snow
And hangs on Dian's temple.* Dear Valeria.

VOLUMNIA [*Indicating young* MARTIUS] This is a poor epitome* of
                                      yours,
Which by th' interpretation* of full time
May show like all yourself.

CORIOLANUS   The god of soldiers,*   70
With the consent of súpreme Jove, inform*
Thy thoughts with nobleness, that thou mayst prove
To shame unvulnerable,* and stick* i' th' wars
Like a great sea-mark,* standing every flaw,*
And saving those that eye thee.*

VOLUMNIA   Your knee, sirrah!*   75

CORIOLANUS That's* my brave boy.

VOLUMNIA Even he, your wife, this lady and myself
Are suitors* to you.

CORIOLANUS   I beseech you, peace.*
Or, if you'd ask, remember this before:
The thing I have forsworn to grant* may never   80
Be held by you denials.* Do not bid me
Dismiss my soldiers, or capitulate*
Again with Rome's mechanics.* Tell me not
Wherein I seem unnatural. Desire not
T'allay* my rages and revenges with   85

86   *colder:* unimpassioned.
90   *fail in:* fail to grant.
92   *we'll* – Shakespeare makes Coriolanus unconsciously adopt the royal 'we' here.
94   *Should we be:* Even if we remained.
94   *raiment . . . bodies:* our clothing and bodily condition (possibly a state of emaciation).
95   *bewray:* reveal.
98   *Are we come . . . sight:* we are who have come here, since the sight of you.
99   *comforts:* cheerfulness.
100   *Constrains them weep:* forces them to weep.
103   *we* for *us,* a grammatical looseness tolerated in Shakespeare's day.
104   *capital:* deadly.
108   *Whereto we are bound:* which we are under an obligation to do.
109   *Alack:* Alas.
109   *or . . . or:* either . . . or.
111   *find:* experience.
112   *evident:* inevitable.
112   *though:* even if.
113   *which:* whichever.
114   *a foreign recreant:* a deserter to a foreign state. – *Recreant,* a chivalric term, was applied to a knight who had broken his faith or allegiance, and carried also connotations of cowardice. Volumnia carefully chooses a word which she knows will sting Coriolanus.
115   *through* – The word must be sounded disyllabically to keep the rhythm and metre of the line. It was often spelt *thorough* at this time to indicate this pronunciation.
117   *bear the palm* – A branch or leaf of the palm tree was carried as a symbol of victory in ancient Greek and Roman times. Cf. the carrying of palm leaves by Christians on Palm Sunday today, commemorating the occasion when the people of Jerusalem went out to greet Jesus as King (*John* 12:13).
119   *purpose . . . fortune:* do not intend to wait to know my fate.
120   *determine:* come to an end.
121   *grace:* favour.
121   *parts:* sides, i.e. Romans and Volscians.
124   *Trust . . . world:* I assure you that you shall not attack Rome without treading on my dead body. – Volumnia is threatening to commit suicide if Coriolanus attacks Rome.

Your colder* reasons.
VOLUMNIA   O, no more, no more!
You have said you will not grant us anything;
For we have nothing else to ask, but that
Which you deny already. Yet we will ask,
That, if you fail in* our request, the blame   90
May hang upon your hardness. Therefore hear us.
CORIOLANUS Aufidius, and you Volsces, mark, for we'll*
Hear nought from Rome in private. [*He sits*] Your
                    request?
VOLUMNIA Should we be* silent and not speak, our raiment*
And state of bodies would bewray* what life   95
We have led since thy exíle. Think with thyself
How more unfortunate than all living women
Are we come* hither, since that thy sight, which should
Make our eyes flow with joy, hearts dance with
                    comforts,*
Constrains them weep* and shake with fear and sorrow,   100
Making the mother, wife, and child, to see
The son, the husband, and the father, tearing
His country's bowels out. And to poor we*
Thine enmity's most capital.* Thou barr'st us
Our prayers to the gods, which is a comfort   105
That all but we enjoy. For how can we,
Alas, how can we for our country pray,
Whereto we are bound,* together with thy victory,
Whereto we are bound? Alack,* or* we must lose
The country, our dear nurse, or else thy person,   110
· Our comfort in the country. We must find*
An evident* calamity, though* we had
Our wish, which* side should win. For either thou
Must as a foreign recreant* be led
With manacles through* our streets, or else   115
Triumphantly tread on thy country's ruin,
And bear the palm* for having bravely shed
Thy wife and children's blood. For myself, son,
I purpose* not to wait on fortune till
These wars determine.* If I cannot persuade thee   120
Rather to show a noble grace* to both parts*
Than seek the end of one, thou shalt no sooner
March to assault thy country than to tread
(Trust* to't, thou shalt not) on thy mother's womb

126   *keep your . . . time:* keep your name alive to the end of time.
127   *'A:* He.
129   *Not of . . . to see:* If one is to avoid being tender like a woman, one must not look at the
           face of a child or woman. – These lines may be said as an aside. The rhyme
           here gives weight to Coriolanus's statement, accentuating the temptation to
           his constancy.
135   *poisonous of:* destructive of.
136   *while:* so that at the same time.
139   *the all-hail:* a universal acclamation.
144   *Whose repetition . . . curses:* the mention of which will be followed by curses.
145   *chronicle:* history.
146   *attempt:* endeavour, undertaking.
146   *it –* i.e. his nobility.
149   *Thou hast . . . oak –* Volumnia is here guiding Coriolanus in what she wants him to say,
           providing a way out of his dilemma, namely that he has displayed an exalted
           sense of honour in order to show god-like mercy, splitting the air with thunder,
           but using his thunderbolt harmlessly to destroy only an oak. Volumnia no
           doubt uses the word *affected* deliberately since it could mean 'imitated' and
           'sought after', both of which meanings she seems to have intended to convey.
149   *strains:* impulses.
150   *graces:* mercies.
150   *gods –* she alludes particularly to Jove, the god of thunder.
151   *To tear . . . th'air –* Shakespeare probably had in mind the maps of the time which repre-
           sented the winds as being blown from the distended cheeks of cherubs.
152   *sulphur:* lightning.
152   *bolt:* thunderbolt.
153   *rive:* split.
155   *Still:* always.
159   *bound to:* (a) under an obligation to (b) closely tied to.
159   *prate:* chatter.
160   *i' th' stocks –* The *stocks* were a device for punishing offenders consisting of two planks,
           the upper one hinged to come down and encase the ankles or legs of the
           offender, who sat with his legs out in front of him. Volumnia is suggesting that
           Coriolanus is treating her ignominiously, and paying no more attention to
           what she says than people pay to the complaints of a prisoner in the stocks.
162   *fond of:* wishing for.

That brought thee to this world.

VIRGILIA   Ay, and mine   125
That brought you forth this boy, to keep your* name
Living to time.

BOY   'A* shall not tread on me.
I'll run away till I am bigger, but then I'll fight.

CORIOLANUS Not of* a woman's tenderness to be,
Requires nor child nor woman's face to see.   130
I have sat too long.

VOLUMNIA   Nay, go not from us thus.
If it were so that our request did tend
To save the Romans, thereby to destroy
The Volsces whom you serve, you might condemn us
As poisonous of* your honour. No, our suit   135
Is that you reconcile them, while* the Volsces
May say, 'This mercy we have showed', the Romans,
'This we received'; and each in either side
Give the all-hail* to thee, and cry, 'Be blest
For making up this peace!' Thou know'st, great son,   140
The end of war's uncertain; but this certain,
That if thou conquer Rome, the benefit
Which thou shalt thereby reap is such a name
Whose repetition* will be dogged with curses,
Whose chronicle* thus writ, 'The man was noble,   145
But with his last attempt* he wiped it* out,
Destroyed his country, and his name remains
To th' ensuing age abhorred.' Speak to me, son.
Thou hast* affected the fine strains* of honour,
To imitate the graces* of the gods,*   150
To tear* with thunder the wide cheeks o' th' air,
And yet to charge thy sulphur* with a bolt*
That should but rive* an oak. Why dost not speak?
Think'st thou it honourable for a nobleman
Still* to remember wrongs? Daughter, speak you;   155
He cares not for your weeping. Speak thou, boy;
Perhaps thy childishness will move him more
Than can our reasons. There's no man in the world
More bound to's* mother, yet here he lets me prate*
Like one i' th' stocks.* Thou hast never in thy life   160
Showed thy dear mother any courtesy,
When she, poor hen, fond of* no second brood,
Has clucked thee to the wars, and safely home

165 *spurn:* kick out of the way.
166 *honest:* honourable.
167 *That thou restrain'st:* because you withhold.
167 *duty:* respect.
168 *He turns away* – He cannot restrain his tears and turns away to hide this; also, defeated
     by her arguments he is unwilling to look her in the eye, although she tries in
     various ways to make him do so.
169 *shame him:* make him ashamed.
170 *longs:* belongs.
173 *behold's:* behold us.
174 *cannot tell what he would have:* does not know what he is begging for.
175 *for fellowship:* to keep us company.
176 *reason:* urge.
178 *to:* for.
180 *Like him by chance:* resembles him only by chance. – Volumnia pretends to believe that
     Coriolanus is a Volscian so that young Martius cannot be his son.
180 *dispatch:* dismissal.
181 *am hushed:* will be silent.
181 *afire:* on fire.
182 S.D. The stage direction in the Folio reads: *Holds her by the hand, silent.*
183 *ope:* open.
184 *unnatural scene* – i.e. because the natural relationship has been inverted, with the mother
     begging favours from the son.
186 *to:* for. – Cf. line 178 above.
189 *mortal:* fatally.
190 *make true wars:* make war as I have promised.
191 *frame convenient peace:* arrange a fitting peace.
192 *stead:* place.
192 *heard/A mother less:* listened less to your mother.
194 *withal:* by it.
196 *sweat compassion* – i.e. shed tears.
199 *Stand to:* support.
201 *At difference:* at odds, in opposition. – Aufidius plans to turn to his own account the inner
     conflict in Coriolanus between honour and mercy.
201 *I'll work . . . fortune:* I'll fashion for myself a fortune like the one I formerly possessed. –
     By *fortune* Aufidius means the reputation and prestige he has lost through
     defeat at Coriolanus's hands, and Coriolanus's more recent successes as
     joint-commander of the Volscians.
202 *Ay, by and by.* – Coriolanus is replying to an unheard remark by his mother, possibly
     assuring them that he will later return to Rome.

Loaden with honour. Say my request's unjust,
And spurn* me back. But if it be not so,   165
Thou art not honest,* and the gods will plague thee,
That thou restrain'st* from me the duty,* which
To a mother's part belongs. He turns away.*   .
Down, ladies,. let us shame him* with our knees.
To his surname Coriolanus longs* more pride   170
Than pity to our prayers. Down! [*They kneel*] An end;
This is the last. So we will home to Rome,
And die among our neighbours. Nay, behold's!*
This boy, that cannot tell what he would have,*
But kneels and holds up hands for fellowship,*   175
Does reason* our petition with more strength
Than thou hast to deny't. Come, let us go.
This fellow had a Volscian to* his mother;
His wife is in Corioli, and his child
Like him by chance.* Yet give us our dispatch.*   180
I am hushed* until our city be afire,*
And then I'll speak a little.

CORIOLANUS [*Holding her silently by the hand*] O mother, mother!
What have you done? Behold, the heavens do ope,*
The gods look down, and this unnatural scene*
They laugh at. O my mother, mother! O!   185
You have won a happy victory to* Rome.
But, for your son, believe it, O believe it,
Most dangerously you have with him prevailed,
If not most mortal* to him. But let it come.
Aufidius, though I cannot make true wars,*   190
I'll frame convenient peace.* Now, good Aufidius,
Were you in my stead,* would you have heard
A mother less?* Or granted less, Aufidius?

AUFIDIUS I was moved withal.*

CORIOLANUS   I dare be sworn you were.
And, sir, it is no little thing to make   195
Mine eyes to sweat compassion.* But, good sir,
What peace you'll make, advise me. For my part,
I'll not to Rome. I'll back with you, and pray you
Stand to* me in this cause. O mother! Wife!

AUFIDIUS [*Aside*] I am glad thou hast set thy mercy and thy honour   200
At difference* in thee. Out of that I'll work*
Myself a former fortune.

CORIOLANUS   Ay, by and by.*

203   *bear . . . countersealed:* carry back with you a stronger proof of my decision than words, namely a written treaty with the same terms I have promised, which we will have sealed by both parties.

207   *a temple built you* – Shakespeare puts into the mouth of Coriolanus a narrative detail from a later passage in Plutarch, who describes how the women, offered any gift they wanted by a grateful Senate, asked for 'a Temple of Fortune of the Women'.

208   *Italy . . . arms:* Rome and the armies of her allies. – In 490 B.C. *Italia* was the name of only a small part of the modern Italian peninsula; Rome was its centre.

v.iv.   Menenius is trying to persuade Sicinius that Volumnia's mission has no hope of success. A messenger enters with the news that the citizens have seized Brutus, threatening him with death if Volumnia fails. A second messenger rushes in with news of her success and they all hurry off to the city gates to welcome her.

        There is dramatic irony in Menenius's pessimism, which we know to be unfounded (see *Introduction*, page xxxvi). The fallibility of his judgement should warn us not to accept at face value his character sketch of Coriolanus, which is coloured by his wretchedness at Coriolanus's rejection of him and the failure of his own peace mission.

1   *yond coign:* that corner.
6   *stay upon:* wait for.
7   *condition:* character.
9   *differency:* difference.
10   *your* – For the undefined use of the pronoun see the note to I.i.114.
11   *creeping thing:* Either (a) man or (b) snake. – Menenius's point is that Coriolanus has become a monster, something non-human.
15   *than an eight-year-old horse:* than an old horse remembers its dam. – The animal image reinforces Menenius's assertion that Coriolanus has become inhuman.
17   *engine:* instrument of war, e.g. battering ram, catapult, ordnance.
17   *shrinks:* (a) cowers (b) gives way. – The word cleverly conveys both the physical and emotional effects of Coriolanus's power.
18   *corslet:* piece of armour covering the trunk only.
18   *knell:* sound announcing someone's death.
19   *his hum:* the way he says 'hum'. See note to v.i.48.
19   *battery:* physical assault, beating.
19   *state:* chair of state, throne.
19   *as a thing made for Alexander:* Either (a) as if it were one made for Alexander the Great, or (b) like a statue of Alexander. – If (a), then Menenius is being sarcastic about Coriolanus's majestic air; if (b), he is stressing Coriolanus's inflexibility.
21   *with his bidding:* while he is still ordering it.
21   *wants:* lacks.
22   *throne:* be enthroned.
23   *Yes, mercy . . . truly* – i.e. Yes, he does lack something, and that is mercy, if your description of him is correct.

But we will drink together, and you shall bear*
A better witness back than words, which we
On like conditions will have countersealed.   205
Come enter with us. Ladies, you deserve
To have a temple built you.* All the swords
In Italy,* and her confederate arms,
Could not have made this peace.

                                                            [*Exeunt*

scene iv

Rome. A public place.

Enter MENENIUS *and* SICINIUS.

MENENIUS See you yond coign* o' th' Capitol, yond cornerstone?
SICINIUS Why, what of that?
MENENIUS If it be possible for you to displace it with your little finger,
there is some hope the ladies of Rome, especially his
mother, may prevail with him. But I say there is no hope   5
in't; our throats are sentenced, and stay upon* execution.
SICINIUS Is't possible that so short a time can alter the condition* of
a man?
MENENIUS There is a differency* between a grub and a butterfly, yet
your* butterfly was a grub. This Martius is grown from   10
man to dragon. He has wings; he's more than a creeping
thing.*
SICINIUS He loved his mother dearly.
MENENIUS So did he me. And he no more remembers his mother now
than an eight-year-old horse.* The tartness of his face   15
sours ripe grapes. When he walks, he moves like an
engine,* and the ground shrinks* before his treading. He
is able to pierce a corslet* with his eye, talks like a knell,*
and his hum* is a battery.* He sits in his state* as a thing
made for Alexander.* What he bids be done is finished   20
with his bidding.* He wants* nothing of a god but
eternity, and a heaven to throne* in.
SICINIUS Yes, mercy,* if you report him truly.

24   *paint him in the character:* I depict him exactly as he is.
27   *'long of:* because of.
34   *hale:* drag.
35   *comfort:* good news.
36   *death by inches:* a slow torturing death.
38   *are dislodged:* have left their camp.
40   *th'expulsion of the Tarquins* – See note to II.i.139.
43   *lurked:* been hiding.
44   *Ne'er through . . . tide:* Never did the tide, propelled by the wind, rush through the arch
         of a bridge. – Shakespeare probably had in mind London Bridge with its
         narrow arches, which forced the Thames to flow through at great speed,
         forming rapids dangerous to boatmen.
45   *the recomforted through:* the reheartened citizens out through.
45   S.D. *hautboys* – The hautboy, a wood-wind instrument, was a coarser form of the modern
         oboe.
46   *sackbuts* were base trumpets with a slide like a trombone for altering the pitch. They are
         now obsolete.
46   *psalteries* were zither-like instruments with strings of varying length over a sounding
         board or box, played by plucking the strings with finger or plectrum.
47   *Tabors:* small side-drums.
50   *of consuls . . . full:* a city full of consuls, senators and patricians.
54   *doit:* small coin of little value. Cf. I.v.6, IV.iv.17.
54   *joy:* rejoice.

MENENIUS I paint him in the character.* Mark what mercy his
mother shall bring from him. There is no more mercy in   25
him than there is milk in a male tiger; that shall our poor
city find. And all this is 'long of* you.
SICINIUS The gods be good to us!
MENENIUS No, in such a case the gods will not be good unto us.
When we banished him, we respected not them; and he   30
returning to break our necks, they respect not us.

Enter a MESSENGER.

MESSENGER Sir, if you'd save your life, fly to your house.
The plébeians have got your fellow-tribune,
And hale* him up and down; all swearing if
The Roman ladies bring not comfort* home   35
They'll give him death by inches.*

Enter another MESSENGER.

SICINIUS   What's the news?
2nd MESSENGER Good news, good news! The ladies have prevailed,
The Volscians are dislodged,* and Martius gone.
A merrier day did never yet greet Rome,
No, not th' expulsion of the Tarquins.*
SICINIUS   Friend,   40
Art thou certain this is true? Is't most certain?
2nd MESSENGER As certain as I know the sun is fire.
Where have you lurked* that you make doubt of it?
Ne'er through* an arch so hurried the blown tide,
As the recomforted through* the gates. Why, hark you!   45
          [*Trumpets, hautboys* and drums sound all together*
The trumpets, sackbuts,* psalteries,* and fifes,
Tabors* and cymbals, and the shouting Romans,
Make the sun dance. Hark you!   [*A shout is heard*
MENENIUS   This is good news.
I will go meet the ladies. This Volumnia
Is worth of consuls,* senators, patricians,   50
A city full; of tribunes such as you,
A sea and land full. You have prayed well today.
This morning for ten thousand of your throats
I'd not have given a doit.* Hark, how they joy!*
          [*Shouting continues*
SICINIUS First, the gods bless you for your tidings; next,   55
Accept my thankfulness.

58   *at point to:* on the point of.
59   *help the joy:* join in the rejoicing.

v.v.   This very brief scene in which all Rome turns out to welcome Volumnia's triumphal
        return is an ironic echo of Coriolanus's triumphant return in II.i. It has tragic overtones,
        since her triumph means her son's ruin, a point which the Romans have not grasped.
        All triumphs in this play are short-lived.

4   *Unshout . . . Martius* – i.e. by shouting now (in support of Volumnia's action) wipe out
       your shouts of approval when Coriolanus was banished.
5   *Repeal him with the welcome of:* recall him (metaphorically) from banishment by welcoming.

v.vi.   In Corioli, Aufidius sends to the Volscian Senate a letter containing his charges against
        Coriolanus. With a number of conspirators he plans to murder Coriolanus on his return
        from the war. When he arrives Coriolanus is given a hero's welcome, but Aufidius
        accuses him before the Lords of the city of treason in betraying the Volscians because of
        the tears of a few women. His insulting term 'boy' infuriates Coriolanus who, ignoring the
        charge of treason, is stung into boasting of his single-handed capture of Corioli. This
        rouses those citizens whose kinsmen he had killed in that action, and Aufidius and his
        fellow-conspirators fan this anger into an uproar in which they kill Coriolanus, despite
        the Senators' attempt to have a judicial hearing of the charges against him. Aufidius,
        stricken with sorrow at his action, helps to bear off Coriolanus's body for an honourable
        funeral.
            This closing scene is the inevitable postscript to Coriolanus's surrender to his mother
        in v.iii. His political ineptitude continues to the last in his assumption that his explanation
        of his action will be acceptable to the Volscian Senate, whereas, as the First Lord says,
        his betrayal 'admits no excuse'. The question is not whether he will die, but rather how
        he will die, and Shakespeare fittingly presents death in an outburst of heroic anger, alone
        in the city which he had captured single-handed, with the boast of that exploit on his
        lips. We are left with the final impression, requisite to tragedy, of the wasteful loss of a
        great man at the hands of lesser mortals.

1   *th' city* – i.e. Antium, the Volscian capital. In Plutarch Coriolanus returns to Antium after
       the meeting with his family and is killed there. Shakespeare sets the beginning
       of the scene in Antium (the home of Aufidius, referred to in lines 49 and 60).
       Later he changed his mind, making Corioli the setting, as is clear from lines
       89 and 150, but failing to go back and make the necessary changes in the first
       part of the scene to fit in with his altered plan.
2   *Having:* When they have.
3   *repair:* go.
4   *theirs:* their.

2nd MESSENGER   Sir, we have all
Great cause to give great thanks.
    SICINIUS   They are near the city?
2nd MESSENGER Almost at point to* enter.
    SICINIUS   We'll meet them,
And help the joy.*
                                              [*Exeunt*

scene v

Rome. A street near the gate.

Enter two SENATORS *with* VOLUMNIA *and her party and a
crowd of Romans, passing over the stage.*

FIRST SENATOR Behold our patroness, the life of Rome!
Call all your tribes together, praise the gods,
And make triumphant fires; strew flowers before them.
Unshout* the noise that banished Martius,
Repeal him with the welcome of* his mother.   5
Cry 'Welcome, ladies, welcome!'
    ALL   Welcome, ladies.
            [*A flourish with drums and trumpets. Exeunt*

scene vi

Corioli. A public place.

Enter AUFIDIUS *with* ATTENDANTS.

AUFIDIUS Go tell the lords o' th' city* I am here.
Deliver them this paper. Having* read it,
Bid them repair* to th' market-place, where I,
Even in theirs* and in the commons' ears,

5   *vouch:* affirm.

5   *Him:* He whom.

6   *ports:* gates.

6   *by this:* by this time.

8   *purge:* clear.

8   *Dispatch:* Hurry.

9   *Even so . . . empoisoned:* I am just like a man destroyed by his own charity. – Aufidius refers to the Elizabethan custom of collecting the remains of drink left in cups and glasses, mixing them together, and giving them to the poor as alms, or *alms-drink.* It was often highly potent.

11   *with:* by.

12   *hold . . . parties:* retain the same purpose with which you wished us to help.

14   *Of:* from.

17   *'Twixt:* between.

17   *difference:* disagreement.

19   *pretéxt . . . construction:* reason for striking at him can be justifiably explained.

20   *pawned:* staked.

21   *for his truth:* on his loyalty.

21   *who . . . heightened,/He:* but having been distinguished in this way he.

22   *new plants* – i.e. new position and honours.

23   *so:* by doing so.

24   *never known . . . free:* always known previously to be rough, inflexible and outspoken.

26   *stoutness:* haughtiness.

28   *lack of stooping:* failure to bend, compromise.

28   *I would have spoke of:* I was going to speak about.

31   *gave him way:* gave him his own way.

33   *files:* ranks.

33   *his projects to accomplish:* to carry out his plans.

34   *designments:* enterprises.

35   *holp:* helped.

36   *end all his:* gather in as if the crop were all his. – *End* is a dialectal variant of *in* or *inn,* to harvest.

Will vouch* the truth of it. Him* I accuse   5
The city ports* by this* hath entered, and
Intends t' appear before the people, hoping
To purge* himself with words. Dispatch.*

[*Exeunt* ATTENDANTS

Enter three or four CONSPIRATORS, *followers of* AUFIDIUS.

Most welcome!

1st CONSPIRATOR   How is it with our general?

AUFIDIUS   Even so*
As with a man by his own alms empoisoned,   10
And with* his charity slain.

2nd CONSPIRATOR   Most noble sir,
If you do hold* the same intent wherein
You wished us parties, we'll deliver you
Of* your great danger.

AUFIDIUS   Sir, I cannot tell.
We must proceed as we do find the people.   15

3rd CONSPIRATOR   The people will remain uncertain whilst
'Twixt* you there's difference;* but the fall of either
Makes the survivor heir of all.

AUFIDIUS   I know it,
And my pretéxt* to strike at him admits
A good construction. I raised him, and I pawned*   20
Mine honour for his truth,* who* being so heightened,
He watered his new plants* with dews of flattery,
Seducing so* my friends; and to this end
He bowed his nature, never known* before
But to be rough, unswayable, and free.   25

3rd CONSPIRATOR   Sir, his stoutness*
When he did stand for consul, which he lost
By lack of stooping* –

AUFIDIUS   That I would have spoke of.*
Being banished for't, he came upon my hearth,
Presented to my knife his throat. I took him,   30
Made him joint servant with me, gave him way*
In all his own desires; nay, let him choose
Out of my files,* his projects to accomplish,*
My best and freshest men, served his designments*
In mine own person; holp* to reap the fame   35
Which he did end all his,* and took some pride
To do myself this wrong; till at the last

39   *He waged . . . mercenary:* he paid me by giving me friendly looks as if I were a hired
soldier, i.e. he did not pay me at all. – Aufidius accuses Coriolanus of being
ungrateful and patronizing. It was common in Shakespeare's time for mer-
cenaries, i.e. hired professional soldiers, to be kept waiting a long time for
their pay.

41   *in the last:* finally.

42   *had carried Rome:* had Rome beaten and at his mercy.

42   *that we looked/For:* when we expected.

43   *There was it:* That was the thing.

44   *sinews shall be stretched upon:* strength shall be fully exerted against.

45   *At:* Either (a) at the sight of, or (b) at the price of, or both.

45   *rheum:* tears.

47   *action:* military campaign.

48   *renew me:* regain my lost authority.

49   *like a post:* like a mere messenger.

51   *patient:* long-suffering.

52   *their base . . . glory:* make themselves hoarse cheering him.

53   *at your vantage:* when you see your opportunity.

54   *Ere:* before.

56   *second:* support (with ours).

56   *along:* stretched at full length.

57   *After . . . pronounced:* his story told as you choose to tell it.

58   *his reasons:* his side of the argument.

63   *made:* committed.

64   *found easy fines:* been met by light punishments.

66   *our levies:* the armies we raised.

66   *answering . . . charge:* paying us back only our expenses (Cf. line 77 and the note on it).

I seemed his follower, not partner, and
He waged* me with his countenance, as if
I had been mercenary.

1st CONSPIRATOR   So he did, my lord.   40
The army marvelled at it, and in the last,*
When he had carried Rome,* and that we looked
For* no less spoil than glory —   ·

AUFIDIUS   There was it,*
For which my sinews shall be stretched upon* him.
At* a few drops of women's rheum,* which are   45
As cheap as lies, he sold the blood and labour
Of our great action.* Therefore shall he die,
And I'll renew me* in his fall. But hark!
[Drums and trumpets sound, with great shouts from the
people.

1st CONSPIRATOR Your native town you entered like a post,*
And had no welcomes home; but he returns   50
Splitting the air with noise.

2nd CONSPIRATOR   And patient* fools,
Whose children he hath slain, their base* throats tear
With giving him glory.

3rd CONSPIRATOR   Therefore, at your vantage,*
Ere* he express himself, or move the people
With what he would say, let him feel your sword,   55
Which we will second.* When he lies along,*
After* your way his tale pronounced shall bury
His reasons* with his body.

AUFIDIUS   Say no more.
Here come the lords.

Enter the LORDS of the city.

LORDS You are most welcome home.

AUFIDIUS   I have not deserved it.   60
But worthy lords, have you with heed perused
What I have written to you?

LORDS   We have.

FIRST LORD   And grieve to hear't.
What faults he made* before the last, I think
Might have found easy fines.* But there to end
Where he was to begin, and give away   65
The benefit of our levies,* answering* us
With our own charge; making a treaty where

69   S.D. *drum* i.e. a drummer.
71   *infected . . . love:* tainted by any love for my country.
72   *parted hence:* left here, i.e. Antium, which he left at the end of IV.v.
72   *subsisting:* remaining.
74   *prosperously I have attempted:* I have been successful in my enterprise.
75   *passage:* passage of arms, military action.
77   *Doth* for *Do.* – See the note to IV.i.4.
77   *more than . . . charges:* exceed the cost by at least a third. – This contradicts the assertion
      of the First Lord (line 66), based on Aufidius's letter, that Coriolanus has
      returned only the cost of the expedition to the Volscians; *counterpoise:*
      balance.
81   *Subscribed:* signed.
83   *compounded on:* agreed.
84   *traitor in the highest degree:* out-and-out traitor.
85   *abused your powers:* misused the powers you deputed to him.
86   *How now?:* What do you mean?
88   *grace:* honour.
90   *perfidiously:* treacherously.
92   *drops of salt* – i.e. the tears of Volumnia and Virgilia. Cf. *drops of rheum,* line 45.
95   *twist:* threads wound round one another.
95   *admitting/Counsel o' th' war:* allowing consultation about the war.
98   *That:* so that.
98   *heart:* courage.
99   *wond'ring:* in astonishment.
99   *others:* the others.
99   *Hear'st thou, Mars?* – In astonishment at these accusations, Coriolanus calls on the god of
      war to hear them.
100 *boy* – This was a highly insulting term in Shakespeare's day when applied to a man.
101 *No more* – i.e. You are no more than a boy.

There was a yielding – this admits no excuse.

AUFIDIUS   He approaches. You shall hear him.

Enter CORIOLANUS *marching with drum* and colours, and the* COMMONERS.

CORIOLANUS   Hail lords! I am returned your soldier,   70
No more infected* with my country's love
Than when I parted hence,* but still subsisting*
Under your great command. You are to know
That prosperously I have attempted,* and
With bloody passage* led your wars even to   75
The gates of Rome. Our spoils we have brought home
Doth* more than* counterpoise a full third part
The charges of the action. We have made peace
With no less honour to the Antiates
Than shame to th' Romans. And we here deliver,   80
Subscribed* by th' consuls and patricians,
Together with the seal o' th' Senate, what
We have compounded on.*

AUFIDIUS   Read it not, noble lords,
But tell the traitor in the highest degree*
He hath abused your powers.*   85

CORIOLANUS   Traitor? How now?*

AUFIDIUS   Ay, traitor, Martius!

CORIOLANUS   Martius?

AUFIDIUS   Ay, Martius, Caius Martius! Dost thou think
I'll grace* thee with that robbery, thy stol'n name
Coriolanus, in Corioli?
You lords and heads o' th' state, perfidiously*   90
He has betrayed your business, and given up,
For certain drops of salt,* your city Rome –
I say 'your city' – to his wife and mother,
Breaking his oath and resolution, like
A twist* of rotten silk, never admitting   95
Counsel o' th' war;* but at his nurse's tears
He whined and roared away your victory,
That* pages blushed at him, and men of heart*
Looked wond'ring* each at others.*

CORIOLANUS   Hear'st thou, Mars?*

AUFIDIUS   Name not the god, thou boy* of tears.

CORIOLANUS   Ha?   100

AUFIDIUS   No more.*

103	*what contains it* – i.e. its containing body.
104	*the first time . . . scold* – He means, of course, among the Volscians.
106	*give . . . lie:* prove that this dog is lying.
106	*notion:* awareness of the truth.
107	*Who wears . . . grave:* who carries on his body the wounds I gave him, and must take the marks of them to his grave.
109	*thrust the lie unto him:* force him to admit that it is a lie.
112	*edges:* swords.
113	*there* – i.e. written in your history books.
114	*dovecote:* pigeon-house.
115	*Fluttered* – i.e. threw into a panic. The image is of frightened pigeons wildly flapping their wings.
117	*blind fortune:* pure luck. – The Roman goddess Fortuna is traditionally represented in art as blindfold.
118	*your shame:* the cause of your disgrace.
119	*'Fore:* Before.
120	*presently:* at once.
124	*folds in . . . earth:* embraces this whole globe, the earth, i.e. his fame has spread all over the world.
125	*last:* recent.
126	*judicious:* judicial.
126	*Stand:* Stop.
127	*O that . . . sword* – Coriolanus wishes that Aufidius (and all the support he wants) were in some place or circumstances where it would be lawful to use his sword on him.
128	*tribe:* his whole family.
130	*Hold:* Stop.
132	*whereat:* at which.
132	*valour will weep* – i.e. because of the cowardly nature of Aufidius's act.

CORIOLANUS   Measureless liar, thou hast made my heart
             Too great for what contains it.* 'Boy?' O slave!
             Pardon me, lords, 'tis the first time* that ever
             I was forced to scold. Your judgements, my grave lords,   105
             Must give* this cur the lie, and his own notion* –
             Who wears* my stripes impressed upon him, that
             Must bear my beating to his grave – shall join
             To thrust the lie unto him.*
FIRST LORD   Peace, both, and hear me speak.   110
CORIOLANUS   Cut me to pieces, Volsces; men and lads
             Stain all your edges* on me. 'Boy'! False hound!
             If you have writ your annals true, 'tis there,*
             That, like an eagle in a dovecote,* I
             Fluttered* your Volscians in Corioli.   115
             Alone I did it. 'Boy'!
AUFIDIUS   Why, noble lords,
             Will you be put in mind of his blind fortune,*
             Which was your shame,* by this unholy braggart?
             'Fore* your own eyes and ears?
ALL THE
CONSPIRATORS   Let him die for't!
ALL THE PEOPLE Tear him to pieces! Do it presently!* He killed my son! – 120
             My daughter! – He killed my cousin Marcus! – He killed
             my father!
SECOND LORD Peace, ho! No outrage. Peace!
             The man is noble, and his fame folds in*
             This orb o' th' earth. His last* offence to us   125
             Shall have judicious* hearing. Stand,* Aufidius,
             And trouble not the peace.
CORIOLANUS   O that* I had him,
             With six Aufidiuses or more, his tribe,*
             To use my lawful sword!
AUFIDIUS   Insolent villain!
ALL THE
CONSPIRATORS Kill kill kill, kill, kill him!

             [*The* CONSPIRATORS *draw their swords and kill* CORIOLANUS,
             who falls. AUFIDIUS *stands on him*
LORDS   Hold,* hold, hold, hold!   130
AUFIDIUS   My noble masters, hear me speak.
FIRST LORD   O Tullus!
SECOND LORD Thou hast done a deed whereat* valour will weep.*
THIRD LORD   Tread not upon him. Masters, all be quiet.

134   *Put up:* sheathe.
137   *did owe you:* possessed for you.
139   *deliver:* demonstrate.
141   *censure:* condemnation.
143   *corse:* corpse.
143   *herald* – an official, one of whose duties was the arranging of funerals.
144   *urn* – burial vase containing the ashes of a deceased person.
144   *impatience:* anger.
148   *I'll be one* – i.e. the fourth.
150   *Trail your steel pikes* – This was a military sign of mourning, the pike butt trailing on the
        ground with the point forward.
151   *unchilded:* deprived of children (by killing them in war).
152   *Which:* who.
152   *memory:* memorial, tomb.

Put up* your swords.

AUFIDIUS My lords, when you shall know (as in this rage   135
Provoked by him you cannot) the great danger
Which this man's life did owe you,* you'll rejoice
That he is thus cut off. Please it your honours
To call me to your Senate, I'll deliver*
Myself your loyal servant, or endure   140
Your heaviest censure.*

FIRST LORD   Bear from hence his body,
And mourn you for him. Let him be regarded
As the most noble corse* that ever herald*
Did follow to his urn.*

SECOND LORD   His own impatience*
Takes from Aufidius a great part of blame.   145
Let's make the best of it.

AUFIDIUS   My rage is gone,
And I am struck with sorrow. Take him up.
Help, three o' th' chiefest soldiers; I'll be one.*
Beat thou the drum, that it speak mournfully,
Trail your steel pikes.* Though in this city he   150
Hath widowed and unchilded* many a one,
Which* to this hour bewail the injury,
Yet he shall have a noble memory.*
Assist.

[*Exeunt, bearing the body of* MARTIUS. *A dead march is
sounded.*

Glossary

(S.D. = Stage direction)

A

'a, he III.i.319, v.iii.127
abated, humbled III.iii.131
abed, in bed III.i.260
abhorred, loathed I.iv.32
abhorring, contempt I.i.154
about, out of the way I.vi.20
abram, dark brown II.iii.17
absolute, positive, unconditional III.i.90
    unrestricted III.i.116
    uncompromising III.ii.39
    complete, perfect IV.v.132
abused, deceived III.i.58
    misused v.vi.85
account, consider I.i.12, II.iii.86, 89
achieve, win I.ix.33
    accomplish a purpose IV.vii.23
act, performance I.ix.19
action, the use of the body in rhetoric
    III.ii.76
    military campaign I.i.265, II.i.126, IV.vii.5,
    15, v.vi.47
addition, title I.ix.65, 71
adieu, goodbye II.iii.75
admire, wonder at I.ix.5
admit, accept II.iii.132
    permit v.vi.19
admitting, allowing v.vi.95
a-doing, being done IV.ii.5
advanced, raised I.vi.61, II.i.150
advantage, opportunity II.iii.187, IV.i.43
adversely, disagreeably II.i.51
aediles, Roman police officials III.i.172 etc.
affect, desire II.ii.20, III.iii.1, IV.vi.32
affected, (a) imitated (b) aimed at v.iii.149
affection, desire, inclination I.i.90,163,
    II.iii.220
affrights, frightens I.i.155
afire, on fire v.iii.181
Afric, Africa I.viii.3
after, following II.iii.219
    according to II.iii.215, v.vi.57
after-meeting, addition to the main meeting
    II.ii.36
against, near III.i.246
age, lifetime III.i.7, IV.vi.52
aged, ancient II.iii.157
agents, bodily instruments I.i.109
agued, trembling I.iv.38

aidless, unaided II.ii.109
alack, alas I.i.63, v.iii.109
alarum, (a) a call to arms, or warning of
    imminent action I.iv.9, S.D. 19, 29 (b)
    the sound of fighting I.iv.19, 42, 47, I.v.3
alias, alternative name II.i.39
allay, diminish v.iii.85
allaying, diluting II.i.43
all-hail, universal acclamation v.iii.139
allow, accept III.iii.45
allowance, acceptance III.ii.57
alms, charity II.iii.75, III.ii.120
    alms-drink (the dregs or remains of drink)
    v.vi.10
along, at full length v.vi.56
Amazonian, like the Amazons, the women
    warriors of ancient Greek times II.ii.88
amplified, exaggerated v.ii.16
ancient, long-standing IV.v.92
Ancus Martius, the fourth of the Roman
    kings II.iii.228
and, if I.i.81, II.i.120, II.iii.77
an-hungry, hungry I.i.191
annals, history books v.vi.113
anon, shortly II.iii.130, 133
    at once IV.v.16
answer, fight I.i.19, I.iv.52
    meet II.iii.248
    answer a charge III.i.162, 323
answering, paying back v.vi.66
Antiates, inhabitants of Antium I.vi.59,
    v.vi.79
antique, ancient, past II.iii.108
apoplexy, paralysis IV.v.213
appeared, became known I.ii.22
    made apparent IV.iii.8
apprehended, arrested III.i.172
apprehension, understanding II.iii.213
approbation, confirmed success II.i.97
    ratification, approval II.iii.133, 240
approve, approve of III.ii.8
apron-men, artisans IV.vi.97
apt, willing III.ii.29
aptness, readiness IV.iii.20
arm, prepare III.i.138
arms, armies v.iii.107
arriving, reaching II.iii.170
article, condition II.iii.185
articulate, negotiate articles of peace
    I.ix.76

217

as, as if I.i.199, I.vi.22, v.i.64
    as that II.i.220
ash, ash spear IV.v.104
aspect, look v.iii.32
assistance, partners IV.vi.33
associated, joined IV.vi.77
assuage, calm v.ii.73
asunder, apart I.i.59
atone, unite IV.vi.73
attach, arrest III.i.174
attained, acquired I.i.251
attempt, undertaking v.iii.139
attend, await I.i.64, 232, I.x.30, II.ii.157,
    III.i.330, III.ii.138
    listen I.ix.4
attend upon, accompany I.i.223
audible, noisy IV.v.212
audience, hearing II.i.66
    pay attention III.iii.40
audit, statement of accounts I.i.130
auger, tool for boring holes in wood IV.vi.88
aught, anything I.i.262, II.iii.186, IV.i.52
augurer, Roman religious official who fore-
    told events II.i.1
author, begetter v.iii.85
authority, those in authority I.i.13
avoid, leave IV.v.20, 28
awe, control I.i.173
awry, distorted III.i.303
ay, yes I.i.128, I.vi.28, II.i.8

B

baas, makes a sound like a lamb II.i.10
babies, dolls III.ii.115
baited with, annoyed by IV.ii.43
baits, snares IV.i.33
bald, (a) hairless (b) trivial III.i.164
    bareheaded IV.v.186
bale, injury, hurt I.i.149
balms, healing ointments I.vi.64
bands, troops I.ii.26, I.vi.53
bare, worthless v.i.20
barred, obstructed III.i.148
bastard, spurious III.ii.56
bate, reduce II.ii.137
bats, cudgels I.i.44, 147
batten, grow fat IV.v.29
battery, physical assault, beating v.iv.19
battle, army I.iv.51
be, be considered I.i.253
be with, go along with, humour III.ii.74
beam of sight, glance III.ii.5
bear, be endowed with II.iii.169
    carry III.i.212
    support III.ii.35
    manage IV.vii.21
bear the business, manage the action I.i.256,
    I.vi.82, v.iii.4
bear with, put up with II.i.54
    endure I.i.86, III.i.249, III.iii.33

beastly, like cattle II.i.88
become, befit I.iii.9, II.i.114, III.i.59, 159
become of, happened to I.iv.48
bedfellow, close friend II.ii.62
bedward, showing the way to bed I.vi.32
before-time, on former occasions I.vi.24
being, since (you are) II.i.87
belonging, equipment, fine trappings I.ix.61
bemock, mock at I.i.243
bench, authority III.i.106, 165
bencher, member of the Senate II.i.75
bended, bowed II.i.254
bent, intended I.ii.16
bereaves, deprives III.i.158
bestrid, stood astride II.ii.89
bestride, cross IV.v.114
bewitchment, bewitching manners II.iii.93
bewray, reveal v.iii.95
billeted, either (a) enrolled, or (b) assigned to
    quarters IV.iii.39
bisson, blind II.i.58
blanks, blank lottery tickets v.ii.10
bleared, dim, poor II.i.194
bleeding, uncured II.i.71
bless, protect I.iii.43
blessed, happy II.ii.55
block, (a) blockhead (b) obstruction v.ii.74
blood, condition I.i.145
    bloodshed III.ii.61
    full cry IV.v.201
bloody, red II.i.69
bolt, thunderbolt v.iii.152
bolted, refined III.i.320
bonnet, hat III.ii.73
bonneted, took off their caps II.ii.24
book, record, chronicle v.ii.15
bore, hole IV.vi.88
borne, controlled I.i.256
    conducted IV.vii.15, v.iii.4
bosom, (a) stomach (b) heart III.i.131
    heart III.ii.57
botcher, mender of old clothes II.i.81
bottom, essence IV.v.189
bound, heading for III.i.54
    under an obligation v.iii.108, 109, 159
    closely tied to v.iii.159
bountiful, bountifully II.iii.93
bower, (a) garden, or (b) room III.ii.92
brace, couple, II.i.38, II.iii.57, III.i.243
bragged, boasted I.viii.12
bran, husks I.i.132
brand, mark of shame, stigma III.i.302
    flaming torch IV.vi.116
brats, children, hence, insignificant men
    IV.vi.94
brave, insolent IV.v.16
brawn, strong arm IV.v.116
break, come out of I.iv.16
    break an agreement, quarrel IV.vi.49
breaking out, bursting into flame IV.iii.23
breath, voice II.i.225
    expression of approval II.ii.148

breathe, rest I.vi.1
briars, prickly bushes III.iii.51
briefly, a short time ago I.vi.16
bring, escort IV.i.47
bristled, bearded II.ii.89
broil, fight III.i.33
    battle III.ii.81
brook, endure I.i.248
brow-bound, decorated with a garland around
    the head II.ii.95
bruising, damaging II.iii.191
brunt, violence II.ii.97
budge, run away I.vi.44
budger, one who gives way I.viii.5
bulks, projecting frameworks in front of
    shops II.i.199
business, war, action I.i.229, 256, I.iii.17,
    v.iii.4
bussing, kissing III.ii.75
but, except II.iii.158, 241, IV.vi.14
    only I.i.15, III.i.4, III.i.215, III.ii.86, 119,
    III.iii.129, IV.v.67, v.ii.61
    simply v.i.44
but is, is not I.vi.78
but it, which does not I.i.139
butcher, killer I.ix.87
buttock, end II.i.46
by the ears, fighting I.i.219

C

calamity, disaster, affliction I.i.63
called up, aroused II.iii.183
calved, born III.i.239
cambric, fine white linen I.iii.81
came off, escaped II.ii.109
cankered, diseased IV.v.87
cannibally, like a cannibal IV.v.181
canon, law I.x.26, III.i.90
canopy, sky IV.v.34, 35
caparison, horse's trappings I.ix.12
capital, deserving death III.iii.81
    deadly v.iii.104
Capitol, the Capitoline Hill in Rome I.i.38,
    178 etc.
capitulate, come to terms v.iii.82
carbonado, meat scored for grilling IV.v.180
carbuncle, ruby I.iv.55
carelessness, indifference II.ii.14
cares, solicitude III.i.137
carried, beaten v.vi.42
carries, brings II.i.147
carry, win II.i.227, II.ii.4, II.iii.34, IV.vii.27
casque, helmet, hence the military life
    IV.vii.43
cast, confer II.i.191
    threw up IV.vi.131
Cato, the famous Roman Censor (234–149
    B.C.) I.iv.57
cats, a term of contempt IV.ii.34

cause, occasion I.vi.83, II.iii.183
    legal case II.i.64
    disease III.i.234
    case III.iii.18
cautelous, crafty IV.i.33
cement, foundations IV.vi.86
censor, Roman official responsible for the
    census and for public morality II.iii.233
Censorinus, Martius Censorinus who was
    Censor about 265 B.C. He was not an
    ancestor of Coriolanus, though of the
    same family II.iii.232
censure, public opinion I.i.254
    punishment III.iii.46
    condemnation v.vi.140
censured, considered II.i.20, 22
centuries, companies I.vii.3
centurion, officer commanding a century, i.e.
    one hundred men IV.iii.38
ceremony, customary ritual II.ii.138
chafed, roused to anger III.iii.63
chair, judgement-seat IV.vii.52
chance, happen III.iii.22
chances, mishaps IV.i.5
changeling, fickle or inconstant person
    IV.vii.11
character, character-sketch II.i.59
charge (v.), press charges against III.iii.1, 42
    urge IV.vi.113
charge (n.), expenses v.vi.67, 78
charges (n.), attacks I.vi.6
    subordinate troops IV.iii.38
charms, magic spells I.v.21
charter, licence granting privileges I.ix.14
    privilege II.iii.172
chats, gossips about II.i.197
choired, in tune with III.ii.113
choler, anger II.iii.187, III.i.83, 84, III.iii.25
chronicle, history v.iii.145
cicatrices, scars II.i.138
circumvention, power to outwit I.ii.6
clapped to, closed up I.iv.51
cleave, split III.ii.28
clip, embrace I.vi.29, IV.v.105
cloven, cut to pieces I.iv.21
clusters, crowds IV.vi.123, 129
coal, cinder IV.vi.138
cockle, weed III.i.70
coffined, in a coffin II.i.165
cog, cheat III.ii.133
coign, cornerstone of a building v.iv.1
coin, mint, turn out III.i.78
cold, dispassionate III.i.219
colder, unimpassioned v.iii.86
colic, stomach-ache II.i.68
come off, acquit oneself I.vi.1
    withdraw successfully II.ii.109
come upon, attack IV.iii.16
comeliness, handsomeness I.iii.6
comely, agreeable IV.vi.27
comes over, falls I.iii.59
comfortable, cheerful I.iii.2

command, troops to be commanded I.vi.84
  air of authority IV.v.57
commend, recommend IV.v.140
commission, letter of authority I.ii.26
  troops under a person's command IV.v.134
  command IV.vii.14
common (n.), common people I.i.137, III.i.29
common (adj.), equal I.ix.39; general (giving
  to everyone) II.iii.87
common (n.), ordinary IV.i.32
commonalty, common people I.i.23
companion, rascal IV.v.11, V.ii.58
competency, supply I.i.125
complainings, complaints I.i.195
complaint, complainant, plaintiff in a law
  suit II.i.45
complexions, types II.i.201
composition, agreement III.i.3
compound, in combination with II.i.53
compound (v.), agree V.vi.83
conclude, make decisions III.i.145
condemned, damnable I.viii.15
condition, reasonable terms I.x.2, 6
  state I.x.5
  quality I.x.5, 6
  mode of behaviour II.iii.89
  character V.iv.7
conduits, channels, pipes II.iii.231
confederate, allied V.iii.208
confirm, make effective IV.ii.46
  installed in office II.iii.198
confirmed, determined I.iii.57
confound, spend I.vi.17
confusion, ruin III.i.110, 189
  destruction IV.vi.29
conies, rabbits IV.v.205
conjure, command V.ii.71
conned, learned IV.i.11
conspectuities, insights II.i.58
constant, loyal, unwavering I.i.226, IV.vi.106,
  V.ii.90
construction, explanation V.vi.20
consume, burn down IV.vi.116
contagion, pestilence, disease I.iv.30
contemn, despise II.ii.154
contemning, contemptuously I.iii.41
content, agreed II.iii.43
  willing (to do or accept something)
  III.iii.45, 47, 48
contradiction, (a) contrariness (b) opposition
  III.iii.27
contrariety, opposites IV.vi.74
contrived, plotted III.iii.63
control, overpower III.i.161
convenient, sufficient I.v.12
  fitting V.iii.190
convented, come together II.ii.51
converse, be conversant with II.i.46
conveyances, channels V.i.54
cormorant (adj.), insatiably greedy I.i.107
cornerstone, stone forming the corner of a
  wall V.iv.1

cornet, a trumpet-like wind instrument
  S.D. I.x, S.D. II.i.193, S.D. II.ii.151
corrected, rebuked V.iii.57
correcting, chastising III.ii.78
corse, corpse V.vi.143
corslet, piece of armour covering the trunk
  V.iv.19
counsellor (adj.), counselling I.i.102
countenance, friendly looks V.vi.39
counterfeit, imitate II.iii.92
counterfeitly, hypocritically II.iii.92
counterpoise, equal, balance II.ii.84, V.vi.77
countersealed, sealed by both sides V.iii.205
course, bout I.v.16
covetous, greedy I.i.34
coxcomb, the cap worn by the domestic fool,
  hence fool, rascal IV.vi.135
coyed, was unwilling V.i.6
crack, lively youngster I.iii.65
cracked, broken V.iii.9
craft, cunning I.x.16
crafted, (a) carried out work (b) plotted
  IV.vi.119
crafts, craftsmen IV.vi.119
cranks, winding channels I.i.123
crest, (a) plumed helmet (b) spirit IV.v.201
crooked, wry II.i.51
cross, oppose III.ii.23
crown, reward II.i.168
crush, oppress II.iii.192
cry (v.), complain III.i.42
  shout III.iii.19
cry (n.), pack III.iii.119, IV.vi.147
cry havoc, authorize general slaughter
  III.i.273
cuckolds, men whose wives have been
  unfaithful to them IV.v.218
cunning, wisdom IV.i.9
cupboarding, hoarding up, shutting up I.i.86
curbs, restraints I.i.58
curdied, congealed V.iii.66
cushions, senatorial seat III.i.101, IV.vii.43

D

dam, mother III.i.291
damask, rosy II.i.205
darken, eclipse II.i.248, IV.vii.5
darts, spears I.vi.61
dastard, cowardly IV.v.71
daws, jackdaws (proverbially foolish birds),
  hence fools IV.v.40
deadly, grievously II.i.55
dearth, famine I.i.55
debile, feeble I.ix.48
declines, descends II.i.150
deed-achieving, acquired by deeds II.i.162
degrees, steps II.ii.23
deliberate, thoughtful I.i.114
deliver, speak I.i.81
  set free I.ix.88, V.vi.13

give up III.iii.130
present V.iii.39
demonstrate V.vi.139
delivered, stated II.i.52
reported IV.vi.64
demand (n.), question III.ii.45
demand (v.), demand to know III.iii.43
demerits, merits I.i.258
denials, refusals V.iii.81
desert, merit II.iii.60
deserved, deserving III.i.290
deserves, earns I.i.163
deserving, merits I.ix.20
design (n.), purpose IV.vii.8
designments, enterprises V.vi.34
despite, (a) contempt (b) injury III.i.163
contempt III.iii.138
determine, be settled III.iii.43
come to an end V.iii.120
decide IV.i.35
determine of, decide about II.ii.34
Deucalion, son of Prometheus in ancient
Greek mythology II.i.84
devise, ponder, deliberate I.i.88
plan for II.ii.121
plan IV.iii.39
devotion, enthusiasm II.ii.17
devour, destroy I.i.244
dews, dampness II.iii.30
Dian, Roman goddess of chastity and the
moon V.iii.67
dieted, fed I.ix.51
prepared by a meal V.i.57
difference, odds, opposition V.iii.201
disagreement V.vi.17
differency, difference V.iv.9
digest, interpret III.i.131
directly, face to face IV.v.178
disbenched, removed from (your) seat II.ii.68
discharge, perform II.iii.131, III.ii.106
disciplined, thrashed II.i.117
disclaim, repudiate III.i.34
discover, reveal II.ii.19
discovery, disclosure I.ii.22
disdain, despise I.i.246
disease, spoil, make uncomfortable I.iii.100
disgest, digest I.i.136
disgrace, misfortune I.i.81
dishonoured, dishonourable III.i.60
dislodged, left camp V.iv.38
dispatch (v.), kill III.i.284
hurry V.vi.8
dispatch (n.), final arrangement I.i.263
dismissal V.iii.180
disposed, inclined III.ii.22
disposing (n.), use IV.vii.40
disposition, state of mind I.vi.74
character II.ii.13
inclination II.i.26, III.ii.21, III.ii.111
dispropertied, dispossessed II.i.237
dissemble with, disguise III.ii.62
dissentious, quarrelsome I.i.150, IV.vi.7

dissolved. melted away I.i.190
distinctly, separately III.i.205, IV.iii.39
distribute, administer III.iii.99
diversely, variously II.iii.18
divide in, share I.vi.87
divines, priests II.iii.54
dogged, followed V.iii.144
doing, action II.ii.136
doit, Dutch coin of low value I.v.6, V.iv.54
trifle IV.iv.17
donation, gift III.i.130
doom (v.), judge I.viii.6
dotant, feeble-minded person V.ii.43
dote on, worship II.i.176
doubled, twice as strong II.ii.113
doublets, close-fitting jackets I.v.6
doubt, fear III.i.152
dovecote, pigeon-house V.vi.114
downright, thoroughly II.iii.148
drachma, Greek coin I.v.5
draw out, select I.vi.84
drawn, gathered III.i.242
drift, aim III.iii.115
droop, be dejected IV.i.20
drum, drummer S.D. V.vi.114
dull, stupid I.ix.6
duty, respect V.iii.51, 55, 167

E

each, every III.i.50
ears, attention II.ii.49
earth, clay V.ii.29
easy, requiring little effort V.ii.41
eat up, consume, destroy I.i.72
edge, sword I.iv.29, V.vi.112
edicts, laws I.i.69
e'er, ever I.x.11
effected, carried out I.ix.18
elders, experienced leaders I.i.212, II.ii.39
election, choice II.iii.208, 218, 244
elements, the world, composed of the four
elements, earth, water, air and fire I.x.10
else, otherwise I.i.173, I.vi.20, III.ii.60
embarquements, prohibitions I.x.22
empiricutic, empirical, quackish II.i.107
empoisoned, poisoned V.vi.10
emulation, envious rivalry I.i.200
rivalry I.x.12
end (v.), harvest V.vi.36
endue, endow II.iii.128
endure, remain always I.vi.58
enforce, emphasize II.iii.208
insist upon III.iii.3, III.iii.3, 21
engine, instrument of war V.iv.17
enigma, riddle II.iii.82
enormity, fault II.i.14
enrolled, written down III.i.290
entered in, familiar with I.i.2
entertainment, state of mobilization IV.iii.39
welcome, reception IV.v.8, V.ii.61

entire, perfect I.iv.55
envied, showed malice III.iii.95
envy, malice III.iii.3
    ill-will IV.v.70
    enmity IV.v.99
epitome, miniature version V.iii.68
ere, before I.i.205, 229, I.v.8 etc.
estimate, reputation III.iii.113
estate, property, lease of life II.i.105
estimation, valuation II.i.83, II.iii.88
    esteem, good books II.ii.25
    respect V.ii.50, 59
eunuch, castrated man III.ii.114
even, exactly I.i.94
    in a balanced manner IV.vii.37
even so, just as I.i.98
event, future II.i.259
ever, always I.i.152, III.iii.26, IV.vi.153 etc.
evident, inevitable IV.vii.52, V.iii.112
evil, illness I.i.165
execution, carrying out III.iii.21
exposture, exposure, IV.i.36
extol, praise I.ix.14, IV.vii.53
extremist, most violent III.iii.82
extremities, extreme situations, crises III.ii.41,
    IV.i.4
extremity, extreme adversity IV.v.75
eye, look for guidance V.iii.75

F

fabric, body I.i.105
    building III.i.246
factionary, active supporter V.ii.29
factions, parties I.i.179
fail in, fail to grant V.iii.90
fair (adj.), clean I.ix.68
    even III.i.241
    fine IV.vi.89
    polite III.ii.96, III.iii.91, V.i.74
fair (adv.), politely III.i.262, III.ii.70
fairly, well IV.vii.21
fairness, best I.ix.72
faith, indeed (short for *in faith*) II.ii.7
fall in, degenerate into III.i.33
fall out, happen II.i.232
false-faced, deceptive I.ix.44
falsely, treacherously III.i.60
familiar, friendly V.ii.81
famously, to win fame I.i.28
fane, temple I.x.20
fast, determined II.iii.173
fatigate, weary II.ii.114
faucet-seller, seller of taps II.i.65
favour, face IV.iii.8
fawn, flattery III.ii.67
fawning, cringing I.vi.38
fear, doubt I.vii.5
feebling, depreciating I.i.181
fell, fierce I.iii.43
fellest, fiercest IV.iv.18

fellows, fellow-servants IV.v.2, 176
fellowship, company V.iii.175
fen, marsh III.iii.20
    marshy lair IV.i.30
fetch off, rescue I.iv.62
feverous, feverish I.iv.61
fidiused, treated like Aufidius II.i.121
fie, shame on you I.iii.73, III.i.195
    shame IV.ii.54
field, battle I.vii.4, I.ix.33, II.ii.118
    battle-field I.vii.17, I.ix.43
fielded, on the battlefield I.iv.12
file, the common soldier, rank and file I.vi.43
files, ranks V.vi.33
fillip, strike V.iii.59
find (v.), understand III.iii.128
find, experience V.iii.111
fires (of heaven), heavenly bodies I.iv.39
first, already II.iii.103
    firstborn IV.i.33
fist, seize with the hand IV.v.121
fit (adj.), ready I.iii.42
    proper II.ii.83, 93
fit (v.), adapt II.ii.139
fit (n.), madness III.ii.33
fitly, aptly I.i.98
fixed, unchanging II.iii.239
flamens, Roman priests II.i.202
flaw, gale V.iii.74
flayed, bloody, like a skinned carcase I.vi.22
flaying, stripping off the skin III.iii.89
fliers, those running away II.ii.100
flour, finest extract I.i.131
flourish, trumpet blast S.D. I.ix.etc.
flouted, expressed contempt II.iii.148
flower, quintessence, perfection I.vi.32
fluttered, threw into a panic V.vi.115
fly out of, change its nature I.x.19
fob off, set aside I.i.80
foiled, beaten I.ix.48
fold in, enfold III.iii.68
    embrace V.vi.124
fond, foolish IV.i.26
fond of, wishing for V.iii.162
fool, play the part of the fool II.iii.110
foolery, folly III.i.245
for, as for I.i.54, 60, III.i.66, IV.vi.112,
    V.ii.102
    because I.i.99, 143, I.ix.47, III.i.10, III.iii.93,
    V.ii.85
    because of III.i.161, III.iii.133, V.iii.44
force, urge III.ii.51
'fore, in the face of IV.iv.3
    before IV.vi.61, IV.vii.3, V.vi.119
fore me, upon my word I.i.106
fore-advised, advised beforehand II.iii.180
forehead, early part II.i.47
foremost, at the front I.i.144
forges, shapes III.i.257
form, ceremony II.ii.141
    procedure III.i.323
former, aforementioned I.i.109

forsook, forsaken, failed to support IV.v.72
forsooth, certainly III.ii.85
forsworn, having broken one's word V.iii.28
forth, out of I.iv.23
fortune, good fortune IV.vii.38
foxship, cunning IV.ii.18
fragments, incomplete men I.i.208
frame, make III.ii.84
 adapt III.ii.97
 form V.iii.63
 arrange V.iii.190
franchise, rights IV.vi.87
frank, free III.i.130
free (adj.), unconcealed II.iii.189
 generous III.ii.88
 frank III.iii.73
 outspoken V.vi.25
free (v.), exonerate IV.vii.47
freedoms, rights II.i.237
freelier, more readily I.iii.3
friendly, in a friendly manner IV.vi.9
fright, frighten IV.v.139
from, against III.i.90
front, oppose V.ii.40
fronts, (a) front ranks (b) faces I.vi.8
full, completely IV.v.79
function, job IV.v.29
fusty, stale-smelling I.ix.7

G

'gainst, in the face of, at I.ix.30
Galen, famous Greek physician (A.D. 129–199), II.i.107
galled, irritated II.iii.184
gan pierce, pierced II.ii.112
gangrened, diseased III.i.305
garb, fashion IV.vii.44
garland, object of admiration I.i.170
 oak wreath worn on victor's head I.ix.59, II.ii.98
garners, granaries I.i.236
gauded, painted, made up II.i.206
generosity, the nobility I.i.197
gentle, gentlemanly II.iii.89
 acting like a gentleman IV.i.8
gentry, high birth III.i.144
getter, begetter IV.v.214
giber, jester II.i.75
gibingly, mockingly II.iii.214
giddy, unreliable I.i.254
gilded, yellow I.iii.59
gird, jibe at I.i.242
give, report I.ix.54
 cause to suspect IV.v.146
give forth, distribute III.i.113
give me way, grant my request IV.iv.25
give out, proclaim as certain I.i.179
give the lie, show to be untrue II.ii.30
given, allowed III.i.93
 inclined IV.v.181

glasses (of sight), eyeballs III.ii.117
glean, deduce II.i.59
go upon, set out on I.i.264
goaded, incited II.iii.252
God-den, good evening (a contraction of 'God give you good even') II.i.86, IV.vi.20, 21
godded, worshipped V.iii.11
gone forth, become IV.vi.35
good, wealthy I.i.11
goodly, imposing IV.v.4
 fine IV.vi.146
gosling, foolish inexperienced person V.iii.35
got, begotten I.iii.31
got off, escaped II.i.119
got on, won from III.iii.4
gown, toga II.ii.134, S.D. II.iii.36
grace (v.), favour I.i.250, V.iii.15
 honour V.vi.88
grace (n.), prayer IV.vii.3
 favour V.iii.121, 150
graceful, divine II.i.210
gracious, lovely II.i.164
grafted, improved II.i.178
grained, straight-grained or close-grained, hence tough IV.v.104
gratify, reward II.ii.37
gratis, free III.i.43, 114, 125
grave (n.), end II.i.81, 145
grave (adj.), reverend III.i.92
graver, more dignified III.i.106
grief-shot, stricken with grief V.i.44
groat, English coin of little value III.ii.10
ground, reason II.ii.10
guard, protection I.x.25
guardant, on guard V.ii.60
guess, think I.i.15
guider, guide I.vii.7
gulf, abyss, bottomless pit I.i.84, III.ii.91

H

ha', have I.i.211
ha't, have it II.iii.73
hale, drag IV.iv.34
handkerchers, handkerchiefs II.i.253
hap, happen III.iii.24
haply, perhaps V.ii.16
happy, lucky IV.vii.39
hardly, with difficulty V.ii.69
harp, keep stressing II.iii.241
hatching, planning I.ii.21
hautboy, oboe S.D. V.iv.45
have with you, let us go II.i.259
haver, possessor II.ii.82
havoc, a cry used in battle ordering a general slaughter III.i.273
hazard, risk of failure II.iii.245
 danger IV.i.28
 risk IV.vii.25
head, army II.ii.85, III.i.1
heard, listened to V.iii.192

heart, true feeling I.ix.8
    (a) intelligence (b) courage II.iii.193
    courage V.vi.98
heat, angry state III.i.63
heavy, sad II.i.173
    oppressive IV.ii.48
Hector, great Trojan warrior and prince
    I.iii.39, I.ix.11
Hecuba, wife of Priam, King of Troy, and
    mother of Hector I.iii.38
heightened, exalted V.vi.21
held in chase, pursued I.vi.19
helms, pilots I.i.65
    helmets IV.v.121
helps, ways of improving the situation
    III.i.220
herald, official whose duties included the
    arranging of funerals V.vi.143
Hercules, a hero of Greek mythology IV.i.17,
    IV.vi.100
hereto, previously II.ii.57
hew down, fell I.i.167
hie, hurry I.ii.26
hint, opportunity III.iii.23
hire, reward II.ii.146, II.iii.103
hitherward, in this direction I.ii.33
hoarded, stored up IV.ii.11
Hob, rustic form of Robert II.iii.105
hold, stick to II.i.229
    view II.i.235
    bear, endure III.ii.80
    stop V.vi.130
holding (n.), defence I.vii.4
holding (v.), considering II.i.237
hollow, call out like a huntsman I.viii.7
holp, helped III.i.275, IV.vi.82, V.iii.63 etc.
home, to the centre I.iv.38
    fully II.ii.100
    hard III.iii.1, IV.i.8
    thoroughly IV.ii.48
honest, honourable I.i.43, 50, V.iii.166
hoo, hooray II.i.98, III.iii.136
hooped out, driven out with derisive shouts
    IV.v.74
hoot, shout contemptuously IV.vi.124, 132
horse-drench, medicine for a horse II.i.109
horsed, with people sitting astride II.i.200
hospitable, pertaining to hospitality I.x.26
host, army I.ix.63, V.iii.2
Hostilius, legendary King of Rome II.iii.229
house, family II.iii.230
housekeeper, (a) stay-at-home (b) one who
    looks after a house I.iii.49
how, with what force I.x.28
    what II.iii.63, III.i.47,75, III.iii.67,
        IV.vi.122, V.ii.77 etc.
how now, hallo II.i.90
howbeit, however I.ix.69
howsoever, although V.ii.30
hum, make a dissenting sound V.i.49, V.iv.19
humanely, out of human feelings I.i.15
humble, make humble III.ii.79

humorous, whimsical II.i.42
hungry, empty, barren V.iii.58
hurry, commotion IV.vi.4
husbandry, management IV.vii.22
hushed, silent V.iii.181
huswife, housewife I.iii.67
Hydra, a poisonous, many-headed water
    snake III.i.93
hyperbolical, exaggerated I.ix.50

I

ignorant, stupid II.iii.163
ill (adv.), badly III.i.51
ill (n.), evil III.i.161
ill-schooled, untrained III.i.319
impatience, anger V.vi.144
impediment, obstruction, hindrance I.i.60
in, by I.i.251, III.i.209
    into II.i.230, III.i.33, 96
    of II.ii.13, II.iii.244
incapable, unable IV.vi.121
incensed, made angry I.ix.55
inclination, disposition II.iii.181
incorporate, united in one body I.i.116
indifferently, neutrally II.ii.16
induced, led on I.ix.17
infant-like, feeble II.i.33
infirmity, imperfection III.i.82
inform, tell I.vi.42
    instruct III.iii.18
    inspire V.iii.71
information, source of information IV.vi.54
ingrate, ungrateful V.ii.83
ingrateful, ungrateful II.ii.29, II.iii.9
inherent, permanent III.ii.123
inheritance, possession III.ii.68
injurious, insulting III.iii.69
injury, insult II.ii.29
    wrongs suffered V.i.64
inkling, suspicion, idea I.i.44
innovator, revolutionary III.i.174
inshelled, drawn into the shell IV.vi.47
insinuating, ingratiating II.iii.91
insolence, arrogance, pride I.i.248, II.i.243
instruction, signal to attack I.iv.22
    knowledge III.ii.53
instruments, bodily organs I.i.87
insurrection, rebellion I.i.207
    disorder IV.iii.12
integrity, unity III.i.159
intelligence, news IV.iii.26
intent, intention II.ii.153
intercession, entreaty V.ii.42
interims, intervals I.vi.5
interjoin, unite IV.iv.22
interrupted, obstructed III.i.248
inventory, catalogue, list I.i.17
inveterate, long-established II.iii.215
iron, sword I.v.6, IV.v.209

issue, offspring I.iii.19
  (a) action or (b) children IV.iv.22
  come out I.iv.23, I.vi.10
Ithaca, Aegean island of which Ulysses was
  king I.iii.81

J

Jack guardant, officious sentry V.ii.60
jot, minute detail II.ii.138
Jove, a sky deity, the chief god of the Romans,
  also called Jupiter II.i.255, III.i.107
joy, rejoice V.iv.59
judgement, administration of justice III.i.158
judicious, judicial V.vi.126
jump, risk III.i.154
Juno, wife of Jove, and chief Roman goddess
  II.i.94, IV.ii.53
Jupiter, I.iii.36, I.ix.89, II.i.98, IV.v.99, see
  under *Jove*

K

kam, crooked III.i.302
keep, protect IV.vi.25
kicked at, spurned, rejected II.ii.121
kind, friendly IV.vi.11
kindle, set fire to II.i.247
  inflame III.i.196
kites, birds of prey of the falcon family
  IV.v.38, 39
knee, move forward on one's knees V.i.5
knell, sound announcing death V.iv.20
know, learn I.v.28

L

la, an exclamation adding emphasis I.iii.64,
  85
lacked, missed IV.i.15
lapsing, collapsing V.ii.19
'larum, alarum, a call to arms I.iv.9
last, latest II.ii.98
  recent V.vi.125
last (n.), end V.vi.41
late, just now III.i.195
latest, last V.iii.11
lay, lodged I.ix.81
leads (n.), roofs II.i.200, IV.vi.83
learned, wise III.i.99
leasing, falsehood V.ii.22
leave, permission III.i.280
lectures, lessons II.iii.224
lenity, mildness III.i.99
lessoned, instructed II.iii.166
let alone, trust I.ii.27
let go, enough of that III.ii.18
let slip, release I.vi.39
lethargy, sluggishness IV.v.213

levies, conscripted armies V.iv.66
lictors, Roman officials serving the magistrates S.D. II.ii.33
lief, soon, willingly IV.v.168
lies, lives IV.iv.8
lies in, is confined in childbed I.iii.74
lies on, is incumbent on III.ii.52
light, descend I.iv.30
  joyful II.i.173
lightly, thoughtlessly IV.i.29
like (adj.), similar I.i.87, III.ii.51
  same I.iv.45, II.i.257
like (adv.), likely I.i.178, I.iii.12, II.i.230,
  III.i.48, 133, 202, IV.v.195
liking, favour I.i.181
limitation, time limit prescribed II.iii.127
linger, stay alive III.iii.29
lip, sneer II.i.106
list, hear I.iv.20
  please III.ii.128
  listen III.iii.40
littered, born III.i.238
lockram, linen II.i.198
'long, because of V.iv.27
longs, belongs V.iii.170
look to it, see to it I.iv.40
looked for, expected V.vi.42
looked to, attended to I.ix.93
looks (v.), promises III.iii.29
lots, lottery tickets winning prizes V.ii.10
lover, dear friend V.ii.14
lurched, stole II.ii.98
lurked, been hiding V.iv.43
Lycurgus, famous Spartan lawgiver II.i.50

M

made, did I.viii.9
  committed V.vi.63
made on, made much of IV.v.184
mailed, covered in mail armour I.iii.33
maims, wounds IV.v.82
make, raise V.i.37
make a head, raise an army II.ii.85, III.i.1
make a lip, sneer II.i.106
make good, secure, capture I.v.12
make much of, value highly II.iii.99
make road, invade III.i.5
make up, prepare I.i.130
make worthy, consider praiseworthy I.i.161
making, saying, making out to be I.i.180
malice, ill-will II.ii.20
  act of ill-will II.ii.29
  enmity IV.v.92
malign, slander I.i.99
malignantly, maliciously II.iii.172
malkin, wench II.i.197
mammocked, tore to pieces I.iii.62
manacles, hand fetters I.ix.56
man-entered, begun like a man II.ii.96
mangles, impairs III.i.158

manifest, obvious I.iii.49

mankind, mad IV.ii.16

mantled, covered as with a cloak I.vi.29

mark (n.), reach, power II.ii.86

mark, wound III.iii.110

Mars, Roman god of war I.iv.10, IV.v.114, 186

marvellous, extremely IV.v.25

mastership, mastery, skill IV.i.7

match, bargain II.iii.74

mean, poor S.D. IV.iv.1

meaner, inferior I.vi.27

measles, scabby eruptions on the skin III.i.78

measure, right amount II.ii.120

extent V.iii.10

mechanics, manual labourers, workmen V.iii.83

meddle, interfere with IV.v.42, V.i.38

have intercourse with IV.v.43

meed, reward II.ii.94

meet, right III.i.167

(i) right (ii) done III.i.169

meiny, mob III.i.66

mellow, soft, juicy IV.vi.101

members, parts I.i.82

memory, memorial IV.v.67, V.i.17, V.vi.152

mend, improve I.iv.38

mercenary, hired soldier V.vi.40

mere, pure IV.v.78

merely, completely III.i.303

merit, virtue IV.vii.48

methinks, I think I.iii.27

methought, it seemed to me IV.v.151

microcosm, literally 'little world', hence body II.i.57

midst, middle III.ii.28

mind, intentions I.v.28

minded, reminded V.i.18

minister unto, supply I.i.89

minnow, tiny fish, hence a type of insignificance III.i.89

miscarry, go wrong I.i.252

mischief, harm IV v.63

misery, miserliness II.ii.124

misguide, misdirect I.v.22

miss, do without II.i.226

modest, chaste I.i.243

moderate I.ix.25

limited III.i.274

moe, more III.iii.114, IV.ii.21

monstered, described as marvels II.ii.74

more than, apart from I.i.264

morrow, morning III.iii.93

mortal, deadly II.ii.108

fatal III.i.295

fatally V.iii.189

motion, reason II.i.46

action II.ii.106

motion toward, influence with II.ii.50

mould, (a) form (b) clay III.ii.103

(a) form (b) womb V.iii.22

mountebank, quack III.ii.132

move, provoke III.iii.52

persuade V.ii.69

moved, angered I.i.242

movers, active men I.v.4

mulberry, a fruit tree III.ii.79

mulled, dulled IV.v.213

multitudinous, of the multitude III.i.156

mummers, actors of mime or dumb-show II.i.69

muniments, defences I.i.104

murrain, plague I.v.3

muse, wonder III.i.7

musty, stale I.i.212, V.i.26

mutable, changeable III.i.66

mutiners, rioters I.i.236

mutiny, disturbance II.iii.245, III.i.126

N

naked, unarmed I.x.20

exposed II.ii.134

name, reputation IV.vi.126

name of, credit for II.i.125

napes, backs of necks II.i.35

napless, threadbare II.i.233

native, origin, cause III.i.129

nature, natural ties, affection V.iii.25, 33

naught, ruined III.i.230

navel, vital centre III.i.123

nay, indeed, II.i.100

ne'er, never II.iii.240

Neptune, Roman god of the sea III.i.255

nerves, sinews, muscles I.i.124

nervy, muscular II.i.149

nicely, skilfully II.i.206

noise, music II.i.147

noisome, smelly V.i.26

nor . . . nor, neither . . . nor I.i.155, I.iv.7, I.x.19 etc.

nose, smell V.i.28

not, not only III.ii.71, III.iii.97

notched, cut notches in IV.v.179

note, notice I.ix.48

nothing, in no way I.iii.95

nothings, insignificant actions II.ii.74

notice, observation III.iii.149

notion, awareness V.vi.106

now, just recently I.i.169, I.ix.78

at one minute III.i.34

Numa, second King of Rome II.iii.228

O

o', of I.iii.104

oak, oak garland I.iii.14, II.ii.95

oaken garland, wreath worn on victor's head II.i.116, S.D. 150

object, sight, spectacle I.i.17

obstinate, hard-hearted V.iii.26

occasion, opportunity II.i.25

occupation, tradesmen IV.vi.98

occupations trades, manual labour IV.i.14

o'erbear, overwhelm III.i.248
o'erbeat, overcome IV.v.127
o'erborne, overcome IV.vi.79
o'erleap, avoid II.ii.133
o'erpeer, see over the top II.iii.110
o'erpressed, overwhelmed II.ii.90
of, about I.i.255, I.ii.17, 68, II.i.66, II.ii.34,
    IV.iv.17
  by I.ii.13, II.i.20, II.ii.3, II.iii.16
  from I.iv.5, II.iii.226, IV.i.39, 40, V.vi.14
  upon II.iii.20
  against I.x.22
  for II.iii.68
off, off the point, irrelevant II.ii.57
  hatless II.iii.91
offence, offensive matter V.i.28
offered, attempted V.i.23
office, drive by virtue of one's office V.ii.60
offices, workplaces I.i.123
  duties III.i.35
officious, interfering I.viii.14
old, long-continued II.iii.209, V.iii.12
Olympus, Mt. Olympus, home of the gods in
    Greek mythology V.iii.30
omit, neglect III.i.146
on, about I.i.10
  go on, I.i.57
  of I.i.211, I.iii.63, II.i.182, IV.vi.71
  to II.ii.92
  in III.i.330
on's, of his II.ii.78
on't, of it III.i.152
once, when II.iii.14
ope, open I.iv.43, III.i.138, V.iii.183
opinion, (a) public opinion (b) reputation
    I.i.257
opposite, opponent II.ii.19
or . . . or, either . . . or I.x.16, III.i.207,
    IV.i.32 etc.
orange-wife, a woman orange-seller II.i.65
orb, globe V.vi.125
ordinance, rank III.ii.12
osprey, a fishing bird IV.vii.34
ostentation, show I.iv.86
ostler, stableman III.iii.32
other, otherwise IV.vi.103
out, away V.iii.24
  speechless V.iii.41
  completely IV.v.117
  out of V.ii.37
out of, as a result of IV.vii.38
  beyond V.ii.48
  astray from III.i.55
over-measure, excess III.i.140
overtaken, surpassed I.ix.19
overture, offer I.ix.46
owe, own, possess III.ii.130, V.ii.79, V.vi.137

P

painful, arduous IV.v.64

palates, tastes like III.i.104
palm, palm branch, symbol of victory
    V.iii.117
palsied, trembling V.ii.42
palt'ring, trickery III.i.58
parcel, part, detachment I.ii.32
  part IV.v.206
parley, discussion S.D. I.iv.12
part, share I.ix.39
  behalf III.i.209
  side I.x.7, V.iii.121
  role IV.iii.44
participate, take part I.i.89
particular, personal IV.v.82, V.ii.66
  personal case IV.vii.13
  affection V.i.3
particularize, list in detail I.i.18
particulars, individuals II.iii.39
parties, factions III.i.313
pass (v.), by-pass II.ii.136
passable, (a) allowing free passage (b) accept-
    able V.ii.13
passage, passage of arms, fighting V.vi.75
passed, passed over II.iii.188
  been accepted by III.i.29
passing, extremely I.i.189
pates, heads IV.vi.83
patience, permission I.iii.71, I.ix.54
patient, calm III.i.85
  long-suffering V.vi.51
patricians, Roman aristocracy I.i.12, II.i.42
pawned, staked V.vi.20
peace, be quiet III.i.187, 191, 192, 216,
    III.iii.41, 75, IV.ii.12, V.vi.123
Penelope, wife of Ulysses, King of Ithaca
    I.iii.79
pent, imprisoned III.iii.89
peradventure, probably II.i.85
peremptory, dictatorial III.i.94
  determined III.i.284
perfecter, better II.i.74
perfidiously, treacherously V.vi.90
peril, penalty III.iii.102
person, handsome body I.iii.9
pertinent, to the point II.ii.60
pest'ring, infesting IV.vi.7
pestilence, plague IV.i.13
petitionary, suppliant V.ii.72
petitioned, prayed to II.i.159
Phoebus, the sun-god in Greek mythology
    II.i.206
physic, medicine III.i.154, III.ii.33
physical, medicinal I.v.18
pick, throw I.i.186
  pick out individually V.i.25
piece, add to II.iii.201
piece (n.), coin III.iii.32
piercing, distressing I.i.71
  wounding I.v.11
pikes, spears with wooden shaft and steel
    head I.i.19
pinched, gripped II.i.68

pinned, secured I.iv.18
pipe, voice III.ii.113
plainly, honestly V.iii.3
plaster, cover like plaster I.iv.31
please you, may it please you II.ii.38
pleasures, wishes II.i.27
plebeians, common people of Rome I.ix.7,
   II.i.8
plebeii, the Latin for *plebeians* II.iii.173
plot, piece of earth, hence body III.ii.102
pluck, evoke II.ii.30
Pluto, god of Hades, the Roman underworld
   I.iv.36
points, detailed instructions IV.vi.126
poisonous, destructive V.iii.135
policy, political expediency III.ii.42
   plan III.ii.48
poll, number of heads III.i.134
   individual voter III.iii.10
polled, cut, cleared IV.v.194
popular, consisting of people II.i.203
   vulgar, plebeian III.i.106, V.ii.38
porch, portico III.i.239
portance, behaviour II.iii.213
ports, gates I.vii.1, V.vi.6
possessed, informed II.i.123
post, messenger V.vi.49
posterity, family IV.ii.26
posture, bearing II.i.210
potch, poke, stab at I.x.15
potency, power II.iii.171
pother, commotion II.i.207
pound, enclose in a pen or pound I.iv.17
pounds, pound-weights III.i.312
pout upon, look sulkily at V.i.52
pow waw, pooh-pooh II.i.132
power, army I.ii.9, 32, I.iii.94 etc.
   strength I.viii.11
practice, treachery IV.i.33
prank, dress up III.i.23
prate, say III.iii.83
   talk foolishly IV.v.44, V.iii.159
   boast, chatter V.iii.48
prating, chattering I.i.38
prattling, talkative II.i.195
pray you, I beg you II.ii.139
precipitation, drop III.ii.4
   being thrown down III.iii.102
preparation, army prepared for war I.ii.15
prerogative, right III.iii.17
present, immediate III.i.211, III.iii.21, IV.iii.42
present (v.), prescribe III.ii.1
presently, immediately II.iii.242, III.iii.12
   etc.
preservative, medicine II.i.108
press, conscript I.ii.9
pressed, impressed, conscripted III.i.122
presume, pretend I.i.177
pretences, intentions I.ii.20
pretext, reason V.vi.19
pretty, pleasing I.i.77
prevailing, overcoming I.iii.95

prithee, literally 'I pray you', hence I beg you
   I.iv.10, III.ii.72, 89, 98
privilege, claim, right I.x.23, V.iii.25
prize (v.), value I.v.4, II.ii.57
probable, credible IV.vi.66
process, process of law III.i.312
progeny, forefathers, ancestry I.viii.12
pronounced, told V.vi.57
proof, tested and found impregnable I.iv.25
proper, own I.ix.56
properly, personally V.ii.80
prosperity, success I.v.23, II.i.160
prosperous, successful II.i.96
prosperously, successfully V.vi.74
proud, high-spirited I.i.156
provand, provender, food II.i.240
prove, put to the proof I.vi.62
   try IV.v.89, V.i.60
psalteries, stringed instruments V.iv.46
puff, get out of breath II.i.203
puling, whining IV.ii.52
pupil-age, boyhood, apprenticeship II.ii.95
purchasing, earning II.i.130
purge, clear V.vi.8
purpose, proposal II.ii.149
   intend V.iii.121
purposed, premeditated III.i.38
put forth, make a fine show I.i.237
put to, force upon II.ii.105
   make III.iii.25
put to it, put to the test I.i.215
   force to do II.ii.138
put to that, put to that extreme test III.i.232
put up, sheathe V.vi.134
put upon, provoked II.i.245
putting on, instigation II.iii.241

Q

quaked, trembled I.ix.6
quarry, heap of dead animals after hunting,
   hence heap of dead men I.i.184
quartered, cut up into parts I.i.185
question (n.), doubt II.i.219
quit of, revenged on IV.v.79
quoth, said I.i.116

R

raise, originate IV.vi.61, 70
ranges, stands III.i.205
rank-scented, foul-smelling III.i.66
rapt, enraptured IV.v.112
rapture, fit, paroxysm II.i.196
rarest, finest IV.v.155
rascal, inferior deer or hound, hence one of
   the rabble I.i.145, I.vi.45
rash, eager IV.vii.32
rates (n.), prices I.i.175
read lectures, instructed II.iii.224

ready, acute II.ii.113
reason, urge V.iii.176
reason with, question IV.vi.48
rebuke, censure II.ii.30
receipt, something received I.i.98
receive, take IV.iii.18
recomforted, reheartened V.iv.45
recommend, commit II.ii.148
recompense, reward III.i.121
recreant, deserter V.iii.114
rectorship, dictates, rule II.iii.194
redress, put right III.i.219
reechy, dirty II.i.198
reek, smelly fog III.iii.120
reeking, smoking II.ii.116
reel, go round II.i.103
refuge, resource V.iii.11
regard, pay attention III.i.67
reined, brought under control III.iii.28
rejourn, adjourn II.i.65
relish, taste, II.i.178
remember, distinguish II.ii.44
   maintain II.ii.55
remembrances, memories II.iii.237
remission, power to forgive V.ii.80
remove, raising of a siege, I.ii.28
render, give I.ix.34, II.ii.18
renew me, regain my lost authority V.vi.48
renown, desire for fame I.iii.11
repair, go, make one's way II.iii.243, V.vi.3
repeal (n.), recall IV.i.41, IV.vii.32
repeal (v.), recall V.v.5
repetition, mention, recital I.i.36, V.iii.144
repined, disapproved III.i.43
   fame I.iii.18
report, reputation I.vi.70
   commendation II.ii.26
   value II.i.108
reproof, disagreement II.ii.30
re-quickened, revived II.ii.114
require, request II.ii.153, II.iii.1
requital, reward II.ii.47
requite, repay IV.ii.12, IV.v.66
rescue, unlawful release of a prisoner III.i.275
rest, stay IV.i.39
restitution, redemption III.i.16
restrain, withhold V.iii.167
retire, withdraw I.iii.25
   retreat I.vi.3, 50, III.i.11
retreat, trumpet call to recall troops in battle
   S.D. I.ix.
revel, rejoice IV.v.203
reverend, worthy of respect II.i.55, II.ii.39
revoke, cancel II.iii.207, 239
revolt, change sides I.i.220
rheum, tears V.vi.45
ridges, roof-tops II.i.200
right, very I.i.233
   altogether II.ii.126
rive, split V.iii.153
road, invasion III.i.5
roared, cried out in fear II.iii.49, IV.vi.125

roted, learned by heart III.ii.55
rotten, worn out through age I.x.23
   unhealthy II.iii.30, III.iii.120
royal, splendid IV.iii.38
rub, obstacle III.i.60
rudely, violently IV.v.138
rumourer, rumour-monger IV.vi.48
rushes, reeds I.i.167, I.iv.19
ruth, pity I.i.183

S

sack, destroy III.i.314
sackbut, bass trumpet V.iv.46
safeguard, safe-conduct III.i.9
safer, sounder II.iii.207
salve, heal III.ii.70
sanctuary, the protection of a sacred place
   I.x.19
sauced, made appetizing I.ix.52
scabs, (a) sores (b) loathsome fellows I.i.152
scaling, weighing II.iii.238
scandalled, slandered III.i.44
scape, escape I.viii.13
scarf, sling S.D. I.ix.1
   neck ornament II.i.253
sconce, head III.ii.99
scorn, refuse contemptuously III.i.267
scotched, slashed IV.v.179
scourge, whip II.iii.83
'sdeath, 'by God's death', an oath I.i.203
seal, confirm (as with a seal) II.iii.98, III.i.142
sea-mark, marker or beacon to guide ships
   V.iii.74
seasoned, (a) long-established (b) moderate
   III.iii.64
second, back up IV.vi.63, V.vi.56
seconds, helpers I.iv.43
   help I.viii.15
seeking, petition I.i.174
seld-shown, rarely seen II.i.202
Senate, the Roman state-council or governing
   body I.i.46
sennet, music accompanying a procession of
   dignitaries S.D II.i.150
senseless, unfeeling I.iv.53
sensible, capable of feeling I.iii.82
sensibly, able to feel I.iv.53
sentence (v.), decree III.iii.22
servanted, subordinated, put at the service
   of V.ii.79
set down, besiege I.ii.28, I.iii.94
   deploy for a siege V.iii.2
   determine IV.v.134
set on, incite III.i.37, 58
set up, spin IV.v.149
several, different I.i.171
   separate IV.v.118, IV.vi.39
shame, be ashamed II.ii.64
   cause of disgrace V.vi.118
shent, rebuked V.ii.94

stored, filled II.i.16
stout, proud III.ii.78
stoutness, obstinacy III.ii.127
   haughtiness v.vi.26
straight, at once II.i.113, II.iii.136, III.i.35 etc.
strains, impulses v.iii.149
stretch, extend, make greater II.ii.48
stretched, held out III.i.74
   fully exerted v.vi.44
stride, bestride I.ix.70
strike, fight I.ii.35, I.vi.4
strong, offensive I.i.49
struck, sounded II.ii.73
strucken, struck IV.v.145
stubble, stumps of grain left after harvesting
   II.i.247
stuck, hesitated II.iii.15
subdue, debase, degrade I.i.161
subjects, (a) citizens (b) subjects for discussion
   II.i.78
subscribed, signed v.vi.81
subsisting, remaining v.vi.72
subtle, crafty I.x.17
   deceptive v.ii.20
success, result, good or bad I.i.246, I.vi.7,
   v.i.62
sudden, hasty II.iii.240
sued-for, sought-after II.iii.197
suffer, allow III.i.40, 301, IV.v.73, v.ii.19
sufferance, suffering, hardship I.i.18
   endurance III.i.24
suffrage, vote II.ii.135
suggest, insinuate to II.i.234
suit, request II.i.227, II.iii.211, v.iii.84 etc.
suitor, (a) one who has a suit or request
   v.iii.78 (b) wooer I.i.48 (both meanings)
sulphur, lightning v.iii.152
summon, call to a parley I.iv.7
superfluity, surplus, excess I.i.14
   superfluous elements I.i.212
supple, compliant II.ii.24
suppler, more flexible v.i.55
suppliants, petitioners III.i.44
supplication, entreaty v.iii.31
surcease (v.), stop III.ii.121
sure, certainly, assuredly II.iii.27, v.i.35
surer, more reliable I.i.158
surety, go bail for III.i.177
surfeit (v.), indulge excessively I.i.13, I.iii.23
surfeit (n.), excessive hardship IV.i.46
sway, authority II.iii.171
sway with, rule over II.i.193
sworn brother, intimate friend II.iii.87
swound, swoon v.ii.64
synod, assembly v.ii.66

T

tabor, small side-drum I.vi.25, v.iv.47
tackle, ship's sails, rigging etc., hence
   clothing IV.v.57

ta'en, taken I.ix.32, 34
tag, rabble III.i.247
take, make an impression II.ii.105
   destroy III.i.111, IV.iv.20
take in, capture I.ii.24, III.ii.59
take up, take on, fight III.i.243
   occupy III.ii.116
taken, approached v.i.50
taken note of, observed IV.ii.10
tapers, candles I.vi.32
target, shield IV.v.116
Tarpeian rock, a rock on the Capitoline Hill
   in Rome III.i.212, 265, III.ii.3
Tarquin, Tarquinius Superbus, the last king
   of Rome, defeated at the Battle of Lake
   Regillus (c. 496 B.C.) II.i.139, II.ii.85, 91,
   v.iv.40
tasked, employed I.iii.34
tauntingly, contemptuously I.i.96
taunts, insults I.i.241
tell, say II.i.56
tell over, rehearse in detail I.ix.1
temperance, self-control, restraint III.iii.28
temporized, compromised principles IV.vi.17
temp'rately, moderately, in a self-controlled
   way II.i.213
tender-bodied, young I.iii.5
tent, probe a wound with lint I.ix.31
   treat III.i.235
   pitch a tent III.ii.116
testy, bad-tempered II.i.39
tetter, cover with scabs III.i.79
that, what I.i.213, III.i.217, v.ii.101
   so that I.vi.8, III.ii.44, v.vi.98
   because II.iii.16
theme, subject, II.i.206
   business II.ii.54
think, think so I.vi.46
think upon, think well of II.iii.52, 177
this, this time, now IV.iii.35, IV.vi:34
though, even if v.iii.112
thou't, you would (a contraction of *thou
   wouldst*) I.ix.2
thread, pass through III.i.124
throat, voice III.iii.112
throne, power, authority IV.vi.32
   be enthroned v.iv.22
throng, fill III.iii.36
through, throughout IV.v.83
throw, in bowls the distance the ball should
   be rolled v.ii.21
thrust forth, present IV.i.40
thwack, thrash IV.v.172
thwartings, obstacles III.ii.21
Tiber, the river on which Rome stands II.i.44,
   III.i.261
tickled, delighted I.i.246
tiger-footed, swift and fierce III.i.310
time-pleasers, time-servers, men acting from
   self interest III.i.45
timed with, accompanied by II.ii.107
tinder-like, apt to flare up II.i.45

titleless, nameless v.i.13
to, about i.i.132
 for v.iii.178, 186
 go to iii.i.31, 334
 against iv.v.123
 before iv.vi.84
toga, long flowing Roman robe ii.iii.104
together, against each other i.i.218
told, told off, scolded iv.ii.48
tongue, voice iv.iii.9
took, made an impression ii.ii.105
 taken iv.vi.79
topping, surpassing ii.i.18
to't, on it iv.ii.48
touch (v.), affects ii.i.50
 inflame ii.i.244
touch (n.), quality iv.i.49
touched, tested ii.iii.180
 threatened iii.i.123
 reached v.ii.11
touching, concerning i.i.137
towards, in dealing with v.i.41
trades, tradesmen iii.iii.134, iv.i.13
traducement, defamation i.ix.22
translated, transform ii.iii.178
transport, maintain, carry through ii.i.213
transported, carried away i.i.63
treaty, proposal ii.ii.52
trencher, wooden plate iv.v.45
tribe, Roman political division iii.iii.11
 fellows iv.ii.24
 family v.vi.128
tribunes, Roman magistrates i.i.201
trick, joke ii.iii.32
trident, three-pronged spear iii.i.255
trim, (a) equipment (n.) (b) fine (adj.) i.ix.61
Triton, a sea-god in Greek mythology iii.i.89
troop, group of citizens i.i.190
trophy, monument i.iii.37
troth, true faith iv.ii.49
 truth ii.i.128, iv.v.178
 faith, word i.iii.56, 102
true, genuine iii.i.134
 faithful v.iii.47
true (n.), truth v.ii.31
truth, loyalty v.vi.21
tumbled, rolled v.ii.21
tuns, barrels iv.v.95
turn, divert iii.i.96
 bring iii.i.282
turn (v.), change iv.vi.60
turn (n.), change iv.iv.12
tush, exclamation of impatience iii.ii.45
twin, be like twins iv.iv.15
twist, skein, plaited thread v.vi.95
'twixt, between ii.ii.16, v.vi.17
tyranny, cruelty v.iii.43

U

Ulysses, King of Ithaca i.iii.80

unaching, healed and no longer painful ii.ii.145
unactive, inactive i.i.85
unapt, unwilling v.i.52
unbarbed, unarmed, bare iii.ii.99
unbruised, uninjured iv.i.47
unbuckling, tearing off iv.v.121
uncertainty, fickleness iii.iii.123
unchilded, deprived of children v.vi.151
unclog, relieve iv.ii.47
under, infernal iv.v.88
undercrest, support as one would a crest, or personal heraldic sign i.ix.71
undo, ruin i.i.51
undone, ruined i.i.52
ungravely, without dignity ii.iii.214
unhearts, discourages v.i.49
unknit, undone iv.ii.31
unless, otherwise iii.ii.27
 except v.i.71
unlike, unlikely iii.i.49
unmeriting, undeserving ii.i.38
unmusical, unpleasing in sound iv.v.54
unproperly, contrary to propriety, unbecomingly v.iii.54
unroof, destroy i.i.204
unscanned, thoughtless iii.i.311
unseparable, inseparable iv.iv.16
unsevered, inseparable iii.ii.42
unshout, wipe out former shouts by fresh ones v.v.4
unstable, wayward iii.i.148
unswayable, inflexible v.vi.25
unvulnerable, unable to be hurt v.iii.73
up, opposed in action iii.i.109
upon, among i.i.220
 under i.x.25
 because of ii.i.217
 against iii.iii.47
 about ii.iii.133
urn, vase containing ashes of a dead person v.vi.144
use, treat i.ix.82, ii.ii.152, ii.iii.151, v.ii.50
usher, male attendant on a lady or gentleman S.D. i.iii.46, ii.i.147
usurers, moneylenders i.i.69
usury, moneylending i.i.69

V

vagabond, wandering iii.iii.89
vail, bow down iii.i.98
value, opinion ii.ii.56
vantage, advantage i.i.146, ii.iii.249, iii.ii.31
 opportunity v.vi.53
variable, different ii.i.201
varlet, rascal v.ii.74
vassals, slaves iii.ii.9
vaward, vanguard i.vi.53
vengeance, excessively ii.ii.5
venomous, stinging iv.i.23

vent (v.), get rid of i.i.211
    express iii.i.257
vent (n.), outlet for energy iv.v.212
vented, voiced i.i.195
venture (v.), risk ii.ii.77
verdict, unanimous decision i.i.9
verified, told the truth about v.ii.17
verily, truly i.iii.88
verity, truth v.ii.18
very, utter i.i.23
    themselves i.iv.49, ii.i.77
    complete iv.v.213
vessel, (a) ship (b) body iv.v.58
vesture, clothing ii.i.223
vexation, torment iii.iii.139
viand, food i.i.86
view, sight ii.ii.90
vigilant, watchful i.i.101
vilde, vile i.i.170
vilely, basely iii.i.10
violentest, most extreme iv.vi.74
viperous, poisonous iii.i.285
virgin, girlish iii.ii.114
virgined, remained chaste v.iii.48
virtue, courage, manliness, manly qualities
    i.i.32, iii.i.73
    power, special quality i.i.160, v.ii.12
visage, face i.ix.92
voice (v.), vote ii.iii.223
voices, votes ii.ii.137, ii.iii.1 etc.
voided, avoided iv.v.78
Volsces, an Italian tribe bordering on Rome
    i.i.210
voluptuously, luxuriously i.iii.22
vouch, utter, word i.ix.24
    affirm iii.i.298, v.vi.5
vouches, testimonials ii.iii.106
vulgar, plebeian i.i.201
    among the crowd ii.i.204
    popular iv.vii.21

W

waged, paid v.vi.39
walking, action iv.v.212
want (v.), lack i.iii.78, v.iv.21
    be lacking ii.i.244
want (n.), lack iii.ii.69, iv.ii.44
wanton, (a) lascivious (b) unrestrained ii.i.206
warrant, assure i.iv.47, ii.i.120, 129, 211
watched, kept watch ii.iii.116
wave, waver ii.ii.16
waving, bowing up and down iii.ii.77
waxed, grew ii.ii.96
ways, procedure iv.v.136
weal, welfare i.i.137, iii.i.175
    commonwealth ii.iii.170
wealsmen, men devoted to the public good
    ii.i.49
wedged up, jammed ii.iii.26
weed, reed ii.ii.102
    garment ii.iii.142, 210
weigh, have worth ii.ii.71

well-found, well-deserved ii.ii.41
were, would be ii.ii.28, 29, iii.ii.87
what, who i.x.28
wheel, take a roundabout route i.vi.19
where,whereas i.i.87,i.x.13
whereat, at which v.vi.132
wherefore, why ii.ii.9
whereto, to which v.iii.108, 109
which, who i.i.173, iv.vi.3, v.i.2, v.vi.152
    whichever v.iii.113
while, whole time iii.i.147
    at the same time iii.iii.136
whip, champion i.viii.12
who, which iii.ii.119
    whoever iv.vi.104
wholesome, sound i.i.70
    reasonable ii.iii.56
why so, just so, exactly v.i.15
wild, rash iv.i.36
win, obtain ii.i.204
win our purpose, gain our objective i.vi.50
win upon, get the better of i.i.206
wind, wriggle, insinuate iii.iii.64
wit, intellect ii.iii.18, iii.i.250
with, by iv.vi.14, v.vi.11
withal, with iii.i.142
    by it v.iii.194
within, off-stage i.i.36 etc.
without, beyond iii.i.144
wolvish, hypocritical ii.iii.104
wondering, in astonishment v.vi.99
wondrous, extremely i.i.75
    remarkably ii.i.32
    wonderful ii.i.128, 129
wont, accustomed ii.i.109, iii.ii.8, iv.i.16
woollen, coarse iii.ii.8
word, password iii.ii.142
work, destruction i.viii.9
worn, exhausted iii.i.6
worshipful, honourable i.i.236
worth, pennyworth, full value iii.iii.26
wot, know iv.i.27
wot on, know of iv.v.157
would, I wish i.i.43
wracked, worked hard with disastrous
    results v.i.16
wreak, vengeance iv.v.81
wrench (v.), tune i.viii.11
wrought, worked ii.iii.235

Y

yet, still iii.i.205
yield, approve ii.ii.51
    give ii.iii.165
    give in approval iii.i.34
yielded, surrendered iii.i.10
yoke, be associated iii.i.57
yond, yonder iii.i.50, v.iii.1
youngly, at a tender age ii.iii.225
your, that you know of v.iv.10
you'st, you shall i.i.112